Praise for
Early Childhood Literacy
The National Early Literacy Panel and Beyond

"If you read the National Early Literacy Panel report, you should read this book. The book offers important perspectives on the panel's findings and takes the field beyond those findings.... This book is notable for its currency, the range of topics represented, and the role it can play in shaping the research agenda in early literacy."
—**Nell K. Duke, Ed.D.,** Professor of Language, Literacy, and Culture, University of Michigan

"An extremely important contribution to early literacy in this country. I am delighted to have the opportunity to endorse this edited book that includes chapters by outstanding researchers in the field of early literacy. The chapters begin with excellent research syntheses about their topic and then go on to describe implications for practice and future research. A very scholarly and reader-friendly document that should be read and kept in the professional library of all who are in the field of early childhood."
—**Lesley Mandel Morrow, Ph.D.,** Professor of Literacy, Rutgers, The State University of New Jersey

"This impressive collection of writings by highly regarded experts provides a solid foundation of research regarding early childhood literacy development. It summarizes large-scale projects and reports and covers important topics. This book has gathered the most important information about early literacy development into one easy-to-read book. It will be a valuable resource to researchers and other literacy professionals."
—**Diane Haager, Ph.D.,** Professor, Division of Special Education and Counseling, California State University, Los Angeles

"Further clarifies the results of the NELP report and expands on vital issues within it, consistently advocating for the importance of young children's early literacy development to future academic success."
—**Andrea DeBruin-Parecki, Ph.D.,** Graduate Program Director, Early Childhood Education, Old Dominion University

Early Childhood Literacy

Early Childhood Literacy
The National Early Literacy Panel and Beyond

edited by

Timothy Shanahan, Ph.D.
University of Illinois at Chicago

and

Christopher J. Lonigan, Ph.D.
Florida State University, Tallahassee

·P A U L·H·
BROOKES
PUBLISHING Cº ®

Baltimore • London • Sydney

Paul H. Brookes Publishing Co., Inc.
Post Office Box 10624
Baltimore, Maryland 21285-0624

www.brookespublishing.com

Typeset by Network Publishing Partners, Inc., Glenview, Illinois.
Manufactured in the United States of America by
Sheridan Books, Inc., Chelsea, Michigan.

Chapter 2 was written by U.S. Government employees within the scope of their official
duties and, as such, shall remain in the public domain. The opinions and assertions
contained herein are the private opinions of the authors and are not to be construed as
official or reflecting the views of the U.S. Government.

Photograph on the cover copyright © Corbis.

Library of Congress Cataloging-in-Publication Data

Early childhood literacy : the National Early Literacy Panel and beyond / edited by
Timothy Shanahan and Christopher J. Lonigan.
    p.   cm.
  Includes bibliographical references and index.
  ISBN 978-1-59857-115-8 (pbk.)
  ISBN 1-59857-115-X (pbk.)
  1. Language arts (Preschool) 2. Language arts (Kindergarten)
  I. Shanahan, Timothy. II. Lonigan, Christopher J.
LB1140.5.L3E27 2012
372.6'049—dc23   2012024567

British Library Cataloguing in Publication data are available from the British Library.

2016   2015   2014   2013   2012

10   9   8   7   6   5   4   3   2   1

Contents

About the Editors

Timothy Shanahan, Ph.D., Distinguished Professor of Urban Education and Chair, Department of Curriculum & Instruction, University of Illinois at Chicago, 1040 West Harrison Street (M/C 147), Chicago, IL 60607

Dr. Shanahan is Director of the University of Illinois at Chicago (UIC) Center for Literacy. Previously, he was Director of Reading for the Chicago Public Schools, serving 437,000 children. He is the author or editor of more than 200 publications, including the books *Developing Literacy in Second-Language Learners: Report of the National Literacy Panel on Language-Minority Children and Youth* (Lawrence Erlbaum Associates, 2006) and *Improving Reading Comprehension in Kindergarten Through 3rd Grade: A Practice Guide* (U.S. Department of Education, Institute of Education Sciences, National Center for Education Evaluation and Regional Assistance, 2010). His research emphasizes the connections between learning to read and learning to write, literacy in the disciplines, and improvement of reading achievement.

Dr. Shanahan is Past President of the International Reading Association (IRA). In 2006 he received a presidential appointment to serve on the advisory board of the National Institute for Literacy, and he serves as a content expert, as an advisor, and on various boards for the National Center for Family Literacy, the Education Resources Information Center, What Works Clearinghouse, National Assessment of Educational Progress, the Partnership for Assessment of Readiness for College and Careers, Reach Out and Read, and Ready to Learn (Barnardo's Northern Ireland). Dr. Shanahan took a leadership role on the National Reading Panel, a group convened by the *Eunice Kennedy Shriver* National Institute of Child Health and Human Development at the request of the U.S. Congress to evaluate research on the teaching of reading. He has chaired two other federal research review panels, the National Literacy Panel on Language-Minority Children and Youth and the National Early Literacy Panel, and was a member of the English Language Arts Work Team for the Common Core State Standards. He serves on the editorial boards of all of the major research journals in literacy and is the coprincipal investigator of the National Title I Study of Implementation and Outcomes: Early Childhood Language Development.

Dr. Shanahan received the Albert J. Harris Award for outstanding research on reading disability from IRA, the Milton D. Jacobson Readability Research Award from IRA, the Amoco Award for Outstanding Teaching, and the University of Delaware Presidential Citation for Outstanding Achievement. In 2009 he was selected as Researcher of the Year at UIC (in social sciences and the humanities). His research and testimony have been cited in federal case law (*Memisovski v. Maram,* 1982), a case lauded by the American Academy of Pediatrics as "an enormous victory" for children's health care. He received his Ph.D. at the University of Delaware in 1980. He was inducted into the Reading Hall of Fame in 2007 and is a former first-grade teacher. For more information, visit his blog: Shanahan on Literacy (http://www.shanahanonliteracy.com).

Christopher J. Lonigan, Ph.D., Distinguished Research Professor of Psychology and Associate Director, Florida Center for Reading Research, Department of Psychology, Florida State University, 1107 West Call Street, Tallahassee, FL 32306-4301

Dr. Lonigan received his Ph.D. in clinical psychology in 1991 from the State University of New York at Stony Brook. After completing his Ph.D., Dr. Lonigan was awarded a 2-year National Institutes of Health (NIH) Postdoctoral Fellowship at the John F. Kennedy Center at Vanderbilt University. Dr. Lonigan's area of expertise concerns the development, assessment, and promotion of preschool early literacy skills.

Dr. Lonigan has authored or coauthored more than 70 research publications. He is or has been the principal investigator for four *Eunice Kennedy Shriver* National Institute of Child Health and Human Development (NICHD)–funded research projects on the development and promotion of early literacy; an Institute of Education Sciences (IES) Preschool Curriculum Evaluation Research project; a U.S. Department of Health and Human Services–funded project on the development and promotion of literacy skills in children attending Head Start; a National Science Foundation (NSF)–funded project on promoting early literacy skills in children at risk for reading failure; an NICHD program project on the impacts of cognitive and socioemotional curricula for 2-, 3-, and 4-year-old children; an IES research project on the impacts of preschool curricula for reducing the need and utilization of special education services; two IES-funded research projects to develop assessments of early literacy skills; and an NICHD-funded research project to evaluate the efficacy of preschool curricula for English language learners. Dr. Lonigan is the principal investigator for the Florida Center for Reading Research's Reading for Understanding Core Research Center, funded by IES.

Dr. Lonigan has served in an advisory capacity on various federal, state, and local committees associated with the development of literacy in young children. He was a member of the National Early Literacy Panel and the principal investigator for the What Works Clearinghouse early childhood education review group. For 3 years he chaired the Reading and Writing Review Panel for the IES grant reviews, and he has served on other grant-review panels for NIH, IES, NSF, the Administration on Children, Youth and Families, and the U.S. Department of Education. Dr. Lonigan has served on various advisory committees for federal research and demonstration projects, including work associated with Reading First, Head Start, the Even Start Family Literacy Program, and the Investing in Innovation Fund. He was part of the advisory committees for the development of preschool learning standards for both Florida and California.

About the Contributors

Mindy Sittner Bridges, Ph.D., Assistant Research Professor, Schiefelbusch Institute for Life Span Studies, University of Kansas, 3001 Dole Center, 1000 Sunnyside Avenue, Lawrence, KS 66045

Dr. Bridges' research interests include the identification and prevention of language disorders and reading disorders.

Kate Cain, D.Phil., Reader, Department of Psychology, Lancaster University, Lancaster, LA1 4YF, United Kingdom

Dr. Cain's research focuses on the development of language comprehension in children, with a particular interest in the cognitive and language issues that lead to reading (and listening) comprehension difficulties. She is the editor of the journal *Scientific Studies of Reading* and author of *Reading Development and Difficulties,* published by Wiley-Blackwell in 2010.

Judith J. Carta, Ph.D., Senior Scientist and Professor, University of Kansas, 444 Minnesota Avenue, Suite 300, Kansas City, KS 66101

Dr. Carta is a senior scientist at Juniper Gardens Children's Project, a professor of special education at the University of Kansas, and Codirector of the Institute of Education Sciences–funded Center for Response to Intervention in Early Childhood. Her major research interests are evidence-based practices to improve the language, literacy, and social competence of young children and approaches for monitoring progress in young children.

Anne E. Cunningham, Ph.D., Professor, Cognition and Development, 4511 Tolman Hall, Graduate School of Education, University of California, Berkeley, Berkeley, CA 94720

Dr. Cunningham earned her Ph.D. in developmental psychology from the University of Michigan and is known for her research on literacy and development across the life span. Her work examines the cognitive and motivational processes underlying reading ability and the interplay of context, development, and literacy instruction. She is a fellow of the American Educational Research Association and the American Psychological Association as well as a recipient of the Reid Lyon Award for Research Excellence and the University of Virginia's George Graham Award. She is a former preschool and elementary school teacher and reading resource specialist.

Catherine L. Darrow, Ph.D., Associate, Abt Associates, 55 Wheeler Street, Cambridge, MA 02138

Dr. Darrow works as an associate in the Social and Economic Policy Division. Dr. Darrow specializes in implementation science and in developing and employing measures of implementation fidelity.

David K. Dickinson, Ed.D., Professor, Peabody College, Vanderbilt University, Peabody #230, 230 Appleton Place, Nashville, TN 37203

Dr. Dickinson has long been interested in the relationship between language and early literacy development. Building on insights gained as part of a longitudinal study, he has developed tools to describe classrooms, coauthored a curriculum, and currently is working on an intervention designed to teach vocabulary by combining book reading and supported play.

Coralie Driscoll, Ph.D., Lecturer, Macquarie University Special Education Centre, Macquarie University, NSW 2109, Australia

Dr. Driscoll was a visiting scholar at Juniper Gardens Children's Project, University of Kansas, during 2010. She has worked in Sydney, Australia, as a teacher, served in senior early childhood intervention roles for the state system, and held positions as a university lecturer and educational consultant. Dr. Driscoll is an editorial consultant for the *Australasian Journal of Special Education.*

Nancy Eisenberg, Ph.D., Regents' Professor of Psychology, Arizona State University, Post Office Box 871104, Tempe, AZ 85287-1104

Dr. Eisenberg's research interests pertain to social, emotional, and moral development. Her books include *The Caring Child* (Harvard University Press, 1992), *The Roots of Prosocial Behavior in Children* (with Paul Mussen; Cambridge University Press, 1989), and *How Children Develop* (with Robert Siegler and Judy DeLoach, 3rd ed.; Worth Publishers, 2010). She has edited Volume 3 of the *Handbook of Child Psychology* (Wiley, 1998, 2006). She has been editor of *Psychological Bulletin* and is the current editor of *Child Development Perspectives.* She has received career contribution awards from Divisions 1 and 7 of the American Psychological Association, the Association for Psychological Science, and the International Society for Research on Behavioral Development.

Beth Anne N. Feldman, Ph.D., Postdoctoral Fellow, Kennedy Krieger Institute and Johns Hopkins School of Medicine, 9801 Patuxent Woods Drive, Columbia, MD 21045

Dr. Feldman provides direct clinical services, parent training, and consultation to children and their families on an outpatient basis. Her research interests include early literacy, behavioral parent training, and school consultation.

Howard Goldstein, Ph.D., Professor of Human Development and Family Science, Schoenbaum Family Center, The Ohio State University, 175 East 7th Avenue, Columbus, OH 43201-2562

Dr. Goldstein's research interests include early intervention and the development of approaches for teaching generalized language, literacy, and social skills to children with or at risk for developmental disabilities.

James A. Griffin, Ph.D., Deputy Chief, Child Development and Behavior Branch, *Eunice Kennedy Shriver* National Institute of Child Health and Human Development, National Institutes of Health, 6100 Executive Boulevard, Suite 4B05D, Rockville, MD 20852-7510

Dr. Griffin is Director of the Early Learning and School Readiness Program at the *Eunice Kennedy Shriver* National Institute of Child Health and Human Development (NICHD). Prior to joining NICHD, Dr. Griffin served as a senior research analyst in the Institute of Education Sciences at the U.S. Department of Education; as Assistant Director for the Social, Behavioral, and Education Sciences in the White House Office of Science and Technology Policy; and as a research analyst at the Administration on Children, Youth and Families.

Tiffany P. Hogan, Ph.D., Assistant Professor, Department of Special Education and Communication Disorders, Munroe-Meyer Institute, University of Nebraska–Lincoln, 271 Barkley Memorial Center, Lincoln, NE 68583

Dr. Hogan is Director of the Link N Literacy Lab and Assistant Director of the Neurogenetic Communication Disorders Consortium at Munroe-Meyer Institute. Dr. Hogan studies the genetic, neurological, and behavioral links between spoken and written language development, with a focus on comorbid speech and language disorders.

Laura M. Justice, Ph.D., Professor, School of Teaching and Learning, The Ohio State University, 357 Arps Hall, 1945 North High Street, Columbus, OH 43210

Dr. Justice is Director of the Children's Learning Research Collaborative at The Ohio State University. Dr. Justice is interested in promoting the early language and literacy skills of children considered at risk for academic challenges, including children with disabilities and children reared in poverty. She has authored more than 100 articles and book chapters on this topic as well as a number of textbooks.

Tanya Kaefer, Ph.D., Postdoctoral Scholar, School of Education, University of Michigan, 610 East University Avenue, Room #3119, Ann Arbor, MI 48109

Dr. Kaefer earned a Ph.D. in developmental psychology from Duke University in 2009. She studies reading development and the influence of content knowledge on early literacy skills.

Peggy McCardle, Ph.D., M.P.H., Chief, Child Development and Behavior Branch, *Eunice Kennedy Shriver* National Institute of Child Health and Human Development, 6100 Executive Boulevard, Suite 4B05H, Rockville, MD 20852-7510

Dr. McCardle directs the Language, Bilingualism, and Biliteracy Research Program at the *Eunice Kennedy Shriver* National Institute of Child Health and Human Development (NICHD). Her publications address various aspects of public health and developmental psycholinguistics (e.g., language development, bilingualism, reading). She was the NICHD liaison to the National Reading Panel, has led or served on various interagency working groups, and serves on various advisory boards and councils. She has coedited volumes on reading, language development, dyslexia, and human–animal interaction and its influence on child health and development, as well as various thematic journal issues on these and related topics.

Susan B. Neuman, Ed.D., Professor, School of Education, University of Michigan, 610 East University Avenue, Room #3119, Ann Arbor, MI 48109

Dr. Neuman is a professor of educational studies specializing in early literacy development. She has served as the U.S. Assistant Secretary for Elementary and Secondary Education. She has directed the Center for the Improvement of Early Reading Achievement and currently directs the University of Michigan's Ready to Learn research program. Her research interests include early childhood policy, curriculum, and early reading instruction (pre-K through Grade 3) for children who live in poverty.

Jill M. Pentimonti, Ph.D., Postdoctoral Researcher, Children's Learning Research Collaborative, The Ohio State University, 356 Arps Hall, 1945 North High Street, Columbus, OH 43210

Prior to receiving a doctoral degree in reading and literacy in early and middle childhood from The Ohio State University, Dr. Pentimonti worked as a reading specialist and an early childhood teacher. Her research interests include child language and literacy development during the preschool years, as well as home and educational interventions.

Beth M. Phillips, Ph.D., Assistant Professor, Department of Educational Psychology and Learning Systems and Florida Center for Reading Research, Florida State University, 2010 Levy Avenue, Suite 100, Tallahassee, FL 32310

Dr. Phillips is a clinical and educational psychologist whose research focuses on the constellation of influences on school readiness for preschool- and early elementary–age children, including early language development, home language and literacy environments, and early childhood curricula and interventions. She is currently involved with several intervention development and efficacy projects that focus on improving children's vocabulary and language skills, as well as on the professional development needed to improve early childhood classrooms serving children at high risk for reading difficulties.

Shayne B. Piasta, Ph.D., Assistant Professor, School of Teaching and Learning, The Ohio State University, 356 Arps Hall, 1945 North High Street, Columbus, OH 43210

Dr. Piasta is Assistant Director of the Children's Learning Research Collaborative at The Ohio State University. Dr. Piasta is a developmental psychologist whose research focuses on early and emergent literacy skill development and empirical validation of classroom literacy programs and practices.

Ashley M. Pinkham, Ph.D., Research Fellow, School of Education, University of Michigan, 610 East University Avenue, Room #3113, Ann Arbor, MI 48109

Dr. Pinkham completed her doctoral studies in cognitive-developmental psychology at the University of Virginia in 2009. Her research focuses on sources of children's knowledge acquisition and conceptual development, including observational learning, adult–child conversations, and book-reading experiences.

Naomi Schneider, Ph.D., Research Scientist, Schoenbaum Family Center, The Ohio State University, 175 East 7th Avenue, Columbus, OH 43201-2562

Dr. Schneider's research focuses on remediating challenging behaviors and facilitating the social communication skills of elementary school children with developmental disabilities as well as language and literacy development.

Elizabeth J. Spencer, Ph.D., Research Scientist, Schoenbaum Family Center, The Ohio State University, 175 East 7th Avenue, Columbus, OH 43201-2562

Dr. Spencer's research interests include early intervention in language and literacy for young children with oral language difficulties, with an emphasis on vocabulary instruction for preschool children.

Trina D. Spencer, Ph.D., Research Coordinator, Institute for Human Development, Northern Arizona University, Post Office Box 5630, Flagstaff, AZ 86001

Dr. Spencer is a school psychologist, a board-certified behavior analyst, and an early childhood special educator. Her research interests include preschool language and literacy assessment and intervention and social communication interventions for children with autism.

Tracy L. Spinrad, Ph.D., Associate Professor, School of Social and Family Dynamics, Arizona State University, Post Office Box 3701, Tempe, AZ 85287-3701

Dr. Spinrad's research focuses on children's emotions, emotion regulation, and social competence. In addition, she has examined the important role of parenting in her research, particularly with regard to the socialization of emotion regulation.

Carlos Valiente, Ph.D., Associate Professor, School of Social and Family Dynamics, Arizona State University, Post Office Box 3701, Tempe, AZ 85287-3701

Dr. Valiente's research interests focus on understanding children's social and academic success, with a particular focus on the contributions of the family environment and children's temperament. He teaches courses on marriage and family relationships, school success, and family theories.

Barbara Hanna Wasik, Ph.D., William R. Kenan Jr. Distinguished Professor, School of Education, University of North Carolina, CB #3500, Chapel Hill, NC 27599

Dr. Wasik is a fellow at the Frank Porter Graham Child Development Institute at the University of North Carolina at Chapel Hill. Her research focuses on early childhood interventions, family literacy, child development, problem solving, home visiting, and classroom observations. She has edited the book *Handbook of Family Literacy* (1st ed., Lawrence Erlbaum Associates, 2004; 2nd ed., Routledge, 2012), coedited the book *Handbook of Child Development and Early Education: Research to Practice* (with Oscar Barbarin; Guilford Press, 2009), and coauthored *Home Visiting: Procedures for Helping Families* (with Donna Bryant and Claudia Lyons, 1st ed., Sage Publications, 1990; with Donna Bryant, 2nd ed., Sage Publications, 2001).

Acknowledgments

We would like to acknowledge and extend our appreciation to several people who participated in the development of this book. Because we used the National Early Literacy Panel report as the book's point of departure, it is fitting that we thank the other members of that panel (Anne E. Cunningham, Kathy C. Escamilla, Janet Fischel, Susan Landry, Victoria J. Molfese, Chris Schatschneider, and Dorothy Strickland) and everyone else at the National Center for Family Literacy and the now-defunct National Institute for Literacy for their support and assistance. (In particular, we wish to thank Laura Westberg, who oversaw that work from beginning to end, and Kelly Coots and Lisa Smith Jackson as well.) Without that panel report, this book would not exist.

We believe that educational practice and policy will only be successful when it is closely attuned to the findings of empirical research. Accordingly, we invited leading scholars in the field to write the chapters for this book. We want to thank them for their fine contributions. Their expertise and commitment to increasing knowledge is evident from what they have written here as well as from their past work. In addition, we want to thank Sarah Shepke, our editor at Paul H. Brookes Publishing Co., for coming up with the idea of this book and for her patience as the writing was done (edited books always take longer than intended).

This book summarizes the most up-to-date research findings and the best current thought on teaching literacy to preschoolers and kindergartners. We assembled this collection in the hopes that it would guide future research directions and help educators to implement more enlightened educational practices effectively. Ultimately, the success of this book depends on how it is received and used by those researchers who aim at increasing understanding of how young children learn literacy and by those educators who spend their days teaching young children. We thank both groups for their enduring commitment and wish them increasing success.

*To Aiden and to all other young
children on their early path to literacy*

1

The National Early Literacy Panel

A Summary of the Report

Timothy Shanahan and Christopher J. Lonigan

The National Early Literacy Panel (NELP) is a group of scholars who were asked by the National Institute for Literacy and the National Center for Family Literacy to review the research on teaching literacy to preschool and kindergarten children. NELP was appointed in 2002 and issued its report in 2008. This chapter summarizes that report, including both discussions of the methodology used to review the evidence and the research findings. Although this chapter strives to provide a clear and accurate summary of the NELP report, we strongly encourage readers to examine the report itself, as it is impossible in a chapter-length treatment to cover all the nuances and details of the full report (available online at http://lincs.ed.gov/publications/pdf/NELPReport09.pdf). Any opinions expressed here about the implications of the NELP findings are the responsibilities of the authors of this chapter and are not necessarily those of the other panelists.

Literacy achievement in the United States has stagnated since the early 1970s (Campbell, Reese, O'Sullivan, & Dossey, 1996; National Center for Education Statistics, 2009). Although literacy demands have increased since then, meaning that individuals need higher levels of literacy than in the past to participate successfully in society (Shanahan & Shanahan, 2008) and that the United States invests more in literacy teaching now than in the past (Snyder, Dillow, & Hoffman, 2008), there has been very little improvement in how well students read. Furthermore, there are a large number of Americans who have such limited literacy that it interferes with their ability to work, to manage their health care, or to provide educational support for their children (Baer, Kutner, & Sabatini, 2009). Given these great learning needs, NELP's goal was to turn to research to find answers on how to improve current practices, particularly with young children.

An earlier panel, the National Reading Panel (NRP), reviewed research on teaching reading to school-age children (National Institute of Child Health and Human Development, 2000). NRP considered whether the explicit teaching of phonemic awareness, phonics, oral reading fluency, vocabulary, and reading comprehension gave students any benefits in learning to read; it also considered the impact of encouraging students to read, the use of technology, and teacher education. However, it did not consider research that focused specifically on children in their early years, although the phonemic awareness section of the report did review some studies on preschoolers. Consequently, NELP was asked to address this part of the research evidence.

NELP carried out an extensive synthesis of research evidence to try to determine what should be taught to young children about literacy and to evaluate the effectiveness of various approaches for teaching these early literacy skills. Although the NELP synthesis was particularly thorough and rigorous in its analysis of the research evidence, there are several reasons both for trying to come to terms with its implications and for trying to go beyond its findings. NELP provided a thorough examination of early correlates of later literacy proficiency and a relatively comprehensive review of the published studies that evaluated interventions for improving early literacy skills. However, research continues to accumulate on many of these issues, and the NELP synthesis, or any synthesis, can never truly be said to be the final word. Also, although the analytic approach that NELP took allowed the panel to answer some major questions (e.g., does code-based literacy instruction help young readers?), it did not allow us to present a very detailed analysis of related questions, such as how or why such instruction may work. Given that limitation, we invited a group of scholars to weigh in, within this volume, on the newest evidence, to discuss issues that NELP did not address, and even to critique the report. Each chapter provides a deeper look at a variety of important issues concerning the literacy learning of young children. But first, this chapter provides a brief review of what NELP did and what it found.

PURPOSES AND METHODOLOGY

The NELP report is really a study of studies or a meta-analysis of existing research on young children's literacy learning. To understand the report and its implications for preschool and kindergarten teaching, it is important to understand the questions that it set out to answer and how it examined the evidence.

Did NELP look at all of the research on early literacy?

No, the panel did not look at all of the research on early literacy. Nevertheless, it is the most comprehensive review of research on this topic yet undertaken. This review had particular questions that it tried to answer, and the panel tried to examine all of the published research that could address those questions and that met certain quality and design criteria.

What questions did NELP try to answer about young children's literacy?

The panel focused on identifying what teachers and parents could do to improve young children's literacy learning and to try to understand how those actions may need to be adjusted for different children or under different circumstances. However, it is difficult to evaluate the effectiveness of instructional routines, programs, materials, or interventions without first identifying which skills or abilities those efforts need to improve. If the children were older, any tests of conventional literacy skills (i.e., decoding, oral reading fluency, reading comprehension, writing quality, and spelling) might be acceptable. But what measures can be used with 3- or 4-year-old children, who most often are not yet reading or writing by any conventional measure? Because of that problem, the panel spent considerable time determining what early skills and abilities were predictive of later literacy achievement.

Can't you prove anything with research?

Many practitioners are skeptical about the value of research evidence, given that different studies sometimes have contradictory outcomes (e.g., is it all right to eat eggs now or should they still be avoided?). The world is complex and research aims to help pierce that complexity, but often it just reveals how complicated things are. Making matters worse, of course, are the self-serving claims of some vendors, consultants, and "experts," all alleging their approaches to be research based but often contradicting each other. That, in fact, was part of the reason why the panel was asked to review this research in the first place: to clear away those contradictions and to let parents and teachers know what the research was really saying. Although it might seem that one can make research "say" anything, there are objective ways of synthesizing studies that can be replicated—meaning other scientists, using the same methods, should get the same results—and that allow scientists to formally evaluate the conclusions. NELP was required to conduct a meta-analysis of these data using explicit meta-analytic methodology.

What is a meta-analysis?

Meta-analysis is a technique that allows scientists to conduct a more objective kind of research synthesis or literature review. Up to the mid-1970s, combining studies together to get a big-picture view of something was a pretty subjective process. The researcher would pick the studies he or she wanted to include—perhaps ignoring contradictory evidence, or dismissing it in some disparaging way—to provide a kind of personal summary of what he or she thought it all meant.

The problem with this method is that you cannot easily account for differences in the studies in any systematic manner. People, scientists included, tend to have beliefs and biases; therefore, when they examine a study that supports their beliefs, they might be less inclined to notice its limitations, and when a study contradicts their beliefs, they may be more critical and less accepting of the study design. With meta-analysis, those decisions are made early in the process, and all studies that meet certain design characteristics are included, even if that means accounting for data that do not support the researcher's own views. Of course, even if a scientist is particularly objective, careful, and dispassionate when it comes to evaluating particular studies, it is very complicated to try to develop an overall outcome for a large and complex collection of research studies. With meta-analysis, the combination of studies is more than a researcher's subjective summary but is actually a statistical combination of the original data; therefore, the overall patterns should be the same no matter who analyzes that particular set of studies. Finally, because meta-analytic methodology is explicit, other scientists can verify the results or can reanalyze the data in different ways to see how well they stand up under different assumptions.

What study selection criteria did NELP use?

To be included in this meta-analysis, "studies" had to be studies, meaning that they had to report on the analysis of empirical data. There is, of course, a broad literature on teaching, which includes opinion pieces, personal accounts, and descriptions of how to teach. As valuable as those kinds of materials may be, ultimately they cannot help answer the questions that the panel set out to answer. Studies collect and analyze data in some formal systematic way, and the NELP report synthesized that kind of evidence; to do this, we had to rely on studies that provided quantitative data on groups of children (no qualitative studies were included). Because NELP was trying to find out what works, the panel focused on studies that examined children, from birth through 5 years or kindergarten age, who represented the typical range of abilities and disabilities that would be common to general education classrooms (as opposed to special education placements). The studies had to focus on literacy in English or some other alphabetic language (i.e., languages in which letters in words represent speech sounds). Finally, the studies had to be published in English in a refereed journal prior to 2004 and had to be free of serious design flaws or confounds that would make it impossible to determine the study outcome. Any study that met those criteria was included in the NELP analysis.

How do you know that NELP found all of the studies that fit those criteria?

The panel carried out extensive searches in the PsycINFO and Education Resources Information Center (ERIC) databases using 284 search terms to identify relevant articles. This process identified 7,313 potential articles that were then screened, often multiple times, using the previously described criteria. In addition, the lists of studies were sent to 14 early childhood literacy experts to see if they knew of any articles that were not included; journals that publish many articles on early literacy were also checked directly to make sure that nothing was missed. As thorough as the panel was in its search, however, it is always possible to miss some articles. That is why it matters that the panel was explicit about how it carried out its searches and why particular articles were rejected; that is what allows other scientists to check the accuracy and completeness of the process.

Does it matter that NELP found all of the studies?

It does, but it matters more some times than others. For example, NELP tried to determine the relationships of various measures administered anytime from birth to the beginning of kindergarten with reading and spelling measures that were administered when the children were a little older (i.e., any time from the end of kindergarten on). For some variables, the panel combined data from nearly 10,000 children from more than 60 independent studies. Therefore, if an article had more such data and NELP missed it, it might not matter very much, because data on a few more children would be unlikely to change the results already obtained. However, NELP also looked at the effectiveness of various literacy interventions; for some types of interventions there were fewer than 20 studies with data on only a few hundred children. In a case such as that, an additional study, especially if it were large and carefully done, could change a result in some important way. NELP was very thorough and careful, but it is always possible that there is another study that was missed for some reason and that has new information to provide.

Is it a problem that NELP only included studies that had been published in refereed journals?

NELP only used refereed studies—that is, studies that had undergone some independent review of quality prior to publication (research journals have editorial review boards that review the studies, without knowing who the authors are, to decide what should be published). One of the benefits of relying on refereed studies is that the studies can be identified systematically, which allows the searches to be replicated by others. Although it is possible to obtain conference presentations, doctoral dissertations, technical reports, and other nonrefereed materials, these are more difficult to find consistently. By sticking with refereed journals, there is also some independent check on quality, although journals may differ in how rigorously or well they are refereed.

There are, however, potential problems with this approach. Studies have revealed a bias in journals toward the publication of statistically significant findings (Rothstein, Sutton, & Borenstein, 2005). Journals are more likely to publish a study that found an intervention to be effective than one that reported that the intervention did not work. Because of this, the effect sizes tend to be higher in meta-analyses that include only published studies than they are in meta-analyses that include both published and unpublished studies. This phenomenon is sometimes referred to as the "file drawer" problem, meaning that the meta-analyst includes published studies (usually with significant findings) but misses the ones that remain in somebody's file drawer (i.e., that were not published because those interventions did not work). Thus, NELP's effect size estimates may be overestimates in some cases, although this is less likely to be a problem with those questions for which NELP had large amounts of data.

If the panel had multiple questions, how does it do one big analysis of these data?

Actually, the panel carried out many meta-analyses. The first question (what early skills predict later literacy achievement?) was answered by combining all of the studies that had correlational data on particular variables (e.g., alphabet knowledge, oral language, phonological awareness). Similarly, what the research was trying to predict might differ; that is, some studies that looked at the predictive power of alphabet knowledge, for instance, may have tried to predict later decoding skills, or comprehension, or spelling ability. Separate meta-analyses were conducted for each predictor variable and its outcome. The second question, concerning what worked in improving literacy achievement, was addressed through five separate analyses that looked at code-based, shared-book, home and parent, preschool, and oral language interventions, and sometimes there were even additional analyses of particular questions on those different kinds of interventions.

Why did the panel include correlational studies?

Correlational studies provide quantitative measurements of the strength of relationships among variables. As such, studies that provide correlational data are useful for answering the question of which early skills are correlated with later literacy abilities. The panel identified such skills so that we could provide an appropriate evaluation of the intervention studies as we checked whether the interventions improved student performance in these correlated skills, as well as with conventional literacy outcomes.

Doesn't that mean that NELP imputed causation using correlations?

No, not really, but this is a complicated point. If NELP claimed that teaching these skills would lead to higher later achievement, then it would be making a causal argument based on these correlations. That is not what NELP did. The panel used the correlations to make sure that its evaluative criteria were broad enough to reveal potentially important instructional outcomes, recognizing that it would be identifying both causal variables (i.e., those that if taught would lead to higher literacy achievement) and correlates (i.e., those that had measurable relationships with literacy but if enhanced or improved would not lead to improvements in later literacy). However, the panel recognized that the outcomes of the correlational studies could be mistaken for the best things to teach to young children, and we analyzed the data in various ways to help interpret the correlations.

What is a correlation coefficient?

A correlation coefficient is a measure of the strength of relationship between two variables. It indicates how much the two variables rise and fall together. Correlation coefficients can range from -1.00 to 1.00. A correlation coefficient of 0 means that there is no relation at all between the two measures. A correlation coefficient of 1.0 means that the variation in the two variables coincides exactly (i.e., every unit of increase in one variable would be matched by a unit of increase in the other) and a correlation coefficient of -1.0 means that the variation in the two variables is exactly inverse (i.e., every unit of increase in one variable would be matched by a unit of decrease in the other). The panel interpreted correlations as being strong if they were .50 or larger (meaning that the predictor variable would explain 25% of the variation in later literacy achievement), moderate if they were .30–.49 (explaining 9%–25% of variance), and small if they were .29 or smaller (explaining less than 9% of the variance in later literacy).

How did the panel evaluate the correlations?

First, we set objective standards for evaluating the strength of the correlations and the amount of data. Data had to be drawn from at least three independent studies to allow descriptive statistics about the correlations to be computed, and the variable had to account for at least 9% of the variance in the later literacy learning. The panel also looked at more complex correlational studies that had controlled for the effects of other variables. We did this because one of the problems with correlations is that the relationships could be due to other variables. For instance, if alphabet knowledge correlates with later reading, is this because knowing the ABCs helps a child to become literate (a causal connection), because smarter children do well with their ABCs and reading, or because parents who help their children learn the alphabet will continue to help them when they enter school? There are studies that test whether such correlations continue to operate if the effects of variables such as socioeconomic status, IQ, or other variables are controlled. The panel reviewed such studies to see which predictor variables had been tested that way. We could put more credence in a variable that had successfully undergone such a test. The panel also considered other evidence on these correlated variables, including whether studies have demonstrated directly a causal impact; for example, studies have shown that teaching some aspects of phonological awareness does lead to clear improvements in later literacy.

Why did the panel decide to look at
the five intervention topics that it included?

Unlike the earlier NRP that selected topics of study (e.g., phonics, teacher education, reading comprehension), NELP did not actually make such choices. It aimed to provide a comprehensive review of all of the experimental studies that met the selection criteria. Thus, NELP identified the universe of studies first and then proceeded to group or categorize these studies based on the nature of the interventions examined in the studies. NELP analyzed the impacts of code-based instruction, book sharing, parent–home interventions, preschool interventions, and programs aimed at facilitating language development because that is what researchers had studied.

Couldn't some studies fit into more than one category?

Yes. The panel did find studies that could have fit in multiple categories (e.g., a study in which parents are taught to read to their children—would that be considered a parent intervention or a shared-reading intervention?). However, for the sake of analysis, it is not a good idea to include studies multiple times; therefore, the panel had to make decisions about where studies best fit. Thus, if code-based teaching was being evaluated in a preschool setting, then NELP treated it as a code-based intervention; if a combination of code-based teaching and shared reading was being evaluated, the study would go into the preschool set.

Were correlational studies used to evaluate the interventions?

No. When it came to testing whether particular approaches to teaching conferred learning advantages, the panel required that experimental evidence (e.g., from experimental or quasi-experimental studies) be provided. This means that the studies used in those syntheses had to provide the instructional support to some children but not to others to see if it made any difference on some outcome measure. For the panel to say that an approach was beneficial, the approach had to consistently lead to better learning for the children who received it across several studies.

What is the difference between experimental and quasi-experimental studies?

Experimental studies randomly assign participants to the treatments or interventions—meaning that all of the participants have an equal chance of being in the experimental treatment group or the control group. This is best because, if the sample is large enough, all of the important background factors that might influence the results are equally distributed across the groups. In contrast, quasi-experimental studies assign participants to groups using some nonrandom form of assignment (i.e., participants who request a specific treatment or participants in a particular location). Because the assignment to one or the other treatment groups in a quasi-experimental study is not random, there are likely to be preexisting differences among the groups, which may influence the outcomes. That is, the reasons why some participants chose to receive a particular treatment can be directly responsible for any observed difference in outcomes (e.g., those who choose to receive a new treatment may be more motivated and this motivation may directly cause better outcomes). Because of this, quasi-experiments have to provide some kind of pretesting to show that the groups are equal before the intervention is delivered, but these studies can only do this for key variables and cannot account for all the ways that individuals could differ. NELP accepted both kinds of data but required that the quasi-experiments show that the groups were sufficiently equal to justify evaluating the intervention; the panel also investigated how much difference was present in the outcomes of the randomized and quasi-experimental studies for the same type of intervention.

How did NELP interpret the meta-analyses of the intervention studies?

Meta-analysis provides a standardized average weighted effect size for the interventions of interest. That means that a meta-analysis tells how large of an effect a category of treatments had on some outcomes across several studies. For example, suppose NELP had a study that was testing the effects on vocabulary learning of a home visit program in which mothers were taught how to play language games with their young children. At the end of the study, the children's vocabulary would be tested and performance could be compared, allowing statements such as "Children in the experimental group knew 10 more words than the children who did not get this support." Of course, different studies use different tests; therefore, a 10-word improvement in one study might represent a big accomplishment reflecting a great deal of student learning, whereas in another it could mean more modest achievement. Thus, the effects have to be standardized; that is, they must be expressed in a standard way that makes them statistically comparable (effect sizes are stated in standard deviation units). Once effect size statistics are calculated they can be weighted by the number of children in the studies and averaged across the studies. That means the effect size for a group of interventions is an average of the effect sizes from that set of studies. Because there is usually variation in those effect sizes, it is possible to correlate various mediators or moderators with the variation to get clues about what influences the outcomes. Thus, it is possible to ask whether randomized or quasi-experimental studies ended up with different outcomes or whether studies that delivered the intervention one way or another did better. NELP provided both average weighted effect sizes for each intervention set, but we also conducted moderator analyses that examined demographic differences and instructional design differences.

How is an effect size interpreted?

Effect sizes are stated in terms of standard deviations (a measure of the amount of variation in a distribution) and they can be interpreted in terms of difference scores (thus, effect sizes are often summarized as d statistics). If an effect size was 1.00, it would mean that the experimental group outperformed the control group by 1 standard deviation. Another way of saying this would be that the average student in the experimental group was now performing at the 84th percentile on the outcome measure, whereas the average student in the control group was still at the 50th percentile—quite an advantage, given that this would be equivalent to a full year's difference on many standardized reading achievement tests. Theoretically, effect sizes could be higher than 3.00, but in education studies effect sizes tend to be lower than 1.00, and they can even be negative (i.e., the control group students gained more than the experimental ones). Effect sizes were characterized as large if they were higher than 0.80, moderate if they were in the 0.50–0.79 range, and small if they were lower than 0.30 (Cohen, 1988).

RESULTS

These meta-analyses allowed the panel to draw some important conclusions about what it is that children need to learn about language and literacy, and the kinds of instructional approaches that help children to learn these during the preschool and kindergarten years.

What variables predicted later literacy proficiency?

The panel identified 10 variables that were moderate-to-strong predictors of either later decoding or later reading comprehension literacy proficiency. Six of these variables maintained their predictive value even when variables such as IQ or socioeconomic status were controlled for: *alphabet knowledge* (knowing the names and sounds of letters), *phonological awareness* (the ability to detect, manipulate, or analyze the auditory aspects of spoken language independent of meaning), *rapid automatized naming of letters or digits* (the ability to name rapidly sequences of random letters or numerals), *rapid automatized naming of objects or colors* (the ability to name rapidly a sequence of repeating random sets of pictures of objects or colors), *writing or name writing* (the ability to write letters in isolation or to write one's own name), and *phonological memory* (the ability to remember spoken information for a short period of time).

Four other variables were moderately correlated with either later decoding or comprehension (there was also a visual processing variable that predicted later spelling), but they either did not maintain their predictor power when other variables were accounted for or had not been evaluated in this way yet: *concepts about print* (knowledge of print conventions, e.g., left–right), *print knowledge* (combination of alphabet knowledge, concepts about print, and early decoding), *reading readiness* (combination of alphabet knowledge, concepts about print, vocabulary, memory, and phonological awareness), and *oral language* (the ability to produce or comprehend oral language).

How well did these variables predict later literacy learning?

Table 1.1 summarizes the information about these variables, showing the correlations each variable had with decoding and reading comprehension, and the numbers of studies and students whose data were used for this analysis.

What can be said about these correlations?

One thing the panel noticed was that there were more studies (with more children) that tried to predict later decoding than studies that tried to predict reading comprehension. Still, for many of the variables there were plenty of data upon which to make sound estimates of the comprehension relationships (although the decoding estimates are somewhat more reliable). It is also notable that many variables had moderate-to-high relationships with later literacy. These variables clearly make useful measures for predicting later literacy, and they all need to be evaluated in terms of what causative role they might play in literacy learning. The panel was also struck by the similarity in predictive power that several variables had with both decoding and reading comprehension. Alphabet knowledge, phonological awareness, and oral language, for example, were equally effective in predicting later decoding and later reading comprehension.

Which of those variables should I teach to young children?

Studies show that teaching phonological awareness has a clear benefit to young children. When this is taught, children not only improve in phonological awareness but also in other literacy variables (and instruction aimed at teaching students to perceive sounds and to manipulate sounds is likely to have a positive impact on the memory for sounds as well). Alphabet knowledge can also be beneficial, at least when taught in

Table 1.1. Correlations of predictor variables with later decoding and reading comprehension

Predictor variables	Numbers of studies[a]	Numbers of students[b]	Correlations with decoding	Correlations with reading comprehension
Alphabet knowledge	52 / 17	7,570 / 2,038	.50	.48
Phonological awareness	69 / 20	8,433 / 2,461	.40	.44
Rapid automatized naming (letters or digits)	12 / 3	2,081 / 333	.40	.43
Rapid automatized naming (objects or colors)	16 / 6	3,100 / 1,146	.32	.42
Writing or name writing	10 / 4	1,650 / 565	.49	.33
Phonological memory	33 / 13	4,863 / 1,911	.26	.39
Concepts about print	12 / 3	2,604 / 535	.34	.54
Print knowledge	6 / 4	683 / 347	.29	.48
Reading readiness	5 / 3	1,988 / 348	.50	.59
Oral language	63 / 30	9,358 / 4,015	.33	.33

Source: National Early Literacy Panel (2008).
[a]Number of studies that provided data on predicting later decoding and reading comprehension outcomes. Listed as decoding studies / reading comprehension studies.
[b]Number of students whose data were used to predict later decoding and reading comprehension outcomes. Listed as decoding studies / reading comprehension studies.

conjunction with phonological awareness. Moreover, given the evidence, it seems to make sense to familiarize children with concepts about print, to get them writing, and to try to expand their oral language ability. Despite the strong correlations of some of the other variables, we would not recommend giving them much or any instructional attention. The tests for rapid automatized naming are meant to reveal how quickly children can process information cognitively; although these tests do predict reading proficiency, there have been no studies showing that teaching these skills eventually leads to improvements in literacy or even that rapid naming can be taught successfully. It would be best to wait on that one. The print knowledge and reading readiness tests are really composite measures of many skills and abilities, and they are redundant with the abilities already mentioned.

Why was the oral language prediction so low? And isn't it puzzling that the results are so similar for decoding and reading comprehension outcomes?

The panel was puzzled by this one, too, and we conducted some additional analyses to try to understand it better. There were many different kinds of oral language measures; therefore, NELP divided studies up on the basis of these differences. There were, for instance, studies that tested only expressive or receptive forms of language, or that looked only at vocabulary, and there were even differences in the kinds of vocabulary assessments that were used. There were also tests of listening comprehension and grammar, and there were composite measures that combined several of these measures of specific components of oral language.

When results were separated out for these different kinds of measures, a very different picture emerged. For example, the panel found that composite measures that addressed multiple skills in both receptive and expressive language evidenced much greater predictive power. These measures had a .70 correlation with reading comprehension and a .58 correlation with decoding; some other oral language measures also were more closely related to reading comprehension than decoding (i.e., listening comprehension, grammar, and expressive language measures). Unfortunately, many of the studies used either receptive or expressive vocabulary measures and these simply did not do a very good job of predicting later literacy (i.e., their correlations ranged from .24 to .34), suggesting that more complex measures of oral language should be used.

Which of these predictor skills matter in kindergarten and which in preschool?

The panel found few differences across those age levels; approximately 75% of the correlations were the same whether the predictor skill was measured in preschool or kindergarten. When there were differences, the preschool predictions tended to be stronger; but in each case, the average correlations were in the moderate or high range at both age levels. These results suggest that the kinds of skills and abilities that should be taught in preschool are the same as those that should be taught in kindergarten.

Are you really saying that children should be taught the same skills at both levels?

Generally, yes, but the devil is in the details. Although it makes sense to teach phonological awareness in both preschool and kindergarten, there is a rough sequence of development that was described in the NELP report. Children typically come to terms with the separations of larger units of sound (e.g., words and syllables) earlier than they do with individual phonemes. Although this is not a hard and fast developmental pattern (i.e., there are many children who deviate from it in various ways), it is reasonably descriptive to suggest that the larger units of sound should be taught earlier and that individual phonemes should come a bit later. Thus, teachers at both levels would be teaching phonological awareness, but different aspects of phonological awareness. Similarly, one would expect preschool teachers to focus on letters, sounds, and oral language concepts that are more distinctive and easier to learn than those that would come a bit later, but there is no reason to avoid working with any of these concepts even with younger children as long as the teaching is sensitive to what the children already know and how they are progressing.

What did the panel find out about code-based interventions?

The panel reviewed 78 studies on interventions that were mainly aimed at teaching skills to young children to help them crack the alphabetic code. The interventions had moderate-to-large effects on outcomes such as phonological awareness (effect size [ES] = 0.82, 51 studies) and alphabet knowledge (ES = 0.38, 24 studies) and on reading measures, too. Code-based interventions were varied, but they usually required children to detect or manipulate units of sound in words. Instructional activities that combined the teaching of phonological awareness with print-related training had the greatest impacts on children's learning.

Which commercial code-focused interventions were best?

For the most part, the studies did not examine commercial products; instead, they looked at experimental programs of instruction that could not be purchased. Even when commercial products were used in the studies, there would not be enough studies of any of these products to be able to say with any reliability which ones work consistently or with which kinds of children. However, the Institute of Education Sciences' What Works Clearinghouse (WWC) does evaluate studies of commercial instructional programs for teaching literacy to young children and for early childhood education; this information can be obtained from the WWC web site (http://ies.ed.gov/ncee/wwc).

Did the studies provide any guidance about how phonological awareness and alphabet knowledge should be taught?

It should be noted that none of these studies examined whole-class teaching of these dimensions of reading with young children. In all of the studies, this teaching was delivered either individually or to small groups of children. Although there was a great deal of variability in the programs of instruction, for the most part they focused on teacher-directed activities that helped children learn the skills through using those skills.

What did the panel find out about shared-book reading interventions?

Parents and teachers are widely advised to read to young children to improve literacy; therefore, the panel examined the experimental studies that have evaluated such practices. There were 19 of these types of studies that met the panel's criteria. Book-sharing interventions produced moderate-size effects on children's oral language skills (ES = 0.57, 15 studies) and print knowledge (ES = 0.50, 4 studies). The impact of shared reading was bigger on simple measures of oral vocabulary and smaller for more complex measures of language, such as listening comprehension—an unfortunate pattern given NELP's finding that there was a closer relationship between these complex measures and reading than there was between measures of receptive or expressive vocabulary and later reading.

Did the studies provide any guidance about how best to read to children?

Shared-reading interventions differed in how much interaction was required of the children. Some of these interventions required some form of dialogic reading, engaging the children in responding to questions or talking about the text in some fashion. In other cases, the children simply were required to listen. The effects on learning were greater when participation was required (ES for dialogic reading was 0.59 and for nondialogic reading it was 0.41), but this was not a statistically significant difference. We do not think that this is convincing evidence for just reading to children instead of engaging them in dialogue about the shared book. The reason for our skepticism is that there was an important difference in how these two sets of studies were executed: The nondialogic studies compared the effects of reading to children with those of not reading to children. Therefore, the effects reported were the effects of reading. In contrast, the dialogic reading studies compared the effects of both reading to and interacting with young children to those of just reading to them. Therefore, the effects reported were the effects of the dialogic portion of the activity, because the control condition takes the effect of just reading into account. Thus, these studies suggest that it is important to engage children in talking about and thinking about what is being read to them.

Who should read to children?

In these studies, parents and preschool or kindergarten teachers were the readers and it did not seem to matter who provided the reading. Effect sizes came out pretty much the same, suggesting that children benefited equally from being read to by both groups and even from being read to by combinations of parents and teachers.

What did the panel find out about parent and home interventions?

The panel examined 32 studies that used parents as the agent of the intervention. This varied set of studies included a wide range of interventions, including those with general goals of improving children's health, behavior, or cognitive functioning, and those with more specific goals (e.g., improving children's oral language skills). These varied studies showed moderate-to-large effects on oral language outcomes (ES = 0.37, 18 studies) and general cognitive abilities (ES = 0.92, 6 studies). As with the shared reading studies, these programs had greater impacts on vocabulary (ES = 0.41) than on complex language outcomes (ES = 0.27). Usually, other outcome measures were not used in these studies.

What were the most important dimensions of successful home literacy programs?

The panel was not able to determine features of the parent-based programs that conferred the greatest literacy advantages. The diversity of interventions was so great that it was not possible to make worthwhile comparisons of the programs by intervention features, for the most part; even when such comparisons could be made they were not very informative. For example, the panel was interested in whether parent-based programs worked better when offered in conjunction with high-quality, center-based early childhood education programs. However, there were only a few studies that could be used to address this question, and the results were inconsistent: Sometimes there was an additive impact, and sometimes there was not.

What did the panel find out about preschool and kindergarten programs?

Preschool and kindergarten programs affected children's development of conventional literacy skills and early literacy skills. Such programs had clear and small-to-moderate impacts on reading (ES = 0.75, 9 studies) and on spelling (ES = 0.34, 3 studies), but the spelling effects were only seen in kindergarten programs, probably due to curriculum coverage at that level. Preschool and kindergarten literacy programs had their greatest impact on the reading readiness measures (ES = 1.22, 3 studies), but they had very little impact on oral language development (ES = 0.13, 12 studies).

What did the panel find out about language enhancement interventions?

Obviously, many of the previously discussed interventions had positive impacts on oral language development. Nevertheless, there are interventions that more explicitly attempt to enhance oral language ability, and NELP examined studies of such efforts. The meta-analysis of these studies indicated that such interventions did increase children's oral language skills to a large and statistically significant degree (ES = 0.63, 19 studies). These interventions enhanced performance on a diverse set of oral language measures.

What were the most important dimensions of successful oral language enhancement programs?

Language interventions were more effective with younger children (3 years of age and younger) than with older ones; therefore, intervening early in this area might be a sound strategy. Play-based strategies, in which toys are provided along with opportunities for the child to explore language, had higher effect sizes than did strategies that were not play-based, but the difference was not statistically significant.

Did any of the interventions work better for some types of children than for others?

With a couple of exceptions, demographic differences did not matter much in the effectiveness of these procedures (i.e., oral language interventions were more effective with younger children and spelling outcomes were more common with kindergarten children). Socioeconomic status, race, ethnicity, language background, and even age were not found to mediate these findings. However, even though these studies examined the learning of diverse groups of youngsters, they often did not separate their data when the study was reported. Without such separation it is impossible to determine whether there were different outcomes. That means that NELP's demographic comparisons were generally weak; that is, there were only a few studies that were actually being compared in these analyses. The studies generally provided no evidence for the idea that different kinds of instruction are needed by different kinds of students.

Did the NELP study have any limitations?

Yes. All studies have some limitations, and the NELP study is no exception. One limitation of a meta-analysis has to do with the availability of studies. Although NELP synthesized literally hundreds of studies, there often were no data on variables or issues that the panel would have liked to pursue. Another limitation has to do with the quality of the original studies. All studies have varying degrees of weakness, and the value of a synthesis is always constrained by the quality of the data that it encompasses. There were significant problems with the quality of much of the research on early childhood literacy instruction. Building a sufficient knowledge base concerning early literacy skill development will require more high-quality research.

CONCLUSION

NELP provided an extensive synthesis of the research on early childhood and kindergarten literacy. Its report described 10 early childhood measures that had moderate and large correlations with later decoding and reading comprehension outcomes. Such measures have value not only as a means for identifying students who are likely to have difficulty in learning to read, but also in helping to determine what skills should be the focus of an early childhood or kindergarten curriculum. The panel also provided reviews of research on code-based, shared-book, home- and parent-based, preschool, kindergarten, and oral language interventions. All of these interventions were successful, although there were varying amounts and quality of evidence supporting each of them. However, different approaches had different patterns of outcomes—an important finding given the varied nature of the skills that students need to develop. Explicit code-based teaching exerted clear and consistent impacts on a variety of skills, particularly on alphabet knowledge, phonological awareness, and conventional reading measures such as decoding. Conversely, shared-book experiences, parent-based programs, and interventions aimed at improving oral language all had notable oral language outcomes. This suggests the possibility that various program elements could be combined into more powerful and complete supports for young children's literacy learning.

REFERENCES

Baer, J., Kutner, M., & Sabatini, J. (2009). *Basic reading skills and the literacy of America's least literate adults: Results from the 2003 National Assessment of Adult Literacy (NAAL) supplemental studies* (NCES 2009-481). Washington, DC: U.S. Department of Education, Institute of Education Sciences, National Center for Education Statistics.

Campbell, J.R., Reese, C.M., O'Sullivan, C., & Dossey, J.A. (1996). *NAEP 1994 trends in academic progress* (NCES 97-583). Washington, DC: U.S. Department of Education, Office of Educational Research and Improvement.

Cohen, J. (1988). *Statistical power for behavioral sciences* (2nd ed.). Mahwah, NJ: Lawrence Erlbaum Associates.

National Center for Education Statistics. (2009). *The nation's report card: Reading 2009* (NCES 2010-458). Washington, DC: U.S. Department of Education, Institute of Education Sciences, National Center for Education Statistics.

National Early Literacy Panel. (2008). *Developing early literacy: Report of the National Early Literacy Panel.* Washington, DC: National Institute for Literacy.

National Institute of Child Health and Human Development. (2000). *Report of the National Reading Panel: Teaching children to read: An evidence-based assessment of the scientific research literature on reading and its implications for reading instruction* (NIH Publication No. 00-4769). Washington, DC: Government Printing Office.

Rothstein, H.R., Sutton, A.J., & Borenstein, M. (Eds.). (2005). *Publication bias in meta-analysis—prevention, assessment and adjustments.* New York, NY: Wiley.

Shanahan, T., & Shanahan, C. (2008). Teaching disciplinary literacy to adolescents: Rethinking content-area literacy. *Harvard Educational Review, 78*(1), 40–59.

Snyder, T., Dillow, S., & Hoffman, C. (2008). *Digest of education statistics 2007* (NCES 2008-022). Washington, DC: U.S. Department of Education, Institute of Education Sciences, National Center for Education Statistics.

2

Contributions of Large-Scale Federal Research Projects to the Early Literacy Knowledge Base

James A. Griffin and Peggy McCardle

Prior to, during the literature review for, and after the publication of the National Early Literacy Panel (NELP; 2008) report, large-scale research and evaluation projects funded by the federal government had been and still are taking place; yet, very little of the knowledge gained from these projects is reflected in the NELP report. This was by design; the literature review that formed the basis of the NELP report purposely examined only research that had appeared in refereed research journals and thus de facto excluded the findings of government reports (Shanahan & Lonigan, 2010). However, most if not all of these large federal studies can make a contribution to what is known about the development of early literacy, including those studies specifically designed to evaluate the effectiveness of programs that have as

Authors' Note: The views expressed in this manuscript are those of the authors and do not purport to represent those of the National Institutes of Health, the *Eunice Kennedy Shriver* National Institute of Child Health and Human Development, or the U.S. Department of Health and Human Services.

their primary or secondary goal the improvement of early literacy skills. Although these studies did not fit NELP's methodology, either because of their lack of peer-reviewed publications (the majority of these studies have resulted in government-published technical reports) or because they were published after the NELP literature review was completed, their findings have value for the field. These projects include descriptive longitudinal studies (e.g., the Early Childhood Longitudinal Study, Birth Cohort), evaluations of national intervention programs (e.g., Head Start, Early Reading First), and large initiatives involving multiple researcher-designed intervention studies (e.g., the Interagency School Readiness Consortium).

This chapter briefly reviews these major research projects and highlights their relevant findings, because they can inform both current efforts to improve early literacy with evidence-based practices and what additional research is needed to continue to move toward evidence-based practice for the nation's preschool children. It is beyond the scope of this chapter to include all large-scale federal data collection efforts (e.g., Zhai, Brooks-Gunn, & Waldfogel, 2011); therefore, we focus on those that include a direct assessment of children's preliteracy and early literacy skills. Finally, we make a case for the use of the datasets generated by these studies for secondary data analyses that can contribute to the peer-reviewed literature.

DESCRIPTIVE LONGITUDINAL STUDIES

Three major federally supported descriptive longitudinal studies provide both important findings on early child development and learning and extremely useful, well-documented datasets available for additional analysis: the National Institute of Child Health and Human Development (NICHD)[1] Study of Early Child Care and Youth Development (SECCYD) and the Early Childhood Longitudinal Studies, Birth Cohort (ECLS-B) and Kindergarten Cohort (ECLS-K).

National Institute of Child Health and Human Development Study of Early Child Care and Youth Development

In the early 1990s, the majority of children began some nonmaternal care by 6 months of age. The NICHD SECCYD, also known as the Child Care Study or the Day Care Study, began in 1991. Its major goal was to exam-

---

[1]Note that the National Institute of Child Health and Human Development (NICHD) was renamed the *Eunice Kenney Shriver* National Institute of Child Health and Human Development by the U.S. Congress in 2008.

ine how differences in child care experiences relate to children's social, emotional, intellectual, and language development, and to their physical growth and health. Researchers collected data on 1,364 children who were born healthy into a variety of backgrounds, in English-speaking families, starting at birth; the data were collected at 10 sites around the country. In addition to child care arrangements and family characteristics, the researchers collected in-depth data on cognitive and language development, social behavior, emotional development, the children's relationships with their parents, and health and physical growth through age 15.

Children who experienced higher-quality child care showed somewhat better cognitive functioning and language development across the first 3 years of life (NICHD Early Child Care Research Network, 2000). The most important feature of quality caregiving was the language used by the caregiver. Caregivers who stimulated language by asking questions and responding to vocalizations were associated with better cognitive and language development in children. Higher-quality child care also predicted greater school readiness at age 4½ years, as measured by standardized tests of early literacy and number skills (NICHD Early Child Care Research Network, 2002). However, child care quality effects were much less predictive of children's early literacy skills than were parent and family characteristics and effects found using similar measures of the quality of parent–child interactions.

One of the SECCYD's strengths was the depth of assessment conducted at multiple time points as the children developed (Vandell et al., 2010). Assessments of children's school readiness and academic achievement from ages 4½ to 15 demonstrated a remarkable level of consistency, with the quality of child care associated with school readiness skills at age 4½ (effect size [d] = 0.06), school readiness skills associated with academic achievement in first grade (d = 0.97), first grade predicting third-grade achievement (d = 0.95), third grade predicting fifth-grade achievement (d = 0.92), and fifth grade achievement predicting academic achievement at age 15 (d = 0.89). Part of this stability may be due to the educational environments children find themselves in after school entry. In a study assessing the quality of teaching the SECCYD children received in school, Pianta, Belsky, Houts, Morrison, and the NICHD Early Child Care Research Network (2007) found that most children received at best mediocre quality of instruction and that children from disadvantaged backgrounds were very unlikely to receive high-quality instruction, only 10% being in classrooms with a high instructional climate across multiple grade levels. Overall, the SECCYD's findings demonstrate both the stability of academic achievement over time as well as the long-term impact that the quality of early care has on academic achievement more than 10 years later.

Early Childhood Longitudinal Study, Birth Cohort

The ECLS-B was the first nationally representative study within the United States to directly assess children's early mental and physical development, the quality of their early care and education settings, and the contributions of their fathers, as well as their mothers, in their lives. The ECLS-B was designed to provide detailed information on children's development, health, and early learning experiences in the years leading up to entry into school. The children were followed from birth through kindergarten entry. As of 2009, when data for birth through age 4 were published (Chernoff, Flanagan, McPhee, & Park, 2007), information had been collected from children and their parents three times: when the children were about 9 months of age (2001), about 2 years of age (2003), and about preschool age (i.e., 4 years of age; 2005). Because we wanted to examine early literacy findings, we did not extensively review reports from the earlier data waves (Flanagan & West, 2004; Mulligan & Flanagan, 2006). Data collected included direct assessment parent reports from mothers and fathers, information from early care and education providers, and observations conducted at early care and education settings (Chernoff et al., 2007).

The ECLS-B assessed performance in language, literacy, mathematics, color knowledge, and fine motor skills when the children were ages 48 months–57 months, although some were as young as 44 months or as old as 65 months. Twenty percent of the children were in no regular child care or educational setting on a regular basis, but 44% were in a Head Start setting, and almost 21% were in home care settings (Chernoff et al., 2007).

Findings on the children's abilities are presented, as noted, only in descriptive, broad-brush proportions. Basically, the majority (63.3%) of children could name five colors without prompting, although relatively more Caucasian and Asian American children were able to do so than African American or Hispanic children. Of particular interest for early literacy are both the language and literacy performance. For language skills, girls outperformed boys both on receptive vocabulary and expressive narrative ability. Unsurprisingly, children from lower socioeconomic status (SES) performed less well than those with the highest SES, and those with very low birth weight performed less well than children with typical and moderately low birth weight. Children from all family types (two parent, single parent, and other) performed equally well.

The study assessed literacy in terms of letter recognition, phonological awareness, and concepts about print (e.g., understanding that reading English text proceeds from left to right). Children in two-parent families outperformed those in single-parent families on overall literacy, and this was also the case for each subarea of literacy activities. On the overall literacy scale, Asian American children performed best (17.5 out of a potential score of 37), with Caucasian children following (14.2), then African American children (12), Hispanic children (10.7), and American Indian and Alaska Native children (9.6). Typical birth weight children performed better than children with moderately low or very low birth weight (13.3, 11.9, and 11.4, respectively). And as might be expected given that poverty is a known risk factor affecting early learning, children from higher SES families outperformed those from middle and lower SES families (18 compared with 12.7 and 9.2, respectively). These patterns held for each of the three component areas: letter recognition, phonological awareness, and concepts about print.

Denton Flanagan and McPhee (2009) report on the data at kindergarten entry (ages 5 and 6 years); these data were collected on 9,850 children across two school years (2006–2007 and 2007–2008) to be able to include those children with "late" birthdays who were not eligible for kindergarten and those who did not enter kindergarten the first year that they were age eligible. For the kindergarten wave of data, information was collected on early reading and mathematics, fine motor skills, and school and classroom characteristics. For the kindergarten assessments, the reading assessment measured such skills as children's letter recognition, letter–sound knowledge, recognition of simple words, phonological awareness, receptive and expressive vocabulary knowledge, and knowledge of concepts about print. Language per se was not assessed, except as part of the overall reading assessment.

Generally, those children who performed best in reading and mathematics came from two-parent households, at or above the poverty level, and had English as the primary home language. Caucasian and Asian American children performed better than children from other racial and ethnic groups. In addition, children who had participated in early care and education arrangements the year prior to kindergarten performed better than children who had not had these experiences (Denton Flanagan & McPhee, 2009). Broadly speaking, both the 4-year-old and the kindergarten entry data on the children in the ECLS-B illustrate that poverty is clearly a risk factor in literacy and learning, and that children with preschool experience prior to kindergarten perform better on literacy tasks at kindergarten entry.

Early Childhood Longitudinal Study, Kindergarten Cohort

Kindergarten and first grade represent a time of rapid growth and learning for children, and often the acquisition of reading knowledge gains greater emphasis at this point. Until the ECLS-K, few national data were available on young children's reading skills. The ECLS-K followed a nationally representative sample of kindergartners in Fall 1998 through eighth grade to obtain such data. The study collected information directly from the children, their families, their teachers, and their schools. The full ECLS-K base-year sample comprised approximately 22,000 children who attended about 1,000 kindergarten programs during the 1998–1999 school year (West, Denton, & Germino-Hausken, 2000).

Of particular interest to us, the ECLS-K assessed children's reading skills and collected detailed information about the children's home literacy environments and the reading instruction they received in school. Denton, West, and Walston (2003) summarized findings from the ECLS-K on the children's reading skills for kindergarten and first grade and on the classroom experiences of these beginning readers.

The ECLS-K assessed various components of reading at the beginning and end of both kindergarten and first grade. The ECLS-K researchers developed an individually administered, untimed adaptive assessment that covered basic reading skills (e.g., recognizing printed words), vocabulary (e.g., knowing the meaning of single words), and reading comprehension. Reading comprehension was broken down into four areas: identifying the main point of a passage or understanding words in the context of simple passages; linking information within a text and focusing on specific information; relating what is in the text to personal background knowledge or experience; and understanding text objectively, such as what events in that text are plausible. The researchers included items that assessed both listening comprehension and comprehension of written text, because kindergartners are just beginning to read. The study did not assess writing, based on the time and cost of scoring such assessments. It also did not assess oral language directly, other than via vocabulary and listening comprehension items (Denton et al., 2003).

At kindergarten entry in Fall 1998, about two thirds of the children already knew the letters of the alphabet, about one third knew the letter–sound relationships for beginnings of words, and about one in five knew this information for the ends of words. Some children could already read single words. By the end of kindergarten, nearly all of the children knew their letters, 70% had letter–sound recognition for word beginnings, and half could recognize letter–sound correspondences at the ends of words. By the beginning of first grade, one fourth of the children could read frequently encountered words and one in 10 could read and understand words in context; these proportions grew to three fourths and four in ten, respectively, by the end of first grade (Denton & West, 2002).

There were several factors examined that might correlate with growth in learning to read. At kindergarten entry, Caucasian children scored higher than African American or Hispanic children on letter and letter–sound correspondence recognition, and children whose mothers had higher levels of education performed better than those whose mothers had less education (West et al., 2000). Similarly, children from nonpoor families outperformed those from poor families, and those with multiple risk factors performed worse than those with one or no risk factors (Zill & West, 2000). During the course of kindergarten, children at risk for school failure did make some gains—most notably in basic reading skills. However, on the more difficult tasks, such as word reading, the gap between those at risk and those not at risk actually widened (Denton & West, 2002).

Those data showed that a literacy-rich home environment—in which children are read and sung to, are told stories frequently, and have a larger supply of books, audiotapes, and CDs—was important to the development of literacy skills. (NELP looked at the correlations of early literacy skills with later literacy achievement, but the ECLS-K considered environmental variables and their correlation with later literacy learning.) Home environments correlated with higher literacy skills for the children in the cohort, regardless of family income level, not only at the beginning of kindergarten but throughout kindergarten and first grade (Denton & West, 2002). Furthermore, children with higher literacy skills at the beginning of kindergarten were more likely to perform well at the end of both kindergarten and first grade—a finding consistent with the NELP conclusions.

Two other factors that correlated with growth in reading were attitude and health. Children who persisted at tasks, paid attention, and appeared eager to learn had higher reading skill scores in the spring of both kindergarten and first grade than did children who exhibited these characteristics less frequently. Children with very good to excellent health at kindergarten entry had higher reading scores at the end of both years as well. Overall, the ECLS-K data, consistent with the SEC-CYD and ECLS-B findings, indicate that reading achievement during kindergarten and first grade was related to child, family, and home literacy characteristics, as well as early literacy skills and attitude toward learning, regardless of poverty status or race and ethnicity.

Additional data on the educational experiences of the ECLS-K children were gathered via teacher reports and classroom observations (Walston & West, 2004). According to data from Spring 1999, full-day classes were more likely than half-day classes to use mixed-level grouping (48% versus 42%), reading achievement grouping (26% versus 14%), and peer tutoring in reading (23% versus 15%) on a daily basis.

The most common reading instructional activities were recognizing alphabet letters and matching letters to sounds. Full-day classes spent more time every day on these and other activities: concepts about print, vocabulary, predicting based on text, using context clues to understand text, rhyming words, reading aloud, and so forth. Overall, findings from the ECLS-K data indicate that public school children in full-day kindergartens learned more during the academic year in both reading and mathematics than those attending half-day programs (Walston & West, 2004).

In summary, analyses of the ECLS-K data from the beginning of kindergarten, end of kindergarten, and first grade indicate that the skills children bring to school at the onset of kindergarten are critically important. Secondary data analysis of the ECLS-B and ECLS-K data sets clearly demonstrates that in the United States, the achievement gap between children from disadvantaged sociodemographic groups and their more advantaged peers emerges by 2 years of age (Fuller et al., 2009; Hillemeier, Farkas, Morgan, Martin, & Maczuga, 2008) and persists through 4 years of age and beyond (Chernoff et al., 2007; Zill & West, 2000). If they start out behind, they are highly likely to remain behind, despite gains; few if any of them close the gap. More time in school with reading instruction makes a positive difference for all kindergarten children, and those gains persist through first grade.

It must be emphasized that there are other large federally funded data sets, such as the Fragile Families and Child Wellbeing Study (Reichman, Teitler, Garfinkel, & McLanahan, 2001) available for secondary data analysis, and that the SECCYD, ECLS-B, and ECLS-K were used as exemplars because of their size and coverage of the early developmental period addressed by the NELP report. The long-term consequences of early childhood poverty (Duncan, Ziol-Guest, & Kalil, 2010) and the importance of school readiness skills for later achievement (Duncan et al., 2007) are coming into clearer focus thanks to the existence of these types of longitudinal data sets. What is less clear, however, is how to intervene meaningfully to ameliorate these early differences and prevent pernicious effects later in life.

NATIONAL PROGRAM EVALUATION STUDIES

There have also been federally funded studies that have evaluated the effect of federally supported preschool programs. Here we report on the findings of the Early Head Start Impact study, the Head Start Impact study, and the two related descriptive longitudinal studies, Head Start Family and Child Experiences Study and Early Head Start Family and Child Experiences Survey (Baby FACES), with particular attention to the findings relevant to early literacy development.

Head Start Impact Study

The Head Start program was begun in 1965 as part of President Lyndon B. Johnson's national "War on Poverty" with the goal of boosting school readiness in low-income children. To give a sense of the size of Head Start, in 2009 approximately 904,153 children attended Head Start programs in 49,200 classrooms across the nation, with nearly half attending full-day programs. Approximately 46% of Head Start children enter the program at age 3 or younger; the rest enter as 4-year-olds. Slightly more than half of the children in Head Start are boys. Approximately one third of the children are African American, one third are Hispanic, and one third are Caucasian (Administration for Children and Families [ACF], 2010a).

In 1998, in reauthorizing the program, Congress mandated that the U.S. Department of Health and Human Services (DHHS) study the national-level impact of Head Start. Specifically, DHHS was tasked with determining what difference the program had made to development and learning (in multiple domains) and parental practices, and under what circumstances (which services and for which children).

After serious consideration of designs that could address the mandated questions, DHHS began a randomized controlled trial of two cohorts (3-year-olds and 4-year-olds eligible for Head Start enrollment; ACF, 2010b). The study collected data from 2002–2006 on a nationally representative sample of programs and children. The sample included 4,667 children from 383 randomly selected programs in 23 states. The children randomized to Head Start programs were compared with a control group of children who were eligible for Head Start but were randomized to have no access to the program. However, control group children were allowed to enroll in other early childhood programs; approximately 60% of these children did so. This enabled the researchers to compare participation in Head Start programs with participation in other preschool programs such as state prekindergarten programs and center-based child care programs. The study examined multiple domains of learning and followed the children through first grade and kindergarten to determine longer-term impact. In this chapter, we examine only those findings that are relevant to literacy.

Among the overall findings, there were some benefits in areas related to early literacy (ACF, 2010b). The study examined cognitive performance via direct assessments of language, literacy, prewriting (in Head Start years only), and mathematics skills; teacher reports of children's school performance; and parent reports of children's literacy skills and grade promotion.

Access to Head Start was found to have positive impacts on several aspects of children's school readiness during their time in the program.

Specifically, benefits for the 4-year-old group at the end of the Head Start year were concentrated in language and literacy, including vocabulary (as measured by the Peabody Picture Vocabulary Test–Third Edition [PPVT-III]; Dunn & Dunn, 1997), letter-word identification, spelling, letter naming (as measured by Oral Language Aptitude and Reading Aptitude subtests of the Woodcock-Johnson III [WJ-III]; Woodcock, McGrew, & Mather, 2000), and parent-reported emergent literacy. For the 3-year-old group, similar benefits were found by the end of the children's first year in Head Start, as well as at 4 years of age. Those findings specific to early literacy included vocabulary (PPVT scores), letter-word identification and letter naming (WJ-III scores), elision (phonological processing) as measured by the Preschool Comprehensive Test of Phonological and Print Processing (TOPEL; Lonigan, Wagner, Torgesen, & Rashotte, 2002), parent-reported emergent literacy, and perceptual motor skills and prewriting (as measured by the McCarthy Draw-A-Design Task, part of the McCarthy Scales of Children's Abilities; McCarthy, 1972). However, for both cohorts these advantages did not persist, and few statistically significant differences in outcomes remained at the end of both kindergarten and first grade for the sample as a whole. By the end of first grade for the 4-year-old cohort, only vocabulary remained significantly different from the control group. For the 3-year-old cohort, by the end of first grade the children performed significantly better as a group only on the WJ-III Test of Oral Comprehension (ACF, 2010b).

To provide some context for these results, the Head Start Impact Study researchers compared skill levels of children in the study with norms for the general population of 3- and 4-year-old children in the United States at that time (including children who did not come from low-income families). The study children scored low in letter identification: only 55% of the 4-year-old Head Start group and 65% of the 3-year-old Head Start group were able to recognize all of the letters of the alphabet by the end of their kindergarten year. Similarly, in the control group 58% of the 4-year-olds and 64% of the 3-year-olds recognized all of the letters of the alphabet by the end of kindergarten. To put this finding in context, the ECLS-K found that 95% of children in the United States know all of the letters of the alphabet by the end of their kindergarten year (ACF, 2010b).

In addition to the Head Start Impact Study, there is also an ongoing descriptive study that provides a snapshot of the progress children make during the time they attend Head Start and during their transition into kindergarten: The Head Start Family and Child Experiences Survey (FACES). The Administration for Children and Families launched FACES in 1997 as a periodic, longitudinal study of Head Start program performance. This survey has been used to examine successive nationally representative samples of Head Start children, their families, and their classrooms. The Head Start programs provide descriptive information about their staff and the population they serve, as well as classroom practices (ACF, 2003, 2006, 2008). FACES also uses measures of quality and child outcomes, including a battery of direct child assessments across several developmental domains. In addition, the study includes interviews with parents, teachers, and Head Start program managers, as well as direct classroom observations. Data from five FACES cohorts have been fielded to date—FACES 1997, 2000, 2003, 2006, and 2009. Although periodic government reports have been released providing descriptive findings based on the FACES data set, it is only recently that data from the 1997–2006 cohorts have been made available to outside researchers for secondary data analysis.

Early Head Start Impact Study

In 1994 the Administration on Children, Youth and Families (ACYF) began the Early Head Start (EHS) program to enhance very young children's development and health, to strengthen family and community partnerships, and to support the staff who would deliver these new services to low-income families with pregnant women, infants, or toddlers (ACF, 2002). This program officially became part of the overall Head Start program in 1995.

To ascertain the effectiveness of the EHS program, ACYF established a consortium of 17 programs (serving approximately 3,000 families) that had partnered with local researchers to participate in a large-scale, rigorous, random-assignment evaluation study. These EHS programs were characterized according to the options they offered families: 1) *center-based,* providing all services to families through center-based child care and education, parent education, and a minimum of two home visits per year to each family; 2) *home-based,* providing all services to families through weekly home visits and at least two group socializations per month for each family; or 3) *mixed approach,* a diverse group of programs providing center-based services to some families, home-based services to other families, or a mixture of center- and home-based services. Although initially the mix of program types was balanced, by Fall 1997 the mix was seven home-based, four center-based, and six mixed (ACF, 2002).

The short-term impact research showed that effects overall were modest, although stronger results were demonstrated for some subgroups in specific domains of development (ACF, 2002). EHS programs showed statistically significant, positive impacts on cognitive development at age 2, and these impacts were sustained to 3 years of age. These children scored higher, on average, on the Bayley Scales of Infant Development (Bayley, 1969) Mental Development Index (MDI; mean of 91.4 for the EHS group compared with 89.9 for the control group), although still functioning below the national typical score of 100. In addition, a smaller percentage of EHS children (27.3% versus 32%) scored in the at-risk range (below 85 on the MDI); this may indicate reduced risk for poor cognitive and educational outcomes in later years, but such speculation must acknowledge these children's still below-average level of functioning. Children in EHS programs also demonstrated sustained (to age 3) impacts in language development, scoring higher in vocabulary (as measured by the PPVT-III; Dunn & Dunn, 1997) than comparison children (the mean PPVT-III score for EHS children at age 3 was 83.3, compared with 81.1 for the comparison group), although still well below the national typical score of 100. As with general cognitive functioning, the proportion of 3-year-old EHS children at risk based on vocabulary scores was lower than for comparison children (51.1% versus 57.1%; ACF, 2002).

Within programs, some differences in impact were noted. Although all program approaches showed benefits to children and parents, some programs showed stronger literacy-related benefits. Center-based programs were seen to enhance cognitive development consistently, and home-based programs showed favorable impacts on language development (vocabulary) at 2 but not 3 years of age. Vocabulary was consistently enhanced (i.e., at both 2 and 3 years of age) in those children who were in mixed-approach programs (ACF, 2002).

When examined by length of time in program, the EHS Impact Study demonstrated that earlier is better. For example, for the group of families enrolled when the mothers were pregnant, impacts on many child outcomes were stronger, including a greater tendency for parents to read on a daily basis to their children. It is interesting to note that the researchers conducting the impact studies found evidence that effects on EHS children were associated with positive parenting impacts. For example, in literacy-related domains, higher cognitive scores were associated with a more supportive cognitive and literacy environment for 2-year-olds and with higher levels of parent supportiveness in play for 3-year-olds (ACF, 2002).

A follow-up study of children who attended EHS programs was conducted at fifth grade, 7 years after the end of the program (Vogel, Xue, Moiduddin, Kisker, & Carlson, 2010). Impacts on the full sample of children and families in the fifth grade follow-up revealed that EHS did not continue to have the broad pattern of impacts for child and family outcomes seen at earlier ages. The overall intent-to-treat analysis demonstrated no significant differences between EHS attendees and control group children in fifth grade (Vogel et al., 2010). Nonexperimental analyses showed that children who attended EHS, received formal care (including Head Start) at ages 3 and 4, and attended a school with fewer children receiving free and reduced-price lunches scored 6 points higher on the PPVT in fifth grade than children who received none of these services early in life and attended a high-poverty school as measured by subsidized lunch program usage (Vogel et al., 2010).

Overall, the findings of the EHS Impact Study suggest that the program had some short-term effects on early language and preliteracy skills, but these gains were not sustained through fifth grade. The study also suggests that when it comes to intervention, earlier is better—enrolling children and families as early as possible, even during pregnancy, is desirable—and that children who are offered services from birth to 3 years of age and beyond can and do make gains in literacy-related domains such as vocabulary and overall cognitive development.

In 2008 the EHS Family and Child Experiences Survey (Baby FACES) was launched by ACF. This study uses a longitudinal cohort design that identifies a representative sample of EHS programs and two cohorts of families in each program: a perinatal group and a group of infants about 1 year old. Data will be collected annually, in spring, until the sample children reach 3 years of age, with a supplemental interview about transition activities with some parents when the children are 3½ years old.

For the first Baby FACES report (Vogel et al., 2011) a nationally representative sample of 89 EHS programs was used to enroll 976 parents of children who were in two age cohorts in Spring 2009: 194 newborns (including pregnant women and children up to 8 weeks old) and 782 1-year-olds (including children ages 10 months–15 months). When the children are 2 and 3 years old, direct child assessments will be used to measure cognitive and language development and record the children's interactions with their parents. EHS staff report that for language development children's vocabulary comprehension is comparable to national norms but vocabulary production is slightly behind typical levels. EHS staff members also report that children from English-speaking homes comprehend more English words than children who are dual language learners (DLLs), for whom the dominant home language is typically Spanish. Children who are DLLs are reported to understand more words in Spanish than in English and to understand more total words, including both English and Spanish words, than children who are not DLLs (Vogel et al., 2011). We anticipate that the Baby FACES data set will be made available for secondary data analysis subsequent to the release of the government summary report for that cohort.

Reading First and Early Reading First Impact Studies

On January 8, 2002, President George W. Bush signed the No Child Left Behind Act of 2001 (PL 107-110) into law, with the hope of ushering in a new era of evidence-based teaching practices that would increase the academic achievement of American students. The law added two important new reading programs to the Elementary and Secondary Education Act of 1965 (PL 89-10, 115 Stat. 1425): Reading First (RF) and Early Reading First (ERF). The ERF program was created to address the reality that many children begin kindergarten without the necessary foundation to fully benefit from formal school instruction. The goal was to support local efforts to enhance the early language, preliteracy, and literacy development of preschool-age children, particularly those from low-income families, through strategies and professional development that were based on scientifically based reading research. Likewise, the goal of the RF program was to provide funding to states and districts to establish scientifically based reading programs (i.e., programs that have been shown by research to be effective) for students enrolled in kindergarten through third grade to ensure that all children learn to read well by the end of third grade. No Child Left Behind also designated funds for the evaluation of both programs, a summary of the results follow.

The ERF program provided targeted funding to early childhood programs that serve primarily low-income children, including Head Start centers, Title I preschools,[2] Even Start centers,[3] state prekindergartens, and child care centers. The ERF Impact Study used a quasi-experimental design (regression discontinuity) to determine an unbiased estimate of the program's impact (Jackson et al., 2011). The evaluation looked at 65 sites that applied for funding in 2003, comparing the child outcomes of 28 sites that received ERF funding with 37 sites that did not receive funding. Data collected included individual assessments of 4-year-old children's early language and literacy skills, classroom observations, and surveys of program staff and the children's parents.

---

[2]Title I refers to a title in the Elementary and Secondary Education Act of 1965 (PL 89-10, 115 Stat. 1425), federal legislation that provides financial assistance to local educational agencies for schools with high numbers or high percentages of children from low-income families to help ensure that these children's educational needs are met.

[3]Even Start centers were established to provide family literacy services. The legislative authority was as follows: The Even Start Family Literacy Program—Title I, Part B, Subpart 3 of the Elementary and Secondary Education Act of 1965 (PL 89-10, 115 Stat. 1425)— was first authorized in 1988 with an appropriation of $14.8 million. The program became state administered in 1992 when the appropriation exceeded $50 million. Most recently, the program was reauthorized by the Literacy Involves Families Together (LIFT) Act of 2000 (as enacted by the Consolidated Appropriations Act of 2001 [PL 106-554]) and the No Child Left Behind Act of 2001 (PL 107-110).

The ERF program was found to have a significant impact on classroom environments and teacher practices related to early literacy development, including the language environment of the classroom, book-reading practices, phonological awareness activities, and educational practices that support print and letter knowledge and writing. Findings for the direct child assessment measures demonstrated that the ERF program had a significant positive impact on children's print and letter knowledge but no discernable impact on phonological awareness or oral language (Jackson et al., 2011). Thus, the ERF program appears to have changed teaching practices in preschool settings serving disadvantaged children, but changes in children's preliteracy skills were limited to print and letter knowledge.

Like the ERF program evaluation, the RF program evaluation utilized a quasi-experimental, regression-discontinuity design (Gamse, Jacob, Horst, Boulay, & Unlu, 2008). School districts nationwide were selected based on their use of a quantifiable rating or ranking process to choose which schools within the district would receive RF funding. The evaluation compared 125 schools scoring above their district's cutoff point for funding with 125 schools scoring below the cutoff point. Data collection included direct student assessments in reading comprehension for Grades 1–3, decoding in the spring of first grade, and classroom observations of reading instruction in the first and second grades. The RF program was found to have a significant impact on classroom environments and teacher practices related to the development of literacy skills, with more instructional time spent on the five essential components of reading instruction (phonemic awareness, phonics, vocabulary, fluency, and reading comprehension). Direct child assessments in the spring of first grade demonstrated significant gains in decoding skills relative to students in the comparison group. However, the RF program did not produce a significant impact on student reading comprehension test scores in Grades 1, 2, or 3 (Gamse et al., 2008).

Taken together, the results of the ERF and RF program evaluations indicate that both programs were successful at changing instructional practices related to preliteracy, literacy, and reading skills in preschools and schools but had limited impacts on children's achievement levels in these areas. The RF, but not the ERF, Impact Study data are available from the National Center for Educational Statistics (NCES) for secondary data analysis.

MULTIPLE INTERVENTION STUDY INITIATIVES

In addition to federally funded descriptive longitudinal studies and evaluations of national intervention programs, periodically federal agencies, often in partnership, create large-scale initiatives to fund a set of research studies on a particular topic in order to spur scientific advancement in that area. Three such initiatives are discussed next to highlight their contributions to the early literacy knowledge base.

Interagency Education Research Initiative

The Interagency Education Research Initiative (IERI) was established in 1999 as a collaboration of the National Science Foundation, the U.S. Department of Education, and NICHD with the goal of supporting a fundamentally new character of research in pre-K–12 education. This initiative would feature interdisciplinary collaborations across learning-related disciplines; focus on key aspects of pre-K–12 reading, mathematics, and science education; and conduct research projects on a scale large enough to produce generalizable lessons about what works and why. From an empirical perspective, IERI's aim was to identify conditions under which effective evidence-based interventions to improve pre-K–12 student learning and achievement succeed when applied on a large scale. Between 2000 and 2007 IERI supported over 200 research studies, approximately half of which were focused on improving preliteracy and reading outcomes. A summary of findings from the IERI projects can be found in two edited volumes (Schneider & McDonald, 2007a, 2007b), and a partial listing of published articles can still be found on the IERI Data Research and Development Center web site (http://drdc.uchicago.edu). Researchers funded by IERI continue to publish their results in peer-reviewed journals (e.g., Lonigan, Farver, Phillips, & Clancy-Menchetti, 2011), but there is no central repository for the data sets generated by these studies.

Preschool Curriculum Evaluation Research Program

Early childhood education intervention research has a rich history of studies demonstrating the value of intervening early in order to increase the school readiness skills, and subsequent academic success, of children from disadvantaged backgrounds who would otherwise be at risk for later school failure (Barnett, 2011). However, a gap remained between the results of these historic focused intervention studies and data on the efficacy of contemporary preschool curricula being used to enhance young children's preliteracy and early reading abilities. In 2002, the U.S. Department of Education's Institute of Education Sciences (IES) began an initiative to address this gap in research evidence, the Preschool Curriculum Evaluation Research (PCER) program. PCER consisted of 12 research teams, each of which tested two or more established curricula against one another in a randomized controlled experimental design; the IES hired two research contractors to do the overarching analyses and report on the results of all of these studies. All told, the 12 PCER studies included a range of Head Start, Title I, state prekindergarten, and private preschool programs serving more than 2,000 children in 20 geographic locations implementing 15 different experimental preschool curricula (Preschool Curriculum Evaluation Research Consortium [PCER-C], 2008).

PCER research teams used common measures and conducted child assessments, classroom observations, teacher interviews, and parent interviews; they also gathered data by teacher report. Direct child assessment measures addressed school readiness and classroom conditions. School readiness measures included reading, phonological awareness, language, mathematics, and behavior; measures of classroom conditions consisted of classroom quality, teacher–child interaction, and instructional practices (PCER-C, 2008). The results of the combined PCER analyses revealed that 10 of the treatment group curricula showed no statistically significant impacts on any of the student-level measures at the end of the prekindergarten year, and only one (*DLM Early Childhood Express* supplemented with *Open Court Reading Pre-K;* SRA/McGraw-Hill, 2003a, 2003b) demonstrated significant impacts across multiple achievement domains (early reading, phonological awareness, language, and mathematics) as well as a positive impact at the classroom level on phonological awareness instruction. *DLM Early Childhood Express* supplemented with *Open Court Reading Pre-K* continued to have positive effects on reading, phonological awareness, and language in kindergarten. Two curricula that showed no impact at the end of the prekindergarten year were found to have effects at the end of the kindergarten year: *Curiosity Corner* (Success for All Foundation, 2003) positively affected reading and the *Early Literacy and Learning Model (ELLM;* Wood, 2002) positively affected language.

Overall, the PCER initiative was an important contribution to the field, because it demonstrated that—in all but one case—the experimental curricula that were thought to produce results superior to the curricula already in use failed to produce a significant impact on child outcomes.

The Interagency School Readiness Consortium

Although the study of curricula targeting specific domains (e.g., preliteracy, early mathematics) contributes to the early education knowledge base, it is divorced from the reality of the typical preschool classroom, in which all preacademic domains are required to be addressed. In order to support the development and evaluation of a range of integrated preschool curricula, the Interagency School Readiness Consortium (ISRC) was formed. ISRC was founded in 2003 by NICHD, ACF, the Office of the

Assistant Secretary for Planning and Evaluation within DHHS, and the Office of Special Education and Rehabilitation Services within the U.S. Department of Education. ISRC was established to fund rigorous scientific studies of the effectiveness of integrative early childhood interventions and programs across a variety of early childhood settings. The ISRC initiative awarded a total of eight research grants featuring interventions implemented in public settings, including Head Start, state prekindergarten, and child care programs (ACF, 2009).

The peer-reviewed ISRC projects were selected based on their approach to systematic, programmatic, multidisciplinary research to determine the most effective early childhood interventions in promoting children's school readiness. Specifically, the research was designed to increase understanding of the types of integrative programs and their components (individually and in combination) that promote child learning and development across multiple domains of early childhood competence, including language and communication, emergent and early literacy, early mathematics, early science, self-regulation of behavior, emotion and attention, social competency, and motivation to learn, as well as the types of programs and components that address teacher, caregiver, or parent behaviors to promote children's development in these areas. To date, five of the ISRC projects have reported short-term impacts for their intervention programs, including those related to early language and preliteracy skills (Bierman et al., 2008; Fantuzzo, Gadsen, & McDermott, 2011; Hamre et al., 2010; McDermott et al., 2009; Raver et al., 2009; Sheridan, Knoche, Edwards, Bovaird, & Kupzyk, 2010). However, information can be found elsewhere on the other studies (Baker, Kupersmidt, Voegler-Lee, Arnold, & Willoughby, 2010; Fuligni, Howes, Lara-Cinisomo, & Karoly, 2009; Lara-Cinisomo, Fuligni, Ritchie, Howes, & Karoly, 2008; Odom et al., 2010).

In addition to the publication of individual impact papers, ISRC has generated two special journal issues on topics that are woefully understudied in early childhood education: the role of professional development in such interventions (Griffin, 2009) and the fidelity of intervention implementation (Griffin, 2010). These special issues provide in one place a description of how professional development and program implementation varied across these diverse school readiness intervention programs, and (we hope) will provide important lessons learned for future intervention studies. The ISRC study data sets are not currently archived in a central repository and would need to be accessed via request to the individual investigators.

Although the PCER and ISRC initiatives made significant contributions to the early childhood education knowledge base, for the most part the children they studied did not include English language learners (ELLs; also referred to as dual language learners [DLLs]). In 2008 NICHD solicited applications for experimental efficacy trials on integrative early childhood programmatic approaches that promote school readiness for children ages 3–5 who are ELLs and are at risk for later school difficulties. The purpose of this solicitation was to increase understanding of the types of integrative programmatic approaches that promote learning and development across multiple domains of early childhood competence for children who are ELLs and that address teacher and parent behaviors that promote these children's development in these areas. Three projects have been funded: one at Florida State University (Christopher Lonigan, Principal Investigator), one at the University of Pennsylvania (Carol Hammer, Principal Investigator), and one at the University of North Carolina at Chapel Hill (Dina Castro, Principal Investigator). These projects are currently underway.

CONCLUSION

This chapter demonstrates how large-scale federal research projects can and have contributed to the knowledge base on early literacy. From descriptive longitudinal studies to targeted intervention studies, all of these projects have provided important information on children at risk for later reading difficulties or low literacy and on the variety of interventions that have been implemented at various levels of scale and with varying degrees of success. Given the continued intractability of these achievement difficulties, it is important that researchers learn all that they can from these projects. We encourage researchers to access archived data for these studies and to use them for secondary data analyses.

RESOURCES

NICHD Study of Early Child Care and Youth Development data sets

All four phases of the SECCYD data set and support information have been archived at the University of Michigan Inter-University Consortium for Political and Social Research: http://www.icpsr.umich.edu/icpsrweb /ICPSR/series/00233

Head Start Impact Study, Early Head Start Impact Study, and Head Start Family and Child Experiences Survey data sets

Data from the Head Start studies, and FACES data from the 1997–2006 cohorts, are archived by Research Connections, a web-based clearinghouse of resources from the many disciplines related to child care and early education (http://www.researchconnections.org/childcare/data.jsp). FACES instruments and other documentation from these cohorts are available as well.

Early Childhood Longitudinal Studies (Birth Cohort and Kindergarten Cohort), Reading First Program Evaluation, and Preschool Curriculum Evaluation Research program data sets

Data from the ECLS-B, ECLS-K, RF evaluation, and PCER are available from the National Center for Educational Statistics (http://nces.ed.gov/pubsearch/licenses.asp).

REFERENCES

Administration for Children and Families. (2002). *Making a difference in the lives of infants and toddlers and their families: The impacts of Early Head Start.* Washington, DC: U.S. Department of Health and Human Services.

Administration for Children and Families. (2003). *Head Start FACES 2000: A whole-child perspective on program performance. Fourth progress report.* Washington, DC: U.S. Department of Health and Human Services.

Administration for Children and Families. (2006). *FACES 2003 research brief: Children's outcomes and program quality in Head Start.* Washington, DC: U.S. Department of Health and Human Services.

Administration for Children and Families. (2008). *Head Start FACES 2003: Recent trends in program performance. Fifth progress report.* Washington, DC: U.S. Department of Health and Human Services.

Administration for Children and Families. (2009). *The Interagency School Readiness Consortium.* Washington, DC: U.S. Department of Health and Human Services. Retrieved from http://www.acf.hhs.gov/programs/opre/hs/interagency/index.html

Administration for Children and Families. (2010a). *Head Start fact sheet fiscal year 2010.* Washington, DC: U.S. Department of Health and Human Services.

Administration for Children and Families. (2010b). *Head Start impact study. Final report.* Washington, DC: U.S. Department of Health and Human Services.

Baker, C.N., Kupersmidt, J.B., Voegler-Lee, M.E., Arnold, D.H., & Willoughby, M.T. (2010). Predicting teacher participation in a classroom-based, integrated preventive intervention for preschoolers. *Early Childhood Research Quarterly, 25*(2), 270–283.

Barnett, W.S. (2011). Effectiveness of early educational intervention. *Science, 333*(6045), 975–978.

Bayley, N. (1969). *Bayley Scales of Infant Development: Birth to two years.* San Antonio, TX: Harcourt Assessment.

Bierman, K.L., Domitrovich, C.E., Nix, R.L., Gest, S.D., Welsh, J.A., Greenberg, M.T., & Gill, S. (2008). Promoting academic and social-emotional school readiness: The *Head Start REDI* program. *Child Development, 79*(6), 1802–1817.

Chernoff, J.J., Flanagan, K.D., McPhee, C., & Park, J. (2007). *Preschool: First findings from the preschool follow-up of the Early Childhood Longitudinal Study, Birth Cohort (ECLS-B)* (NCES 2008-025). Washington, DC: U.S.

Department of Education, Institute of Education Sciences, National Center for Education Statistics.

Denton, K., & West, J. (2002). *Children's reading and mathematics achievement in kindergarten and first grade* (NCES 2002-125). Washington, DC: Government Printing Office.

Denton, K., West, J., & Walston, J. (2003). *Reading—young children's achievement and classroom experiences* (NCES 2003-070). Washington, DC: Government Printing Office.

Denton Flanagan, K., & McPhee, C. (2009). *The children born in 2001 at kindergarten entry: First findings from the Kindergarten Data Collections of the Early Childhood Longitudinal Study, Birth Cohort (ECLS-B)* (NCES 2010-005). Washington, DC: U.S. Department of Education, Institute of Education Sciences, National Center for Education Statistics.

Duncan, G.J., Dowsett, C.J., Claessens, A., Magnuson, K., Huston, A.C., Klebanov, P.,...Japel, C. (2007). School readiness and later achievement. *Developmental Psychology, 43*(6), 1428–1446.

Duncan, G.J., Ziol-Guest, K.M., & Kalil, A. (2010). Early-childhood poverty and adult attainment, behavior and health. *Child Development, 81*(1), 306–325.

Dunn, L.M., & Dunn, L.M. (1997). *Peabody Picture Vocabulary Test–Third Edition (PPVT-III)*. Circle Pines, MN: American Guidance Service.

Elementary and Secondary Education Act of 1965, 20 U.S.C. §§ 241 *et seq.*

Fantuzzo, J.W., Gadsen, V.L., & McDermott, P.A. (2011). An integrated curriculum to improve mathematics, language, and literacy for Head Start children. *American Educational Research Journal, 48*(3), 763–793.

Flanagan, K.D., & West, J. (2004). *Children born in 2001: First results from the base year of the Early Childhood Longitudinal Study, Birth Cohort (ECLS-B)* (NCES 2005-036). Washington, DC: U.S. Department of Education, Institute of Education Sciences, National Center for Education Statistics.

Fuligni, A.S., Howes, C., Lara-Cinisomo, S., & Karoly, L. (2009). Diverse pathways in early childhood professional development: An exploration of early educators in public preschools, private preschools, and family child care. *Early Education and Development, 20*(3), 507–526.

Fuller, B., Bridges, M., Bein, H.J., Jung, S., Rabe-Hesketh, S., Halfon, N., & Kuo, A. (2009). The health and cognitive growth of Latino toddlers: At risk or immigrant paradox? *Maternal and Child Health Journal, 13*(6), 755–768.

Gamse, B.C., Jacob, R.T., Horst, M., Boulay, B., & Unlu, F. (2008). *Reading First Impact Study final report executive summary* (NCEE 2009 4039). Washington, DC: U.S. Department of Education, Institute of Education Sciences, National Center for Education Evaluation and Regional Assistance.

Griffin, J.A. (2009). Professional development and preschool intervention research: I would rather have a talking frog. *Early Education and Development, 20*(3), 373–376.

Griffin, J.A. (2010). Research on the implementation of preschool intervention programs: Learning by doing. *Early Childhood Research Quarterly, 25*(3), 267–269.

Hamre, B.K., Justice, L.M., Pianta, R.C., Kilday, C., Sweeney, B., Downer, J.T., & Leach, A. (2010). Implementation fidelity of *My Teaching Partner* literacy and language activities: Association with preschoolers' language and literacy growth. *Early Childhood Research Quarterly, 25*(3), 329–347.

Hillemeier, M.M., Farkas, G., Morgan, P.L., Martin, M.A., & Maczuga, S.A. (2008). Disparities in the prevalence of cognitive delay: How early do they appear? *Paediatric and Perinatal Epidemiology, 23*(3), 186–198.

Jackson, R., McCoy, A., Pistorino, C., Wilkinson, A., Burghardt, J., Clark, M.,... Swank, P. (2011). *National evaluation of Early Reading First: Final report to Congress* (NCEE 2007-4007rev). Washington, DC: Government Printing Office.

Lara-Cinisomo, S., Fuligni, A.S., Ritchie, S., Howes, C., & Karoly, L. (2008). Getting ready for school: An examination of early childhood educators' belief systems. *Early Childhood Education Journal, 35*(4), 343–349.

Lonigan, C.J., Farver, J.M., Phillips, B.M., & Clancy-Menchetti, J. (2011). Promoting the development of preschool children's emergent literacy skills: A randomized evaluation of a literacy-focused curriculum and two professional development models. *Reading and Writing, 24*(3), 305–337.

Lonigan, C.J., Wagner, R.K., Torgesen, J.K., & Rashotte, C.A. (2002). *Preschool Comprehensive Test of Phonological & Print Processing.* Austin, TX: PRO-ED.

McCarthy, D.A. (1972). *Manual for the McCarthy Scales of Children's Abilities.* San Antonio, TX: Harcourt Assessment.

McDermott, P.A., Fantuzzo, J.W., Waterman, C., Angelo, L.E., Warley, H.P., Gadsen, V.L., & Zhang, X. (2009). Measuring preschool cognitive growth while it's still happening: The Learning Express. *Journal of School Psychology, 47,* 337–366.

Mulligan, G.M., & Flanagan, K.D. (2006). *Age 2: Findings from the 2-year-old follow-up of the Early Childhood Longitudinal Study, Birth Cohort (ECLS-B)* (NCES 2006-043). Washington, DC: U.S. Department of Education, Institute of Education Sciences, National Center for Education Statistics.

National Early Literacy Panel. (2008). *Developing early literacy: Report of the National Early Literacy Panel.* Washington, DC: National Institute for Literacy.

NICHD Early Child Care Research Network. (2000). The relation of child care to cognitive and language development. *Child Development, 71*(4), 960–980.

NICHD Early Child Care Research Network. (2002). Early child care and children's development prior to school entry: Results from the NICHD Study of Early Child Care. *American Educational Research Journal, 39*(1), 133–164.

No Child Left Behind Act of 2001, 20 U.S.C. §§ 6301 *et seq.*

Odom, S.L., Fleming, K., Diamond, K., Lieber, J., Hanson, M., Butera, G., ...Marquis, J. (2010). Examining different forms of implementation in early childhood curriculum research. *Early Childhood Research Quarterly, 25*(3), 314–328.

Pianta, R.C., Belsky, J., Houts, R., Morrison, F., & the NICHD Early Child Care Research Network. (2007). Opportunities to learn in America's elementary classrooms. *Science, 315*(5820), 1795–1796.

Preschool Curriculum Evaluation Research Consortium. (2008). *Effects of preschool curriculum programs on school readiness* (NCER 2008-2009). Washington, DC: Government Printing Office.

Raver, C.C., Jones, S.M., Li-Grining, C., Zhai, F., Metzger, M.W., & Solomon, B. (2009). Targeting children's behavior problems in preschool classrooms: A cluster-randomized controlled trial. *Journal of Consulting and Clinical Psychology, 77*(2), 302–316.

Reichman, N.E., Teitler, J.O., Garfinkel, I., & McLanahan, S.S. (2001). Fragile Families: Sample and design. *Children and Youth Services Review, 23*(4), 303–326.

Schneider, B., & McDonald, S.-K. (2007a). Scale-up in practice: An introduction. In B. Schneider & S.-K. McDonald (Eds.), *Scale-up in education: Issues in practice* (Vol. 2, pp. 1–15). Lanham, MD: Rowman & Littlefield.

Schneider, B., & McDonald, S.-K. (2007b). Scale-up in principle: An introduction. In B. Schneider & S.-K. McDonald (Eds.), *Scale-up in education: Ideas in principle* (Vol. 1, pp. 1–12). Lanham, MD: Rowman & Littlefield.

Shanahan, T., & Lonigan, C.J. (2010). The National Early Literacy Panel: A summary of the process and the report. *Educational Researcher, 39*(4), 279–285.

Sheridan, S.M., Knoche, L.L., Edwards, C.P., Bovaird, J.A., & Kupzyk, K.A. (2010). Parent engagement and school readiness: Effects of the Getting Ready Intervention on preschool children's social-emotional competencies. *Early Education and Development, 21*(1), 125–156.

SRA/McGraw-Hill (2003a). *DLM Early Childhood Express.* Desoto, TX: Author.

SRA/McGraw-Hill (2003b). *Open Court Reading Pre-K.* Desoto, TX: Author.

Success for All Foundation. (2003). *Curiosity Corner.* Baltimore, MD: Author.

Vandell, D.L., Belsky, J., Burchinal, M., Steinberg, L., Vandergrift, N., & the NICHD Early Child Care Research Network. (2010). Do effects of early child care extend to age 15 years? Results from the NICHD Study of Early Child Care and Youth Development. *Child Development, 81*(3), 737–756.

Vogel, C.A., Boller, K., Xue, Y., Blair, R., Aikens, N., Burwick, A.,...Stein, J. (2011). *Learning as we go: A first snapshot of Early Head Start programs, staff, families, and children* (OPRE 2011-7). Washington, DC: U.S. Department of Health and Human Services, Administration for Children and Families, Office of Planning, Research, and Evaluation.

Vogel, C.A., Xue, Y., Moiduddin, E.M., Kisker, E.E., & Carlson, B.L. (2010). *Early Head Start children in Grade 5: Long-term follow-up of the Early Head Start Research and Evaluation Study sample* (OPRE 2011-8). Washington, DC: U.S. Department of Health and Human Services, Administration for Children and Families, Office of Planning, Research, and Evaluation.

Walston, J.T., & West, J. (2004). *Full-day and half-day kindergarten in the United States: Findings from the Early Childhood Longitudinal Study, Kindergarten Class of 1998–99* (NCES 2004-078). Washington, DC: Government Printing Office.

West, J., Denton, K., & Germino-Hausken, E. (2000). *America's kindergartners* (NCES 2000-070). Washington, DC: Government Printing Office.

Wood, J. (2002). *Early Literacy and Learning Model.* Jacksonville: Florida Institute of Education and the University of North Florida.

Woodcock, R.W., McGrew, K.S., & Mather, N. (2000). *Woodcock-Johnson III: Complete Battery.* Itasca, IL: Riverside.

Zhai, F., Brooks-Gunn, J., & Waldfogel, J. (2011). Head Start and urban school readiness: A birth cohort study in 18 cities. *Developmental Psychology, 47,* 134–152.

Zill, N., & West, J. (2000). *Entering kindergarten* (NCES 2001-035). Washington, DC: Government Printing Office.

3

Identifying Early Literacy Learning Needs

Implications for Child Outcome Standards and Assessment Systems

Elizabeth J. Spencer, Trina D. Spencer, Howard Goldstein, and Naomi Schneider

The origins of conventional literacy skills are evident in early childhood development. Emergent literacy skills, as measured in preschool and kindergarten, are strong predictors of later literacy achievement. Current educational research and policy (e.g., No Child Left Behind Act of 2001, PL 107-110, 115 Stat. 1425, 2001) emphasize assessment of preschool children to inform identification and instruction. The assessment of emergent literacy skills can serve to identify those children who may be at risk for later reading difficulties. Furthermore, assessment can guide the content and delivery of early literacy instruction. Failure to identify children early and provide appropriate intervention to promote emergent literacy skills is likely to have serious repercussions for later development of conventional reading skills.

Acknowledgment: Preparation of this chapter was supported by Cooperative Agreement R324C080011 from the U.S. Department of Education, Institute of Education Sciences, awarded to The Ohio State University.

Effective early literacy assessment can provide valuable information. However, decisions about what to assess must be guided by evidence. The National Early Literacy Panel (NELP; 2008) report identifies those emergent literacy skills that are reliable predictors of later reading skill. In this chapter we review the predictors identified by NELP and make recommendations for assessment relative to those predictors. We discuss the different purposes of early literacy assessment and provide guidelines for the implementation of a measurement framework that encompasses these purposes in light of the availability of well-developed assessments. We also discuss the alignment of assessment with state early childhood education standards.

WHAT INFORMATION DOES THE NELP REPORT PROVIDE TO INFORM EARLY LITERACY ASSESSMENT?

One purpose of the NELP report was to identify preschool and kindergarten predictors of conventional literacy skills (i.e., later reading, writing, and spelling outcomes). To address this research question, the panel conducted a meta-analysis of empirical studies published in refereed journals (see Chapter 1). The selected studies provided information to allow for the calculation of average correlations to identify predictors that were interpreted as strong (average correlations of .50 or larger), moderate (between .30–.49), and small (less than .30); a minimum of three studies examining a predictor variable were required to compute an effect size. In addition, the panel analyzed information provided by multivariate studies; these studies provided information about the strength of predictors when additional variables (e.g., IQ) were controlled.

The panel identified a set of skills that are precursors to later literacy achievement in decoding, reading comprehension, and spelling. A review of correlational evidence identified skills with high predictive validity, including *alphabet knowledge* (knowledge of letter names and sounds), *phonological awareness* (the ability to detect, manipulate, or analyze spoken words independent of meaning, including syllable and phoneme-level tasks), *rapid automatized naming* (the ability to rapidly name a repeating sequence of random sets of letters, numbers, colors, or pictures), *early writing or name writing* (the ability to write letters in isolation or write one's own name), and *phonological memory* (the ability to remember spoken information for a short time). Skills with moderate predictive validity included *concepts about print* (knowledge of print conventions and concepts, such as reading from left to right), *print knowledge* (combination of alphabet knowledge, concepts about print, and early decoding ability), *oral language* (the ability to produce and comprehend spoken language, including semantics and syntax), *visual processing* (the ability to match or discriminate symbols), and *reading readiness* (combination of alphabet knowledge, concepts about print, vocabulary, memory, and phonological awareness).

As the authors of the NELP report point out, this approach is limited by the research available. If there is a lack of research on a particular emergent literacy skill, it is not possible to examine that skill as a predictor. Moreover, different statistical methods for identifying predictors of later literacy development may reveal different information (Paris & Luo, 2010).

The panel is careful to caution against drawing causal conclusions about the relationships between predictors and outcomes. We encourage this caution as well. Experimental research is needed to determine causality. The first step is to establish the efficacy of intervention approaches on what are thought to be important predictors. When there are robust intervention approaches, it is easier to determine their immediate and long-term effects on conventional literacy development (e.g., decoding, fluency, comprehension, writing). Identifying predictors is helpful but does not always fully inform the goal of promoting the full complement of literacy skills. For example, within the important domain of phonological awareness, phoneme awareness may be a stronger predictor of decoding than rhyme awareness (Macmillan, 2002).

At least three domains with predictive validity remain poor candidates for emergent literacy instruction given the current knowledge base: rapid automatized naming, phonological memory, and visual processing tasks. Interventions that target these skills and produce robust short- and long-term learning effects have yet to appear in the literature. Moreover, it is difficult to imagine practical tasks that could be taught to improve these skills in ways that relate to literacy development. Therefore, practitioners would be wise to focus on teaching skills that appear to have functional or causal relationships to later reading acquisition (e.g., phonological awareness).

Two additional domains with predictive validity warrant further explanation. Alphabet knowledge involves the naming of letters and their associated sounds. Identifying the names of letters, as an isolated skill, does not have a direct influence on learning to read. Learning letter names is a strong predictor of learning to read because it facilitates learning letter sounds (Ehri & Wilce, 1979), but naming letters without phonological awareness and letter–sound association has little effect on reading development. Concepts about print play a similar role in the development of reading. Knowing the directionality of print, differences between print and pictures, and other print conventions are indicators of children's familiarity with books and can help in learning other more critical literacy skills, but they do not have a direct causal link to reading development (Neuman & Roskos, 2005). Although research indicates that concepts about print and letter names can be taught successfully to young children, in this chapter we focus on those predictors that have the greatest relevance for early literacy instruction.

The domains of phonological awareness, alphabet knowledge (with emphasis on letter–sound correspondence), oral language, and early writing are the focus of this chapter because the NELP report identifies them as moderate or strong predictors of later reading performance and because there is substantial evidence supporting their causal role in literacy development, thus highlighting their relevance to early literacy instruction. As we discuss the predictors of later reading in the context of early childhood assessment, the potential value of assessing the less practical predictors of reading ability (e.g., rapid automatized naming, concepts about print) should not be ignored. They may be especially good in discriminating among children who should be eligible for special education services, for example. On the other hand, practitioners might be expected to give little priority to tracking those skills. This is discussed further in the context of the various purposes of assessment described next.

EMERGENT LITERACY STANDARDS

Recognition of critical emergent literacy skills has substantial implications for early childhood educational practices. One way the NELP report is likely to influence practice is through the development or revision of states' early learning guidelines (also called child outcome standards). With encouragement from federal initiatives to improve early childhood education such as *Good Start, Grow Smart* (White House, 2002), states began developing early childhood standards that resemble those mandated for K–12 education. Initially, though, many standards were crafted by a consensus of content experts instead of referencing research evidence (Neuman & Roskos, 2005). This is understandable for content domains lacking well-developed literature bases, but the release of the NELP report eliminates a lack of scientific evidence as a feasible excuse for neglecting key emergent literacy skills in state early childhood standards.

At present, all 50 states have developed, are developing, or are revising their early childhood guidelines (Barnett, Carolan, Fitzgerald, & Squires, 2011). Of those states that are implementing early learning standards, many have not included guidelines for all key emergent literacy skills. Some states, however, paid close attention to early literacy research and either created a new domain called emergent literacy (e.g., Florida) or expanded their language and literacy domain to include phonological awareness, alphabet knowledge, print recognition, and writing strategies (e.g., California). California and Florida's early learning standards, for example, reflect rather comprehensive coverage of the essential precursors of conventional literacy skills.

The importance of including all of the critical emergent literacy skills is evident when considering the purpose of state standards. Child outcome standards describe the development and learning expectations for young children. Standards guide curriculum, assessment, and professional development (Bodrova, Leong, & Shore, 2004). Thus, standards prescribe what should happen in classrooms. In the standards-based education reform movement, standards are believed to lead to higher student achievement. In K–12 education, states that implemented standards-aligned instruction have shown improved student achievement (Education Commission of the States, 2000). Moreover, students taught by teachers whose professional development matched state standards and reform plans demonstrated impressive gains in reading (U.S. Department of Education, 2001). Early learning guidelines have the potential to have a similar impact for preschool children. However, if critical emergent literacy skills are neglected from the standards as key child outcomes, they are likely to be neglected in preschool classrooms as key instructional objectives. Because of the foundation that emergent literacy provides for later reading achievement, educational programs incur substantial risk of poor outcomes if they fail to teach skills identified in the NELP report as moderate or strong predictors of later reading performance (i.e., alphabet knowledge, phonological awareness, oral language, and early writing skills).

The identification of early predictors of later reading and writing achievement also amplifies the need to assess them. In general, educators and policy makers agree that assessment is an integral component of an effective early childhood educational program, but there is little agreement on how assessment should be carried out. For example, there is no consensus on how assessment data should be collected, who should collect assessment data, or how assessment information should be interpreted and reported. Several books and policy papers have addressed the challenges to effective early childhood assessments (Bagnato, Neisworth, & Pretti-Frontczak, 2010; Epstein, Schweinhart, DeBruin-Parecki, & Robin, 2004; National Association for the Education of Young Children [NAEYC] & National Association of Early Childhood Specialists in State Departments of Education [NAECS/SDE], 2009; National Research Council, 2008; Shepard, Kagan, & Wurtz, 1998). Concerns regarding the resources necessary to properly assess young children, the appropriateness of norm-referenced, standardized tests, and questionable reliability and validity associated with assessment alternatives for young children are paramount (Bagnato et al., 2010; Burns, Midgette, Leong, & Bodrova, 2003; Epstein et al., 2004).

Perhaps the most fundamental and consistent recommendation is that assessment instruments should be used for their intended purposes. Using tests for reasons other than their intended purpose is an unfortunate and common misuse of assessment instruments in early childhood. To reduce this risk and help prepare all children for kindergarten, practitioners need psychometrically sound and socially valid instruments to accomplish each educationally relevant purpose.

In this climate of accountability and increasing calls for scientifically based education, effective applications of assessment will be essential for early identification and instruction of emergent literacy. The NELP report suggests which early literacy skills are worthy of thoughtful assessment. As a next step, this chapter describes three major purposes of assessment and focus on how those purposes relate to identifying early literacy needs for children in early childhood educational programs. In Table 3.1, we overlay the purposes of assessment onto the alphabet knowledge, phonological awareness, oral language, and early writing domains to help guide practitioners in the responsible use of available early literacy assessment instruments. Although it is not an exhaustive list, the table includes many of the assessment tools used in preschool for early literacy assessment. In addition, the following analysis of the intersection of assessment purposes and key emergent literacy skills helps identify areas of need in research and development.

PURPOSEFUL ASSESSMENT OF EMERGENT LITERACY SKILLS

This section discusses three primary purposes of early childhood assessment: 1) informing instructional decisions, 2) identifying children who require intensified intervention, and 3) helping educational programs make systematic improvements (NAEYC & NAECS/SDE, 2009). In the context of early learning guidelines, the focus of assessment remains on promoting successful outcomes for children and facilitating positive programmatic changes (Bodrova et al., 2004).

Informing Instructional Decisions

Early childhood educators use assessment data to inform two types of instructional decisions. Before delivering instruction, teachers first assess children's strengths and needs with respect to the classroom curriculum. This type of information helps identify what to teach and informs how to teach it (i.e., instructional planning). Once instruction begins, teachers use assessment data to monitor the effect their instruction has on

Table 3.1. Standardized early literacy instruments for preschoolers

Purpose	Phonological awareness	Alphabet knowledge	Oral language	Early writing	Composite of early literacy
Information instruction					
Instructional planning	GGG PALS-PreK	PALS-PreK	GGG NLM:P	CELF-P2 supplemental subtest PALS-PreK	CELF-P2 PALS-PreK
Progress monitoring	GGG		GGG NLM:P		
Identification					
Screening	GGG GRTR-R PALS-PreK	GRTR-R PALS-PreK	DELV–Screening Test Fluharty-2 GGG LAP-D PLS-4 Screen SPELT-3	PALS-PreK	GRTR-R PALS-PreK
Eligibility	CELF-P2 TOPEL	TERA-3 TOPEL	CELF-P2 DELV–Screening Test EVT LAP-D OWLS PLS-4 PPVT-4 TOLD-P:4 TOPEL		TERA-3 TOPEL

Program improvement	Program-level instruments: CLASS Pre-K, ECERS-R, ELLCO Pre-K

Key: CELF-P2, Clinical Evaluation of Language Fundamentals, Preschool—Second Edition (Wiig, Secord, & Semel, 2004); CLASS Pre-K, Classroom Assessment Scoring System™ Pre-K (Pianta, La Paro, & Hamre, 2008); DELV–Screening Test, Diagnostic Evaluation of Language Variation–Screening Test (Seymour, Roeper, & de Villiers, 2003); ECERS-R, Early Childhood Environment Rating Scale—Revised Edition (Harms, Clifford, & Cryer, 2005); ELLCO Pre-K, Early Language and Literacy Classroom Observation Tool, Pre-K (Smith, Brady, & Anastasopoulos, 2008); EVT, Expressive Vocabulary Test–Second Edition (Williams, 2007); Fluharty-2, Fluharty Preschool Speech and Language Screening Test–Second Edition (Fluharty, 2000); GGG, Get it, Got it, Go! (Early Childhood Research Institute on Measuring Growth and Development, 1998); GRTR-R, Get Ready to Read! Revised (National Center for Learning Disabilities, 2009); LAP-D, Learning Accomplishment Profile–Diagnostic–Third Edition (Hardin, Peisner-Feinberg, & Weeks, 2005); NLM:P, Narrative Language Measures: Preschool (Spencer & Petersen, 2010); OWLS, Oral and Written Language Scales (Carrow-Woolfolk, 1995); PALS-PreK, Phonological Awareness Literacy Screening for Preschool (Invernizzi, Sullivan, Meier, & Swank, 2004); PLS-4, Preschool Language Scale–Fourth Edition (Zimmerman, Steiner, & Pond, 2002); PLS-4 Screen, Preschool Language Scale-4 Screening Test–Fourth Edition (Zimmerman, Steiner, & Pond, 2005); PPVT-4, Peabody Picture Vocabulary Test–Fourth Edition (Dunn & Dunn, 2007); SPELT-3, Structured Photographic Expressive Language Test 3 (Dawson, Stout, & Eyer, 2003); TERA-3, Test of Early Reading Ability–Third Edition (Reid, Hresko, & Hammill, 2001); TOLD-P:4, Test of Language Development–Primary: Fourth Edition (Newcomer & Hammill, 2008); TOPEL, Test of Preschool Early Literacy (Lonigan, Wagner, Torgesen, & Rashotte, 2007).

student learning. Progress monitoring via repeated probes of student performance further informs decisions regarding when and how to make instructional adjustments.

In early childhood education, criterion-referenced tests (CRTs) that compare student performance to a set of preestablished learning objectives or criteria (Sattler, 2000) often are used to document students' progress and identify targets that need to be taught. Many comprehensive preschool curricula include companion CRTs that Bagnato et al. (2010) call curriculum-embedded assessments. Examples of curriculum-embedded CRTs include *The Creative Curriculum Developmental Continuum for Ages 3–5* (Dodge, Colker, & Heroman, 2006) and *The Carolina Curriculum for Preschoolers with Special Needs* (Johnson-Martin, Attermeier, & Hacker, 2004). Often, curriculum-embedded assessments lack standardized administration procedures, as well as evidence of reliability and validity. In contrast, early childhood developmental CRTs that are not companions to specific curricula are more likely to have standardized administration and scoring procedures and established norms so that they can also be used to determine eligibility for intensive services (e.g., the Battelle Developmental Inventory–Second Edition (BDI-2) [Newborg, 2005] and the BRIGANCE Inventory of Early Development II [Brigance & Glascoe, 2010]). Even though developmental CRTs and comprehensive curriculum-embedded CRTs can be used to plan instruction and monitor progress, the extent to which CRTs capture children's performance in key emergent literacy domains is restricted. Comprehensive curriculum-embedded CRTs and CRTs with norms typically cover multiple developmental domains such as personal-social, cognition, communication, fine motor, and gross motor domains. If included, emergent literacy skills may be buried among many other equally weighted skills. Thus, although general developmental inventories and curriculum-embedded tests are useful in early childhood assessment, they may not be sufficient for informing emergent literacy instruction.

As of 2012, there are only a few publicly available assessment tools designed to inform instructional decisions that target emergent literacy skills specifically and have adequate psychometric properties (see Table 3.1). The Phonological Awareness Literacy Screening for Preschool (PALS-PreK; Invernizzi, Sullivan, Meier, & Swank, 2004) has brief, simple, and standardized administration and scoring procedures and includes early writing, alphabet knowledge, print knowledge, and phonological awareness tasks. Another assessment tool, Get it, Got it, Go! (GGG; Early Childhood Research Institute on Measuring Growth and Development, 1998), also has brief and standardized administration and scoring procedures and assesses two of the domains identified by NELP: phonological awareness and oral language. GGG includes three

Individual Growth and Development Indicators (IGDIs): rhyming, alliteration (both of which are measures of phonological awareness), and picture naming (a measure of expressive vocabulary). A third assessment tool, Narrative Language Measures: Preschool (NLM:P; Spencer & Petersen, 2010) includes personal narrative, narrative retell, and story comprehension subtests, all of which fall into the oral language domain. The NLM:P administration and scoring procedures also are brief and standardized.

The assessment schedule or frequency of test administration affects the extent to which results can be used to inform instructional decisions. Assessment schedules vary according to decisions made at local levels and the measurement tools available. In early childhood education, an assessment schedule of three times per year (e.g., fall, winter, spring) is common because the majority of available tools have lengthy administration times, making them impractical for more frequent measurement (e.g., curriculum-embedded CRTs, developmental CRTs). The time necessary to administer PALS-PreK and GGG is sufficiently brief to be practical for more frequent monitoring of early literacy skills; however, neither assessment tool includes multiple equivalent forms to be used weekly. Repeated administrations of GGG are allowed, but the developers recommend that repetition be limited to once per month.

An infrequent assessment schedule may not be sufficient for all early literacy progress-monitoring needs or to inform strategic planning of emergent literacy instruction. Research has shown that frequent monitoring of students' progress enhances teachers' ability to plan instruction and make timely instructional changes that have positive effects on student achievement (Connor et al., 2009; Fuchs, Deno, & Mirkin, 1984; Fuchs, Fuchs, & Hamlett, 1993; VanDerHeyden, Snyder, Broussard, & Ramsdell, 2008). NLM:P was specifically designed for frequent monitoring of language growth over time and has 40 equivalent forms. In a recent study, researchers administered NLM:P daily to preschoolers receiving an oral language intervention and found the test to be sensitive to intervention effects (Spencer & Slocum, 2010).

To inform instructional decision making around early literacy, there is a need for instruments that measure preschoolers' performance on key early literacy skills, that have simple procedures and brief testing times, and that can be administered with a frequency sufficient to provide an index of progress. GGG and PALS-PreK meet several of these criteria. However, neither of these measures assesses all key domains (phonological awareness, alphabet knowledge, early writing, and oral language) nor were they designed for frequent administration. NLM:P has multiple equivalent forms for repeated administration, but it does not measure children's performance in areas of emergent literacy besides language. Therefore, additional measures will need to be developed to inform instructional decision making.

In addition to measures that can be administered more frequently, there is a need for measures that assess multiple emergent literacy domains. Currently, researchers are developing measures that will be similar to the IGDI tasks in GGG but that will assess additional domains, including alphabet knowledge and comprehension. Investigators in Minnesota are working on additional IGDIs that will be appropriate for assessing several emergent literacy skills (McConnell, Missall, Rodriguez, & Wackerle-Hollman, 2010). In contrast to the current GGG versions of IGDIs, the new items are scaled using an item response theory approach. This permits scaling of items for screening that covers a broad developmental age range. For the quarterly measures, the items selected can be scaled to take into account expected progress in critical language and literacy skills. Thus, the item pool would be different for different points in the school year or for different developmental levels.

There is a specific need for measures that can serve as progress-monitoring tools. Ideally, these measures could yield information to serve multiple purposes, assess skills in a number of early language and literacy domains, and align with early learning standards and other measurement tools. These measures should be able to be administered and scored quickly and reliably by practitioners (Deno, 2003). Additional research about the development of early literacy skills is necessary to guide the design of progress-monitoring measures that are appropriate for young children. For example, progress monitoring in the domain of early writing may not be appropriate for many preschool children if early writing skills are not expected to develop until late in the prekindergarten year.

Curriculum-based assessment (CBA) tools that include test stimuli drawn from the local classroom curriculum provide a viable alternative for monitoring progress to inform instruction. CBA is a general term encompassing methods to collect information about student performance in reference to the curriculum for the purpose of informing instruction (Tucker, 1985). Under this general umbrella of curriculum-relevant assessment, CBA can involve a variety of teacher-made tools such as observation recording forms, worksheets, and portfolios, as well as standardized, objective tests (McLoughlin & Lewis, 2008; Tucker, 1985). The direct correspondence between what is taught and what is assessed is an advantage of CBA. Teachers may use these tools to monitor mastery of the lessons taught each week or in each unit and use this information to differentiate instruction for children who may lack skills to progress to more advanced lessons. However, these mastery-monitoring CBAs may lack standardized administration and scoring procedures and evaluations of their reliability and validity. Because this mastery-monitoring approach to assessment may provide limited information about the extent to which students have learned beyond the explicit context of the classroom curriculum (Fuchs & Deno, 1991), it should be supplemented with other standardized measures.

As is evident in Table 3.1, assessments for monitoring progress are limited in the phonological awareness and oral language areas and are absent in the alphabet knowledge and early writing areas. Consequently, early childhood education professionals may need to rely on general CRTs or CBAs that they develop themselves or that are recommended within existing curricula.

Identifying Children Who Require Intensified Intervention

Identifying young children who need additional instructional support occurs in two ways. The traditional method involves screening and follow-up eligibility testing. Screening, typically a first step, involves a brief sampling of the young children's principal developmental skills for the purpose of detecting possible delays. If potential delays are detected, further in-depth eligibility assessment is conducted to determine the allocation of intensified intervention (Bagnato et al., 2010; National Research Council, 2008; Shepard et al., 1998).

Within the last decade, an alternative way to identify children who require intensified intervention has emerged in early childhood education based on response to intervention (RTI) conceptualizations. Although eligibility determinations are necessary before students receive special education services, early detection and prevention efforts such as RTI involve expanded options for children identified as needing intervention via screening measures. An at-risk identification at screening also could lead to increased monitoring or an immediate increase in instructional support without necessitating time- and resource-intensive eligibility assessments. As part of a RTI framework, universal screening occurs on a quarterly schedule (consistent with common early childhood assessment schedules). Assessment that is carried out in fall, winter, and spring is sometimes called benchmarking because students' development, skills, and achievements are compared with specific criteria or benchmarks for learning. In a RTI context, the extent to which student performance meets benchmarks and the extent to which students have progressed since the previous assessment point can be considered when determining students' needs for intensified literacy instruction.

The allocation of supplemental instruction and intervention is contingent upon screening and eligibility assessment results. Because financial and personnel resources necessary to provide intensified intervention are valuable and scarce, the consequence of an identification error can be costly. Therefore, screening and eligibility assessment instruments have stringent psychometric requirements. Educators will want to select screening tools (e.g., Get Ready to Read! Revised [GRTR-R]; National Center for Learning Disabilities, 2009) and eligibility instruments (e.g., Test of Preschool Early Literacy [TOPEL]; Lonigan, Wagner, Torgesen, & Rashotte, 2007) with sufficient evidence of reliability and validity. With respect to emergent literacy skills, screening instruments also should have evidence of predictive validity with conventional reading and writing. Screening tools should involve standardized administration and scoring procedures and yield either criterion-referenced or norm-referenced scores to help determine when potential delays exist. Nearly all tests used as the primary method for determining eligibility for special education are norm-referenced and standardized. To identify children who require intensive intervention, such as special education, educators will want to select measures that also have evidence of good sensitivity and specificity. Sensitivity and specificity are indicators of a test's accuracy in identifying a condition. If a test is sensitive, a person with a condition will test positive for the condition on the measure. If a test is specific, a person without a condition will test negative for the condition on the measure. Test development methods, such as receiver operating characteristic (ROC) analysis (Catts, Petscher, Schatschneider, Bridges, & Mendoza, 2009; Compton et al., 2010; Johnson, Jenkins, & Petscher, 2010), have improved practitioners' ability to design instruments that optimize sensitivity and specificity, as well as the accuracy of predicting developmental delays.

Screening Instruments   Several assessments are available for screening purposes in early language and literacy. As can be seen in Table 3.1, the domain with the most screening measures is oral language; the majority of measures provide a score cutpoint to identify children who need further assessment. Other screening instruments sample skills across multiple domains. For example, GRTR-R is a composite instrument that measures alphabet knowledge, concepts about print, and phonological awareness and provides a score cutpoint.

Several of the measures discussed in the previous section on informing instruction have the potential to be useful as a first step in the identification of children who require intensive intervention. PALS-PreK and GGG, administered in the fall, might provide information to educators about children who should receive additional assessment. However, neither PALS-PreK nor GGG provide score cutpoints or benchmarks to identify such children. PALS-PreK provides a developmental range for spring of the prekindergarten year. GGG suggests using local normative information to create benchmarks. Educators will need to make decisions about a child's performance on these measures to determine if additional testing is necessary. There is a need for the further development of instruments for early literacy screening purposes, especially instruments that provide norm-referenced or benchmark scores to indicate children who may be eligible for additional intervention.

Eligibility Instruments There are many norm-referenced and standardized measures available for the purpose of eligibility determination in the domains of early language and literacy. Educators also will need to make careful decisions about the domains of early language and literacy that are assessed to determine eligibility. NELP has identified key predictors for assessment; educators will need to determine which of these predictors will be assessed to identify children who require intensified intervention. It may be most appropriate to assess those domains that are potential intervention targets. However, educators may supplement eligibility evaluations with measures of rapid automatized naming, phonological memory, and visual processing, which NELP identified as moderate or strong predictors of later reading. Although they are less functional for emergent literacy instruction, rapid automatized naming, phonological memory, and visual processing are good indicators of risk and may be helpful in the identification of children who require intensive literacy intervention (Weismer et al., 2000).

Often, measures that assess a broad range of early language and literacy skills will be most appropriate. For example, some students may struggle to acquire many early literacy skills, including alphabet knowledge, phonological awareness, and vocabulary. Other students may have a weakness only in a particular domain, such as oral language. Educators will need to select assessments that determine not only eligibility for additional services but also the type of services (e.g., early literacy intervention, speech-language services). Tests that provide both a composite score and scores for subtests that relate to particular domains might serve this purpose. Table 3.1 provides examples of available measures that can assist with eligibility determination and that have adequate psychometric properties. More comprehensive information about assessment tools can be found in the report *Early Childhood Assessment: Why, What, and How* (National Research Council, 2008).

TOPEL is an example of a measure that can be useful for the purpose of eligibility determination. It assesses skills in several of the domains identified by NELP and includes three subtests: print knowledge, definitional vocabulary, and phonological awareness. Children receive standard scores for each subtest and a composite score. Although the test manual reports strong reliability and validity, it does not provide information about sensitivity and specificity in identification.

NELP reports that measures of complex oral language skills (i.e., grammar and listening comprehension) have been found to be stronger predictors of later decoding and reading comprehension than simple measures of vocabulary. Therefore, measures of oral language that assess a broad range of skills may be most appropriate for determining children's eligibility for intensified intervention. The Clinical Evaluation of Language Fundamental, Preschool–Second Edition (CELF-P2; Wiig, Secord, & Semel, 2004) is an example of a widely used measure for determining eligibility in the domain of oral language. CELF-P2's core language subtests assess the language skills of sentence comprehension, word structure, and expressive vocabulary. Children receive standard scores for each subtest and a composite standard score based on performance on the core language subtests. CELF-P2 also has subtests and supplemental measures that could be used to assess other early literacy skills, including phonological awareness and early writing. The test manual provides strong evidence of reliability and validity. Sensitivity and specificity are high (.85 and .82, respectively) in identification of children with language disorders when the criterion for a disorder was set at 1 standard deviation below the mean.

Educators selecting assessment tools for oral language also will need to consider dialectical variations. Assessments of oral language, both for screening and eligibility purposes, may overidentify children who speak a dialectical variation as needing intervention. Measures such as the Diagnostic Evaluation of Language Variation—Screening Test (DELV–Screening Test; Seymour, Roeper, & de Villiers, 2003) have been developed to distinguish between children who are speakers of a dialectical variation and children who have language impairments.

In summary, assessments developed to serve the function of identifying children's eligibility for additional services comprise the greatest concentration of assessments in Table 3.1. This is especially evident in the oral language area. As can be seen in the table, early writing assessment has been included only in one screening assessment (PALS-PreK). It also was sampled in a supplemental subtest of the CELF-P2. The findings of the NELP report have provided an impetus for further development in this area. Puranik and Lonigan (2011) are among the investigators who are working on the development of a test of early writing skills.

Helping Programs Make Systematic Improvements

Improving the quality of early childhood educational programs is a third purpose of assessment. However, the use of assessment data for the formative evaluation of a program's early literacy curriculum and instruction is not commonplace. A major reason for this is that few assessment instruments are designed with this specific purpose in mind. Nonetheless, making data-based systematic changes can utilize child-level data combined with program-level measures of teacher behavior, literacy environment, and curriculum content (Epstein et al., 2004).

Although child-level data serve as a reasonable basis for program improvement, there are a number of issues to be considered. First, using child-level data should not be an afterthought. Instead, administrators should plan assessment data collection using valid designs and procedures to properly answer questions about program effectiveness. Second, it is not necessary to test all children in the program, which can be costly for programs with limited resources. With large or more homogeneous programs, sampling procedures can be used strategically to assess enough children to represent the population in the program. Third, child-level data should be aggregated in meaningful ways that reflect the impact of teachers, classrooms, or curricula. Examining an individual child's assessment data reflects the child's ability to learn, but examining a class's annual progress compared with a different class's annual progress may reflect differences in instructional quality. Fourth, children's gains over time as opposed to a static performance assessment provide the best estimate of programmatic impact. Assessment of program effectiveness for the purpose of program improvement is similar to progress monitoring of student performance to determine the effectiveness of that student's instruction, but it occurs on a much larger scale (National Research Council, 2008). Because growth cannot be established using a single assessment score, it is necessary to design program improvement measurements with at least two (beginning and end of year) or three (quarterly evaluation) data collection times across a year. Fifth, to effectively address program improvement goals, results of child-level data should be used to identify professional development needs, because results can be analyzed to reveal strengths and weaknesses in curriculum and instruction (Epstein et al., 2004; NAEYC & NAECS/SDE, 2009).

Many of the assessment instruments discussed in the previous two sections, if executed properly, can be used in the collection of child-level program improvement data. However, the results of these assessments offer only one source of information for evaluation. Program-level information, such as the quality of the classroom literacy environment, the breadth and depth of emergent literacy coverage in the program's curriculum, and the quality of teacher–student literacy interactions, also should inform systemic improvement efforts. These types of data should inform systematic and focused professional development and the selection of evidence-based curricula and instructional approaches. For example, programmatic data indicating that a teacher provides limited opportunities for shared book-reading experiences and makes little effort to expand children's spoken vocabulary should lead to customized training and coaching on how to encourage vocabulary development and incorporate shared book reading into classroom activities. Likewise, if an examination of the program's curriculum finds that it does not include instructional suggestions and objectives for teaching phonological awareness, then selection of a curriculum that does is warranted.

A number of environmental inventories require raters to observe classroom environments to characterize the availability of materials and organization conducive to learning (e.g., the Early Childhood Environment Rating Scale–Revised Edition [ECERS-R; Harms, Clifford, & Cryer, 2005], the Early Language and Literacy Classroom Observation Tool, Pre-K [ELLCO Pre-K]; Smith, Brady, & Anastasopoulos, 2008). ELLCO Pre-K was developed for the purpose of characterizing the classroom literacy environment in particular. It consists of an observational checklist and supplemental teacher interview with items that relate to classroom structure, curriculum, language environment, books and book reading, and print and early writing. The content of ELLCO Pre-K overlaps with the predictors identified by NELP. Although these instruments give general information about the classroom environment, they are limited in their ability to capture details of instructional and classroom quality. For example, observational indicators in the domain of print and early writing describe the availability of writing materials, the display of written material, and opportunities for children to practice early writing skills. These indicators do not directly measure instruction in early writing.

The Classroom Assessment Scoring System, Pre-K (CLASS Pre-K; Pianta, La Paro, & Hamre, 2008) also is used to inform early childhood educational program improvement. This measure is an observational recording system designed to characterize teacher–student interactions in three domains: emotional support, classroom organization, and instructional support. CLASS Pre-K measures aspects of teacher–student interactions that relate to the development of early literacy skill. However, CLASS Pre-K is designed to measure characteristics of classroom interactions across all content domains.

To inform program improvement, there is a need for measures that can more accurately describe the instructional experiences of children in relation to the early language and literacy skills identified by NELP. Classroom CIRCLE: Code for Interactive Recording of Children's Learning Environments (Atwater, Lee, Montagna, Reynolds, & Tapia, 2009) is an example of an observational tool that can provide detailed information about instructional quality in the domain of early language and literacy. Using an event-recorder device (e.g., a personal digital assistant), the observer codes teacher and child behavior every 15 seconds for three

10-minute observations. The coding scheme allows observers to capture information on the focus of classroom instruction, the interactions of teachers and children, and the engagement, academic or otherwise, of children. Classroom CIRCLE yields a time-sampled record of teacher behavior and calculates the amount of time teachers spend teaching domains of early language and literacy instruction, including phonological awareness, alphabetic and print concepts, vocabulary, comprehension, or reading. This measure also provides estimates of the amount of time that children are engaged in early writing and early reading as well as other activities.

Several research groups have developed tools for the evaluation of preschool curricula. Some measures are designed to provide educators with a tool to examine curricular practices across content domains (e.g., socioemotional, mathematics, early literacy). For example, the Curriculum Rating Rubric (Pretti-Frontczak, Robbins, Jackson, Korey-Hirko, & Harjusola-Webb, 2008) allows educators to rate curricular practices as they relate to assessment, scope and sequence, activities and instruction, and progress monitoring. Other measures have focused on early language and literacy domains. Another curriculum evaluation tool, the Preschool Curriculum Review Rubric and Planning Tool (Virginia Department of Education, 2007) helps educators compare preschool curricula in the domains of oral language and vocabulary, phonological awareness, alphabet knowledge, print knowledge, and comprehension. Although the Preschool Curriculum Review Rubric and Planning Tool can provide information about early language and literacy instruction, the rubric's items are general and lack the level of specificity necessary to make decisions about program improvement. For example, in the domain of phonological awareness, the item related to rhyming is simply whether rhyming is taught in the curricula.

The extent to which curricula provide instructional support that teachers find useful (e.g., suggestions for explicit teaching strategies, recommendations for teacher- and child-led activities) is likely to guide programs in the selection of curricula. The Preschool Curricula Checklist (PCC; Kaminski & Carta, 2010) is a tool for examining the instructional design evident in preschool curricula in early language and literacy. Using the checklist, educators can evaluate the instructional support provided by a curriculum in the domains of phonological awareness, alphabet knowledge, vocabulary and oral language, and comprehension. The checklist can provide information about the scope of skills addressed, the sequence of lessons to address those skills, and the materials provided to teachers. PCC also gives an indication of the adaptations suggested for teachers to address the needs of children who struggle to acquire early literacy skills. Items on the checklist are specific and can capture details that will assist educators in the selection of curricula. For example, in each domain educators rate the curriculum resources provided for implementing activities, including the materials required for the lesson or activity, a description of skills to be taught, suggested wording for how to teach the skills, and specific examples and content for teaching. Tools such as PCC can guide educators in the selection of curricula that provide strong support for instruction in early language and literacy.

In summary, evaluations of educational program quality can be informed by several sources of data: 1) test information about children's achievement and development, 2) instruments that rate the quality of literacy environments and teacher–student interactions, 3) instruments that summarize the extent to which teachers and students are engaged in literacy instruction, and 4) analyses of the adequacy of literacy instruction in classroom curricula. The results can be used to make decisions about targeted professional development and selection of new curricular programs.

EDUCATIONAL IMPLICATIONS

This chapter is meant to help early education professionals construct a system of assessment that can address the multiple purposes of assessment: informing instructional decisions, identifying children who require intensive intervention, and helping educational programs make systematic improvements. The focus of the system of assessment should be on promoting successful outcomes for children and facilitating positive programmatic changes. Although the NELP findings help inform the selection of early language and literacy assessments that can guide decision making, they also highlight gaps in the availability of suitable assessments. Further research and development is necessary to provide educators with reliable and valid measures for assessment in early childhood. Optimally, teachers need measures that will allow them to easily and reliably assess how children are developing phonological awareness skills, alphabet knowledge (especially letter–sound correspondence), oral language, and early writing skills.

Recommendations for a System of Assessment

In the next section, we make recommendations for a system of assessment that can address the multiple purposes of assessment. This system includes measures for universal screening, for instructional planning and progress monitoring, for determining eligibility, and for program improvement.

Universal Screening   All children entering prekindergarten should be screened using measures that can be administered reliably and yield a score that can serve as a first step in identifying children who may need additional intervention. Many children enter early childhood educational programs with limited emergent literacy skills. For many children who have limited language and literacy experiences, early childhood education could facilitate rapid development of emergent literacy skills. Other children may fail to make significant progress. Thus, screening should be readministered on the same assessment schedule that is already common in early childhood education (i.e., fall, winter, and spring) to make sure that children who are struggling are detected in a timely manner. Aggregated universal screening results at the local level could inform program improvement and can be used to establish benchmarks to help identify children in need of intervention.

Instructional Planning and Progress Monitoring   Measures selected for this purpose should be brief assessments that align closely with the instruction provided in the classroom, which in turn should align with early learning standards. All children should participate in quarterly progress monitoring (fall, winter, and spring). Depending on the instruments employed, universal screening and progress monitoring can be accomplished using the same tests (e.g., GGG IGDIs). Quarterly progress monitoring can address general classroom needs as well as the needs of individual children. First, performance of the group of children in a class can inform educators about the effectiveness of classroom instruction. For example, if a classroom of children has made progress in the domain of alphabet knowledge but demonstrates limited improvement in phonological awareness, educators can modify instruction to emphasize phonological awareness. Thus, instructional planning can be reflected in revisions in the scope and sequence of emergent literacy skills targeted in the general classroom curriculum. Second, quarterly progress monitoring can identify children who fail to respond to instruction or who are falling behind in certain emergent literacy areas. This would allow teachers to target areas of need for children who require additional instruction.

More frequent progress monitoring is necessary for children who have, or are at risk for, limited early language and/or early literacy skills, whether they receive intensified instruction or not. For example, a child who performed below benchmark on a screening measure at the beginning of preschool should be monitored more frequently to determine if he or she needs a more intensified level of instruction. Alternatively, educators can provide extra support immediately and monitor the child's progress.

In contrast to screening assessments that provide cutpoints, progress-monitoring assessments should provide a means of evaluating whether children are making progress consistent with their peers. For example, Figure 3.1 provides an example of vocabulary development based on the GGG picture-naming IGDI. The example shows a child who may have experienced limited home literacy opportunities and performed well below normative levels in August. After an opportunity to see the effects of the preschool's general curriculum, little progress was evident in October. With no progress evident a month later in November, the teacher decided that the child required supplemental language instruction. The effects of implementing this intervention were readily evident from IGDI measures over the next 3 months. Monthly IGDI assessments in December, January, and February reflected an upward trajectory as evidenced by the steep trend line. When the child reached the aim line for typical development in February, the supplemental language intervention ceased. IGDI measures were then administered quarterly, and the child showed development consistent with typical development at the end of the year and the beginning of the following school year. Figure 3.1 offers an illustration of how progress-monitoring measures could be examined to determine whether more intensive instruction is needed and whether it is successful in improving a child's developmental trajectory.

Eligibility Assessment   Timely, comprehensive assessments are necessary to determine whether developmental delays are significant enough to warrant eligibility for intensive intervention services. Intensive intervention services typically include special education services (e.g., speech-language pathology services, reading specialists). Eligibility assessments work best in conjunction with screening and progress monitoring. If universal screening and progress-monitoring measures are in place, rather than a "wait-to-fail" model, educators should be able to efficiently identify the children for whom more information is needed. Consistent with RTI models, how well a child responds to small group or individual instruction may help determine the need for a comprehensive eligibility assessment. Assessments that are used to determine eligibility should yield information about the array of children's developmental needs. Therefore, these assessments need to be comprehensive, in that they assess across and within developmental domains. These assessments should serve to provide a profile with estimates of developmental status across domains that are indicative of areas of strength and the particular instructional needs of a child. Reading specialists, school psychologists, and speech-language pathologists are among the professionals who should have sufficient expertise in emergent literacy to contribute to this process.

Program Improvement Decisions about educational program improvement should be made using a combination of child-level assessments and program-level assessments of instructional quality and curricular support. Child-level data need to be reported in ways that can be meaningful for this purpose. For example, rather than only reporting the mean score of the classroom or center, distributions of child data should be provided. This information would inform program improvement that addresses the needs of all children in a classroom. Child-level data might identify classrooms in which teachers could benefit from professional development in a particular early language or literacy domain (e.g., phonological awareness) or in instructional strategies for a particular subgroup of children (e.g., English language learners). Data that are aggregated across the classrooms within a center might identify domains of early language and literacy that are not sufficiently addressed in the curriculum. As part of a coherent system of assessment, measures that inform program improvement should align with early learning standards.

In summary, an effective system of assessment in early language and literacy can only be put into place if appropriate measures exist to be a part of this system. As we have highlighted in this chapter, there is a need for further research to develop reliable, valid measures of early language and literacy.

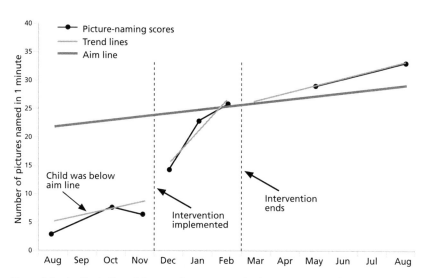

Figure 3.1. An illustration of the use of progress-monitoring assessment to direct intervention efforts, based on the Get it, Got it, Go! picture-naming Individual Growth and Development Indicator (Early Childhood Research Institute on Measuring Growth and Development, 1998). The trend lines indicate the slope of growth before, during, and after intervention.

CONCLUSION

An effective system of assessment in early language and literacy includes instruments that provide coherent information (National Research Council, 2008). Coherence should be demonstrated in multiple ways. First, educators should strive for consensus on goals for children's learning and the purposes of assessment. Second, educators should strive for assessments that align with early learning standards as well as curriculum and instruction. Third, educators should strive for assessments that provide in-depth information at the child's developmental level but have the ability to relate to a broader range of development. Fourth, educators should strive for alignment among measures. If educators are screening for a particular skill (e.g., phonological awareness), then they will want a measure that allows them to monitor progress of that skill.

One reason that educators may develop a system of assessment is to implement a RTI model. Although an in-depth discussion of RTI models is beyond the scope of this chapter, the recommendations we make for a system of assessment align closely with those that would be part of a RTI model. Additional recommendations for assessment in RTI for reading are available in the Institute of Education Sciences practice guide on assisting school-age children who are struggling with reading (Gersten et al., 2008). With an increasing acceptance of RTI in early childhood, it will be important to examine the extent to which assessment systems for school-age children apply to early childhood education (Greenwood et al., 2008). To a great extent, this chapter's recommendations for assessment of young children's early literacy skills are consistent with those applied in primary grades. Unfortunately, the availability of assessment tools in early childhood that can fulfill RTI assessment functions currently is limited. The importance of addressing literacy early, the extension of RTI to early childhood, and the need for increased early childhood assessment options make the development of preschool early literacy assessment instruments an urgent priority.

REFERENCES

Atwater, J., Lee, Y., Montagna, D., Reynolds, L.H., & Tapia, Y. (2009). *Classroom CIRCLE: Code for Interactive Recording of Children's Learning Environments.* Kansas City: University of Kansas, Juniper Gardens Children's Project.

Bagnato, S.J., Neisworth, J.T., & Pretti-Frontczak, K. (2010). *LINKing authentic assessment and early childhood intervention: Best measures for best practices* (2nd ed.). Baltimore, MD: Paul H. Brookes Publishing Co.

Barnett, W.S., Carolan, M.E., Fitzgerald, J., & Squires, J.H. (2011). *The State of Preschool 2011: State Preschool Yearbook.* National Institute for Early Education Research. Retrieved from http://nieer.org/yearbook

Bodrova, E., Leong, D., & Shore, R. (2004, March). Child outcome standards in pre-k programs: What are standards; what is needed to make them work? *Preschool Policy Matters.* Retrieved from http://nieer.org/resources/policybriefs/5.pdf

Brigance, A.H., & Glascoe, F.P. (2010). *BRIGANCE Inventory of Early Development II.* North Billerica, MA: Curriculum Associates.

Burns, M.S., Midgette, K., Leong, D., & Bodrova, E. (2003). *Prekindergarten benchmarks for language and literacy: Progress made and challenges to be met.* Washington, DC: National Institute for Early Education Research.

Carrow-Woolfolk, E. (1995). *Oral and Written Language Scales.* Circle Pines, MN: American Guidance Service.

Catts, H., Petscher, Y., Schatschneider, C., Bridges, M., & Mendoza, K. (2009). Floor effects associated with universal screening and their impact on the early identification of reading disabilities. *Journal of Learning Disabilities, 42*(2), 163–176.

Compton, D., Fuchs, D., Fuchs, L., Bouton, B., Gilbert, J., Barquero, L.,...Crouch, R. (2010). Selecting at-risk first-grade readers for early intervention: Eliminating false positives and exploring the promise of a two-stage gated screening process. *Journal of Educational Psychology, 102*(2), 327–340.

Connor, C., Piasta, S., Fishman, B., Glasney, S., Schatschneider, C., Crowe, E.,... Morrison, F. (2009). Individualizing student instruction precisely: Effects of Child x Instruction interactions on first graders' literacy development. *Child Development, 80*(1), 77–100.

Dawson, J., Stout, C., & Eyer, J. (2003). *Structured Photographic Expressive Language Test 3.* DeKalb, IL: Janelle.

Deno, S.L. (2003). Developments in curriculum-based measurement. *Journal of Special Education, 37,* 184–192.

Dodge, D.T., Colker, L.J., & Heroman, C. (2006). *The Creative Curriculum Developmental Continuum.* Washington, DC: Teaching Strategies.

Dunn, L.M., & Dunn, D.M. (2007). *Peabody Picture Vocabulary Test–Fourth Edition (PPVT-4).* Minneapolis, MN: NCS Pearson Assessments.

Early Childhood Research Institute on Measuring Growth and Development. (1998). *Research and development of individual growth and development indicators for children between birth and age eight* (Technical Report No. 4). Minneapolis: University of Minnesota, Center for Early Education and Development.

Education Commission of the States. (2000). Setting the standard: Will higher expectations improve student achievement? *The Progress of Education Reform, 1*(5), 1–6. Denver, CO: Education Commission of the States.

Ehri, L., & Wilce, L. (1979). The mnemonic value of orthography among beginning readers. *Journal of Educational Psychology, 71*(1), 26–40.

Epstein, A.S., Schweinhart, L.J., DeBruin-Parecki, A., & Robin, K.B. (2004, July). Preschool assessment: A guide to developing a balanced approach. *Preschool Policy Matters.* Retrieved from http://nieer.org/resources/policybriefs/7.pdf

Fluharty, N.B. (2000). *Fluharty Preschool Speech and Language Screening Test* (2nd ed.). Austin, TX: PRO-ED.

Fuchs, L.S., & Deno, S.L. (1991). Paradigmatic distinctions between instructionally relevant measurement models. *Exceptional Children, 57*(6), 488–500.

Fuchs, L.S., Deno, S.L., & Mirkin, P. (1984). Effects of frequent curriculum-based measurement and evaluation on pedagogy, student achievement, and student awareness of learning. *American Educational Research Journal, 21*(2), 449–460.

Fuchs, L.S., Fuchs, D., & Hamlett, C.L. (1993). Technological advances linking the assessment of students' academic proficiency to instructional planning. *Journal of Special Education Technology, 12*(1), 49–62.

Gersten, R., Compton, D., Connor, C.M., Dimino, J., Santoro, L., Linan-Thompson, S., & Tilly, W.D. (2008). *Assisting students struggling with reading: Response to intervention and multi-tier intervention for reading in the primary grades. A practice guide* (NCEE 2009-4045). Washington, DC: U.S. Department of Education, Institute of Education Sciences, National Center for Education Evaluation and Regional Assistance.

Greenwood, C.R., Carta, J.J., Baggett, K., Buzhardt, J., Walker, D., & Terry, B. (2008). Best practices integrating progress monitoring and response-to-intervention concepts into early childhood. In A. Thomas, J. Grimes, & J. Gruba (Eds.), *Best practices in school psychology V* (pp. 535–548). Washington, DC: National Association of School Psychology.

Hardin, B.J., Peisner-Feinberg, E.S., & Weeks, S.W. (2005). *Learning Accomplishment Profile–Diagnostic (LAP-D)* (3rd ed.). Lewisville, NC: Kaplan Early Learning.

Harms, T., Clifford, R.M., & Cryer, D. (2005). *Early Childhood Environment Rating Scale* (Rev. ed.). New York, NY: Teachers College Press.

Invernizzi, M., Sullivan, A., Meier, J., & Swank, L. (2004). *Phonological Awareness Literacy Screening for Preschool.* Charlottesville: University of Virginia.

Johnson, E., Jenkins, J., & Petscher, Y. (2010). Improving the accuracy of a direct route screening process. *Assessment for Effective Intervention, 35*(3), 131–140.

Johnson-Martin, N.M., Attermeier, S.M., & Hacker, B.J. (2004). *The Carolina Curriculum for Preschoolers with Special Needs* (2nd ed.). Baltimore, MD: Paul H. Brookes Publishing Co.

Kaminski, R., & Carta, J. (2010). *The Preschool Curricula Checklist.* Unpublished manuscript. Dynamic Measurement Group, Eugene, Oregon.

Lonigan, C.L., Wagner, R.K., Torgesen, J.K., & Rashotte, C.A. (2007). *Test of Preschool Early Literacy (TOPEL).* Austin, TX: PRO-ED.

Macmillan, B. (2002). Rhyme and reading: A critical review of the research methodology. *Journal of Research in Reading, 25*, 4–42.

McConnell, S., Missall, K., Rodriguez, M., & Wackerle-Hollman, A. (2010, February). Monitoring progress on progress monitoring: Recent innovations in the design and evaluation of individual growth and development indicators. Panel presentation at the 7th Biennial Conference on Research Innovations in Early Intervention (CRIEI), San Diego, CA.

McLoughlin, J.A., & Lewis, R.B. (2008). *Assessing students with special needs* (7th ed.). Upper Saddle River, NJ: Pearson Prentice Hall.

National Association for the Education of Young Children & National Association of Early Childhood Specialists in State Departments of Education. (2009). *Where we stand on curriculum, assessment, and program evaluation.* Retrieved from http://www.naeyc.org/files/naeyc/file/positions/StandCurrAss.pdf

National Center for Learning Disabilities. (2009). *Get Ready to Read! Revised.* Minneapolis, MN: NCS Pearson Assessments.

National Early Literacy Panel. (2008). *Developing early literacy: Report of the National Early Literacy Panel.* Washington, DC: National Institute for Literacy.

National Research Council. (2008). *Early childhood assessment: Why, what, and how.* Washington, DC: National Academies Press.

Neuman, S.B., & Roskos, K. (2005). The state of state pre-kindergarten standards. *Early Childhood Research Quarterly, 20,* 125–145.

Newborg, J. (2005). *Battelle Developmental Inventory–Second Edition (BDI-2).* Itasca, IL: Riverside.

Newcomer, P.L., & Hammill, D.D. (2008). *Test of Language Development–Primary: Fourth Edition (TOLD-P:4).* Austin, TX: PRO-ED.

No Child Left Behind Act of 2001, 20 U.S.C. §§ 6301 *et seq.*

Paris, S., & Luo, S. (2010). Confounded statistical analyses hinder interpretation of the NELP report. *Educational Researcher, 39,* 316–322.

Pianta, R.C., La Paro, K.M., & Hamre, B.K. (2008). *Classroom Assessment Scoring System (CLASS), Pre-K.* Baltimore, MD: Paul H. Brookes Publishing Co.

Pretti-Frontczak, K., Robbins, S.H., Jackson, S., Korey-Hirko, S., & Harjusola-Webb, S. (2008). *Curriculum Rating Rubric.* Kent, OH: Kent State University, Center for Excellence in Early Childhood Research and Training. Retrieved from http://www.ehhs.kent.edu/odec/documents/CurriculumFrameworkRatingRubric_000.pdf

Puranik, C., & Lonigan, C.J. (2011). From scribbles to scrabble: Preschool children's developing knowledge of written language. *Reading and Writing: An Interdisciplinary Journal. 24*(5), 567–589. doi:10.1007/s11145-009-9220-8

Reid, D.K., Hresko, W.P., & Hammill, D.D. (2001). *Test of Early Reading Ability–Third Edition (TERA-3).* Austin, TX: PRO-ED.

Sattler, J.M. (2000). *Assessment of children: Cognitive applications* (4th ed.). San Diego, CA: Jerome M. Sattler.

Seymour, H.N., Roeper, T.W., & de Villiers, J. (with de Villiers, P.). (2003). *Diagnostic Evaluation of Language Variation—Screening Test (DELV–Screening Test).* San Antonio, TX: Harcourt Assessment.

Shepard, L., Kagan, S.L., & Wurtz, E. (Eds.). (1998). *Principles and recommendations for early childhood assessments.* Washington, DC: National Education Goals Panel.

Smith, M.W., Brady, J.P., & Anastasopoulos, L. (2008). *Early Language and Literacy Classroom Observation Tool, Pre-K (ELLCO Pre-K).* Baltimore, MD: Paul H. Brookes Publishing Co.

Spencer, T.D., & Petersen, D.B. (2010). *Narrative Language Measures: Pre-school.* Retrieved from http://www.languagedynamicsgroup.com

Spencer, T.D., & Slocum, T.A. (2010). The effect of a narrative intervention on story retelling and personal story generation skills of preschoolers with risk factors and language delays. *Journal of Early Intervention, 32,* 178–199.

Tucker, J.A. (1985). Curriculum-based assessment: An introduction. *Exceptional Children, 52,* 199–204.

U.S. Department of Education. (2001). *The Longitudinal Evaluation of School Change and Performance (LESCP) in Title I schools.* Washington, DC: Author.

VanDerHeyden, A., Snyder, P., Broussard, C., & Ramsdell, K. (2008). Measuring response to early literacy intervention with preschoolers at risk. *Topics in Early Childhood Special Education, 27,* 232–249.

Virginia Department of Education. (2007). *Preschool Curriculum Review Rubric and Planning Tool.* Richmond: Department of Education, Commonwealth of Virginia.

Weismer, S.E., Tomblin, J., Zhang, X., Buckwalter, P., Chynoweth, J., & Jones, M. (2000). Nonword repetition performance in school-aged children with and without language impairment. *Journal of Speech, Language, and Hearing Research, 43,* 865–878.

White House. (2002). *Good Start, Grow Smart: The Bush administration's early childhood initiative.* Washington, DC: Government Printing Office.

Wiig, E.H., Secord, W.A., & Semel, E. (2004). *Clinical Evaluation of Language Fundamentals—Preschool–Second Edition (CELF-Preschool-2).* San Antonio, TX: Harcourt Assessment.

Williams, K.T. (2007). *Expressive Vocabulary Test (EVT)* (2nd ed.). Minneapolis, MN: NCS Pearson Assessments.

Zimmerman, I.L., Steiner, V.G., & Pond, R.E. (2002). *Preschool Language Language Scale–Fourth Edition (PLS-4).* San Antonio, TX: Harcourt Assessment.

Zimmerman, I.L., Steiner, V.G., & Pond, R.E. (2005). *Preschool Language Scale-4 Screening Test (PLS-4 Screening Test).* San Antonio, TX: Harcourt Assessment.

4

Relations of Children's Socioemotional Development to Academic Outcomes

Tracy L. Spinrad, Carlos Valiente, and Nancy Eisenberg

T he National Early Literacy Panel (NELP) emphasized the importance of children's early cognitive abilities in early learning. This chapter focuses on the role of socioemotional skills in children's school readiness. Specifically, we review research on the relations of children's effortful control (dispositional self-regulation) to factors involved in school success. In addition, we consider the relations of children's emotion understanding, emotionality, peer and teacher relationships, and academic motivation to children's school readiness. Findings thus far support the view that effortful control has a positive association with children's academic readiness and that such associations may be

Acknowledgment: Work on this chapter was supported by grants from the National Institute of Mental Health, the *Eunice Kennedy Shriver* National Institute of Child Health and Development (NICHD), and the National Science Foundation.

mediated by factors such as social competence, the quality of children's relationships with teachers and peers, and children's liking of school. We argue that policy makers should not ignore the importance of socio-emotional skills in children's literacy and school success.

In addition to early literacy skills such as alphabet knowledge and writing skills, there is growing appreciation for the role of social and emotional development in children's school readiness. A successful school transition requires that children begin school not only ready to learn but also able to listen to instructions, sit still, be attentive, and get along with new peers and adults. Therefore, children's socioemotional skills, particularly self-regulation abilities, are critical for success in school. The purpose of this chapter is to examine children's self-regulation and aspects of socioemotional functioning in relation to literacy and, given the lack of research on how these factors relate to literacy per se, to academic outcomes more broadly.

Despite the importance of socioemotional development to children's academic functioning and the transition to school, the NELP (2008) report did not consider socioemotional variables in relation to young children's literacy skills; instead, it focused on early cognitive factors. This omission was likely due to the relatively few studies prior to 2002 that examined these relations, as most of the relevant research has been conducted in the last decade. Moreover, few investigators prior to this period had examined the relations of *preschool-level* social functioning to kindergarten literacy outcomes—the focus of the panel's report.

Our emphasis in this chapter is on several facets of socio-emotional functioning. In particular, we focus on the constructs of regulation (i.e., effortful control) and reactive control (i.e., impulsivity and behavioral inhibition) in relation to children's academic outcomes. We also focus, albeit briefly, on other socioemotional factors—specifically, emotional reactivity, emotion understanding, social competence, quality of relationships with teachers and peers, and academic motivation—in relation to academic success (see Figure 4.1).

EMOTION-RELATED SELF-REGULATION: CONCEPTUAL ISSUES

Emotion-related regulation is defined as the process of initiating, avoiding, inhibiting, maintaining, or modulating the occurrence, form, intensity, or duration of internal feeling states, emotion-related physiological processes, and/or the behavioral concomitants of emotion, generally in the service of accomplishing one's goals (Eisenberg & Spinrad, 2004). Some researchers have also distinguished between effortful or voluntary regulation as opposed to more reactive processes (Rothbart & Bates, 2006). Rothbart and Bates defined *effortful control* as "the effi-

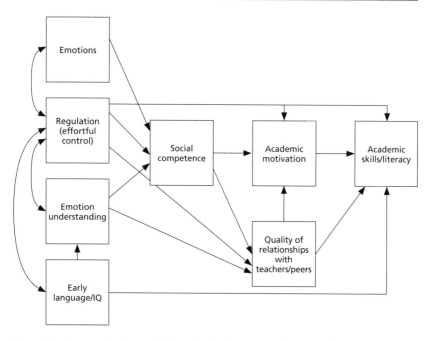

Figure 4.1. A conceptual model of the relations between socioemotional variables and academic competence. One also would expect negative emotions to moderate the relation between regulation (effortful control) and social competence.

ciency of executive attention—including the ability to inhibit a dominant response and/or to activate a subdominant response, to plan, and to detect errors" (2006, p. 129). Effortful control is characterized by the ability to shift and focus attention as needed, to inhibit inappropriate behavior, and to activate or perform an action, as well as some aspects of executive function (Evans & Rothbart, 2007; Rothbart, Ahadi, Hersey, & Fisher, 2001). Some aspects of executive function skills (including executive attention) are believed to be components of effortful control. That is, the roots of effortful control lie in children's executive attention networks, which function to promote and suppress the activation in other networks (Rothbart, Sheese, & Posner, 2007). Tasks that require cognitive control (e.g., executive function tasks such as Stroop tasks, or tasks in which the participant is required to name the ink color of a printed word which may be incongruent with the text, for example, the word *blue* in red ink) appear to activate areas of the anterior cingulated gyrus and regions of the prefrontal cortex—areas also thought to underlie self-regulation (Rothbart et al., 2007).

On the other hand, reactive control reflects relatively involuntary approach and avoidance systems reflecting impulsive undercontrol or

rigid overcontrol (e.g., behavioral inhibition). Empirical data support
the distinction between effortful (voluntary) and reactive (involuntary)
control processes. For example, reactive overcontrol and/or undercontrol appear to load on different factors in confirmatory factor analyses
than does either effortful control or negative emotionality (Rothbart
et al., 2001). Similarly, using structural equation modeling, Eisenberg
et al. (2004) and Valiente et al. (2003), with different samples of children, have obtained separate latent constructs for effortful and reactive
control, with some unique prediction of maladjustment, at least in the
early school years. These aspects of reactive control overlap conceptu-
ally with Nigg's (2000) discussion of impulsivity and overcontrol and
Gray's (Pickering & Gray, 1999) Behavioral Activation System (BAS)
and Behavioral Inhibition System (BIS).

Researchers have found that effortful control appears to increase
with age. Attentional control, one aspect of effortful control, appears to
improve during the toddler and preschool years as children show increased
levels of sustained attention and are able to concentrate for longer periods of time (Kannass, Oakes, & Shaddy, 2006; Ruff & Capozzoli, 2003).
In addition, children's performance on effortful control tasks improves in
the toddler and preschool years (Kochanska, Murray, & Harlan, 2000).
Moreover, there are improvements in executive function in the late preschool years (Mezzacappa, 2004), but some of these skills may level off by
early elementary school. For example, Rueda et al. (2004) found that one
measure of executive attention improved until age 7 but not from age 8 to
adulthood. Nonetheless, effortful control, including the ability to effort-
fully inhibit behavior (inhibitory control), appears to improve somewhat
throughout childhood and adolescence and into adulthood (Crone, Ridderinkhof, Worm, Somsen, & van der Molen, 2004; Murphy, Eisenberg,
Fabes, Shepard, & Guthrie, 1999; Williams, Ponesse, Schachar, Logan, &
Tannock, 1999).

RELATIONS OF EFFORTFUL
CONTROL TO ACADEMIC READINESS

There are a number of reasons to expect a relation between children's
effortful control and academic readiness. In particular, researchers have
argued that attentional skills are critical for academic success, with the
premise that children who can focus attention are likely to be able to pay
attention to lessons, stay on task, listen to instructions, and complete
assignments. In turn, these children are likely to master the reading
and mathematics material taught in school (Raver, 2002).

A growing body of empirical work supports this idea, although the
majority of researchers in this area have used correlational (albeit some-

times longitudinal) designs. Children who have high levels of effortful control tend to have relatively high academic skills. Specifically, attentional skills (i.e., the ability to shift and focus attention as needed), an aspect of effortful control, appear to play an important role in children's academic readiness and skills (Coplan, Barber, & Lagacé-Séguin, 1999; NICHD Early Childcare Research Network, 2003). Using a meta-analysis examining data from six studies, attentional skills at school entry were found to be a modest, but consistent, predictor of later achievement, even when controlling for early cognitive ability (Duncan et al., 2007).

Several investigators have found that other aspects of effortful control (e.g., inhibitory control) have a positive relation to academic competence. Ponitz, McClelland, Matthews, and Morrison (2009) found that behavior regulation in the fall semester of kindergarten predicted academic achievement during the spring semester; children's emotion regulation also has been found to predict higher grade point average (GPA; Gumora & Arsenio, 2002; Valiente, Lemery-Chalfant, Swanson, & Reiser, 2008) and academic competence (Fabes, Martin, Hanish, Anders, & Madden-Derdich, 2003; Fantuzzo et al., 2007; Valiente, Lemery-Chalfant, & Castro, 2007). Children's executive function skills as assessed with tasks involving attention and inhibitory control also have been associated with relatively high levels of on-task behavior (Blair, 2003).

Specific to early literacy skills, some researchers have found that indices of effortful control have a positive relation to measures of children's reading and linguistic skills. Even in infancy, regulation skills have been found to predict language skills 8–9 months later (Dixon & Smith, 2000). Howse, Lange, Farran, and Boyles (2003) found in a sample of low-income families, children's attentional self-regulation to be related to reading achievement in kindergarten, even after controlling for prekindergarten reading achievement. Aspects of effortful control also have been linked to children's letter knowledge (Blair & Razza, 2007; Smith-Donald, Raver, Hayes, & Richardson, 2007), higher reading performance (Alexander, Entwisle, & Dauber, 1993; Hill & Craft, 2003), and language skills (NICHD Early Childcare Research Network, 2003), as well as emergent literacy and vocabulary skills (Bierman, Nix, Greenberg, Blair, & Domitrovich, 2008; Diamond, Barnett, Thomas, & Munro, 2007; McClelland et al., 2007; Smith-Donald et al., 2007). Lonigan et al. (1999) reported that symptoms of attention-deficit/hyperactivity disorder (particularly inattention) were associated with impairments in early literacy, even after controlling for cognitive abilities.

Although there is some evidence of a link between effortful control and emergent literacy skills, some researchers have posited that effortful control may more strongly predict children's emergent mathematics skills than their literacy skills. For example, Ponitz et al. (2009) found that early regulation predicted gains in mathematics skills, but not language or literacy skills, across the kindergarten year. Similarly, Blair and Razza (2007) found that although aspects of effortful control predicted children's literacy skills, the role of effortful control was more substantial for mathematics outcomes. Investigators have argued that the relations between effortful control and children's academic competence may become domain-specific over time. Moreover, it is possible that children may receive more instruction in literacy skills than in mathematics skills; this exposure may make letter knowledge and vocabulary more automatic than the cognitive processes required for mathematics (Ponitz et al., 2009). Alternatively, similar cortical areas (prefrontal) may underlie both mathematics abilities and executive function and/or effortful control skills (Blair & Razza, 2007). It should be noted, however, that in a meta-analytic study, children's attentional skills predicted achievement in both mathematics and reading; thus, a stronger link between effortful control and mathematics outcomes has not always been found (Duncan et al., 2007).

The Mediating Role of Social Competence and Peer Relationships

Although there have been a number of studies examining the direct effects of effortful control on children's academic success, it is likely that this relation is at least partially mediated by children's social competence. For the purposes of this discussion, social competence refers to children's ability to engage in socially appropriate behavior, such as complying with demands and being well-behaved. In a series of studies, emotion regulation has been found to relate to children's social competence and popularity (Eisenberg, Guthrie, et al., 1997; Eisenberg et al., 2003; Spinrad et al., 2006) and relatively low levels of maladjustment (Eisenberg et al., 2001; Eisenberg, Sadovsky, Spinrad, Fabes, et al., 2005; Eisenberg et al., 2004; Spinrad et al., 2007). In one study, Spinrad et al. (2006) found that effortful control predicted greater popularity over time, even when accounting for prior levels of popularity 2 years earlier. Thus, children who are more self-regulated tend to be relatively well-liked by their peers.

Literature also supports the idea that children's relationships with peers have implications for learning and school success (Ladd, Herald, & Kochel, 2006; Welsh, Parke, Widaman, & O'Neil, 2001). The number of mutual friends and the amount of peer acceptance has been found to predict children's achievement (Ladd, Birch, & Buhs, 1999; Wentzel & Caldwell, 1997), even after controlling for earlier academic competence

(O'Neil, Welsh, Parke, Wang, & Strand, 1997). Similarly, Buhs and Ladd (2001) found that rejection by peers during kindergarten was linked to children's school adjustment, and that this link was at least partially mediated through classroom participation and negative treatment by peers. In other words, children who are rejected by peers appear to be treated more negatively by their classmates and are less likely to participate in classroom activities. In turn, these children may be disengaged in the classroom or frequently off task, leading to lower scholastic performance.

Few investigators have formally tested whether children's peer behaviors mediate the relation between effortful control and academics. As an exception, Valiente et al. (2008) found that children's social competence (including a measure of popularity) partially mediated the relations between effortful control and academic achievement; these findings have been replicated with different samples in which mediation could be tested over time (Valiente, Lemery-Chalfant, & Swanson, 2010; Zhou, Main, & Wang, 2010).

The Mediating Role of the Teacher–Child Relationship

Children with relatively high levels of effortful control should be able to engage with, initiate contact with, and comply with their teachers. Moreover, as noted earlier, children who lack regulation skills are more likely to engage in antisocial behavior than their more regulated peers and are perceived as having higher levels of maladjustment by teachers (Eisenberg et al., 2001; Eisenberg, Fabes, Bernzweig, & Karbon, 1993; Eisenberg, Sadovsky, Spinrad, Fabes, et al., 2005; Eisenberg et al., 2009). As a consequence, children who are disruptive receive less instruction and less positive feedback from teachers (Arnold et al., 1999; McEvoy & Welker, 2000)—that is, children who are disruptive are simply harder to teach. There is some evidence that regulation is related to positive teacher–child relationships (Graziano, Reavis, Keane, & Calkins, 2007; Valiente et al., 2008). Similarly, Rudasill and Rimm-Kaufman (2009) found that effortful control had a positive relation to teacher–child closeness and frequency of teacher-initiated interactions.

It is likely that high-quality teacher–child relationships are linked to higher performance because teachers may invest more in children to whom they feel close and may provide more nurturance to these children. Moreover, children who feel a connection with their teacher are likely to feel more engaged in the classroom and approach school with enthusiasm. The quality of teacher–child relationships can vary and has been characterized by closeness (i.e., support and warmth) or conflict (i.e., struggle between the teacher and child; Pianta, Steinberg, & Rollins, 1995). More positive teacher–child relationships have been related to children's higher academic performance (Birch & Ladd, 1997; Hamre & Pianta, 2001), classroom participation and engagement (Furrer & Skinner, 2003; Ladd et al., 1999; Ryan, Stiller, & Lynch, 1994), and positive attitudes about, or liking of, school (Birch & Ladd, 1997; Silva et al., 2011). In one notable investigation, teacher–child conflict was related to relatively high levels of disruptive peer play (Griggs, Gagnon, Huelsman, Kidder-Ashley, & Ballard, 2009), which may create difficulties with school adjustment (Ladd, Kochenderfer, & Coleman, 1996). There have been two attempts to test whether the teacher–child relationship mediates the link between effortful control and academic achievement, with some investigators finding support for mediation (Valiente et al., 2008) and others finding no evidence of mediation (Graziano et al., 2007). There is a need for additional data, in which effortful control, the teacher–child relationship, and index of achievement are all measured at different assessments, to provide more definitive conclusions about the interrelations of these variables.

The Mediating Role of Children's Academic Motivation

In addition to children's relationships with their peers and teachers, academic motivation may play an important mediating role in children's school success. Children's school liking and classroom participation are thought to reflect their motivation to learn and their goal orientation in regard to success in school (Dweck, 1989; Wentzel, 1999). There is consistent evidence that school liking and classroom participation predict academic achievement (Buhs & Ladd, 2001; Ladd, Buhs, & Seid, 2000; Ladd et al., 1999; Valiente et al., 2007; Valiente et al., 2008). Ladd et al. (2000) found that children's liking of school had a positive relation to classroom participation and, in turn, predicted relatively high achievement in school; they also tested an alternative model that showed less support for the hypothesis that school liking was a consequence of academic achievement and classroom participation.

Effortful control may be linked with academic motivation because children who can modulate their emotions are likely to feel more comfortable in the school environment than children who lack regulation skills (Eisenberg, Sadovsky, & Spinrad, 2005). Indeed, in two studies, Valiente and colleagues found a positive association between effortful control, school liking, and classroom participation (Valiente et al., 2007; Valiente et al., 2008). However, it is likely that the relation between effortful control and children's academic motivation is mediated by other factors. For example, Silva et al. (2011) found that the quality of teacher–child relationships mediated the association between effortful control and the school liking of preschoolers from low-income families.

That is, children with high levels of effortful control had closer relationships with their teachers; in turn, these children tended to have higher levels of school liking and lower levels of school avoidance. Thus, the relation between effortful control and children's liking of school is probably not direct.

THE ROLE OF CHILDREN'S EMOTION UNDERSTANDING IN ACADEMICS

Emotion understanding refers to the ability to identify one's own and others' experienced and expressed emotions, understand which emotions are appropriate for a given context, and understand the causes and consequences of emotions. Children's effortful control is likely to be involved in the ability to focus on relevant verbal and nonverbal emotional cues in order to develop emotion understanding. In addition, self-regulation may prevent children from becoming overly aroused during emotion-laden events and enable them to use such circumstances to learn about emotions (Hoffman, 2000). In support of this idea, Schultz, Izard, Ackerman, and Youngstrom (2001) found that children's regulation during preschool predicted emotion understanding 2 years later. Moreover, emotion understanding is thought to contribute to the ability to self-regulate (Eisenberg, Sadovsky, & Spinrad, 2005).

Relatively few researchers have examined the link between emotion understanding and children's school readiness. However, the limited amount of work that has been done in this area has shown emotion understanding to have a positive relation to academic achievement (Garner & Waajid, 2008; Izard et al., 2001; Shields et al., 2001). In one study examining specific literacy measures, Blair, Granger, and Razza (2005) found that emotion understanding had a positive relation to preschoolers' vocabulary and letter knowledge.

It is important to determine the processes that account for the relation between emotion understanding and children's academic competence. It is likely that emotion understanding contributes to academic skills through children's social competence and/or academic motivation (Eisenberg, Sadovsky, & Spinrad, 2005). Investigators have found that emotion understanding has a positive relation to peer acceptance and friendships (Denham, McKinley, Couchoud, & Holt, 1990), social skills (Izard et al., 2001; Mostow, Izard, Fine, & Trentacosta, 2002), and lower levels of maladjustment (Denham, Blair, Schmidt, & DeMulder, 2002). Thus, emotion understanding is likely to facilitate positive social interactions, which in turn contribute to children's learning.

It is also important to note that language skills are likely to contribute to children's emotion understanding (Denham, Zoller, & Couchoud,

1994; Izard et al., 2001; Smith & Walden, 1998; Trentacosta & Izard, 2007) and self-regulation (Kopp, 1982), particularly in the early years of life when basic and emotion-related language skills are developing. Emotion understanding has been related to preschoolers' vocabulary (Cutting & Dunn, 1999; Denham et al., 1994; Smith & Walden, 1998), syntax in 3-year-olds (Ruffman, Slade, Rowlandson, Rumsey, & Garnham, 2003), and language skills in children 4–11 years old (Pons, Lawson, Harris, & de Rosnay, 2003). In addition, mean lengths of utterance and verbal ability have been found to predict later emotion understanding (Laible & Thompson, 2002; Schultz et al., 2001). Pons et al. (2003) suggested that the link between language and emotion understanding is due to the fact that 1) language is an instrument of cognitive representation (i.e., emotions are just objects for language to represent), and/ or 2) language may be a measure of social communication. Therefore, children who are better able to communicate with others have more opportunities to learn about mental states, including emotions. Moreover, particularly in early research, measures of emotion understanding often relied on verbal responses. In the last decade, however, work has often involved measures that allow the child to nonverbally identify emotions by pointing as well as to verbally name emotions (Denham, 2006). Thus, children's verbal abilities undoubtedly contribute to children's performance on emotion-understanding tasks, particularly when verbal responses are required. It is also possible that a third variable, such as IQ, can explain the link between emotion understanding and cognitive outcomes, although some researchers have found relations between emotion understanding and academics after controlling for indices of intelligence such as verbal ability and cognitive concentration and/or attention (Izard et al., 2001; Trentacosta & Izard, 2007). An important task for future research is to examine the transactional relations between early literacy, language development, emotion understanding, and regulation.

THE ROLE OF CHILDREN'S EMOTIONALITY IN ACADEMICS

Negative emotionality (e.g., fear, sadness, anger), an aspect of temperament that is believed to be regulated by effortful control (Rothbart & Bates, 2006), undoubtedly plays a role in at least some aspects of children's adjustment to school. When children are prone to experiencing negative emotionality, they may have difficulties thinking clearly and feeling comfortable in the classroom; this anxiety may reduce their ability to perform. Children who are overaroused emotionally are more likely to attend to their own emotional experiences (Hoffman, 2000) and would be expected to be less able to learn in the classroom environment (Blair,

2003). Gumora and Arsenio (2002) found that a high GPA was predicted by children's higher levels of positive mood and lower levels of negative mood and negative academic affect (i.e., negative affect when performing school-related tasks such as homework, quizzes, and classwork). In a sample of Chinese students, Zhou et al. (2010) found that teachers' (but not parents') reports of students' anger were prospectively related to GPA. Therefore, it is likely that emotionality plays an important role in children's academic functioning.

In addition to considering the direct effects of effortful control and negative emotionality on academic achievement, consistent with Rothbart and Bates's (2006) discussion of the importance of considering temperament-by-temperament interactions (especially those involving regulatory and reactive systems), we believe it will be useful to test whether effortful control moderates relations between negative emotionality and achievement. Eisenberg and Fabes (1992) argued that even if children are prone to anger, they may not display disruptive behavior if they are able to regulate their emotions; research supports this prediction for children's social competence and challenging behavior (Eisenberg, Fabes, Guthrie, & Murphy, 1996; Eisenberg, Guthrie, et al., 1997). Fabes and colleagues (2003) posited that high levels of effortful control may aid students in enjoying school and participating appropriately. When it comes to considering achievement outcomes, findings are inconsistent. Some investigators have not found evidence that regulation abilities moderate the links between negative affect and academic achievement (Gumora & Arsenio, 2002), whereas others have found positive relations between distress and school readiness in children who have high, but not low, levels of effortful control (Belsky, Friedman, & Hsieh, 2001). In contrast, Valiente and colleagues (2010) found negative relations between anger and achievement in children with high, but not low, levels of effortful control.

It is important to note that children who experience more positive and less negative emotions are perceived as more likable by peers (Denham et al., 1990; Eisenberg et al., 1993; Eisenberg et al., 1996; Spinrad et al., 2004). Thus, children who experience more negative emotions may be at risk for poor relationships with peers, which in turn predicts poor adjustment to school (Rubin, Bukowski, & Parker, 2006). Clearly, children who are prone to intense negative emotions are less likely to have good social skills at school (Eisenberg et al., 1993; Jones, Eisenberg, Fabes, & MacKinnon, 2002; Spinrad et al., 2004), which is likely to undermine their relationships with peers and teachers. Consistent with this idea, Zhou et al. (2010) found that the negative association between Chinese students' feelings of anger and frustration and their academic achievement was mediated by externalizing behaviors.

PROMOTING CHILDREN'S EMOTION
REGULATION THROUGH INTERVENTION

Given the associations between regulation and children's social and academic outcomes, it is important to understand the ways in which teachers and parents can foster children's regulation skills. There is evidence that interventions can indeed promote self-regulation. For example, researchers have examined the effects of the *Promoting Alternative Thinking Strategies (PATHS)* curriculum, in which teachers are provided with lessons that foster emotional literacy, social competence, problem solving, and positive peer relationships (Greenberg, Kusché, Cook, & Quamma, 1995). More specifically, the *PATHS* curriculum provides explicit instructions for children to learn to control their emotions and behavior—for example, lessons that teach children how to stop, calm down, take deep breaths, and express the problem and their emotions in response to challenging situations. In addition, *PATHS* focuses on prosocial friendship skills and problem-solving skills (Conduct Problems Prevention Research Group, 2010). The *PATHS* curriculum has been found to be effective for improving children's executive function skills (Riggs, Greenberg, Kusché, & Pentz, 2006) and emotion understanding (Domitrovich, Cortes, & Greenberg, 2007).

The *PATHS* curriculum also has been used with preschool-age children. Domitrovich et al. (2007) showed that children in classrooms receiving *PATHS* exhibited better emotion understanding and were rated by teachers as less socially withdrawn and more socially competent compared with control groups; however, significant intervention effects were not found for children's performance on tasks assessing inhibitory control or sustained attention. In terms of researching the effects of the *PATHS* curriculum's socioemotional intervention on academic and cognitive skills, work has mostly been conceptual, presuming that changes in socioemotional skills will promote cognitive skills (Greenberg et al., 1995). However, Riggs et al. (2006) found that the *PATHS* curriculum had a positive impact on children's verbal fluency, offering support for the idea that these programs may promote academic achievement.

In a year-long school readiness intervention, Bierman and colleagues (Bierman, Domitrovich, et al., 2008; Bierman, Nix, et al., 2008) examined the effects of the *Head Start Research-Based, Developmentally Informed Intervention (Head Start REDI)* curriculum (Bierman, Domitrovich, et al., 2008) on children's executive function skills, as well as the relations of executive function skills to school-related outcomes. In this intervention, preschool teachers used the *Preschool PATHS* curriculum (Domitrovich et al., 2007) and also utilized an interactive reading program. Findings showed that children in intervention classrooms scored higher on vocabulary and parents' reports of language use at home than children in control classrooms (Bierman, Domitrovich, et al., 2008). In addition, the intervention led to improvements in some executive function tasks, although the effect sizes were small. Furthermore, improvements in executive function skills mediated the intervention effects on emergent literacy skills (Bierman, Nix, et al., 2008). This study provides evidence that interventions designed to improve children's regulation skills may, in turn, have effects on children's school readiness skills.

Another program focusing on children's socioemotional development is the teacher-administered *Emotion-Based Prevention Program* (*EBP;* Izard, Trentacosta, King, & Mostow, 2004; Izard et al., 2008). This program was designed to promote emotion understanding and regulation strategies with school-based lessons, observations and consultations with teachers, parental involvement through messages summarizing the lessons, and four monthly discussion meetings. Findings indicated that *EBP* produced increases in emotion understanding (for children who were at least 4 years old at the pretest) and emotion regulation and decreases in the expression of negative emotions, aggression, and anxious or depressed behavior. *EBP* was also compared with a social-cognitive intervention program, *I Can Problem Solve* (*ICPS;* Shure, 1993). Children who received the *EBP* intervention rather than *ICPS* demonstrated significant gains in emotion understanding, teacher-rated emotion regulation skills, and positive behavioral outcomes. No differences were found for teacher-rated lability (i.e., shifts in mood), negative emotionality, expression of negative emotions, or externalizing or internalizing problems. Izard et al. (2008) also found evidence for mediation by emotion understanding of the *EBP* treatment effect on change in emotion regulation.

Rather than focusing on emotion understanding, Diamond et al. (2007) reported promotion of preschoolers' executive function through use of the teacher-administered *Tools of the Mind* curriculum (Bodrova & Leong, 2009) curriculum in classrooms of children from low-income families. This curriculum focuses on challenge, training, and support of executive function. Children who received the *Tools of the Mind* curriculum for 1–2 years performed more accurately on tasks assessing aspects of executive function than children who received their school district's curriculum. Barnett et al. (2008) showed that *Tools of the Mind* was also found to improve various aspects of the classroom environment, such as the quality of literacy instruction, teachers' use of scaffolding techniques, and global quality, but it did not show strong links to cognitive outcomes. Specifically, although *Tools of the Mind* was shown to improve some aspects of children's language development, the results were relatively weak and in some cases insignificant in multilevel models (Barnett et al., 2008).

Thus, interventions designed to promote emotion understanding and regulation show promise in fostering children's socioemotional skills. Given the association of children's effortful control and emotion understanding to academic competence, these skills are likely to mediate the effect of the interventions on children's performance in school, perhaps through factors such as social competence, relationships with peers and teachers, or academic motivation, although this link has seldom been tested. As some interventions become more established, researchers should also consider the factors that might moderate the interventions' effectiveness, such as pretest levels of self-regulation or challenging behavior.

What is relatively unknown, however, is whether literacy-based or cognitively based intervention programs impact children's regulation and social adjustment. Some investigators have expressed concern that such programs might be detrimental to children's development of social skills, regulation skills, and peer relationships (Stipek, Feiler, Daniels, & Milburn, 1995), although no studies to date have supported this claim. However, there is good reason to believe that there is a positive relation between literacy skills and children's social behavior. For example, aggressive and disruptive behaviors have been associated with low literacy (Arnold et al., 1999; Doctoroff, Greer, & Arnold, 2006). In addition, Ladd et al. (1999) found that children's cognitive and language skills predicted positive social functioning (including relationships with teachers and peers). Similarly, Welsh et al. (2001) showed that children's social and academic competence reciprocally predicted each other over time. Thus, it is possible that vocabulary/language and academic skills promote regulation and emotion understanding, just as children's academic challenges may lead to children's increased frustration and lack of regulation (Arnold et al., 1999; Doctoroff et al., 2006). Consequently, interventions designed to increase both academic and social competence, in theory, should be particularly effective, although the effects of literacy-based and socioemotional-based interventions (separately and in combination) should be compared. What is certain, however, is that emotional development, particularly effortful control, is an important factor for school readiness, perhaps nearly as important as learning to read. Therefore, policy makers must recognize that children's emotional development, as well as cognitive development, are important contributors to school readiness.

CONCLUSION

A number of questions remain regarding research on the relations between children's socioemotional skills and academic readiness. For example, there is a need to examine the processes and mechanisms that support the relations between students' effortful control and their academic success. Few researchers have examined links between complex mediated pathways and the unique effects of the multiple factors (e.g., social behavior at school, quality of relationships with peers and teachers, children's liking of school) that may mediate the association between self-regulation (or emotionality) and children's academic success.

Another important area to consider is children's development. It is likely that children's early socioemotional behavior plays an important role during the transition to formal schooling. Few researchers have examined the role of regulation skills in children's school adjustment over time (at least longer than 1 or 2 years), and it is probable that the relations between regulation and school success vary with age. Therefore, researchers should begin to focus on very early predictors of children's academic readiness, perhaps in infancy or toddlerhood. Moreover, investigators should confirm whether regulation and related socioemotional factors continue to contribute to academic outcomes during the elementary school years and adolescence, particularly after controlling for the stability in academic competence. Perhaps regulation, emotionality, and related social skills are most predictive of children's academic performance during periods of rapid change in effortful control and executive function. If this is true, because of the fairly marked changes in executive function in the adolescent years (Keating, 2004; Sowell, Trauner, Gamst, & Jernigan, 2002), regulation may be an important correlate and predictor of school functioning and school dropout in adolescence.

Finally, more work needs to be done on the relations of regulation and emotion-related factors to school readiness for children who are members of racial and ethnic minority populations. Researchers such as Rabiner, Murray, Schmid, and Malone (2004) have found significant gaps between these children and their European American peers in academic skills and school readiness. Children from some racial and ethnic minority groups in the United States may be at risk for having low levels of regulation skills in preschool and the early school years (Ispa et al., 2004; Sulik et al., 2010). It will be important to identify factors related to these disparities, as the findings would have implications for children's academic performance and socioemotional functioning.

In summary, evidence that children's socioemotional development is important to school readiness and academic success is mounting. There is a need to continue to develop programs designed to improve children's socioemotional functioning and to test whether programs that promote literacy also support children's socioemotional skills (and vice versa). Moreover, the effectiveness of programs may depend on factors such as children's initial emotionality and regulation or maladjustment (Greenberg et al., 1995). Finally, the processes involved in improving children's school readiness skills through a focus on socioemotional functioning need to be examined in future research.

REFERENCES

Alexander, K.L., Entwisle, D.R., & Dauber, S.L. (1993). First-grade classroom behavior: Its short- and long-term consequences for school performance. *Child Development, 64*(3), 801–814. doi:10.2307/1131219

Arnold, D.H., Ortiz, C., Curry, J.C., Stowe, R.M., Goldstein, N.E., Fisher, P.H.,...Yershova, K. (1999). Promoting academic success and preventing disruptive behavior disorders through community partnership. *Journal of Community Psychology, 27*(5), 589–598. doi:10.1002/(SICI)1520-6629(199909)27:5<589::AID-JCOP6>3.0.CO;2-Y

Barnett, W.S., Jung, K., Yarosz, D.J., Thomas, J., Hornbeck, A., Stechuk, R., & Burns, S. (2008). Educational effects of the *Tools of the Mind* curriculum: A randomized trial. *Early Childhood Research Quarterly, 23*(3), 299–313. doi:10.1016/j.ecresq.2008.03.001

Belsky, J., Friedman, S.L., & Hsieh, K. (2001). Testing a core emotion-regulation prediction: Does early attentional persistence moderate the effect of infant negative emotionality on later development? *Child Development, 72*(1), 123–133. doi:10.1111/1467-8624.00269

Bierman, K.L., Domitrovich, C.E., Nix, R.L., Gest, S.D., Welsh, J.A., Greenberg, M.T.,...Gill, S. (2008). Promoting academic and social-emotional school readiness: The *Head Start REDI* program. *Child Development, 79*(6), 1802–1817. doi:10.1111/j.1467-8624.2008.01227.x

Bierman, K.L., Nix, R.L., Greenberg, M.T., Blair, C., & Domitrovich, C.E. (2008). Executive functions and school readiness intervention: Impact, moderation, and mediation in the *Head Start REDI* program. *Development and Psychopathology, 20*(3), 821–843. doi:10.1017/S0954579408000394

Birch, S.H., & Ladd, G.W. (1997). The teacher–child relationship and children's early school adjustment. *Journal of School Psychology, 35*(1), 61–79. doi:10.1016/S0022-4405(96)00029-5

Blair, C. (2003). Behavioral inhibition and behavioral activation in young children: Relations with self-regulation and adaptation to preschool in children attending Head Start. *Developmental Psychobiology, 42*(3), 301–311. doi:10.1002/dev.10103

Blair, C., Granger, D., & Razza, R.P. (2005). Cortisol reactivity is positively related to executive function in preschool children attending Head Start. *Child Development, 76*(3), 554–567. doi:10.1111/j.1467-8624.2005.00863.x

Blair, C., & Razza, R.P. (2007). Relating effortful control, executive function, and false belief understanding to emerging math and literacy ability in kindergarten. *Child Development, 78*(2), 647–663. doi:10.1111/j.1467-8624.2007.01019.x

Bodrova, E. & Leong, D.J. (2007). *Tools of the Mind: The Vygotskian approach to early childhood education* (2nd ed.). Upper Saddle River, NJ: Prentice-Hall.

Buhs, E.S., & Ladd, G.W. (2001). Peer rejection as an antecedent of young children's school adjustment: An examination of mediating processes. *Developmental Psychology, 37*(4), 550–560. doi:10.1037/0012-1649.37.4.550

Conduct Problems Prevention Research Group. (2010). The effects of a multiyear universal social–emotional learning program: The role of student and school characteristics. *Journal of Consulting and Clinical Psychology, 78*(2), 156–168. doi:10.1037/a0018607

Coplan, R.J., Barber, A.M., & Lagacé-Séguin, D.G. (1999). The role of child temperament as a predictor of early literacy and numeracy skills in preschoolers.

Early Childhood Research Quarterly, 14(4), 537–553. doi:10.1016/S0885-2006(99)00025-3

Crone, E.A., Ridderinkhof, K.R., Worm, M., Somsen, R.J.M., & van der Molen, M.W. (2004). Switching between spatial stimulus-response mappings: A developmental study of cognitive flexibility. *Developmental Science, 7*(4), 443–455. doi:10.1111/j.1467-7687.2004.00365.x

Cutting, A.L., & Dunn, J. (1999). Theory of mind, emotion understanding, language, and family background: Individual differences and interrelations. *Child Development, 70*(4), 853–865. doi:10.1111/1467-8624.00061

Denham, S.A. (2006). Social-emotional competence as support for school readiness: What is it and how do we assess it? *Early Education and Development, 17*(1), 57–89. doi:10.1207/s15566935eed1701_4

Denham, S.A., Blair, K., Schmidt, M., & DeMulder, E. (2002). Compromised emotional competence: Seeds of violence sown early? *American Journal of Orthopsychiatry, 72*(1), 70–82. doi:10.1037/0002-9432.72.1.70

Denham, S.A., McKinley, M., Couchoud, E.A., & Holt, R. (1990). Emotional and behavioral predictors of preschool peer ratings. *Child Development, 61*(4), 1145–1152. doi:10.2307/1130882

Denham, S.A., Zoller, D., & Couchoud, E.A. (1994). Socialization of preschoolers' emotion understanding. *Developmental Psychology, 30*(6), 928–936. doi:10.1037/0012-1649.30.6.928

Diamond, A., Barnett, W.S., Thomas, J., & Munro, S. (2007). Preschool program improves cognitive control. *Science, 318*(5855), 1387–1388. doi:10.1126/science.1151148

Dixon, W.E., Jr., & Smith, P.H. (2000). Links between early temperament and language acquisition. *Merrill-Palmer Quarterly: Journal of Developmental Psychology, 46*(3), 417–440.

Doctoroff, G.L., Greer, J.A., & Arnold, D.H. (2006). The relationship between social behavior and emergent literacy among preschool boys and girls. *Journal of Applied Developmental Psychology, 27*(1), 1–13. doi:10.1016/j.appdev.2005.12.003

Domitrovich, C.E., Cortes, R.C., & Greenberg, M.T. (2007). Improving young children's social and emotional competence: A randomized trial of the *Preschool "PATHS"* curriculum. *The Journal of Primary Prevention, 28*(2), 67–91. doi:10.1007/s10935-007-0081-0

Duncan, G.J., Dowsett, C.J., Claessens, A., Magnuson, K., Huston, A.C., Klebanov, P.,...Japel, C. (2007). School readiness and later achievement. *Developmental Psychology, 43*(6), 1428–1446. doi:10.1037/0012-1649.43.6.1428

Dweck, C.S. (1989). Motivation. In A. Lesgold & R. Glaser (Eds.), *Foundations for a psychology of education* (pp. 87–136). Hillsdale, NJ: Lawrence Erlbaum Associates.

Eisenberg, N., Cumberland, A., Spinrad, T.L., Fabes, R.A., Shepard, S.A., Reiser, M.,...Guthrie, I.K. (2001). The relations of regulation and emotionality to children's externalizing and internalizing problem behavior. *Child Development, 72*(4), 1112–1134. doi:10.1111/1467-8624.00337

Eisenberg, N., & Fabes, R.A. (1992). Emotion, regulation, and the development of social competence. In M.S. Clark (Ed.), *Emotion and social behavior* (pp. 119–150). Thousand Oaks, CA: Sage Publications.

Eisenberg, N., Fabes, R.A., Bernzweig, J., & Karbon, M. (1993). The relations of emotionality and regulation to preschoolers' social skills and sociometric status. *Child Development, 64*(5), 1418–1438. doi:10.2307/1131543

Eisenberg, N., Fabes, R.A., Guthrie, I.K., & Murphy, B.C. (1996). The relations of regulation and emotionality to problem behavior in elementary school children. *Development and Psychopathology, 8*(1), 141–162. doi:10.1017/S095457940000701X

Eisenberg, N., Guthrie, I.K., Fabes, R.A., Reiser, M., Murphy, B.C., Holgren, R.,...Losoya, S. (1997). The relations of regulation and emotionality to resiliency and competent social functioning in elementary school children. *Child Development, 68*(2), 295–311. doi:10.2307/1131851

Eisenberg, N., Sadovsky, A., & Spinrad, T. (2005). Associations among emotion-related regulation, language skills, emotion knowledge, and academic outcomes. *New Directions in Child and Adolescent Development, 109,* 109–118.

Eisenberg, N., Sadovsky, A., Spinrad, T.L., Fabes, R.A., Losoya, S.H., Valiente, C.,...Shepard, S.A. (2005). The relations of problem behavior status to children's negative emotionality, effortful control, and impulsivity: Concurrent relations and prediction of change. *Developmental Psychology, 41*(1), 193–211. doi:10.1037/0012-1649.41.1.193

Eisenberg, N., & Spinrad, T.L. (2004). Emotion-related regulation: Sharpening the definition. *Child Development, 75*(2), 334–339.

Eisenberg, N., Spinrad, T.L., Fabes, R.A., Reiser, M., Cumberland, A., Shepard, S.A.,...Thompson, M. (2004). The relations of effortful control and impulsivity to children's resiliency and adjustment. *Child Development, 75*(1), 25–46. doi:10.1111/j.1467-8624.2004.00652.x

Eisenberg, N., Valiente, C., Fabes, R.A., Smith, C.L., Reiser, M., Shepard, S.A.,...Cumberland, A.J. (2003). The relations of effortful control and ego control to children's resiliency and social functioning. *Developmental Psychology, 39*(4), 761–776. doi:10.1037/0012-1649.39.4.761

Eisenberg, N., Valiente, C., Spinrad, T.L., Cumberland, A., Liew, J., Reiser, M.,...Losoya, S.H. (2009). Longitudinal relations of children's effortful control, impulsivity, and negative emotionality to their externalizing, internalizing, and co-occurring behavior problems. *Developmental Psychology, 45*(4), 988–1008. doi:10.1037/a0016213

Evans, D.E., & Rothbart, M.K. (2007). Developing a model for adult temperament. *Journal of Research in Personality, 41*(4), 868–888. doi:10.1016/j.jrp.2006.11.002

Fabes, R.A., Martin, C.L., Hanish, L.D., Anders, M.C., & Madden-Derdich, D.A. (2003). Early school competence: The roles of sex-segregated play and effortful control. *Developmental Psychology, 39*(5), 848–858. doi:10.1037/0012-1649.39.5.848

Fantuzzo, J., Bulotsky-Shearer, R., McDermott, P.A., McWayne, C., Frye, D., & Perlman, S. (2007). Investigation of dimensions of social-emotional classroom behavior and school readiness for low-income urban preschool children. *School Psychology Review, 36*(1), 44–62.

Furrer, C., & Skinner, E. (2003). Sense of relatedness as a factor in children's academic engagement and performance. *Journal of Educational Psychology, 95*(1), 148–162. doi:10.1037/0022-0663.95.1.148

Garner, P.W., & Waajid, B. (2008). The associations of emotion knowledge and teacher–child relationships to preschool children's school-related developmental competence. *Journal of Applied Developmental Psychology, 29*(2), 89–100. doi:10.1016/j.appdev.2007.12.001

Graziano, P.A., Reavis, R.D., Keane, S.P., & Calkins, S.D. (2007). The role of emotion regulation in children's early academic success. *Journal of School Psychology, 45*(1), 3–19. doi:10.1016/j.jsp.2006.09.002

Greenberg, M.T., Kusché, C.A., Cook, E.T., & Quamma, J.P. (1995). Promoting emotional competence in school-aged children: The effects of the *PATHS* curriculum. *Development and Psychopathology, 7*(1), 117–136. doi:10.1017/S0954579400006374

Griggs, M.S., Gagnon, S.G., Huelsman, T.J., Kiddler-Ashley, P., & Ballard, M. (2009). Student–teacher relationships matter: Moderating influences between temperament and preschool social competence. *Psychology in the Schools, 46*(6), 553–567. doi:10.1002/pits.20397

Gumora, G., & Arsenio, W.F. (2002). Emotionality, emotion regulation, and school performance in middle school children. *Journal of School Psychology, 40*(5), 395–413. doi:10.1016/S0022-4405(02)00108-5

Hamre, B.K., & Pianta, R.C. (2001). Early teacher–child relationships and the trajectory of children's school outcomes through eighth grade. *Child Development, 72*(2), 625–638. doi:10.1111/1467-8624.00301

Hill, N.E., & Craft, S.A. (2003). Parent–school involvement and school performance: Mediated pathways among socioeconomically comparable African American and Euro-American families. *Journal of Educational Psychology, 95*(1), 74–83. doi:10.1037/0022-0663.95.1.74

Hoffman, M.L. (2000). *Empathy and moral development: Implications for caring and justice.* New York, NY: Cambridge University Press.

Howse, R.B., Lange, G., Farran, D.C., & Boyles, C.D. (2003). Motivation and self-regulation as predictors of achievement in economically disadvantaged young children. *Journal of Experimental Education, 71*(2), 151–174.

Ispa, J.M., Fine, M.A., Halgunseth, L.C., Harper, S., Robinson, J., Boyce, L.,…Brady-Smith, C. (2004). Maternal intrusiveness, maternal warmth, and mother–toddler relationship outcomes: Variations across low-income ethnic and acculturation groups. *Child Development, 75*(6), 1613–1631.

Izard, C., Fine, S., Schultz, D., Mostow, A., Ackerman, B., & Youngstrom, E. (2001). Emotion knowledge as a predictor of social behavior and academic competence in children at risk. *Psychological Science, 12*(1), 18–23. doi:10.1111/1467-9280.00304

Izard, C.E., King, K.A., Trentacosta, C.J., Morgan, J.K., Laurenceau, J., Krauthamer-Ewing, E.S., & Finlon, K.J. (2008). Accelerating the development of emotion competence in Head Start children: Effects on adaptive and maladaptive behavior. *Development and Psychopathology, 20*(1), 369–397. doi:10.1017/S0954579408000175

Izard, C.E., Trentacosta, C.J., King, K.A., & Mostow, A.J. (2004). An emotion-based prevention program for Head Start children. *Early Education and Development, 15*(4), 407–422. doi:10.1207/s15566935eed1504_4

Jones, S., Eisenberg, N., Fabes, R.A., & MacKinnon, D.P. (2002). Parents' reactions to elementary school children's negative emotions: Relations to social and emotional functioning at school. *Merrill-Palmer Quarterly: Journal of Developmental Psychology, 48*(2), 133–159. doi:10.1353/mpq.2002.0007

Kannass, K.N., Oakes, L.M., & Shaddy, D.J. (2006). A longitudinal investigation of the development of attention and distractibility. *Journal of Cognition and Development, 7*(3), 381–409. doi:10.1207/s15327647jcd0703_8

Keating, D. (2004). Cognitive and brain development. In R. Lerner & L. Steinberg (Eds.), *Handbook of adolescent psychology* (2nd ed., pp. 45–84). New York, NY: Wiley.

Kochanska, G., Murray, K.T., & Harlan, E.T. (2000). Effortful control in early childhood: Continuity and change, antecedents, and implications for social development. *Developmental Psychology, 36*(2), 220–232.

Kopp, C.B. (1982). Antecedents of self-regulation: A developmental perspective. *Developmental Psychology, 18*(2), 199–214. doi:10.1037/0012-1649.18.2.199

Ladd, G.W., Birch, S.H., & Buhs, E.S. (1999). Children's social and scholastic lives in kindergarten: Related spheres of influence? *Child Development, 70*(6), 1373–1400. doi:10.1111/1467-8624.00101

Ladd, G.W., Buhs, E.S., & Seid, M. (2000). Children's initial sentiments about kindergarten: Is school liking an antecedent of early classroom participation and achievement? *Merrill-Palmer Quarterly: Journal of Developmental Psychology, 46*(2), 255–279.

Ladd, G.W., Herald, S.L., & Kochel, K.P. (2006). School readiness: Are there social prerequisites? *Early Education and Development, 17*(1), 115–150. doi:10.1207/s15566935eed1701_6

Ladd, G.W., Kochenderfer, B.J., & Coleman, C.C. (1996). Friendship quality as a predictor of young children's early school adjustment. *Child Development, 67*(3), 1103–1118. doi:10.2307/1131882

Laible, D.J., & Thompson, R.A. (2002). Mother–child conflict in the toddler years: Lessons in emotion, morality, and relationships. *Child Development, 73*(4), 1187–1203. doi:10.1111/1467-8624.00466

Lonigan, C.J., Bloomfield, B.G., Anthony, J.L., Bacon, K.D., Phillips, B.M., & Samwel, C.S. (1999). Relations among emergent literacy skills, behavior problems, and social competence in preschool children from low- and middle-income backgrounds. *Topics in Early Childhood Special Education, 19*(1), 40–53. doi:10.1177/027112149901900104

McClelland, M.M., Cameron, C.E., Connor, C.M., Farris, C.L., Jewkes, A.M., & Morrison, F.J. (2007). Links between behavioral regulation and preschoolers' literacy, vocabulary, and math skills. *Developmental Psychology, 43*(4), 947–959. doi:10.1037/0012-1649.43.4.947

McEvoy, A., & Welker, R. (2000). Antisocial behavior, academic failure, and school climate: A critical review. *Journal of Emotional and Behavioral Disorders, 8*(3), 130–140. doi:10.1177/106342660000800301

Mezzacappa, E. (2004). Alerting, orienting, and executive attention: Developmental properties and sociodemographic correlates in an epidemiological sample of young, urban children. *Child Development, 75*(5), 1373–1386.

Mostow, A.J., Izard, C.E., Fine, S., & Trentacosta, C.J. (2002). Modeling emotional, cognitive, and behavioral predictors of peer acceptance. *Child Development, 73*(6), 1775–1787. doi:10.1111/1467-8624.00505

Murphy, B.C., Eisenberg, N., Fabes, R.A., Shepard, S., & Guthrie, I.K. (1999). Consistency and change in children's emotionality and regulation: A longitudinal study. *Merrill Palmer Quarterly, 45*(3), 413–444.

National Early Literacy Panel. (2008). *Developing early literacy: Report of the National Early Literacy Panel.* Washington, DC: National Institute for Literacy.

NICHD Early Childcare Research Network. (2003). Does amount of time spent in child care predict socioemotional adjustment during the transition to kindergarten? *Child Development, 74*(4), 976–1005.

Nigg, J.T. (2000). On inhibition/disinhibition in developmental psychopathology: Views from cognitive and personality psychology and a working inhibition taxonomy. *Psychological Bulletin, 126*(2), 220–246.

O'Neil, R., Welsh, M., Parke, R.D., Wang, S., & Strand, C. (1997). A longitudinal assessment of the academic correlates of early peer acceptance and rejection. *Journal of Clinical Child Psychology, 26*(3), 290–303.

Pianta, R.C., Steinberg, M.S., & Rollins, K.B. (1995). The first two years of school: Teacher–child relationships and deflections in children's classroom adjustment. *Development and Psychopathology, 7*(2), 295–312. doi:10.1017 /S0954579400006519

Pickering, A.D., & Gray, J.A. (1999). The neuroscience of personality. In L.A. Pervin and O.P. John (Eds.), *Handbook of Personality* (pp. 277–279). New York, NY: Guilford Press.

Ponitz, C.C., McClelland, M.M., Matthews, J.S., & Morrison, F.J. (2009). A structured observation of behavioral self-regulation and its contribution to kindergarten outcomes. *Developmental Psychology, 45*(3), 605–619. doi:10.1037 /a0015365

Pons, F., Lawson, J., Harris, P.L., & de Rosnay, M. (2003). Individual differences in children's emotion understanding: Effects of age and language. *Scandinavian Journal of Psychology, 44*(4), 347–353. doi:10.1111/1467-9450.00354

Rabiner, D.L., Murray, D.W., Schmid, L., & Malone, P.S. (2004). An exploration of the relationship between ethnicity, attention problems, and academic achievement. *School Psychology Review, 33*(4), 498–509.

Raver, C.C. (2002). Emotions matter: Making the case for the role of young children's emotional development for early school readiness. *Social Policy Report, 16*(3), 3–18.

Riggs, N.R., Greenberg, M.T., Kusché, C.A., & Pentz, M.A. (2006). The mediational role of neurocognition in the behavioral outcomes of a social-emotional prevention program in elementary school students: Effects of the *PATHS* curriculum. *Prevention Science, 7*(1), 91–102. doi:10.1007/s11121-005-0022-1

Rothbart, M.K., Ahadi, S.A., Hersey, K.L., & Fisher, P. (2001). Investigations of temperament at three to seven years: The Children's Behavior Questionnaire. *Child Development, 72*(5), 1394–1408.

Rothbart, M.K., & Bates, J.E. (2006). Temperament. In N. Eisenberg, W. Damon, & R.M. Lerner (Eds.), *Handbook of child psychology: Social, emotional, and personality development* (6th ed., Vol. 3, pp. 99–166). Hoboken, NJ: Wiley.

Rothbart, M.K., Sheese, B.E., & Posner, M.I. (2007). Executive attention and effortful control: Linking temperament, brain networks, and genes. *Child Development Perspectives, 1*(1), 2–7.

Rubin, K.H., Bukowski, W.M., & Parker, J.G. (2006). Peer interactions, relationships, and groups. In N. Eisenberg, W. Damon, & R.M. Lerner (Eds.), *Handbook of child psychology: Social, emotional, and personality development* (6th ed., Vol. 3, pp. 571–645). Hoboken, NJ: Wiley.

Rudasill, K.M., & Rimm-Kaufman, S.E. (2009). Teacher–child relationship quality: The roles of child temperament and teacher–child interactions. *Early Childhood Research Quarterly, 24*(2), 107–120.

Rueda, M., Fan, J., McCandliss, B.D., Halparin, J.D., Gruber, D.B., Lercari, L.P., & Posner, M.I. (2004). Development of attentional networks in childhood. *Neuropsychologia, 42*(8), 1029–1040.

Ruff, H.A., & Capozzoli, M.C. (2003). Development of attention and distractibility in the first 4 years of life. *Developmental Psychology, 39*(5), 877–890. doi:10.1037/0012-1649.39.5.877

Ruffman, T., Slade, L., Rowlandson, K., Rumsey, C., & Garnham, A. (2003). How language relates to belief, desire, and emotion understanding. *Cognitive Development, 18*(2), 139–158.

Ryan, R.M., Stiller, J.D., & Lynch, J.H. (1994). Representations of relationships to teachers, parents, and friends as predictors of academic motivation and self-esteem. *The Journal of Early Adolescence, 14*(2), 226–249. doi:10.1177/027243169401400207

Schultz, D., Izard, C.E., Ackerman, B.P., & Youngstrom, E.A. (2001). Emotion knowledge in economically disadvantaged children: Self-regulatory antecedents and relations to social difficulties and withdrawal. *Development and Psychopathology, 13*(1), 53–67. doi:10.1017/S0954579401001043

Shields, A., Dickstein, S., Seifer, R., Giusti, L., Magee, K.D., & Spritz, B. (2001). Emotional competence and early school adjustment: A study of preschoolers at risk. *Early Education and Development, 12*(1), 73–96. doi:10.1207/s15566935eed1201_5

Shure, M.B. (1993). *I Can Problem Solve (ICPS):* Interpersonal cognitive problem solving for young children. *Early Child Development and Care, 96,* 49–64 doi: 10.1080/0300443930960106

Silva, K.M., Spinrad, T.L., Eisenberg, N., Sulik, M.J., Valiente, C., Huerta, S.,...Taylor, H.B. (2011). Relations of children's effortful control, teacher–child relationship quality and school attitudes in a low-income sample. *Early Education and Development, 22*(3), 434–460. doi: 10.1080/10409289.2011.578046

Smith, M., & Walden, T. (1998). Developmental trends in emotion understanding among a diverse sample of African-American preschool children. *Journal of Applied Developmental Psychology, 19*(2), 177–198. doi:10.1016/S0193-3973(99)80035-5

Smith-Donald, R., Raver, C.C., Hayes, T., & Richardson, B. (2007). Preliminary construct and concurrent validity of the Preschool Self-Regulation Assessment (PSRA) for field-based research. *Early Childhood Research Quarterly, 22*(2), 173–187. doi:10.1016/j.ecresq.2007.01.002

Sowell, E.R., Trauner, D.A., Gamst, A., & Jernigan, T.L. (2002). Development of cortical and subcortical brain structures in childhood and adolescence: A structural MRI study. *Developmental Medicine and Child Neurology, 44*(1), 4–16.

Spinrad, T.L., Eisenberg, N., Cumberland, A., Fabes, R.A., Valiente, C., Shepard, S.A.,...Guthrie, I.K. (2006). Relation of emotion-related regulation to children's social competence: A longitudinal study. *Emotion, 6*(3), 498–510. doi:10.1037/1528-3542.6.3.498

Spinrad, T.L., Eisenberg, N., Gaertner, B., Popp, T., Smith, C.L., Kupfer, A.,...Hofer, C. (2007). Relations of maternal socialization and toddlers' effortful control to children's adjustment and social competence. *Developmental Psychology, 43*(5), 1170–1186. doi:10.1037/0012-1649.43.5.1170

Spinrad, T.L., Eisenberg, N., Harris, E., Hanish, L., Fabes, R.A., Kupanoff, K.,...Holmes, J. (2004). The relation of children's everyday nonsocial peer play behavior to their emotionality, regulation, and social functioning. *Developmental Psychology, 40*(1), 67–80.

Stipek, D., Feiler, R., Daniels, D., & Milburn, S. (1995). Effects of different instructional approaches on young children's achievement and motivation. *Child Development, 66*(1), 209–223.

Sulik, M.J., Huerta, S., Zerr, A.A., Eisenberg, N., Spinrad, T.L., Valiente, C.,... Taylor, H.B. (2010). The factor structure of effortful control and measurement invariance across ethnicity and sex in a high-risk sample. *Journal of Psychopathology and Behavioral Assessment, 32*(1), 8–22. doi:10.1007 /s10862-009-9164-y

Trentacosta, C.J., & Izard, C.E. (2007). Kindergarten children's emotion competence as a predictor of their academic competence in first grade. *Emotion, 7*(1), 77–88. doi:10.1037/1528-3542.7.1.77

Valiente, C., Eisenberg, N., Haugen, R.G., Spinrad, T., Hofer, C., Liew, J., & Kupfer, A. (2011). Children's effortful control and academic achievement: Mediation through social functioning. *Early Education and Development, 22*(3), 411–433. doi: 10.1080/10409289.2010.505259

Valiente, C., Eisenberg, N., Smith, C.L., Reiser, M., Fabes, R.A., Losoya, S.,... Murphy, B.C. (2003). The relations of effortful control and reactive control to children's externalizing problems: A longitudinal assessment. *Journal of Personality, 71*(6), 1171–1196.

Valiente, C., Lemery-Chalfant, K., & Castro, K.S. (2007). Children's effortful control and academic competence: Mediation through school liking. *Merrill-Palmer Quarterly: Journal of Developmental Psychology, 53*(1), 1–25. doi:10.1353 /mpq.2007.0006

Valiente, C., Lemery-Chalfant, K.S., & Swanson, J. (2010). Prediction of kindergartners' academic competence from their effortful control and negative emotionality: Evidence for direct and moderated relations. *Journal of Educational Psychology, 3*, 550–560. doi: 10.1037/a0018992 .

Valiente, C., Lemery-Chalfant, K., Swanson, J., & Reiser, M. (2008). Prediction of children's academic competence from their effortful control, relationships, and classroom participation. *Journal of Educational Psychology, 100*(1), 67–77. doi:10.1037/0022-0663.100.1.67

Welsh, M., Parke, R.D., Widaman, K., & O'Neil, R. (2001). Linkages between children's social and academic competence: A longitudinal analysis. *Journal of School Psychology, 39*(6), 463–482. doi:10.1016/S0022-4405(01)00084-X

Wentzel, K.R. (1999). Social-motivational processes and interpersonal relationships: Implications for understanding motivation at school. *Journal of Educational Psychology, 91*(1), 76–97. doi:10.1037/0022-0663.91.1.76

Wentzel, K.R., & Caldwell, K. (1997). Friendships, peer acceptance, and group membership: Relations to academic achievement in middle school. *Child Development, 68*(6), 1198–1209.

Williams, B.R., Ponesse, J.S., Schachar, R.J., Logan, G.D., & Tannock, R. (1999). Development of inhibitory control across the life span. *Developmental Psychology, 35*(1), 205–213. doi:10.1037/0012-1649.35.1.205

Zhou, Q., Main, A., & Wang, Y. (2010). The relations of temperamental effortful control and anger/frustration to Chinese children's academic achievement and social adjustment: A longitudinal study. *Journal of Educational Psychology, 102*(1), 180–196. doi:10.1037/a0015908

5

Phonological Awareness and Alphabet Knowledge

Key Precursors and Instructional Targets to Promote Reading Success

Beth M. Phillips and Shayne B. Piasta

One of the underlying principles of an emergent literacy approach is the idea that early childhood home- and school-based experiences support the continued growth of key foundational skills related to later reading, spelling, and comprehension (Phillips & Lonigan, 2005; Whitehurst & Lonigan, 1998). Phonological awareness (PA) and alphabet knowledge (AK) have received substantial attention as two of the most important of these early skills. This chapter summarizes the relevant National Early Literacy Panel (NELP; 2008) results on the efficacy of teaching PA and AK in preschool and kindergarten classrooms and extends this work by 1) highlighting a number of empirically supported instructional design elements for teaching PA and AK, 2) reviewing observational research on the implementation of PA and AK instruction in early childhood, and 3) offering some suggestions for future research on both PA and AK instructional design and professional development. We generally limit our review to studies of children learning literacy in English but also highlight selected work on other languages where appropriate. Furthermore, our focus in this chapter is limited to the development of children's early code-focused "inside-out" skills (Storch & Whitehurst, 2002; Whitehurst & Lonigan, 1998), although we readily acknowledge that such instruction is just one element of a comprehensive early literacy program (Graue, Clements, Reynolds, & Niles, 2004; Phillips, Clancy-Menchetti, & Lonigan, 2008).

We begin our discussion of PA and AK by summarizing briefly what is meant by these terms and what is known about the predictive and causal roles they play in children's progress toward mastery of the decoding and spelling processes. Consistent with the NELP report, PA is considered to represent an umbrella term that includes children's sensitivity to, and capacity to manipulate, sounds within spoken language at varying levels of linguistic complexity, from the whole word to the phoneme. PA may be measured by a wide range of tasks asking children to match, identify, segment, blend, and delete sound elements within words (Anthony, Lonigan, Driscoll, Phillips, & Burgess, 2003; Lonigan, Burgess, Anthony, & Barker, 1998; Wagner, Torgesen, & Rashotte, 1994). We define AK specifically as the recognition and production of the names and sounds of letters, although we also recognize the importance of other related concepts about print, such as identifying the distinction between letters and other symbols and knowing about the left-to-right orientation of English print (Lonigan, Schatschneider, & Westberg, 2008b). Together, considerable evidence suggests that PA and AK intertwine to allow children to comprehend the basic idea of the alphabetic principle, learn the regularities of the associations between sounds and letters, and apply these understandings to the process of phonemic decoding and "sounding out" words in print (Ehri, 2002; Phillips & Torgesen, 2006; Share, 1995). In the sections that follow, we summarize research findings that support the complementary roles of PA and AK in promoting early literacy and then turn to the discussion of instructional strategies that best enable children to master these two areas.

THE DEVELOPMENTAL CONTINUUM OF PHONOLOGICAL AWARENESS

The available evidence suggests that PA represents a single underlying construct (Anthony & Lonigan, 2004; Anthony et al., 2003; Schatschneider, Francis, Foorman, Fletcher, & Mehta, 1999). In other words, although PA may be assessed using a range of linguistic complexity and a variety of tasks, these multiple methods of assessment all measure the same developing skill. Furthermore, although children's success in demonstrating

PA skills typically progresses from larger to smaller linguistic units and from easier to more complex tasks, this progress does not occur in a series of discrete stages in which movement to the next stage is predicated on complete mastery of the previous stage (Anthony et al., 2002; Anthony et al., 2003; Lonigan, Burgess, & Anthony, 2000; Lonigan et al., 1998; Webb, Schwanenflugel, & Kim, 2004) but is instead continuous and overlapping, with children developing across multiple levels in tandem (Bowey, 2002; Carroll, Snowling, Hulme, & Stevenson, 2003; Lonigan et al., 1998). Although formal reading instruction may accelerate the development of PA, particularly at the phonemic level, some children do demonstrate this level of PA ability before such instruction begins at school (Anthony et al., 2002; Hulme, Caravolas, Málková, & Brigstocke, 2005). Together, these results demonstrate that PA ability is reliably detectable in young children and follows a general developmental progression that may have instructional implications.

Longitudinal Predictions of Phonological Awareness and Alphabet Knowledge to Reading Outcomes

Both PA and AK demonstrate consistent concurrent and longitudinal relations with conventional literacy skills. In summarizing research published prior to 2004, the NELP report indicated that PA, as measured in both preschool and kindergarten, significantly and uniquely predicted decoding, spelling, and reading comprehension outcomes measured at the end of kindergarten or later (Lonigan et al., 2008b). Similar moderate-to-strong predictive relations were found for AK. These findings, along with multivariate results, support PA and AK as being among the primary unique predictors of conventional reading skill that are known to be malleable and appropriate targets for early intervention. More recent studies published in 2004 or later have augmented the conclusions drawn by NELP (Kaplan & Walpole, 2005; Missall et al., 2007; Schatschneider, Fletcher, Francis, Carlson, & Foorman, 2004; Speece, Ritchey, Cooper, Roth, & Schatschneider, 2004), with some studies also indicating unique relations of PA and AK to later reading comprehension skill via both direct and indirect pathways mediated by decoding accuracy and fluency (Burke, Hagan-Burke, Kwok, & Parker, 2009; Furnes & Samuelsson, 2009). The importance of PA and AK as foundational skills is also supported in research samples of English language learners learning to read in English (Chiappe, Siegel, & Wade-Woolley, 2002; Linklater, O'Connor, & Palardy, 2009) and of children learning to read in orthographies of varying transparency such as Finnish and Norwegian (Lervåg, Bråten, & Hulme, 2009; Manolitsis, Georgiou, Stephenson, & Parrila, 2009; Puolakanaho et al., 2008; Torppa et al., 2007).

The NELP report presented some additional evidence supporting the characterization of PA as a single underlying construct. For example, follow-up analyses to those described previously showed that PA measures that combined task and linguistic levels were the best predictors of decoding. Furthermore, phoneme- and subphoneme-level tasks (i.e., syllable-level manipulation) were statistically indistinguishable in predicting decoding and reading comprehension, although some weaker relations were evident for rhyming (Lonigan et al., 2008b). Additional follow-up analyses showed that analysis tasks (e.g., segmenting, deleting) demonstrated stronger relations to decoding and reading comprehension than synthesis tasks (blending), whereas synthesis tasks appeared to be equivalent to identity tasks. Significantly, these findings were not interpreted as suggesting that instruction in analysis tasks is likely to be more beneficial than synthesis tasks, a conclusion borne out by the intervention findings discussed next. Rather, Lonigan et al. (2008b) interpreted these findings to indicate that success at analytic manipulation suggests a child who is closer to—or is already—demonstrating understanding of the alphabetic principle. Together, these results highlight the potential importance of attending to children's developmental level when designing instructional programs.

Efficacy of Phonological Awareness Instruction in Preschool and Kindergarten

The NELP report summarized research on the efficacy of PA interventions for both emergent literacy (e.g., PA, AK) and conventional literacy (e.g., decoding, spelling) outcomes. Overall, results indicated that code-focused interventions (including training on PA alone, PA with AK training, and in some cases PA with phonics training) had moderate-to-large effects on PA, AK, decoding, spelling, and writing (Lonigan et al., 2008a). The largest effect was on PA skill itself, with the effects on reading, spelling, and writing all being somewhat lower but still significant, moderate, and comparable to one another. Findings were quite consistent with the work of the earlier National Reading Panel (NRP) that had investigated PA interventions in a meta-analysis focusing on a wider range of grade levels (Ehri et al., 2001; NRP, 2000) and with the previous meta-analytic summary provided by Bus and van IJzendoorn (1999). In all three reviews, PA training was found to be significantly effective for children as young as preschool age and effective for children who had or did not yet have any reading skills. In fact, all three reviews suggest that PA instruction may be more effective for younger, preschool-age children rather than older children. This convergent finding runs counter to concerns voiced by some early childhood educators that preschool children are not developmentally ready to benefit from PA instruction (Elkind, 1987; Olfman, 2003).

Results from studies completed since the publication of the NELP report support these general conclusions. Findings of significant effects are derived from studies that addressed PA instruction alone (Castiglioni-Spalten & Ehri, 2003; Gillon, 2005; Hesketh, Dima, & Nelson, 2007; Koutsoftas, Harmon, & Gray, 2009; McIntosh, Crosbie, Holm, Dodd, & Thomas, 2007) and from studies that included PA along with letter and/or phonics instruction, and in some cases also decoding instruction itself (Bowyer-Crane et al., 2008; Craig, 2006; Farver, Lonigan, & Eppe, 2009; Hatcher, Hulme, & Snowling, 2004; Simmons et al., 2007; Simmons, Kame'enui, Stoolmiller, Coyne, & Harn, 2003). This large body of literature supports the idea that, across ages, formats of instruction, duration, and other characteristics of the children, instructors, and schools, PA instruction can be effective for the development of PA and reading abilities in young children, including English language learners and children who have already been identified as performing behind peers in reading ability.

Efficacy of Letter-Knowledge Instruction in Preschool and Kindergarten

NELP found a significant impact of code-focused instruction on children's AK, with statistically similar impacts when such instruction was provided to preschool and kindergarten children. When code-focused instruction was separated by training components, significant impacts on AK development were apparent for PA training with AK and PA training with phonics but not for PA training alone. Results concerning the causal impacts of AK training were limited, given the availability of only two studies that provided training in AK alone and met all other NELP selection criteria. These results indicated positive effects of AK training on oral language skills but not on PA or reading skills. A recent meta-analysis (Piasta & Wagner, 2010a) expands understanding of the efficacy of AK training on both AK and other literacy outcomes (i.e., PA, reading, and spelling). The impact of code-focused instruction on AK outcomes was actually slightly larger than the effects reported by NELP. More noteworthy were the impact estimates of pure AK training on various outcomes. Although the meta-analysis yielded positive effects of AK training on AK outcomes, only the effect on letter–sound knowledge was statistically reliable, and this effect was significantly greater than the estimate for letter–name knowledge. Analysis of additional outcomes showed small but significant short-term effects on reading skills but not PA or spelling skills. Together, these findings indicate that the incorporation of early AK training does lead to literacy skill growth for children but that the direct impact of AK training may apply only to letter–sound correspondences unless combined with other components of code-focused instruction, such as PA.

DESIGN FEATURES THAT MAY ENHANCE THE IMPACT OF PHONOLOGICAL AWARENESS AND ALPHABET KNOWLEDGE INSTRUCTION

One of the primary questions related to PA and AK instruction is what type and focus of instruction is best for enabling children to learn not only these skills but also to transfer this knowledge to the process of decoding. In this section, we address some universal features of effective instructional programs, summarize the conclusions drawn from separate research bases on PA and AK, and, finally, discuss some further areas in which findings overlap. We caution that although these recommendations are supported by the available research, many of them have not been tested using the most rigorous research designs; therefore, continued research on their efficacy is required.

Systematic Explicit versus Implicit Instruction

Virtually all studies included in the NRP and NELP reports can be considered systematic programs in which the sequence, nature, and materials used in the teaching episodes were predetermined and relatively standardized across intervention groups or classrooms. Most of these studies include strategies for instruction that would be considered explicit (Lonigan et al., 2008a; NRP, 2000; Phillips et al., 2008). In a direct comparison across levels of systematicity, Simmons et al. (2007) found differential benefits of greater systematicity and specificity of PA instruction with phonics for children at risk for reading difficulties in the comparison of 30-minute supplements that only differed on these design dimensions. Likewise, a handful of studies have compared AK instruction delivered explicitly and with a set scope and sequence to methods using a more implicit approach. Systematic, explicit instructional approaches were found to be most beneficial for children's letter–sound learning (Ball & Blachman, 1988, 1991; Walton & Walton, 2002). However, results for letter–name learning have been mixed, with some studies showing benefits of systematic, explicit instruction (Aram, 2006; Aram & Biron, 2004; Justice, Chow, Capellini, Flanigan, & Colton, 2003) and others showing no differences between explicit and implicit approaches (Ball & Blachman, 1988, 1991). Taken together, these results indicate, with the possible exception of letter–name learning, that less systematic and less explicit instruction may be less effective, particularly for students who have low initial emergent literacy ability and characteristics associated with risk for difficulties in learning to read (Ehri et al., 2001; Foorman & Torgesen, 2001).

Part of systematicity includes allocating sufficient time to allow mastery of key learning goals; this rate is likely to vary across skills and children (Byrne, Fielding-Barnsley, & Ashley, 2000), and there may be some diminishing returns (NRP, 2000). Whereas Hatcher et al. (2006) found that 10 weeks of explicit and systematic PA, AK, and phonics instruction was as beneficial as 20 weeks, other studies found that the children with the lowest initial skills needed more extended training time to realize generalizable benefits (Hindson et al., 2005; Simmons et al., 2007; Whiteley, Smith, & Connors, 2007). More research is needed on thresholds of instruction in PA, AK, and phonics that appear sufficient for most children; however, these thresholds are unlikely to apply to all children, given individual differences and the probability that the appropriate amount of PA or AK or phonics instruction may depend on how much instruction a child has received in the other areas (Hatcher et al., 2004; Hindson et al., 2005; Xue & Miesels, 2004).

Small-Group Instruction versus Individual or Large-Group Instruction

The NELP report did not explicitly compare instruction delivered in small groups of students with instruction delivered to individual students. However, results from both the NRP report and Bus and van IJzendoorn (1999) indicated that instruction in small groups was actually more effective than instruction delivered in one-to-one tutoring. Vadasy & Sanders (2008) also found one-to-two tutoring to be as effective as one-to-one. Likewise, NRP also found that small-group instruction was significantly more effective than whole-class instruction (Ehri et al., 2001; Elbaum, Vaughn, Hughes, & Moody, 2000). Notably, very few of the studies reviewed by NELP included code-focused instruction delivered in whole-class contexts. The absence of these studies does not necessarily indicate that whole-class instruction is not effective (Shapiro & Solity, 2008), but more research on whole-class instruction is warranted to allow confidence that this format affords all children equivalent opportunities to learn the targeted skills and to efficiently transfer this acquired ability to reading and spelling applications (Lonigan et al., 2008a; Phillips et al., 2008). Working in groups may afford children who are performing at lower levels than their peers the benefit of repeated exposure to more difficult skills before being expected to master these skills themselves (Shapiro & Solity, 2008), but too large a group may be challenging for classroom management and time on task for children who are at risk (Connor, Morrison, & Slominski, 2006; Foorman & Torgesen, 2001).

Modularity of Phonological Awareness and Alphabet Knowledge Instructional Effects

There is ample evidence that PA (perhaps especially phonemic awareness) and AK (perhaps especially knowledge of letter sounds) are reciprocally supportive across development (Foy & Mann, 2006; McBride-Chang, 1999; Torppa et al., 2007). Likewise, the acquisition of the alphabetic principle and the act of phonemic decoding itself appears to support further growth in PA skill (Blaiklock, 2004; Ehri et al., 2001; Wagner et al., 1994; Wagner et al., 1997). However, evidence from several preschool studies suggests that one cannot assume that PA or AK instruction will automatically lead to growth in the other dimension (Lonigan, 2003; Piasta & Wagner, 2010a). This supports the idea of modularity and the likely need to explicitly attend to both skills for children with low initial abilities (Hatcher et al., 2004; but cf. Johnston & Watson, 2004).

Inclusion of Alphabet Knowledge
Focus in Phonological Awareness Instruction

Substantial variations exist in PA instruction regarding whether AK is taught, and if so, whether it is integrated as with phonics instruction or kept as a separate module. Findings from the NELP report indicate no differences across three types of instruction (oral PA alone, PA with letters taught separately, and integrated phonics-like instruction) on PA outcomes; in contrast, the NRP results did suggest some advantage to the inclusion of letters on PA outcomes. Yet, the NELP report does converge with prior meta-analyses on the finding that training in PA tasks that included any type of AK instruction was more effective for reading outcomes than oral PA tasks alone. This repeated finding suggests that children must already have, or concurrently acquire, knowledge of some grapheme–phoneme links, and of how these links relate to the blending and segmenting of the sounds in words, in order to most readily apply their new PA skills to the task of decoding real or nonsense words (Blaiklock, 2004; Ehri, 2002).

Linguistic and Task Complexity in
Phonological Awareness Instruction

Unlike the NRP report, which only considered studies involving PA instruction at the phoneme level of linguistic complexity (inclusive of onset–rime tasks), the NELP report also included studies in which PA instruction focused on both larger and smaller sound segments or exclusively on larger linguistic units (e.g., syllables, compound words) and found comparable effects on multiple relevant literacy outcomes. This suggests that PA instruction for children in preschool and kindergarten does not always need to include phoneme-level tasks to have a positive impact on reading and spelling outcomes. Whereas it may be true that phonemic-level manipulation skill is necessary for mastering and applying the alphabetic principle, this may not necessarily mean that PA instruction must use this most complex skill level to be effective; some children are likely to achieve this level of ability without precisely matching instruction (Bus & van IJzendoorn, 1999; Lonigan et al., 2008a; O'Connor, Jenkins, & Slocum, 1995). However, children who begin the instructional program with the lowest levels of PA may require more explicit attention to phonemic-level tasks (Denne, Langdown, Pring, & Roy, 2005; Hatcher et al., 2004; Hindson et al., 2005; O'Connor et al., 1995).

The NELP report, in some contrast to the NRP report, also found no significant difference between interventions that targeted tasks of varying cognitive complexity (e.g., blending, segmenting, identity). NELP did not replicate NRP's analyses indicating that teaching a smaller number of phoneme-manipulation skills (blending and segmenting) was more beneficial than teaching a wider array of tasks. Aspects of instruction related to the type of cognitive operations for larger-unit tasks should all be considered in the context of the linguistic complexity of tasks children are asked to perform, and vice versa, because there is evidence of a developmental progression for both (Anthony et al., 2002, 2003); there is also evidence that certain tasks require greater memory retention than others. More research is needed with younger children on both the level of linguistic complexity and cognitive operations to determine issues related to pedagogical focus, sequencing, and whether mastery-learning or time-linked instructional design optimizes children's benefits for PA and reading. Children appear to learn the specific PA skill that is taught in the instruction but may not always generalize the learning to untaught PA skills of different cognitive task type or level of linguistic complexity (Anthony, Hecht, Schoger, Mukherjee, & Williams, 2009). Acquiring skills at a lower developmental level may enhance learning of phoneme-level skills once they are taught, although some evidence suggests that teaching rhyming alone may not sufficiently promote advancement in overall PA skills (Hatcher et al., 2004; Hindson et al., 2005; Phillips et al., 2008). There is some conflicting data regarding whether or not children need to have attained a threshold level of letter–sound knowledge before becoming competent at phoneme-manipulation tasks (Foy & Mann, 2006; Hulme et al., 2005); although there is no prerequisite need to know a letter sound before identifying it as a word's onset, some letter sounds may be particularly facilitative of the acquisition of "deeper" types of phonemic awareness. Similarly, some preliminary findings suggest that segmenting and blending of syllables and phonemes may be easier, and thus potentially better taught earlier, when manipulated as body–coda (e.g., goa-t) versus onset–rime (e.g., g-oat) or when students are asked to segment the phonemes in VC versus CV words or nonwords

(Cassady & Smith, 2004; Geudens, Dominiek, & Van den Broeck, 2004). Geudens et al. (2004) note that children may more readily stretch a vowel sound and hear the demarcation with the subsequent consonant than separate onset consonants from subsequent vowels, thus experiencing phoneme segmentation in a more phonetically transparent context. It may also be important to key instructional decisions to the frustration level of the children; if they are having difficulty with tasks of a higher linguistic or cognitive demand, it may be beneficial to move to somewhat easier tasks that evoke success and perhaps more motivation and engagement from the children (Hesketh et al., 2007; Phillips et al., 2008). The question turns to what can be concluded about effectively teaching AK to young children. In the following sections, we provide our preliminary recommendations drawn from the relatively small amount of available literature that could inform the specifics of AK instruction.

Sequence of Teaching Letters   There is very little empirical evidence to inform the order in which letters are best taught. The results of a single study (Carnine, 1976) support separating the introduction of letters associated with phonologically similar sounds (e.g., short *e*, short *i*). With respect to visual similarity, such as *b* and *p,* the available research evidence is inconclusive; one study found no effect of introducing these letters simultaneously or separately (Evans & Bilsky, 1975) and another found mixed effects (Farrell, 1978). No studies appear to investigate an optimal sequencing of teaching uppercase versus lowercase letters.

Teaching Letter Names versus Sounds   A growing body of evidence is beginning to suggest that there is indeed an advantage to teaching children letter names. Two studies have demonstrated that children who learn letter names use sound cues contained in the names (e.g., /b/ in *B,* /f/ in *F*) to benefit their learning of letter sounds (Share, 2004; Treiman, Tincoff, Rodriguez, Mouzaki, & Francis, 1998; see also Levin, Shatil-Carmon, & Asif-Rave, 2006). Additional studies by Piasta and colleagues (Piasta, Purpura, & Wagner, 2010; Piasta & Wagner, 2010b) lend tentative support to teaching both letter names and sounds as opposed to sounds alone.

Mnemonics and Multisensory Teaching   By and large, the use of mnemonics appears to support children's AK development. Studies by Ehri and colleagues (Ehri, Deffner, & Wilce, 1984; Shmidman & Ehri, 2010) showed benefits to children's letter–sound knowledge via use of pictorial representations in which letter shapes and sounds were embedded; these results transferred to application of AK to reading and spelling tasks. Hetzroni and Shavit (2002) showed benefits of mnemonics for letter–name learning, although an effect on letter–sound learning was not apparent. Despite widespread support for multisensory AK instruction, the research base for such an approach is minimal and mixed. McMahon, Rose, and Parks (2003) demonstrated an advantage for AK when children used gross motor body movements as part of learning letter sounds, and Kratochwill, Severson, and Demuth (1978) demonstrated similar AK learning benefits when allowing preschool children to physically manipulate letters. A similar advantage was not found for Kratochwill et al.'s kindergarten sample, however. Moreover, studies by Bara and colleagues (Bara, Gentaz, & Colé, 2007; Bara, Gentaz, Colé, & Sprenger-Charolles, 2004) have provided conflicting results as to whether haptic exploration of letters is beneficial in AK learning. Finally, there appear to be no benefits of asking children to trace letter shapes during the learning process (Beech, Pedley, & Barlow, 1994; Kratochwill et al., 1978).

Shared (Alphabet) Book Reading   In general, shared book reading as typically implemented by teachers and parents does not appear to impact children's print knowledge, including AK (Aram, 2006; also see Chapter 6); attempts to use shared reading as an opportunity to develop AK have produced mixed results. Although some studies have found no effects of implicitly or explicitly drawing children's attention to letters during shared reading (Justice & Ezell, 2000), others have demonstrated small-to-moderate effects (Justice & Ezell, 2002; Justice, Kaderavek, Fan, Sofka, & Hunt, 2009). To our knowledge, only one study has specifically investigated whether simply reading alphabet books benefits AK (Murray, Stahl, & Ivey, 1996); despite positive trends, the results were not statistically significant or conclusive.

Use of Technology in Teaching Phonological Awareness and Alphabet Knowledge   Although both the NRP and NELP reports included studies that used computer-based delivery of instruction for PA and AK, only NRP specifically compared the effect sizes for computer- and teacher-delivered instruction and found a smaller effect size on average for computer-delivered instruction (Ehri et al., 2001). Few, if any, experimental studies have directly compared the efficacy of the same PA or AK instruction between teacher- and computer-based delivery, and none included children in preschool or kindergarten. Despite substantial limitations to current knowledge, a body of literature does suggest the promise for instruction with full or partial computer-based delivery, such as interactive and self-paced games, on children's PA and AK (Anthony et al., 2009; Foster, Erikson, Foster, Brinkman, & Torgesen, 1994; Lonigan, 2003). Results for specific code-focused instructional software are varied, however, with some studies suggesting potential benefits (Cassady & Smith, 2005; Mioduser, Tur-Kaspa, & Leitner, 2000; Savage, Abrami,

Hipps, & Deault, 2009) and others showing no effects (Dynarski et al., 2007). A meta-analysis by Blok, Oostdam, Otter, and Overmaat (2002) indicated poor quality in many prior studies of technology-assisted literacy instruction and a small average effect size across studies targeting a wide range of ages, languages, skills, and outcomes. Furthermore, some prior studies suggest that preschool children needed close proctoring to remain on task and understand how to manipulate the game (e.g., using the mouse, advancing screens). At best, therefore, the evidence is decidedly mixed on the efficacy, efficiency, and added value of integrated or supplemental computer-assisted instruction for early childhood literacy.

IS RESEARCH-BASED
INSTRUCTION HAPPENING IN SCHOOLS?

Since the publication of the NRP report and the passage of the No Child Left Behind Act of 2001 (PL 107-110), with its component Reading First initiatives, there seems to be an observable increase in the amount of code-focused instruction in kindergarten classrooms, in commercially available core reading programs, and in pedagogical books for K–3 teachers (Al Otaiba et al., 2008; Al Otaiba, Kosanovich-Grek, Torgesen, Hassler, & Wahl, 2005; Vaughn & Linan-Thompson, 2004). Al Otaiba et al.'s 2008 observational study of kindergarten instruction demonstrated a substantial amount of code-focused instruction in Reading First classrooms. Yet there remains variability in the systematicity, intensity, and differentiation in core curricula as well as disparities in the type and quality of supplemental reading instruction available to elementary school children who are at risk for reading difficulties (La Paro et al., 2009; Xue & Meisels, 2004). The impact of the NELP report, and other federal initiatives such as the Early Reading First (ERF) program, on practices in preschool classrooms seems less certain, and it is perhaps too early to tell whether they might lead to widespread improvements in classroom instruction. As discussed in Chapter 2, the ERF demonstration projects were by design small and distributed across the United States. Results from the first cohort were underwhelming, with the national ERF Impact Study finding child-outcome effects on only print knowledge; in addition, at most 37% of the ERF classrooms in the study were observed to include practice in blending or segmenting at any linguistic level (Jackson et al., 2007).

Findings from other observation studies conducted within the last decade indicate that attention to PA and AK in intentional, meaningful, and explicit instructional episodes remains quite low in preschool classrooms (Howes et al., 2008; LoCasale-Crouch et al., 2007). In an observation of more than 2,000 classrooms in 11 states, Howes et al. (2008) found that the proportion of time devoted to this type of instruction averaged less than 5%! Similarly, Connor et al. (2006) found that the amount of time spent on code-focused instruction, let alone small-group implementation, was quite low even within school-based prekindergarten classrooms with certified teachers. Although the representative Head Start survey findings (e.g., the Head Start Family and Child Experiences Survey [FACES]; Tarullo, West, Aikens, & Hulsey, 2008) indicated an increase from 2003–2006 in the frequency of code-focused instruction, this is primarily focused on AK and concepts about print, with a lesser increase in rhyming, the only aspect of PA even addressed in the survey.

One key reason why the adoption of research-based literacy instruction methods is variable may be teachers' lack of knowledge about the benefit of various teaching methods and about the construct of reading and its phonological and orthographic dimensions (Bos, Mather, Dickson, Podhajski, & Chard, 2001; Cunningham, Perry, Stanovich, & Stanovich, 2004; Joshi et al., 2009). For example, survey results from more than 700 K–3 teachers found teachers' implicit and explicit understanding of phonemes, irregular words, and even children's literature to be quite low (Cunningham et al., 2004). Results may be comparable or even weaker for preschool teachers, particularly those who do not have a bachelor's degree, much less a teaching certificate (and who are still in the majority in many contexts; Clifford et al., 2005; Dickinson & Brady, 2005). Joshi et al.'s (2009) recent report on the relatively low knowledge base of teacher educators is perhaps particularly disheartening, as it suggests that future traditionally certified teachers may be armed with insufficient knowledge and may inadvertently teach incorrectly or make poor choices of example words and sounds when working with children (Cunningham et al., 2004; Cunningham, Zibulsky, & Callahan, 2009; Moats, 2009).

The promise of early childhood education for preventing reading failure and closing achievement gaps for children who are at risk is unlikely to be realized without a concerted and lasting professional development and curricular enhancement effort. Although recent correlational and experimental studies support the positive impact that high-quality, research-based instruction in PA and AK can have on the growth trajectories of young children's emergent literacy skills (Burchinal et al., 2008; Lonigan, Farver, Phillips, & Clancy-Menchetti, 2011), the observational findings suggest that there are low rates of high-quality preschool instruction and that teachers have moderate-at-best pedagogical content knowledge. On a favorable note, several recent professional development studies with preschool or kindergarten teachers suggest that improvement in teachers' knowledge and instructional quality is possible (Cunningham et al., 2009; Neuman & Cunningham, 2009; Pianta, Mashburn, Downer, Hamre, & Justice, 2008). The positive impact of this professional development on children, however, is less certain and is likely to require an integration of high-quality professional development and efficacious curricular materials (see Chapter 8; Dickinson & Brady, 2005; Pianta et al., 2008).

CONCLUSION

In summary, findings from the NELP report as well as more recent experimental and predictive research underscore the substantial impact that PA and AK instruction can have on the trajectories of young children's reading development. The evidence converges on the benefits of systematic, explicit, and differentiated instruction in these core foundational literacy skills within preschool and kindergarten settings. However, there is notably less evidence available to help move these basic research findings into practice. This suggests the need for additional research on instructional design and for high-quality, instructionally linked professional development programs to help classroom teachers of all backgrounds translate these findings into teaching plans and strategies. In classrooms that have such programs already in place, preliminary evidence (Al Otaiba et al., 2008; Lonigan et al., 2011) suggests that the achievement gap for children who are at risk for reading difficulties can be narrowed, if not closed, and that more children can be put on the pathway to successful decoding, spelling, and comprehension. There is a need for future research that will further extend these possibilities— for example, by exploring the impact of multiple years of research-based early instruction, or by enhancing the impact of PA and AK instruction with equally explicit and systematic instruction in language and vocabulary (see Chapters 9 and 10).

REFERENCES

Al Otaiba, S., Connor, C., Lane, H., Kosanovich, M.L., Schatschneider, C., Dyrlund, A.K.,...Wright, T.L. (2008). Reading First kindergarten classroom instruction and students' growth in phonological awareness and letter naming–decoding fluency. *Journal of School Psychology, 46,* 281–314.

Al Otaiba, S., Kosanovich-Grek, M.L., Torgesen, J.K., Hassler, L., & Wahl, M. (2005). Reviewing core kindergarten and first-grade reading programs in light of No Child Left Behind: An exploratory study. *Reading & Writing Quarterly, 21,* 377–400.

Anthony, J.L., Hecht, S., Schoger, K.D., Mukherjee, A.D., & Williams, J.M. (February, 2009). *Efficacy of computerized Earobics and Real Math instruction for kindergartners from low SES, minority backgrounds: Year 1 results.* Paper presented at the Pacific Coast Research Conference, San Diego, CA.

Anthony, J.L., & Lonigan, C.J. (2004). The nature of phonological sensitivity: Converging evidence from four studies of preschool and early grade-school children. *Journal of Educational Psychology, 96*, 43–55.

Anthony, J.L., Lonigan, C.J., Burgess, S.R., Driscoll Bacon, K., Phillips, B.M., & Cantor, B.G. (2002). Structure of preschool phonological sensitivity: Overlapping sensitivity to rhyme, words, syllables, and phonemes. *Journal of Experimental Child Psychology, 82*, 65–92.

Anthony, J.L., Lonigan, C.J., Driscoll, K., Phillips, B.M., & Burgess, S.R. (2003). Phonological sensitivity: A quasi-parallel progression of word structure units and cognitive operations. *Reading Research Quarterly, 38*, 470–487.

Aram, D. (2006). Early literacy interventions: The relative roles of storybook reading, alphabetic activities, and their combination. *Reading and Writing: An Interdisciplinary Journal, 19*, 489–515.

Aram, D., & Biron, S. (2004). Joint storybook reading and joint writing interventions among low SES preschoolers: Differential contributions to early literacy. *Early Childhood Research Quarterly, 19*, 588–610.

Ball, E.W., & Blachman, B.A. (1988). Phoneme segmentation training: Effect on reading readiness. *Annals of Dyslexia, 38*, 208–225.

Ball, E.W., & Blachman, B.A. (1991). Does phoneme awareness training in kindergarten make a difference in early word recognition and developmental spelling? *Reading Research Quarterly, 26*, 49–66.

Bara, F., Gentaz, E., & Colé, P. (2007). Haptics in learning to read with children from low socio-economic status families. *British Journal of Developmental Psychology, 25*, 643–663.

Bara, F., Gentaz, E., Colé, P., & Sprenger-Charolles, L. (2004). The visuo-haptic and haptic exploration of letters increases the kindergarten-children's understanding of the alphabetic principle. *Cognitive Development, 19*, 433–449.

Beech, J.R., Pedley, H., & Barlow, R. (1994). Training letter-to-sound connections: The efficacy of tracing. *Current Psychology, 13*, 153.

Blaiklock, K.E. (2004). The importance of letter knowledge in the relationship between phonological awareness and reading. *Journal of Research in Reading, 27*, 36–57.

Blok, H., Oostdam, R., Otter, M.E., & Overmaat, M. (2002). Computer-assisted instruction in support of beginning reading instruction: A review. *Review of Educational Research, 72*, 101–130.

Bos, C., Mather, N., Dickson, S., Podhajski, B., & Chard, D. (2001). Perceptions and knowledge of preservice and inservice educators about early reading instruction. *Annals of Dyslexia, 51*, 97–120.

Bowey, J.A. (2002). Reflections on onset–rime and phoneme sensitivity as predictors of beginning word reading. *Journal of Experimental Child Psychology, 82*, 29–40.

Bowyer-Crane, C., Snowling, M.J., Duff, F.J., Fieldsend, E., Carroll, J.M., Miles, J.,...Hulme, C. (2008). Improving early language and literacy skills: Differential effects of an oral language versus a phonology with reading intervention. *Journal of Child Psychology and Psychiatry, 49*(4), 422–432.

Burchinal, M., Howes, C., Pianta, R., Bryant, D., Early, D., Clifford, R., & Barbarin, O. (2008). Predicting child outcomes at the end of kindergarten from the quality of pre-kindergarten teacher–child interactions and instruction. *Applied Developmental Science, 12*, 140–153.

Burke, M.D., Hagan-Burke, S., Kwok, O., & Parker, R. (2009). Predictive validity of early literacy indicators from the middle of kindergarten to second grade. *Journal of Special Education, 42*, 209–226.

Bus, A.G., & van IJzendoorn, M.H. (1999). Phonological awareness and early reading: A meta-analysis of experimental training studies. *Journal of Educational Psychology, 91,* 403–414.

Byrne, B., Fielding-Barnsley, R., & Ashley, L. (2000). Effects of preschool phoneme identity training after six years: Outcome level distinguished from rate of response. *Journal of Educational Psychology, 92,* 659–667.

Carnine, D.W. (1976). Similar sound separation and cumulative introduction in learning letter-sound correspondences. *Journal of Educational Research, 69,* 368–372.

Carroll, J.M., Snowling, M.J., Hulme, C., & Stevenson, J. (2003). The development of phonological awareness in preschool children. *Developmental Psychology, 39,* 913–923.

Cassady, J.C., & Smith, L.L. (2004). The impact of a reading-focused integrated learning system on phonological awareness in kindergarten. *Journal of Literacy Research, 35,* 947–964.

Cassady, J.C., & Smith, L.L. (2005). Acquisition of blending skills: Comparisons among body–coda, onset–rime, and phoneme blending tasks. *Reading Psychology, 25,* 261–272.

Castiglioni-Spalten, M.L., & Ehri, L., (2003). Phonemic awareness instruction: Contribution of articulatory segmentation to novice beginners' reading and spelling. *Scientific Studies of Reading, 7,* 25–52.

Chiappe, P., Siegel, L.S., & Wade-Woolley, L. (2002). Linguistic diversity and the development of reading skills: A longitudinal study. *Scientific Studies of Reading, 6*(4), 369–400.

Clifford, R., Barbarin, O., Chang, F., Early, D., Bryant, D., Howes, C.,...Pianta, R. (2005). What is pre-kindergarten? Characteristics of public pre-kindergarten programs. *Applied Developmental Science, 9*(3), 126–143.

Connor, C.M., Morrison, F.J., & Slominski, L. (2006). Preschool instruction and children's emergent literacy growth. *Journal of Educational Psychology, 98,* 665–689.

Craig, S.A. (2006). The effects of an adapted interactive writing intervention on kindergarten children's phonological awareness, spelling, and early reading development: A contextualized approach to instruction. *Journal of Educational Psychology, 98,* 714–731.

Cunningham, A.E., Perry, K.E., Stanovich, K.E., & Stanovich, P.J. (2004). Disciplinary knowledge of K–3 teachers and their knowledge calibration in the domain of early literacy. *Annals of Dyslexia, 54,* 139–167.

Cunningham, A.E., Zibulsky, J., & Callahan, M.D. (2009). Starting small: Building preschool teacher knowledge that supports early literacy development. *Reading and Writing: An Interdisciplinary Journal, 22,* 487–510.

Denne, M., Langdown, N., Pring, T., & Roy, P. (2005). Treating children with expressive phonological disorders: Does phonological awareness therapy work in the clinic? *Journal of Language and Communication Disorders, 40,* 493–504.

Dickinson, D.K., & Brady, J.P. (2005). Toward effective support for language and literacy through professional development. In M. Zaslow & I. Martinez-Beck (Eds.), *Critical issues in early childhood professional development* (pp. 141–170). Baltimore, MD: Paul H. Brookes Publishing Co.

Dynarski, M., Agodini, R., Heaviside, S., Novak, T., Carey, N., Campuzano, L.,... Sussex, W. (2007). *Effectiveness of reading and mathematics software products: Findings from the first student cohort: Report to Congress*

(NCEE 2007-4005). Washington, DC: U.S. Department of Education, Institute of Education Sciences, National Center for Education Evaluation and Regional Assistance.

Ehri, L.C. (2002). Phases of acquisition in learning to read words and implications for teaching [Monograph]. *British Journal of Education Psychology Monograph Series, 1,* 7–28.

Ehri, L.C., Deffner, N.D., & Wilce, L.S. (1984). Pictorial mnemonics for phonics. *Journal of Educational Psychology, 76,* 880–893.

Ehri, L.C., Nunes, S.R., Willows, D.M., Schuster, B.V., Yaghoub-Zadeh, Z., & Shanahan, T. (2001). Phonemic awareness instruction helps children learn to read: Evidence from the National Reading Panel's meta-analysis. *Reading Research Quarterly, 36,* 250–287.

Elbaum, B., Vaughn, S., Hughes, M.T., & Moody, S.W. (2000). How effective are one-to-one tutoring programs in reading for elementary students at risk for reading failure? A meta-analysis of the intervention research. *Journal of Educational Psychology, 92*(4), 605–619.

Elkind, D. (1987). *Miseducation: Preschoolers at risk.* New York, NY: Alfred A. Knopf.

Evans, R.A., & Bilsky, L.H. (1975). Effects of letter-reversals training on the discrimination performance of EMR children. *American Journal of Mental Deficiency, 80,* 99–108.

Farrell, F.E. (1978). *An investigation of letter identification and two methods of instruction for students in second, third, fourth, and fifth grades in ESEA Title I schools in a rural county in Northwest Florida* (Unpublished doctoral dissertation). Florida State University, Tallahassee.

Farver, J.M., Lonigan, C.J., & Eppe, S. (2009). Effective early literacy skill development for young Spanish-speaking English language learners: An experimental study of two methods. *Child Development, 80,* 703–719.

Foorman, B.R., & Torgesen, J. (2001). Critical elements of classroom and small-group instruction promote reading success in all children. *Learning Disabilities Research & Practice, 16,* 203–212.

Foster, K.C., Erikson, G.C., Foster, D.F., Brinkman, D., & Torgesen, J.T. (1994). Computer-administered instruction in phonological awareness: Evaluation of the DaisyQuest program. *Journal of Research and Development in Education, 27,* 126–137.

Foy, J.G., & Mann, V. (2006). Changes in letter sound knowledge are associated with development of phonological awareness in pre-school children. *Journal of Research in Reading, 29*(2), 143–161.

Furnes, B., & Samuelsson, S. (2009). Preschool cognitive and language skills predicting kindergarten and Grade 1 reading and spelling: A cross-linguistic comparison. *Journal of Research in Reading, 32*(3), 275–292.

Geudens, A., Dominiek, S., & Van den Broeck, W. (2004). Segmenting two-phoneme syllables: Developmental differences in relation with early reading skills. *Brain and Language, 90,* 338–352.

Gillon, G. (2005). Facilitating phoneme awareness development in 3- and 4-year-old children with speech impairment. *Language, Speech, and Hearing Services in Schools, 36,* 308–324.

Graue, E., Clements, M.A., Reynolds, A.J., & Niles, M.D. (2004). More than teacher directed or child initiated: Preschool curriculum type, parent involvement, and children's outcomes in the child–parent centers. *Education Policy Analysis Archives, 12,* 1–38.

Hatcher, P.J., Hulme, C., Miles, J.N.V., Carroll, J.M., Hatcher, J., Gibbs, S.,...
Snowling, M.J. (2006). Efficacy of small group reading intervention for begin-
ning readers with reading delay: A randomized controlled trial. *Journal of
Child Psychology and Psychiatry, 47,* 820–827.

Hatcher, P., Hulme, C., & Snowling, M. (2004). Explicit phoneme training combined with phonic reading instruction helps young children at risk of reading
failure. *Journal of Child Psychology and Psychiatry, 45,* 338–358.

Hesketh, A., Dima, E., & Nelson, V. (2007). Teaching phoneme awareness to
pre-literate children with speech disorder: A randomized controlled trial.
International Journal of Language & Communication Disorders, 42(3),
251–271.

Hetzroni, O.E., & Shavit, P. (2002). Comparison of two instructional strategies
for acquiring form and sound of Hebrew letters by students with mild mental
retardation. *Education and Training in Mental Retardation and Developmental Disabilities, 37,* 273–282.

Hindson, B., Byrne, B., Fielding-Barnsley, R., Newman, C., Hine, D.W., &
Shankweiler, D. (2005). Assessment of early instruction of preschool children at risk for reading disability. *Journal of Educational Psychology, 97,*
687–704.

Howes, C., Burchinal, M., Pianta, R., Bryant, D., Early, D., Clifford, R., & Barbarin, O. (2008). Ready to learn? Children's pre-academic achievement in
pre-kindergarten programs. *Early Childhood Research Quarterly, 23,*
27–50.

Hulme, C., Caravolas, M., Málková, G., & Brigstocke, S. (2005). Phoneme isolation
ability is not simply a consequence of letter-sound knowledge. *Cognition, 97,*
B1–B11.

Jackson, R., McCoy, A., Pistorino, C., Wilkinson, A., Burghardt, J., Clark, M.,...
Swank, P. (2007). *National evaluation of Early Reading First: Final
report to Congress* (NCEE 2007-4007). Washington, DC: U.S. Department
of Education, Institute of Education Sciences, National Center for Education
Evaluation and Regional Assistance.

Johnston, R.S., & Watson, J.E. (2004). Accelerating the development of reading, spelling and phonemic awareness skills in initial readers. *Reading and
Writing: An Interdisciplinary Journal, 17,* 327–357.

Joshi, R.M., Binks, E., Hougen, M., Dahlgren, M.E., Ocker-Dean, E., & Smith,
D.L. (2009). Why elementary teachers might be inadequately prepared to
teach reading. *Journal of Learning Disabilities, 42,* 392–402.

Justice, L.M., Chow, S.-M., Capellini, C., Flanigan, K., & Colton, S. (2003).
Emergent literacy intervention for vulnerable preschoolers: Relative effects
of two approaches. *American Journal of Speech-Language Pathology,
12,* 320–332.

Justice, L.M., & Ezell, H.K. (2000). Enhancing children's print and word
awareness through home-based parent intervention. *American Journal of
Speech-Language Pathology, 9,* 257–269.

Justice, L.M., & Ezell, H.K. (2002). Use of storybook reading to increase print
awareness in at-risk children. *American Journal of Speech-Language
Pathology, 11,* 17–29.

Justice, L.M., Kaderavek, J.N., Fan, X., Sofka, A., & Hunt, A. (2009). Accelerating preschoolers' early literacy development through classroom-based
teacher–child storybook reading and explicit print referencing. *Language,
Speech, and Hearing Services in Schools, 40,* 67–85.

Kaplan, D., & Walpole, S. (2005). A stage-sequential model of reading transitions: Evidence from the Early Childhood Longitudinal Study. *Journal of Educational Psychology, 97,* 551–563.

Koutsoftas, A.D., Harmon, M.T., & Gray, S. (2009). The effect of Tier 2 intervention for phonemic awareness in a response-to-intervention model in low-income preschool classrooms. *Language, Speech, and Hearing Services in Schools, 40,* 116–130.

Kratochwill, T.R., Severson, R.A., & Demuth, D.M. (1978). Children's learning as a function of variation in stimulus characteristics and motor involvement. *Contemporary Educational Psychology, 3,* 144–153.

La Paro, K.M., Hamre, B.K., LoCasale-Crouch, J., Pianta, R.C., Bryant, D., Early, D.,…Burchinal, M. (2009). Quality in kindergarten classrooms: Observational evidence for the need to increase children's learning opportunities in early education classrooms. *Early Education and Development, 20,* 657–692.

Lervåg, A., Bråten, I., & Hulme, C. (2009). The cognitive and linguistic foundations of early reading development: A Norwegian latent variable longitudinal study. *Developmental Psychology, 45,* 764–781.

Levin, I., Shatil-Carmon, S., & Asif-Rave, O. (2006). Learning of letter names and sounds and their contribution to word recognition. *Journal of Experimental Child Psychology, 93,* 139–165.

Linklater, D.L., O'Connor, R.E., & Palardy, G.J. (2009). Kindergarten literacy assessment of English only and English language learner students: An examination of the predictive validity of three phonemic awareness measures. *Journal of School Psychology, 47,* 369–394.

LoCasale-Crouch, J., Konold, T., Pianta, R., Howes, C., Burchinal, M., Bryant, D.,…Barbarin, O. (2007). Observed classroom quality profiles in state-funded pre-kindergarten programs and associations with teacher, program, and classroom characteristics. *Early Childhood Research Quarterly, 22,* 3–17.

Lonigan, C. (2003). Development and promotion of emergent literacy skills in children at-risk of reading difficulties. In B. Foorman (Ed.), *Preventing and remediating reading difficulties: Bringing science to scale* (pp. 23–50). Timonium, MA: York Press.

Lonigan, C.J., Burgess, S.R., & Anthony, J.L. (2000). Development of emergent literacy and early reading skills in preschool children: Evidence from a latent-variable longitudinal study. *Developmental Psychology, 36,* 596–613.

Lonigan, C., Burgess, S., Anthony, J., & Barker, T. (1998). Development of phonological sensitivity in 2- to 5-year-old children. *Journal of Educational Psychology, 90,* 294–311.

Lonigan, C.J., Farver, J.M., Phillips, B.M., & Clancy-Menchetti, J. (2011). Promoting the development of preschool children's emergent literacy skills: A randomized evaluation of a literacy-focused curriculum and two professional development models. *Reading and Writing: An Interdisciplinary Journal, 24,* 305–337.

Lonigan, C.J., Schatschneider, C., & Westberg, L. (with the National Early Literacy Panel). (2008a). Identification of children's skills and abilities linked to later outcomes in reading, writing, and spelling. In *Developing early literacy: Report of the National Early Literacy Panel* (pp. 55–106). Washington, DC: National Institute for Literacy.

Lonigan, C.J., Schatschneider, C., & Westberg, L. (with the National Early Literacy Panel). (2008b). Impact of code-focused interventions on young children's early literacy skills. In *Developing early literacy: Report of the National*

Early Literacy Panel (pp. 107–151). Washington, DC: National Institute for Literacy.

Manolitsis, G., Georgiou, G., Stephenson, K., & Parrila, R. (2009). Beginning to read across languages varying in orthographic consistency: Comparing the effects of non-cognitive and cognitive predictors. *Learning and Instruction, 19,* 466–480.

McBride-Chang, C. (1999). The ABCs of the ABCs: The development of letter-name and letter-sound knowledge. *Merrill-Palmer Quarterly, 45,* 285–308.

McIntosh, B., Crosbie, S., Holm, A., Dodd, B., & Thomas, S. (2007). Enhancing the phonological awareness and language skills of socially disadvantaged preschoolers: An interdisciplinary programme. *Child Language Teaching and Therapy, 23*(3), 267–286.

McMahon, S.D., Rose, D.S., & Parks, M. (2003). Basic Reading through Dance program: The impact on first-grade students' basic reading skills. *Evaluation Review, 27,* 104–125.

Mioduser, D., Tur-Kaspa, H., & Leitner, I. (2000). The learning value of computer-based instruction of early reading skills. *Journal of Computer Assisted Learning, 16,* 54–63.

Missall, K., Reschly, A., Betts, J., McConnell, S., Heistad, D., Pickart, M.,... Marston, D. (2007). Examination of the predictive validity of preschool early literacy skills. *School Psychology Review, 36*(3), 433–452.

Moats, L. (2009). Knowledge foundations for teaching reading and spelling. *Reading and Writing: An Interdisciplinary Journal, 22,* 379–399.

Murray, B.A., Stahl, S.A., & Ivey, M.G. (1996). Developing phoneme awareness through alphabet books. *Reading and Writing: An Interdisciplinary Journal, 8,* 307–322.

National Early Literacy Panel. (2008). *Developing early literacy: Report of the National Early Literacy Panel.* Washington, DC: National Institute for Literacy.

National Reading Panel. (2000). *Teaching children to read: An evidence-based assessment of the scientific research literature on reading and its implications for reading instruction.* Washington, DC: Government Printing Office.

Neuman, S.B., & Cunningham, L. (2009). The impact of professional development and coaching on early language and literacy instructional practices. *American Educational Research Journal, 46,* 532–566.

No Child Left Behind Act of 2001, PL 107-110, 115 Stat. 1425, 20 U.S.C. §§ 6301 *et seq.*

O'Connor, R.E., Jenkins, J.R., & Slocum, T.A. (1995). Transfer among phonological tasks in kindergarten: Essential instructional content. *Journal of Educational Psychology, 87,* 202–217.

Olfman, S. (2003). *All work and no play: How educational reforms are harming our preschoolers.* Westport, CT: Praeger.

Phillips, B.M., Clancy-Menchetti, J., & Lonigan, C.J. (2008). Successful phonological awareness instruction with preschool children: Lessons from the classroom. *Topics in Early Childhood Special Education, 28,* 3–17.

Phillips, B.M., & Lonigan, C.J. (2005). Social correlates of emergent literacy. In M. Snowling & C. Hulme (Eds.), *The science of reading: A handbook* (pp. 173–187). Oxford, United Kingdom: Blackwell Publishing.

Phillips, B.M., & Torgesen, J.T. (2006). Phonemic awareness and reading: Beyond the growth of initial reading accuracy. In S. Neuman & D. Dickinson

(Eds.), *Handbook of early literacy research* (Vol. 2, pp. 101–112).New York, NY: Guilford Press.

Pianta, R.C., Mashburn, A.J., Downer, J.T., Hamre, B.K., & Justice, L. (2008). Effects of web-mediated professional development resources on teacher–child interactions in pre-kindergarten classrooms. *Early Childhood Research Quarterly, 23,* 431–451.

Piasta, S.B., Purpura, D.J., & Wagner, R.K. (2010). Fostering alphabet knowledge development: A comparison of two instructional approaches. *Reading and Writing: An Interdisciplinary Journal, 23,* 607-626.

Piasta, S.B., & Wagner, R.K. (2010a). Developing emergent literacy skills: A meta-analysis of alphabet learning and instruction. *Reading Research Quarterly, 45,* 8–38.

Piasta, S.B., & Wagner, R.K. (2010b). Learning letter names and sounds: Effects of instruction, letter type, and phonological processing skill. *Journal of Experimental Child Psychology, 105,* 324–344.

Puolakanaho, A., Ahonen, T., Aro, M., Eklund, K., Leppänen, P., Poikkeus, A.,... Lyytinen, H. (2008). Developmental links of very early phonological and language skills to second grade reading outcomes. *Journal of Learning Disabilities, 41*(4), 353–370.

Savage, R.S., Abrami, P., Hipps, G., & Deault, L. (2009). A randomized controlled trial study of the ABRACADABRA reading intervention program in Grade 1. *Journal of Educational Psychology, 101*(3), 590–604.

Schatschneider, C., Fletcher, J.M., Francis, D.J., Carlson, C.D., & Foorman, B.R. (2004). Kindergarten prediction of reading skills: A longitudinal comparative analysis. *Journal of Educational Psychology, 96,* 265–282.

Schatschneider, C., Francis, D.J., Foorman, B.R., Fletcher, J.M., & Mehta, P. (1999). The dimensionality of phonological awareness: An application of item response theory. *Journal of Educational Psychology, 91*(3), 439–449.

Shapiro, L.R., & Solity, J. (2008). Delivering phonological and phonics training within whole-class teaching. *British Journal of Educational Psychology, 78,* 597–620.

Share, D.L. (1995). Phonological recoding and self-teaching: Sine qua non of reading acquisition. *Cognition, 55,* 151–218.

Share, D.L. (2004). Knowing letter names and learning letter sounds: A causal connection. *Journal of Experimental Child Psychology, 88,* 213–233.

Shmidman, A., & Ehri, L. (2010). Embedded picture mnemonics to learn letters. *Scientific Studies of Reading, 14,* 159–182.

Simmons, D.C., Kame'enui, E.J., Harn, B., Coyne, M.D., Stoolmiller, M., Santoro, L.E.,...Kaufman, N.K. (2007). Attributes of effective and efficient kindergarten reading intervention: An examination of instructional time and design specificity. *Journal of Learning Disabilities, 40,* 331–347.

Simmons, D.C., Kame'enui, E.J., Stoolmiller, M., Coyne, M.D., & Harn, B. (2003). Accelerating growth and maintaining proficiency: A two-year intervention study of kindergarten and first grade children at risk for reading difficulties. In B.R. Foorman (Ed.), *Preventing and remediating reading difficulties: Bringing science to scale* (pp. 197–228). Timonium, MD: York Press.

Speece, D.L., Ritchey, K.D, Cooper, D.H., Roth, F.P., & Schatschneider, C. (2004). Growth in early reading skills from kindergarten to third grade. *Contemporary Educational Psychology, 29,* 312–332.

Storch, S.A., & Whitehurst, G.J. (2002). Oral language and code-related precursors to reading: Evidence from a longitudinal structural model. *Developmental Psychology, 38*(6), 934–947.

Tarullo, L., West, J., Aikens, N., & Hulsey, L. (2008). *Beginning Head Start: Children, families, and programs in Fall 2006.* Washington, DC: U.S. Department of Health and Human Services, Administration for Children and Families, Office of Planning, Research, and Evaluation.

Torppa, M., Poikkeus, A.-M., Laakso, M.-L., Tolvanen, A., Leskinen, E., Leppänen, P.H.T.,...Lyytinen, H. (2007). Modeling the early paths of phonological awareness and factors supporting its development in children with and without familial risk of dyslexia. *Scientific Studies of Reading, 11,* 73–103.

Treiman, R., Tincoff, R., Rodriguez, K., Mouzaki, A., & Francis, D.J. (1998). The foundations of literacy: Learning the sounds of letters. *Child Development, 69,* 1524–1540.

Vadasy, P.F., & Sanders, E.A. (2008). Code-oriented instruction for kindergarten students at risk for reading difficulties: A replication and comparison of instructional groupings. *Reading and Writing: An Interdisciplinary Journal, 21,* 929–963.

Vaughn, S., & Linan-Thompson, S. (2004). *Research-based methods of reading instruction, Grades K–3.* Alexandria, VA: Association for Supervision and Curriculum Development.

Wagner, R.K., Torgesen, J.K., & Rashotte, C.A. (1994). Development of reading-related phonological processing abilities: New evidence of bidirectional causality from a latent variable longitudinal study. *Developmental Psychology, 30,* 73–87.

Wagner, R.K., Torgesen, J.K., Rashotte, C.A., Hecht, S.A., Barker, T.A., Burgess, S.R.,...Garon, T. (1997). Changing relations between phonological processing abilities and word-level reading as children develop from beginning to skilled readers: A 5-year longitudinal study. *Developmental Psychology, 33*(3), 468–479.

Walton, P.D., & Walton, L.M. (2002). Beginning reading by teaching in rime analogy: Effects on phonological skills, letter-sound knowledge, working memory, and word-reading strategies. *Scientific Studies of Reading, 6,* 79–115.

Webb, M.Y.L., Schwanenflugel, P.J., & Kim, S. (2004). A construct validation study of phonological awareness for children entering prekindergarten. *Journal of Psychoeducational Assessment, 22,* 304–319.

Whitehurst, G.J., & Lonigan, C.J. (1998). Child development and emergent literacy. *Child Development, 68,* 848–872.

Whiteley, H.E., Smith, C.D., & Connors, L. (2007). Young children at risk of literacy difficulties: Factors predicting recovery from risk following phonologically based intervention. *Journal of Research in Reading, 30*(3), 249–269.

Xue, Y., & Meisels, S.J. (2004). Early literacy instruction and learning in kindergarten: Evidence from the Early Childhood Longitudinal Study–Kindergarten Class of 1998–1999. *American Educational Research Journal, 41,* 191–229.

6

Sharing Books
with Children

Jill M. Pentimonti, Laura M. Justice, and Shayne B. Piasta

E xposure to books begins very early in life for many children in the United States. Most parents, pediatricians, early childhood educators, and related professionals believe that books have a unique role in child development, despite variable perspectives on what this role might be. To some, books stimulate early symbolic development. To others, books encourage joint engagement between adults and children and foster healthy attachment relationships. And to still others, books are an important means of promoting young children's early attainment of key language and literacy skills, such as vocabulary knowledge and print knowledge.

Interestingly, only in the last several decades has the research community begun to explicitly test, using both correlational and experimental research designs, whether exposure to books does in fact elevate certain child achievements. During this time there have also been efforts to aggregate the findings from this work, spanning from Scarborough and Dobrich's 1994 review that synthesized the body of research on this topic from 1960–1993 to Mol, Bus, and de Jong's 2009 meta-analysis that synthesized the research through 2007. The results of both individual studies and meta-analyses provide important tools for helping to increase understanding of what is known about sharing books with children as well as what remains unknown.

The goal of this chapter is to describe the research base on sharing books with children, with a particular focus on summarizing the experimental evidence linking specific reading approaches to improvements in children's early language and literacy skills. We first provide an overview of noteworthy syntheses in regard to sharing books with children, including the 2008 National Early Literacy Panel (NELP) report. We then describe several specific approaches to sharing books with children that are substantiated in the experimental literature and discuss the strength of the evidence in regard to effects of these approaches on children's reading achievement and its precursors. Finally, we discuss how sharing books with children fits within the early childhood and early primary classroom as a pedagogical practice and a potential therapeutic technique.

SYSTEMATIC REVIEWS OF RESEARCH ON SHARING BOOKS WITH CHILDREN

During the 1980s and 1990s, both the popular press (e.g., Bush, 1990) and scholars (e.g., Anderson, Hiebert, Scott, & Wilkinson, 1985) espoused sharing books with children as a critical component of early childhood education; this led to the first systematic review of this topic. Scarborough and Dobrich (1994) surveyed 31 available research studies with respect to the relations between parent–preschooler shared book reading and language and literacy outcomes. Each study was described and reviewed qualitatively. In addition, Scarborough and Dobrich estimated correlational effect sizes (r) and conducted corresponding significance tests. Counts of significant effects and median rs were reported for sets of studies, based on design (correlational, experimental), measurement of shared book reading (frequency, quality), and outcome (emergent literacy, reading achievement, oral language).

With respect to frequency of shared book reading, Scarborough and Dobrich found mixed results supporting links to literacy and oral language outcomes. Correlational research supported median rs of .27 and .28 for emergent literacy and reading achievement outcomes, respectively, yet only slightly more than half (55%) of these comparisons were statistically reliable. For oral language outcomes, correlational research supported an overall median r of .22, with only 23% of comparisons being statistically reliable. Reviews of studies relating the quality of shared book reading to the outcomes of interest were less conclusive: Median rs could not be computed due to the limited information reported in the original studies, and only 10% and 14% of estimated comparisons were statistically reliable in the studies of emergent literacy and oral language outcomes, respectively. Finally, intervention research supported median rs of .16 (21% of comparisons statistically reliable) and .28 (52% of comparisons statistically reliable) for effects of shared book reading on emergent literacy and oral language outcomes, respectively. There was little evidence to suggest appreciable effects of such interventions on reading achievement. These results led Scarborough and Dobrich to conclude that although there is a reliable, positive relation between parent–preschooler shared book reading and literacy and language outcomes, this relation "is probably not as strong and consistent as generally supposed" (p. 285) and accounts for no more than 8% of the variance in children's literacy and oral language abilities.

Responses to this review included a surge of new studies investigating the effects of shared book reading as well as additional research syntheses. For example, Lonigan (1994) reanalyzed the pool of studies reviewed by Scarborough and Dobrich and derived less conservative estimates using mean, rather than median, rs (.23–.36 in correlational research; .13–.21 in intervention research). Moreover, he argued that such modest relations between shared book reading and literacy and language outcomes may have great practical significance: As the modest estimates do not take into account indirect effects of shared book reading via impacts on other aspects of children's development and are likely to perpetuate over time, the true effect on children's literacy and language outcomes is likely to be much larger in magnitude. Finally, Lonigan also pointed out a number of statistical and methodological issues that may have led to conservatively biased results, including equal weighting of all effect estimates, failure to account for heterogeneity among studies, and lack of statistical precision.

Subsequent reviews were able to overcome many of the latter issues by using quantitative meta-analytic techniques. Bus, van IJzendoorn, and Pellegrini (1995) reviewed 29 studies that examined the relations of parent–preschooler shared book reading to oral language, emergent literacy, and reading achievement. Their analyses revealed statistically significant relations of effect size (d) = 0.59 (r = .28) across all studies and outcomes, d = 0.67 (r = .32) for oral language outcomes, d = 0.58 (r = .28) for emergent literacy outcomes, and d = 0.55 (r = .27) for reading achievement outcomes; none of these estimates reliably differed from one another. Statistical contrasts investigating heterogeneity across studies (in methodological quality, measurement of shared book reading, and participant characteristics) indicated significantly larger estimates in studies that involved younger children, as well as a potential bias toward larger estimates for language outcomes only. These results upheld Scarborough and Dobrich's (1994) original conclusions that parent–preschooler shared book reading accounts for an estimated 8% of variance in children's literacy and language skills, that literacy and language outcomes are affected to a similar extent, and that alternative measures of shared book reading lead to similar findings. A more recent meta-analysis by Mol, Bus, de Jong, and Smeets (2008) expanded these conclusions with respect to the effects of parent–child shared book reading on oral language outcomes. Mol et al. limited their review to the 16 available studies premised on "interactive" shared book reading, which involves training adult readers to use prompts to actively engage children during the reading process and evoke their thoughts and responses to the reading (a concept we discuss more extensively in the next section). Mol et al. found a significant effect of $d = 0.42$ across all language outcomes. Notably, effects were reliably stronger when expressive vocabulary was the outcome of interest ($d = 0.59$) as opposed to receptive vocabulary ($d = 0.22$). Moreover, effects were reliably stronger for younger children and those children who were not considered to be at risk for later reading or language difficulties.

Another set of syntheses reviewed studies that implemented shared book reading within school settings, as opposed to focusing solely on parent–preschooler reading. A review by Blok (1999) yielded 10 studies of this topic, which were analyzed according to whether reading or language constituted the outcome of interest. Significant effects of $d = 0.41$ and $d = 0.63$ were estimated for reading and language outcomes, respectively. Examinations of heterogeneity across studies revealed reliably stronger effects on language outcomes in studies that involved younger children and smaller reading groups; no differences were found based on children's risk status or details of the reading program, such as duration or whether pre- or postreading activities were used. Converging results were found in a second, more recent meta-analysis of school-based shared book reading conducted by Mol and colleagues (2009). Similar to Mol et al. (2008), this synthesis by Mol and colleagues also focused specifically on early childhood interventions that involved interactive shared book reading including dialogic reading, as specified by Whitehurst et al. (1988). The survey reviewed 31 studies in regard to effects on children's emergent literacy and oral language outcomes and detected significant effects for all outcomes: $d = 0.39$ for alphabet knowledge, $d = 0.43$ for phonological awareness, $d = 0.41$ for orthographic awareness, and $d = 0.54$ for oral language. None of these effects reliably differed from one another, including separate estimates for expressive and receptive vocabulary ($d = 0.62$ and $d = 0.45$, respectively). Examinations of heterogeneity across studies indicated reliably stronger effects on alphabet knowledge for younger children and stronger effects on phonological sensitivity for interventions of longer duration (> 16 weeks) but no differences due to intervention administrator or group size. Studies that utilized oral language outcomes showed reliably stronger effects when shared book reading 1) was administered by research staff to individual children rather than by teachers to small or large groups of children and 2) used either dialogic reading techniques as specified by Whitehurst et al. and implemented by research staff or an adapted version of such techniques, rather than dialogic reading implemented by teachers or broader-interaction reading interventions involving classroom extension activities. There were no differences based on child age or intervention duration.

In summary, the available reviews of shared book reading support reliable, moderate-to-strong effects on children's emergent literacy and language outcomes, whether implemented by parents or in school-based contexts. These results are consistent with NELP's oral language findings, which indicated an overall effect of $d = 0.73$ and also reported no reliable differences as to whether shared book reading was implemented by parents or teachers. Despite sometimes failing to meet traditional significance levels, all results, including those reported by NELP, show fairly consistent patterns in reporting greater effects for vocabulary, as opposed to more complex or composite measures of language, and for children who are not considered at risk for language or literacy difficulties. Less consistent are the results for emergent literacy outcomes. Although NELP reported a reliable effect of $d = 0.50$ for print knowledge, no effects of shared book reading were found for two other measures of emergent literacy: alphabet knowledge and phonological awareness. Differences in study selection are likely to account for this variation, as only two studies met NELP's criteria for each of these two outcomes. Finally, firm conclusions regarding the impact of shared book reading on later reading achievement require additional research attention, because there are too few studies that address this issue to warrant meta-analysis at this time.

SPECIFIC LITERACY- AND LANGUAGE-ORIENTED APPROACHES TO SHARING BOOKS WITH CHILDREN

The previous section discussed conclusions drawn from aggregating results of the collective literature in regard to sharing books with children. Generally, these reviews show that children derive benefits from being read to, but these findings do not necessarily provide specific guidance on the exact techniques that seem to benefit children the most. This section will focus in depth on three specific approaches to sharing books with children that are empirically validated for enhancing children's language and literacy development. For the purposes of this discussion, an approach is considered "empirically validated" if two or more rigorous efficacy studies have shown positive impacts on children's development relative to a control group or comparison condition (Chambless & Hollon, 1998); although there are likely to be some valuable approaches that do not meet this minimum criterion, the criterion of two or more studies provides some assurance that positive impacts attributable to a given approach have been replicated at least once.

Dialogic Reading

Dialogic reading, also called interactive reading, is perhaps the most well-studied approach to sharing books with children, at least with respect to establishing efficacy of the practice (Lonigan & Whitehurst, 1998; Whitehurst et al., 1994; Whitehurst et al., 1988). As the name suggests, dialogic reading is an approach in which the adult reader uses specific techniques to create a dialogue between the adult and the child; these techniques make the child a more active participant and the experience a more interactive one for both adult and child. Primarily, the goal of this approach is to promote children's verbal participation in book sharing and, in turn, to increase children's language skills, encompassing both vocabulary and grammar.

Implementation of a dialogic-reading approach involves adult use of a set of three types of prompts that elicit the child's participation in dialogues: cloze procedures (i.e., the adult makes a statement and leaves off final word[s] for the child to complete), questions (*wh-* questions, open-ended questions, and recall questions), and text-to-life connections (also called distancing prompts; i.e., the adult connects the book's events or words to the child's own experiences). Following a prompt and the child's subsequent response, the adult repeats, recasts, and/ or extends the child's contribution, thereby leading to a cycle of dialogue. A small set of studies has shown that participation in book sharing that features a dialogic approach to reading has positive benefits to children's language development (e.g., Wasik & Bond, 2001; Whitehurst et al., 1994; Whitehurst et al., 1988).

Dialogic reading has considerable promise as an approach that serves to create book-sharing experiences that entice children to participate more fully and that enable adults to more intentionally and explicitly promote children's lexical and grammatical development. Although the NELP report found no statistically significant difference between dialogic and nondialogic reading in key child outcomes, the effect size differences were substantial. However, there are also a few caveats regarding this approach that warrant careful attention; these caveats are based on key limitations in this literature base. First, in some studies of dialogic reading, children who experienced this approach did not show a significant boost in language skills compared with children in control group conditions (Lonigan & Whitehurst, 1998). Second, preschool educators did not necessarily show strong fidelity of implementation when asked to use this reading approach, even when they had received training in its methods and were provided with materials to support implementation (Lonigan & Whitehurst). This is important because implementation fidelity has been associated with children's gains. Moreover, to achieve high levels of implementation fidelity, teachers may need a great deal of support, such as in-class mentoring (Wasik & Bond, 2001). Finally, studies that have assessed the efficacy of dialogic reading for children with significant language challenges have also failed to show a significant positive benefit of this approach (Crain-Thoreson & Dale, 1999). It is important to note, therefore, that this approach to sharing books with children may not offer benefits to all children, including those who have developmental disabilities.

Word Elaborations

Word elaborations, also called rich instruction (Beck & McKeown, 2007) and embed instruction (Coyne, McCoach, Loftus, Zipoli, Jr., & Kapp, 2009), is also a well-studied approach to sharing books with children (e.g., Biemiller & Boote, 2006; Justice, Meier, & Walpole, 2005). Word elaborations involve, as the term suggests, embedding explicit discussions (elaborations) about words within the context of sharing books with children. The goal behind elaborating words is to increase children's interest in vocabulary words and to promote not only the overall breadth of children's vocabulary knowledge but also their depth of knowledge about certain words.

Implementation of word elaborations generally involves the following procedures. First, the adult reader selects a book that contains a variety of Tier 2 words. Tier 2 words are "sophisticated words of high utility" (Beck & McKeown, 2007, p. 256). These tend to be words that occur with relatively low frequency but are considered to be very useful; they often offer a more precise and mature way of describing a basic concept or idea. Second, the adult reads the book with the children, either in a small- or large-group setting, and embeds extratextual discussions about Tier 2 words right into the reading (Coyne et al., 2009; Justice et al., 2005) or engages children in a discussion about the words immediately following the reading (Beck & McKeown, 2007). Third, these procedures are typically repeated in additional readings of the book, usually at least two or four more times within a few weeks of the initial reading. Finally, discussion of words beyond the reading context—for instance, group activities that involve additional discussions of the target words or their use in play activities—is also advocated (Coyne et al., 2009). This extended instruction provides children with additional exposure to words outside of the book-sharing context and seems to play an important role in developing depth of knowledge.

A handful of studies have shown that children are more likely to learn words that are elaborated within books that are read to them by adults than words that are not elaborated (e.g., Coyne et al., 2009; Justice et al., 2005). Studies show that receiving more instruction is better than receiving less instruction (e.g., instruction in words for 6 days rather than 3 days; Beck & McKeown, 2007) and that extended instruction that elaborates words beyond the book-sharing context (i.e., extended instruction) further improves vocabulary growth (Coyne et al., 2009). Despite the consistency of such findings, which together provide considerable convergence indicating that explicit elaboration of vocabulary words embedded within or occurring shortly after book-sharing events supports vocabulary development, it is important to address a few limitations of this work. First, these studies provide very little guidance on how many words should be elaborated within book-sharing events; in fact, there is wide variability across studies in regard to this particular aspect of methodology. In a study that involved small-group book-reading sessions with 5-year-old children, Justice et al. (2005) taught three words within each session; Biemiller and Boote (2006), in a study that involved whole-class reading sessions with children in kindergarten through second grade, taught 7–10 word meanings within each session. It is not known whether there is a threshold of instruction at which elaboration of words is no longer effective for children or is even detrimental to children's comprehension and enjoyment of the story.

Second, although this body of work generally shows that children profit from elaborations of word meanings within book sharings, it is also important to note that the boost to children's vocabulary knowledge is actually quite modest. By some estimates, children only learn about 20% of the words taught through this approach (Biemiller & Boote, 2006). Children might need more robust vocabulary instruction than this method provides, particularly those children who have significant needs in this area. Nonetheless, it is also necessary to point out that it is very difficult to measure children's learning of new words, because vocabulary development occurs very incrementally. Some studies of word elaborations have employed quite rigorous methods to examine children's learning of new words (e.g., production of definitions of words; Justice et al., 2005) and in fact may underestimate children's gains from this book-sharing approach.

Print Referencing

Print referencing represents the third well-studied approach to sharing books with children (e.g., Girolametto, Weitzman, Lefebvre, & Greenberg, 2007; Justice & Ezell, 2000). Print referencing involves making explicit verbal and nonverbal references to print when sharing books with children. The goal of print referencing is to draw children's interest toward, and increase their awareness of, print within storybooks as well as to provide explicit instruction regarding forms and functions of print within a meaningful context (Justice & Ezell, 2004). A large body of research has shown that when children are read storybooks, even those children who have fairly sophisticated knowledge about print, they rarely talk about or look at print within the book (e.g.., Evans, Williamson, & Pursoo, 2008). This finding in and of itself may not be surprising, because storybook illustrations are more compelling than print (and correspondingly, the illustrations are where children most focus their attention). However, it is interesting to note that when adults share books with children, even books with interesting print features, the adults seldom draw any attention to these features of the book (Justice, Kaderavek, Fan, Sofka, & Hunt, 2009). For instance, preschool teachers who read to their students in whole-class, read-aloud sessions make no or only one reference to letters within the book, despite the fact that letters (and other forms of print) are a salient characteristic of books (Zucker, Justice, & Piasta, 2009).

Implementation of print referencing generally involves consideration of three issues: materials, targets, and techniques. In regard to materials, referencing print when sharing books with children occurs more meaningfully and naturally when the books being read have salient print features. These include, for example, speech bubbles for character dialogue, font changes, and illustrations embedded in print (Zucker et al., 2009). These types of features seem to naturally evoke more attention to print by adult readers and children, and thus can be leveraged in the print-referencing approach to facilitate children's learning about print.

Second, in regard to targets, print referencing is used to facilitate children's attention to, and learning about, specific aspects of print. In general, these aspects transcend 1) general concepts about print (e.g., title of the book, direction of print), 2) letters (e.g., learning the names of certain letters, differentiating letters from words as print units), and 3) words (e.g., recognizing some contextualized words, understanding the concept of a word). Recent implementations of print referencing have involved preschool teachers who follow an explicit scope and sequence of targets to address children's learning across these areas (Justice et al., 2009). In so doing, this book-sharing approach can be used in a systematic way as a curriculum supplement to address emergent-literacy goals.

Third, in regard to techniques, as noted earlier in this chapter adults can reference print using both verbal and nonverbal means. Verbal references, such as questions about print (e.g., "Can you find the word *danger* on this cage?") and comments about print ("I see the word *danger* on the cage."), are designed to facilitate verbal interactions focused on print. Nonverbal references (e.g., tracking the print while reading, pointing to print) are designed to facilitate children's visual attention to print. Both verbal and nonverbal references cause children to look more often at print within books (Justice, Pullen, & Pence, 2008) and, when used as a package over repeated readings of books, facilitate children's learning about print (Justice et al., 2009).

A number of studies have suggested that exposure to print referencing has positive impacts on children's emergent literacy skills, with research lines that include both experimental (Justice & Ezell, 2000, 2002; Justice et al., 2009; Lovelace & Stewart, 2007) and nonexperimental treatments concerning children with low-incidence disabilities (Ezell, Justice, & Parsons, 2000). Studies that involve larger-scale implementations with preschoolers who are at risk for reading difficulties show that such effects are replicated but attenuated when this approach to book sharing is implemented by classroom teachers in whole-class reading sessions (Justice et al., 2009); significantly, this early boost in print knowledge appears to have a positive impact on children's reading achievement in first grade (Piasta, Justice, McGinty, & Kaderavek, 2012).

Although this approach offers promise for promoting print knowledge within the context of book sharing—an area of development that seems to be only implicitly addressed in typical reading practices—a few limitations to these studies warrant mention. First, it is unclear from this literature whether an increase in children's attention to print has an inverse impact on their attention to and comprehension of the storyline of a book. Second, studies of the use of print referencing in teaching children with disabilities have largely involved nonexperimental research; one exception, which involved implementation of a 12-week reading program by parents of children with specific language impairments, showed relatively modest effects compared with what is found in studies of children without such impairments (Justice, Skibbe, McGinty, Piasta, & Petrill, 2011).

CONSIDERATIONS IN THE CLASSROOM

Given the potential promise of sharing books with children, it seems reasonable to argue that this practice has a rightful place in every classroom. However, children's experiences with shared book reading in the classroom context vary in terms of quantity and quality. First, observational studies indicate that shared book reading is not always a regular part of the curriculum, specifically in those programs that serve children from low-income homes (Dickinson, McCabe, & Anastasopoulos, 2003; Neuman, 1999). In fact, the study conducted by Dickinson et al. (2003) indicated that early childhood teachers spent only about 8% of the day reading books in any setting. Second, the quality of shared book reading that occurs in the classroom can also vary substantially depending on a number of factors, such as the teachers' reading style and focus (Dickinson & Smith, 1994; Martinez & Teale, 1993) and the children's access to a variety of high-quality texts within the classroom (McGill-Franzen, Lanford, & Adams, 2002). McGill et al. found that children from low-income families were offered very limited experiences with books and had less access to culturally relevant literature compared with their peers.

Given the importance of promoting not only the frequency of sharing books with children in early childhood classrooms but also the quality of this practice, in this section we provide recommendations, empirically and theoretically driven to the extent that this is possible, for implementation of book sharing within early childhood classrooms.

Genre of Books to Be Shared

Both researchers and practitioners have emphasized the need to increase children's experiences with a variety of books, because the ability to understand various book genres is vital for becoming a proficient reader (Teale, 2003). Books within a genre share some common characteristics, regardless of the time or place of composition, the author, or the subject matter (Mitchell, Waterbury, & Casement, 2003). Within the early childhood classroom, young children may be exposed to a variety of book genres. *Narrative books* (i.e., books that are designed to entertain or convey an experience) may provide an opportunity for instructing young children in story structure or comprehension strategies (Baumann & Bergeron, 1993). *Information books* (i.e., books that are used to convey accurate information about the natural or social world) serve a function quite different from narrative books because they present children with reasons to read and write beyond purely aesthetic purposes (Duke, 2007). Exposure to information books may provide children with learning opportunities that promote greater understanding of information books' purpose and structure, language abilities (i.e., exposure to technical vocabulary), conceptual knowledge, comprehension skills, and interest and engagement in reading (Duke, 2000; Pappas, 1993). Finally, *dual-purpose books,* or books that contain elements of both information books and narrative books (i.e., they include facts and tell a story), offer benefits similar to information books in terms of acquisition of scientific language and concept development by embedding accurate information about the natural or social world in a familiar story format (Donovan & Smolkin, 2002).

Experts argue that different genres of books represent different discourse styles that children must master (Gee, 2001; Pentimonti, Zucker, & Justice, 2011). This mastery of discourse style helps children understand the goals and purposes of a book (Pappas, 1993). Although these goals may be clear to adults, recognizing the genre of a book and its intended purpose may be difficult for young children. For example, studies have shown that children in preschool and kindergarten often attempt to apply narrative structure to information books, such as looking for "characters" (e.g., Pappas, 1993). An awareness of the various functions of genre is vital if children are to use books to accomplish multiple communicative goals.

Despite the benefits that exposure to a variety of book genres can provide, teachers' use of different genres is disproportionate in early childhood classrooms. Specifically, studies show that teachers infrequently use information books and spend very small percentages of their day reading information books aloud (Duke, 2000; Pentimonti et al., 2011). In fact, one analysis of preschool teachers' whole-class, shared book reading conducted across an entire academic year found that only 5% of books used were information books (Pentimonti, Zucker, Justice, & Kaderavek, 2010). These findings suggest that the genre of books selected for use in early childhood classrooms should receive thoughtful consideration in order to ensure that young children receive exposure to a variety of genres. In turn, this exposure can guarantee that children benefit from the learning opportunities unique to each genre.

In summary, early childhood teachers should be encouraged to consider the genre of books they select when sharing books with children in their classrooms. Ensuring that shared book reading includes a well-balanced combination of book genres will maximize the potential learning opportunities that young children may receive through these book-sharing experiences.

Frequency of Shared Book Reading

Although there is little empirical evidence regarding the exact frequency with which shared book reading should occur in early childhood classrooms, national standards as well as educational researchers offer important suggestions. For example, the U.S. Department of Education recommends that young children be read to several times a day and that early childhood educators establish regular times for shared book reading to take place in the classroom (U.S. Department of Education Early Childhood–Head Start Task Force, 2002). In addition, educational researchers recommend that young children participate in three sessions of shared book reading per day, for a total of 45 minutes, to ensure that shared book readings are a regular part of an early childhood classroom curriculum (Dickinson & Tabors, 2001).

Furthermore, repeated readings of the same storybook may have benefits for children's emergent literacy and language skills. As discussed earlier in this chapter, repeated readings may have a positive influence on children's receptive vocabulary, because several exposures to a book and its vocabulary provide children with additional opportunities to encode, associate, and store new information (Biemiller & Boote, 2006). In addition, a series of case studies conducted by Phillips and McNaughton (1990) suggest that familiarity with the story content due

to repeated readings may create opportunities to shift children's attention to, and learn about, other features of the book.

A number of preschool-oriented programs and curricula have built-in
methods for ensuring that children have repeated exposure to books. For
example, the *Sit Together and Read (STAR)* program is designed to have
teachers read a book four times in a week (Justice et al., 2009). Similarly,
as part of the *Opening the World of Learning (OWL)* curriculum, teachers read a book four times over a period of time; this allows the teachers to advance from discussing an initial sense of story and vocabulary
with students to more active interactions with the book (Schickedanz,
Dickinson, & Charlotte–Mecklenburg Schools, 2006). Although there is
certainly some room for individualizing these matters, the importance
of ensuring that children hear books repeatedly and are exposed to the
concepts within them on a variety of occasions is supported in a number
of developmental studies.

Contexts of Reading

There is some debate concerning the most effective context in which to
conduct shared book reading. Researchers who support the idea that
shared book reading should be conducted in small groups argue that it
may be challenging for teachers to engage all children in whole-group
conversations that are appropriate for all levels of learners (Dickinson
& Sprague, 2001). More specifically, children who are at risk for reading impairments may have difficulty paying attention in a whole-group
setting, because they may have had fewer opportunities to practice
focused attention in this type of setting (Bodrova & Leong, 2007). In
fact, reading in small-group settings may provide even greater benefits
than reading in individual settings; Morrow and Smith (1990) found
that children who are read to in small groups made even greater gains
in story comprehension than children who are read to in individual
sessions.

In contrast, other research suggests that shared book reading is in
fact more effective in a whole-group setting. For example, Karweit and
Wasik (1996) found that teachers provided more redirection of the discussion of the story and provided more positive comments when reading
to whole groups. Similarly, a meta-analysis by Mol et al. (2009) suggests
that children benefited from whole-group interactive reading sessions
as part of book reading interventions compared with children in control
groups. These results suggest that in a whole-group setting teachers
may intentionally focus on events directly related to the story in order
to maintain control over the reading session, whereas in a smaller-group
session a larger amount of extraneous talk and opportunities for each
child to elaborate on personal experiences may provide distraction.

In light of these inconsistent findings, coupling small-group experiences with larger-group experiences could provide maximum benefits for young children. Through conducting shared book reading in both large- and small-group settings, young children will be exposed to environments in which they are able to learn from their peers. When young children are read to along with their peers, they are given the opportunity to hear their peers who are more advanced model new words and ideas (Mashburn, Justice, Downer, & Pianta, 2009). In fact, peer interaction may also provide benefits for young children in terms of narrative development, because their peers can influence preschoolers' narratives (McGregor, 2000).

Age-Level Differences

There is evidence to suggest that differences in the benefits of shared book reading may exist across age levels (Mol et al., 2008; Raikes et al., 2006). Findings in regard to these differences may have implications for shared book reading that occurs in the classroom setting, as well as for recommendations that educators may make to parents about sharing books with children in their homes. The research base on shared book reading with very young children (i.e., from birth to 3 years) largely pertains to parent–child shared book reading. Converging evidence in this relatively limited body of literature suggests that the younger the age of a child when shared book reading begins, the better the child's future language and literacy abilities will be (Debaryshe, 1993; Payne, Whitehurst, & Angell, 1994). Shared book reading with very young children may enhance later language and literacy abilities via multiple processes, such as increased episodes of joint attention, exposure to a broader vocabulary, and establishment of regular reading habits (Karrass & Braungart-Rieker, 2005). Despite the evidence suggesting that shared book reading with young children is beneficial in the home environment, a meta-analysis of interactive shared reading in the classroom context by Mol et al. (2009) found smaller effect sizes for preschoolers than for kindergartners in alphabet knowledge. However, Mol and colleagues hypothesize that these differences may be due to kindergarten teachers making more references to print than preschool teachers, or that older children with some print knowledge may have elicited richer discussion of print features. In summary, it appears that there are benefits of sharing books with children across age levels. These benefits may be most salient for younger children in the home environment. Therefore, teachers and school administrators should endeavor to find ways to communicate the advantages of such activities to parents.

CONCLUSION

Within early childhood literacy instruction, there is perhaps no practice that is more widely recommended than sharing books with children. The goal of this chapter has been to carefully examine what can be learned from research about this highly endorsed practice. Overall, evidence taken from studies of shared book reading indicates reliable, moderate effects on children's emergent literacy and language outcomes. Furthermore, research supports several empirically validated approaches to reading with young children, including dialogic reading, word elaborations, and print referencing. Finally, studies show that shared-reading practices should involve varied genres of books, frequent and repeated readings of books, and a combination of both large- and small-group contexts; they also should be conducted with children across different age levels. In summary, implications from the research reviewed here indicate that teachers and parents of young children should endeavor to use this empirically supported practice to promote children's early language and literacy skills.

REFERENCES

Anderson, R.C., Hiebert, E.H., Scott, J.A., & Wilkinson, I.A.G. (with members of the Commission on Reading). (1985). *Becoming a nation of readers: The report of the Commission on Reading.* Washington, DC: U.S. Department of Education, National Institute of Education.

Baumann, J.F., & Bergeron, B.S. (1993). Story map instruction using children's literature: Effects on first graders' comprehension of central narrative elements. *Journal of Reading Behavior, 25*(4), 407–437.

Beck, I.L., & McKeown, M.G. (2007). Increasing young low-income children's oral vocabulary repertoires through rich and focused instruction. *The Elementary School Journal, 107*(3), 251–273.

Biemiller, A., & Boote, C. (2006). An effective method for building meaning vocabulary in primary grades. *Journal of Educational Psychology, 98*(1), 44–62.

Blok, H. (1999). Reading to young children in educational settings: A meta-analysis of recent research. *Language Learning, 49*(2), 343–371.

Bodrova, E., & Leong, D.J. (2007). *Tools of the Mind: The Vygotskian approach to early childhood education* (2nd ed.). Upper Saddle River, NJ: Prentice-Hall.

Bus, A.G., van IJzendoorn, M.H., & Pellegrini, A.D. (1995). Joint book reading makes for success in learning to read: A meta-analysis on intergenerational transmission of literacy. *Review of Educational Research, 65*(1), 1–21.

Bush, B. (1990). Parenting's best-kept secret: Reading to your children. *Reader's Digest, 137*, 67–70.

Chambless, D.L., & Hollon, S.D. (1998). Defining empirically supported therapies. *Journal of Consulting and Clinical Psychology, 66*(1), 7–18.

Coyne, M.D., McCoach, D.B., Loftus, S., Zipoli, Jr., R., & Kapp, S. (2009). Direct vocabulary instruction in kindergarten: Teaching for breadth versus depth. *The Elementary School Journal, 110*(1), 1–18.

Crain-Thoreson, C., & Dale, P.S. (1999). Enhancing linguistic performance: Parents and teachers as book reading partners for children with language delays. *Topics in Early Childhood Special Education, 19*(1), 28–39.

Debaryshe, B.D. (1993). Joint picture-book reading correlates of early oral language skill. *Journal of Child Language, 20*(2), 455–461.

Dickinson, D.K., McCabe, A., & Anastasopoulos, L. (2003). A framework for examining book reading in early childhood classrooms. In A. van Kleeck, A.A. Stahl, & E.B. Bauer (Eds.), *On reading books to children: Parents and teachers* (pp. 95–113). Mahwah, NJ: Lawrence Erlbaum Associates.

Dickinson, D.K., & Smith, M.W. (1994). Long-term effects of preschool teachers' book readings on low-income children's vocabulary and story comprehension. *Reading Research Quarterly, 29*(2), 104–122.

Dickinson, D.K., & Sprague, K.E. (2001). The nature and impact of early childhood care environments on the language and early literacy development of children from low-income families. In S. Neuman & D. Dickinson (Eds.), *Handbook for research on early literacy* (pp. 263–280). New York, NY: Guilford Press.

Dickinson, D.K., & Tabors, P.O. (Eds.). (2001). *Beginning literacy with language: Young children learning at home and school.* Baltimore, MD: Paul H. Brookes Publishing Co.

Donovan, C.A., & Smolkin, L.B. (2002). Considering genre, content, and visual features in the selection of trade books for science instruction. *Reading Teacher, 55*(6), 502–520.

Duke, N.K. (2000). 3.6 minutes per day: The scarcity of informational texts in first grade. *Reading Research Quarterly, 35*(2), 202–224.

Duke, N.K. (2007). Let's look in a book: Using nonfiction reference materials with young children. *Young Children, 62*(3), 12–16.

Evans, M.A., Williamson, K., & Pursoo, T. (2008). Preschoolers' attention to print during shared book reading. *Scientific Studies of Reading, 12*(1), 106–129.

Ezell, H.K., Justice, L.M., & Parsons, D. (2000). Enhancing the emergent literacy skills of pre-schoolers with communication disorders: A pilot investigation. *Child Language Teaching & Therapy, 16*(2), 121–140.

Gee, J.P. (2001). Reading as situated language: A sociocognitive perspective. *Journal of Adolescent & Adult Literacy, 44*(8), 714–725.

Girolametto, L., Weitzman, E., Lefebvre, P., & Greenberg, J. (2007). The effects of in-service education to promote emergent literacy in child care centers: A feasibility study. *Language, Speech, and Hearing Services in Schools, 38*(1), 72–83.

Justice, L.M., & Ezell, H.K. (2000). Enhancing children's print and word awareness through home-based parent intervention. *American Journal of Speech-Language Pathology, 9*(3), 257–269.

Justice, L.M., & Ezell, H.K. (2002). Use of storybook reading to increase print awareness in at-risk children. *American Journal of Speech-Language Pathology, 11*(1), 17–29.

Justice, L.M., & Ezell, H.K. (2004). Print referencing: An emergent literacy enhancement strategy and its clinical applications. *Language, Speech, and Hearing Services in Schools, 35*(2), 185–193.

Justice, L., Kaderavek, J., Fan, X., Sofka, A., & Hunt, A. (2009). Accelerating preschoolers' early literacy development through classroom-based teacher–child storybook reading and explicit print referencing. *Language, Speech, and Hearing Services in Schools, 40*, 67–85.

Justice, L.M., Meier, J., & Walpole, S. (2005). Learning new words from storybooks: An efficacy study with at-risk kindergarteners. *Language, Speech, and Hearing Services in Schools, 36*, 17–32.

Justice, L.M., Pullen, P.C., & Pence, K. (2008). Influence of verbal and nonverbal references to print on preschoolers' visual attention to print during storybook reading. *Developmental Psychology, 44*(3), 855–866.

Justice, L.M., Skibbe, L.E., McGinty, A.S., Piasta, S.B., & Petrill, S. (2011). Feasibility, efficacy, and social validity of home-based storybook reading intervention for children with language impairment. *Journal of Speech, Language, and Hearing Research, 54*(2), 523–528.

Karrass, J., & Braungart-Rieker, J.M. (2005). Effects of shared parent–infant book reading on early language acquisition. *Journal of Applied Developmental Psychology, 26*(2), 133–148.

Karweit, N., & Wasik, B.A. (1996). The effects of story reading programs on literacy and language development of disadvantaged preschoolers. *Journal of Education for Students Placed at Risk, 1*(4), 319–348.

Lonigan, C.J. (1994). Reading to preschoolers exposed: Is the emperor really naked? *Developmental Review, 14*(3), 303–323.

Lonigan, C.J., & Whitehurst, G.J. (1998). Relative efficacy of parent and teacher involvement in a shared-reading intervention for preschool children from low-income backgrounds. *Early Childhood Research Quarterly, 13*(2), 263–290.

Lovelace, S., & Stewart, S.R. (2007). Increasing print awareness in preschoolers with language impairment using non-evocative print referencing. *Language, Speech, and Hearing Services in Schools, 38*(1), 16–30.

Martinez, M., & Teale, W. (1993). Teacher storybook reading style: A comparison of six teachers. *Research in the Teaching of English, 27*(2), 175–199.

Mashburn, A.J., Justice, L.M., Downer, J.T., & Pianta, R.C. (2009). Peer effects on children's language achievement during pre-kindergarten. *Child Development, 80*(3), 686–702.

McGill-Franzen, A., Lanford, C., & Adams, E. (2002). Learning to be literate: A comparison of five urban early childhood programs. *Journal of Educational Psychology, 94*(3), 434–464.

McGregor, K.K. (2000). The development and enhancement of narrative skills in a preschool classroom: Towards a solution to clinician–client mismatch. *American Journal of Speech-Language Pathology, 9*(1), 55–71.

Mitchell, D., Waterbury, P., & Casement, R. (2003). *Children's literature: An invitation to the world.* Boston, MA: Allyn & Bacon.

Mol, S.E., Bus, A.G., & de Jong, M.T. (2009). Interactive book reading in early education: A tool to stimulate print knowledge as well as oral language. *Review of Educational Research, 79*(2), 979–1007.

Mol, S.E., Bus, A.G., de Jong, M.T., & Smeets, D.J.H. (2008). Added value of dialogic parent–child book readings: A meta-analysis. *Early Education and Development, 19*(1), 7–26.

Morrow, L.M., & Smith, J.K. (1990). The effects of group size on interactive storybook reading. *Reading Research Quarterly, 25*(3), 213–231.

National Early Literacy Panel. (2008). *Developing early literacy: Report of the National Early Literacy Panel.* Washington, DC: National Institute for Literacy.

Neuman, S. (1999). Books make a difference: A study of access to literacy. *Reading Research Quarterly, 34*(3), 286–311.

Pappas, C.C. (1993). Is narrative "primary"? Some insights from kindergartners' pretend readings of stories and information books. *Journal of Reading Behavior, 25*(1), 97–129.

Payne, A.C., Whitehurst, G.J., & Angell, A.L. (1994). The role of home literacy environment in the development of language ability in preschool children from low-income families. *Early Childhood Research Quarterly, 9*(3–4), 427–440.

Pentimonti, J.M., Zucker, T.A., & Justice, L.M. (2011). What are preschool teachers reading in their classrooms? *Reading Psychology, 32*(3), 197–236.

Pentimonti, J.M., Zucker, T.A., Justice, L.M., & Kaderavek, J.N. (2010). Information text use in preschool read-alouds. *The Reading Teacher, 63*(8), 656–665.

Phillips, G., & McNaughton, S. (1990). The practice of reading to preschool children in mainstream New Zealand families. *Reading Research Quarterly, 25*(3), 196–212.

Piasta, S.B., Justice, L.M., McGinty, A.S., & Kaderavek, J.N. (2012). Increasing young children's contact with print during shared reading: Longitudinal effects on literacy achievement. *Child Development, 83,* 810–820.

Raikes, H., Pan, B.A., Luze, G., Tamis-LeMonda, C.S., Brooks-Gunn, J., Constantine, J.,...Rodriguez, E.T. (2006). Mother–child bookreading in low-income families: Correlates and outcomes during the first three years of life. *Child Development, 77*(4), 924–953.

Scarborough, H.S., & Dobrich, W. (1994). On the efficacy of reading to preschoolers. *Developmental Review, 14*(3), 245–302.

Schickedanz, J.A., Dickinson, D.K., & Charlotte–Mecklenburg Schools (2006). *Opening the World of Learning (OWL).* Upper Saddle River, NJ: Pearson Education.

Teale, W.H. (2003). Reading aloud to young children as a classroom instructional activity: Insights from research and practice. In A. van Kleeck, A.A. Stahl, & E.B. Bauer (Eds.), *On reading books to children: Parents and teachers* (pp. 114–139). Mahwah, NJ: Lawrence Erlbaum Associates.

U.S. Department of Education Early Childhood–Head Start Task Force. (2002). *Teaching our youngest: A guide for preschool teachers and child care and family providers.* Retrieved from http://www2.ed.gov/teachers/how/early/teachingouryoungest/index.html

Wasik, B.A., & Bond, M.A. (2001). Beyond the pages of the book: Interactive book reading and language development in preschool classrooms. *Journal of Educational Psychology, 93*(2), 243–250.

Whitehurst, G.J., Arnold, D.S., Epstein, J.N., Angell, A.L., Smith, M., & Fischel, J.E. (1994). A picture book reading intervention in day care and home for children from low-income families. *Developmental Psychology, 30*(5), 679–689.

Whitehurst, G.J., Falco, F., Lonigan, C., Fischel, J.E., Debaryshe, B.D., Valdez-Menchaca, M.C., & Caulfield, M. (1988). Accelerating language development through picture-book reading. *Developmental Psychology, 24*(4), 552–558.

Zucker, T.A., Justice, L.M., & Piasta, S.B. (2009). Prekindergarten teachers' verbal references to print during classroom-based, large-group shared reading. *Language, Speech, and Hearing Services in Schools, 40*(4), 376–392.

7

Parent Education and Home-Based Efforts to Improve Children's Literacy

Barbara Hanna Wasik and Beth Anne N. Feldman

During the 1960s, a heightened awareness developed in the United States for the difficulties many young children growing up in poverty experience in school, including poor academic performance, grade retention, and later dropout. Two major factors, home environment and parent–child interactions, were identified as contributing to children's success in school. This recognition resulted in the initiation of many early-intervention efforts during the preschool years to change children's projected educational pathways. These interventions tended to focus on 1) direct intervention with children through programs such as Head Start, 2) home-visiting parent-education programs such as the Mother–Child Home Program (Levenstein, 1989) and Gordon's home-visiting programs (Lazar, Darlington, Murray, Royce, & Snipper, 1982), or 3) a combination of services, as seen in the Perry Preschool Project that included a center-based intervention and parent education (Muennig, Schweinhart, Montie, & Neidell, 2009).

Throughout the 1970s, interest in early intervention continued to increase, resulting in the initiation of several major experimental studies of this topic. Some of these studies focused on center-based interventions, such as the Abecedarian Project (Campbell & Ramey, 1994), some examined both center-based and home-visiting interventions (Wasik, Ramey, Bryant, & Sparling, 1990), and others examined only home visiting (e.g., Olds, Henderson, & Kitzman, 1994). By the 1980s, there was a major expansion of home-visiting programs, such as Parents as Teachers, Home Instruction for Parents of Preschool Youngsters, and Healthy Families America. These three programs, as well as Early Head Start (established in 1995), the Nurse-Family Partnership (Olds et al., 1994), and the Mother–Child Home Program (now the Parent–Child Home Program), have all obtained national prominence and have established local programs across the country.

Many of these initiatives were undertaken prior to the establishment of considerable research evidence on the relation between children's early home environment and their later language and literacy development. Hart and Risley's (1995) publication on early language development, with its compelling support for the role of parents in children's early language and literacy development, provided some of the strongest evidence on the important role of the family in helping children develop these skills. In spite of such strong evidence linking parent behaviors and children's outcomes, considerably less is known about specific strategies that can be used to influence the home environment and parent–child interactions to bring about significant positive developmental outcomes for children.

Although compelling evidence from correlational and genetic studies supports the role of children's early environment and the role that parents play in such environments, many interventions have not resulted in significant child literacy and language outcomes. The reasons why an intervention might not have positive outcomes for parents and/or children can result from many factors. Although many descriptive and quantitative studies have shown how parents from middle-income families tend to interact with their children and have shown many characteristics of the home environment, these findings do not necessarily mean that practitioners can know with certainty which factors are important to include in an intervention. Is reading to children as significant a factor as some of the literature would suggest? Or do the most important contributions to children's development arise through the verbal and nonverbal parent–child interactions that take place throughout the day? Can the significant factors, once isolated, be taught to or implemented by parents with fidelity? Will parents view such factors as significant and be motivated to follow specific strategies? Other implementation variables also influence outcomes, including ensuring that program staff are trained to implement the procedures, monitoring program fidelity, delivering the intervention at an intensity level that is sufficient for change, and determining whether parents and children participate at a level essential for change. These factors lead to caution in interpreting program effectiveness. As we discuss in this chapter, before deeming an intervention ineffective, many aspects of program implementation and participation levels must be examined.

FINDINGS OF THE NATIONAL EARLY LITERACY PANEL

The National Early Literacy Panel (NELP; 2008) report included an analysis of the overall effects of home-based and parent programs on children's literacy development. NELP analyzed 23 intervention studies that met three inclusion criteria: 1) studies had to implement a group-comparison design (either a randomized controlled trial or a quasi-experimental design), 2) outcome measures had to assess the early literacy skills identified by NELP as developmental precursors to conventional forms of reading (e.g., oral language, phonological awareness) or assess conventional reading skills (e.g., decoding, reading comprehension), and 3) studies had to report sufficient data for an effect size to be computed. The variables of interest in the NELP report included alphabet knowledge, cognitive ability, memory, oral language, phonological awareness, reading, reading readiness, spelling, and writing.

The first NELP analyses examined the effects of parent- and home-based programs on the nine dependent variables shown in Table 7.1. Home and parent programs had the strongest effect size on cognitive outcomes, with moderate-to-large gains. Eighteen studies taken together produced an effect, albeit small, on oral language skills. In addition, NELP found that the impact of home- and parent-based education programs was statistically equivalent for these two outcomes. In analyzing predictors of later reading skills, NELP found that measures of more complex oral language skills (e.g., grammar, ability to define words, reading comprehension) were more predictive of later reading skill than measures of simple vocabulary. In light of this finding, NELP examined the effects of home and parent programs on a composite measure of language compared with measures of simple vocabulary; the results showed no significant difference between the more complex measure and the simple measure.

In another analysis, NELP examined whether intervention effects varied for home and parent programs by children's age. When comparisons

Table 7.1. Estimates of effect sizes across outcomes for home and parent literacy programs for nine dependent variables

Dependent variable	Fixed effect size	Random effect size	95% confidence interval		Number of studies	p-value for effect size
			Lower bound	Upper bound		
Alphabet knowledge	-0.03	-0.03	-.31	.24	1	.81
Cognitive ability	0.65	0.92	.22	1.62	6	.01
Memory	1.17	1.17	.50	1.84	1	.0006
Oral language	0.28	0.37	.18	.55	18	.0001
Phonological awareness	0.22	0.21	-.12	.54	2	.21
Reading	0.28	0.28	-.12	.68	1	.17
Reading readiness	-0.05	0.05	-.33	.22	1	.71
Spelling	0.09	0.09	-.18	.37	1	.51
Writing	0.52	0.52	.23	.81	1	.0005

From National Early Literacy Panel. (2008). *Developing early literacy: Report of the National Early Literacy Panel* (p. 175). Washington, DC: National Institute for Literacy; reprinted by permission.

were made between children ages birth to 3 years and children ages 4–5 years, no statistically significant differences were obtained between younger and older children. NELP also investigated the effects on oral language by type of intervention, but differences in intervention focus, duration, and content made it difficult for the panel to examine additional possible moderators of treatment.

The interventions NELP analyzed included six home-visiting programs that taught parents either general stimulation activities or more specific oral language activities and five programs that taught parents general stimulation or language strategies in a university or hospital. One intervention focused on children from infancy to school entrance, two interventions taught parents to serve as speech-language clinicians for their children who had speech-language delays, two interventions included parent activities coordinated with activities in their child's preschool or kindergarten classroom, and one intervention considered the effects of combining parent training with weekly parent–child interaction time at a preschool. Among this diverse group of interventions, NELP obtained moderate-to-large effect sizes for more than half of the studies but small or negative effect sizes for the remaining studies; in the latter group, the studies were found to share no common features to explain their poor results.

CONCLUSIONS AND IMPLICATIONS OF THESE FINDINGS

Overall, NELP's meta-analysis of parent- and home-based literacy programs showed that some of these programs produced statistically significant positive effects on children's cognitive ability and, to a lesser degree, oral language. NELP also found that parent programs produced positive effects on memory and writing, although there were too few studies to draw conclusive recommendations.

The variability in parent and home programs, the small number of studies, and lack of experimental replication made it difficult for the panel to evaluate the effects that such programs might have on other child outcomes and to draw meaningful conclusions. The NELP report urged researchers to further explore the effect of coordinating home and parent programs with high-quality early childhood education, a finding that we discuss later in this chapter. The panel's report also raised a concern that, for a majority of the studies, the program's developer delivered the intervention or supervised the staff responsible for delivering the intervention, leaving unanswered the question of whether the interventions can be successfully implemented on a broad scale.

Many of the more commonly cited interventions that are designed to enhance parent involvement in children's language and literacy development were not included in NELP's analysis, yet they can still inform the field. Consequently, the remainder of this chapter reviews three categories of parent and home interventions that were not included in the NELP report, to determine whether this broader literature expands on the NELP findings: 1) parent education or parent training provided as stand-alone services, 2) home-visiting interventions, and 3) family literacy interventions, defined as intergenerational programs that include parent education and early childhood education, combined, at times, with adult education.

Parent Education Interventions

Knowledge accumulated in the past 40 years on children's early language and literacy development shows the effects of parent–child interactions on children's later literacy skills and reading. The field struggles, however, with ensuring effective interventions for children and families who are at risk for poor developmental outcomes. The NELP analysis showed that some interventions did enhance oral language and cognitive development but rarely influenced other early literacy skills. Even the successful interventions left many questions unanswered. In this section, we examine some of the experimental studies not included in the NELP analysis that provided interventions to help parents enhance their children's language and literacy development.

Possibly the most salient finding among these studies is that parent–child interactive book reading is predictive of positive, short-term outcomes on aspects of children's language and literacy in both low- and middle-income families (Bennett, Weigel, & Martin, 2002; Burgess, 1997; Bus, van IJzendoorn, & Pellegrini, 1995; Lonigan & Whitehurst, 1998; Sénéchal, LeFevre, Thomas, & Daley, 1998). Much of this research has focused on the nature of the parent–child verbal interaction that accompanies reading and the specific interactions between the adult and the child during reading. This research also laid the groundwork for interventions that encourage parents to read more often to their children and, most significantly, to engage children to be more active participants during storybook reading (Aram & Levin, 2004).

Research conducted on parent–child book-reading interventions has mainly focused on low-income or racial and ethnic minority families. In one early study (Henderson & Garcia, 1973), Mexican American mothers received individual training for book reading with their first-grade children in modeling, cuing, and reinforcing questions asked during reading. The goal was to shift children's questions from nominal-physical questions (e.g., "What is this?" "What color is this?") to causal questions (e.g., "Why?" "How come?"). The children in the experimental group asked significantly more causal questions compared with children in the control group.

Parents in federally funded programs for low-income families have also been participants in literacy intervention studies. In a study by Taverne and Sheridan (1995), a group of mothers of 3-, 4-, and 5-year-old children who were enrolled in an Even Start Family Literacy Program were taught interactive book-reading strategies that included general discussion, modeling, role playing, and performance feedback. Using a single-case A–B replication design, the researchers reported an increase in the frequency of interactive book reading among all parents and qualitative gains in responsive communication between parents and children during book reading. Furthermore, the mothers improved their ability to structure the book reading, obtain their children's cooperation, and sustain the children's focus; all of the children made gains in their receptive language.

In another study, parents of children who were enrolled in Head Start participated in a 12-week book club that provided literacy materials and opportunities for storybook reading with their preschool children (Neuman, 1996). Each week, parents met in a group at a Head Start center and observed a facilitator reading a storybook aloud in a dramatic and interactive manner. The facilitator then guided a discussion with the parents about how to read the book, after which the parents had opportunities to practice reading the book and then to read the book to their children. The results showed that children made gains in receptive language and concepts about print regardless of the parents' reading proficiency.

Other researchers (Hockenberger, Goldstein, & Haas, 1999) helped a group of low-socioeconomic-status mothers relate storybooks to the experiences of their 4- and 5-year-old children and facilitate an interactive conversation during book reading. Results from a single-case design showed that the reciprocal nature of the interaction between the mothers and their children improved and that the children became more engaged in the storybook reading, producing more comments, questions, and responsive utterances.

An alternative objective of parent education programs is to help parents learn to use decontextualized language with their children. Decontextualized language plays a role in helping children learn to read because it is more similar to book reading, in which only the language conveys meaning, not facial expressions or body language. One relatively recent study (Morgan & Goldstein, 2004) found that teaching mothers to use decontextualized language during storybook reading with their preschool-age children increased the mothers' use of these language strategies and improved the content of talk between mother and child during storybook reading. In addition, this study found that children's use of decontextualized language was dependent on how frequently mothers used such language during storybook reading.

Some of the most rigorous research with parents has been with dialogic book reading (Lonigan & Whitehurst, 1998; Whitehurst et al., 1994; Whitehurst et al., 1999). The NELP report found dialogic reading to be a promising intervention, whether delivered by early childhood teachers or by parents. Given the initial strong evidence base in support of dialogic reading, researchers have extended this work to examine whether using training videotapes is a viable alternative to live training. Parents consistently rated the videos as an acceptable and effective mode of delivery (Blom-Hoffman, O'Neil-Pirozzi, & Cutting, 2006) and used the dialogic reading strategies during storybook reading after viewing the video (Briesch, Chafouleas, Lebel, & Blom-Hoffman, 2008).

It is questionable, however, how reliably parents use the strategies after receiving the video training; parents may need additional live sessions to reinforce the strategies (Briesch et al., 2008). Furthermore, these studies are limited because they did not examine whether video training had effects on child outcomes.

Although the studies on book reading discussed previously do provide evidence for improvements in parent responses and children's oral language, examination of children's skills such as letter knowledge or phonological awareness have not yielded significant outcomes, nor has parent–child book reading been shown to influence children's later reading (Hood, Conlon, & Andrews, 2008). Instead, it seems that *direct teaching* of literacy skills (e.g., teaching letter names and sounds) contributes to children's development of emergent literacy and reading skills that are necessary for children to read print independently (Haney & Hill, 2004). Specifically, evidence suggests that parental teaching predicts children's vocabulary and concepts about print (Haney & Hill, 2004) as well as alphabet knowledge, phonological sensitivity, word reading, and spelling (Hood et al., 2008). Given these findings, interventions may need to provide parents with formal teaching strategies to become effective "teachers" of literacy skills, moving beyond just increasing a child's opportunity to read, engage with, and take interest in books. Yet few empirical studies have evaluated programs that educate parents in the direct teaching of literacy skills to their children. Nor is there clear consensus in regard to what parents should do, beyond just reading to their children, to most effectively ensure positive child outcomes (Fitton & Gredler, 1996; Toomey, 1993).

Studies with elementary school–age children suggest that parent-implemented reading interventions that explicitly teach reading skills result in significant increases in first graders' fluency and comprehension (Leach & Siddall, 1990; Rasinski & Stevenson, 2005; Resetar, Noell, & Pellegrin, 2006). Resetar et al. (2006), for example, trained parents in a tutoring procedure that included modeling, practice, phonics, fluency building, comprehension, and reinforcement. Results showed that four of the five first graders demonstrated an increase in fluency, namely the number of words read correctly per minute on tutored reading passages. Rasinski and Stevenson (2005) tested the effects of a fluency-based home reading program called Fast Start with 30 first-grade students. In the experimental group, parents and students received specific training, weekly materials, and weekly telephone support. Results showed significant effects on letter-word recognition and reading fluency for students who were most at risk for reading difficulties. Although the data are not extensive, the strategy of equipping parents with the knowledge and skills to teach literacy skills directly has shown potential for teaching children to read. These promising results suggest that researchers should examine parental teaching of preschoolers, taking into consideration such factors as children's development skills, parent motivation, and cultural practices.

In addition to interactive book reading and parental teaching of early literacy skills as important components of intervention programs, research also suggests that teaching preschool children to write predicts early literacy and reading in the first and third grades (Sénéchal et al., 1998; Sénéchal & LeFevre, 2002). For instance, Israeli kindergartners performed better on measures of word writing and linguistic knowledge when their mothers were better writing mediators (e.g., they referred to and explained alphabetic and orthographic principles, provided their children with more independence in writing letters) (Aram, & Levin, 2001). Following these children into second grade, the researchers found that maternal mediation of writing predicted children's spelling and reading comprehension. This developing body of research suggests that teaching phonological awareness in combination with teaching letters and the connection between graphemes and phonemes may be one of the more effective approaches for helping children learn to read (Aram & Levin, 2004).

The studies on interactive book-reading strategies previously reviewed have demonstrated positive outcomes, especially among mothers, yet long-term effects on children's language and literacy were rarely considered. Furthermore, these studies infrequently examined parents' fidelity to the program, making it difficult to draw conclusions about the interventions. On the other hand, these techniques have shown positive outcomes on several maternal behaviors as well as child outcomes. Given that parental behavior is viewed as the pathway for children's development, these studies provide support for continuing this line of intervention with parents and children, while also emphasizing the need for more clarity about the important parental behaviors that are necessary for children's success.

Home Visiting as a Strategy

Home visiting has a long history in the United States, dating back to at least the 1900s, as a strategy for providing information to parents of young children (Wasik & Bryant, 2001). In the late 1920s, home-visiting services became less common because many services for families were moved to clinic settings. But concerns in the 1960s about children reared in poverty and the detrimental effects on their educational and social outcomes led to an increased interest in home visiting as a strategy for reaching parents. From the 1960s to the 1990s, there was considerable growth in the number of home-visiting programs, and many initiatives launched during that time have expanded into nationally recognized programs. These programs include Parents as Teachers (PAT), Home Instruction for Parents of Preschool Youngsters (HIPPY), Healthy Families America (HFA), the Nurse-Family Partnership (NFP), the Parent–Child Home Program, and Early Head Start (EHS) (Wasik, Villagomez, Berry, & Mulholkar, 2012).

Home visiting remains a significant part of family services, providing programs that reach out to a variety of populations, including pregnant women, parents of newborns, preschool children, or children with special needs. As evidence of the prevalence of home visiting, a recent survey (Johnson, 2009) noted that at least 40 states provided some type of statewide home-visiting program. In addition, within all states there are other home-visiting services sponsored by a variety of agencies.

Recent interest in home visiting has expanded considerably, based in part upon national efforts to provide home-visiting services to address several key child developmental outcomes, including health and school readiness. The Patient Protection and Affordable Care Act of 2010 (PPACA; PL 111-148) established the Maternal, Infant, and Early Childhood Home Visiting Program (MIECHV; U.S. Department of Health and Human Services, Administration for Children and Families, 2012) to provide $1.5 billion over 5 years for home-visiting programs to serve women and children from birth to age 5 in at-risk communities to improve maternal and child outcomes. Goals include better outcomes related to maternal and child health, improvement in school readiness, child abuse prevention, reduction in crime or domestic violence, improvements in family self-sufficiency, and improvements in coordination and referrals for community resources and supports. At-risk communities are identified at the state level and might include such factors as poverty levels, school dropouts, poor birth outcomes, or child maltreatment that are higher than state averages. Because the PPACA requires that 75% of the funds be used for programs with evidence of effectiveness, intensive evaluations have been conducted of the home-visiting research and the results are published on the U.S. Department of Health and Human Services Home Visiting Evidence of Effectiveness web site (http://homvee.acf.hhs.gov/). As of 2012, analyses of 22 home-visiting programs for families and young children have resulted in the identification of 9 programs as evidence-based programs (i.e., Child FIRST; EHS Home Visiting; Early Intervention Program for Adolescent Mothers; Family Check-Up; HFA; Healthy Steps; HIPPY; NFP; and PAT). Though some of these programs have a strong health focus, most are also concerned with children's school readiness, often identified by measures of early literacy and language.

Parents as Teacher   PAT (2010) is a national program, implemented through local sites, that promotes children's school readiness and school success by increasing parents' knowledge of early childhood development, improving parenting practices, and helping parents support their child's language and literacy development. The PAT program has expanded to all 50 states and 7 other countries, serving children from the prenatal period to their third birthday. In their 2010–2011 summary report, PAT (2011) reported serving approximately 250,000 children and over 200,000 families. Among the earlier studies on PAT were three randomized experiments; Wagner and Clayton (1999) reported two of them. In these studies the overall effects were not large and few significant child or parent outcomes were obtained. Wagner, Cameto, and Gerlach-Downie (1996), however, did find several instances of positive parenting practice outcomes in an experimental study of PAT with adolescent parents and their children.

Pfannenstiel, Seitz, and Zigler (2002), in a quasi-experimental study, found that children in both PAT and center-based early childhood services scored significantly higher on school readiness than their peers in kindergarten. Following these children through the third grade, Zigler, Pfannenstiel, and Seitz (2008) found that the intervention children performed better on the School Entry Profile (Phannenstiel, 1999), an assessment of school readiness, and the Missouri Assessment Program (MAP; Missouri Department of Elementary and Secondary Education, 1999), a measure of third-grade achievement, compared with children who were exposed to neither PAT or center-based preschool. Parents of children who received this intervention also had more books in the home and engaged in more literacy-related activities with their children. In one of the few randomized experimental studies on PAT, positive outcomes for children were obtained on mastery motivation (task competence) at 36 months and children from low versus high socioeconomic status (SES) obtained higher scores on mastery motivation and cognitive development at 24 months (Drotar, Robinson, Jeavons, & Lester Kirchner, 2009).

Home Instruction for Parents of Preschool Youngsters   HIPPY (2012) is a 2-year, home-based, family-focused program that centers on enhancing parents' ability to provide educational enrichment for their preschool children at home. HIPPY originated in Israel and is now implemented in 25 states, the District of Columbia, and several other countries, serving over 16,000 children and their families. Several experimental studies have been conducted on HIPPY with mixed findings. Within a two-cohort study of HIPPY, children in the first cohort in a quasi-experimental designed study scored higher than children in the comparison group on measures of cognitive skills, class-room adaptation, and standardized reading (Baker & Piotrkowski, 1996; Baker, Piotrkowski, & Brooks-Gunn, 1998). The effects, however, were not replicated for the second cohort of children who were enrolled in a randomized controlled trial (Baker & Piotrkowki, 1996).

Favorable results of HIPPY were demonstrated in a longitudinal quasi-experimental designed study that used a post hoc matching design (Bradley & Gilkey, 2002). In this study, children who participated in HIPPY were compared with children from the same classrooms who had no preschool experience and children who had preschool experiences other than HIPPY. The findings suggested that the HIPPY program produced modest positive impacts on decreasing school suspensions for children in third grade and sixth grade, as well as improving these children's grades, classroom behavior, and achievement test scores. More recently, Necoechea (2007) reported on a randomized control trial of children in HIPPY that resulted in mixed outcomes, namely no effect on the Peabody Picture Vocabulary Test (Dunn & Dunn, 1997), a statistically significant effect on a measure of children's ability to name pictures of common objects, and no effect on school readiness tasks such as letter identification.

Healthy Families America   HFA (2012) is a national home-visiting program that targets new and expectant mothers in order to promote positive parenting, enhance child health and development, and prevent child abuse and neglect. It offers weekly home visits to families at risk for child maltreatment. Services begin prenatally or during the first three months of life and continue for three to five years. Like PAT and HIPPY, this program's focus is on direct intervention with the mothers rather than the children. HFA operates programs in over 430 communities in 35 states, Washington, D.C., and Canada (Healthy Families America, 2012). A comprehensive summary of 33 evaluations of HFA indicates that the program is most effective for parents but has mixed impacts on children (Harding, Galano, Martin, Huntington, & Schellenbach, 2007). One study of a statewide program on parenting child health and development found few positive outcomes related to maltreatment, but did find significant positive outcomes on some measures of child development and behavior (Caldera et al., 2007). Positive significant outcomes were found for children's mental development at 1 year in another experimental study of HFA (Landsverk et al., 2002). Harding et al. (2007) note that synthesizing data on HFA is difficult because of the implementation variability, given that local programs have considerable flexibility in program implementation.

Nurse-Family Partnership The NFP (2011) is the most documented home-visiting program with nurses providing home visits to first-time parents throughout pregnancy and continuing until the child's second birthday. The partnership aims to support children's health and development, mothers' prenatal health, and parental life management. Researchers have conducted studies on NFP for more than 3 decades, including three major randomized treatment–control studies in Elmira, New York; Memphis; and Denver (NFP, 2011). NELP included one of these three studies in its report: the third study, which was conducted in Denver. (In the Denver study the researchers did not obtain significant outcomes for literacy and language for the entire sample but did obtain positive outcomes for children who were born to a subset of mothers with low psychological resources (Olds et al., 2007; Olds, Robinson, et al., 2004). As a result of nurse visits, children in these families benefited in several ways, including having a home environment that was more conducive to early learning (Olds, Robinson, et al., 2004). Children who received nurse visits demonstrated more advanced language skills on the Peabody Picture Vocabulary Test–Third Edition (PPVT-III; Dunn & Dunn, 1997) and higher reading and mathematics achievement scores on the Kaufman Assessment Battery for Children (K-ABC; Kaufman, 1983), received fewer reports of challenging behavior in the elevated range on the Achenbach Child Behavior Checklist (Achenbach, 1991, 1992), and were more likely to be enrolled in structured child care or preschool prior to starting kindergarten (Olds, Kitzman, et al., 2004). These findings are similar to the earlier NFP Memphis study, which found that as a result of nurse visits, children who were born to mothers with low psychological resources had better achievement test scores in mathematics and reading in Grades 1–3 (Olds et al., 2007).

Early Head Start The federal EHS program, initiated in 1994 by the Administration on Children, Youth and Families, has been extensively evaluated through a large-scale randomized study of 17 local programs (Love et al., 2005) to assess the effects on parenting and child development. These programs provided a variety of educational, health, and social services delivered through home-visiting programs, center-based programs, or a combination of the two. Each local EHS program determined its own intervention strategy. The findings showed that parents whose children were enrolled in EHS were more emotionally supportive, provided more language and learning stimulation, and read to their children more often. Child outcomes showed significantly higher cognitive and language development, higher levels of emotional engagement and sustained attention, and lower levels of aggressive behavior. Love et al. (2005) also found significant and positive differences in the

PPVT-III standard score and the average Bayley Scales of Infant Development Mental Development Index (MDI) score (Bayley, 1969) for children who were enrolled in EHS. The strongest outcomes were found in programs that had a mix of home-visiting and center-based services and that more fully implemented the performance standards early. Although these positive and significant findings were modest, they provide a foundation for continuing to offer such services and for examining factors that will enhance parent and child outcomes.

Home-visiting services more often produce positive outcomes for parents. Given that the focus of home visiting is on the parent, these outcomes are not surprising. The targeted parenting behaviors, such as positive parent–child relationships and reading with children, are often found to be associated with higher language and literacy outcomes for children, thus providing a rationale for continuing to provide such services. Positive child outcomes have been realized in home-visiting programs, and these findings are providing a foundation for funding these programs. Nevertheless, with a few exceptions, there are often many insignificant outcomes in these studies and the positive findings are not always robust.

Combining home visits with early childhood center-based programs has gained considerable support (Brooks-Gunn & Markham, 2005; Sweet & Appelbaum, 2004; Gomby, 2012). Nevertheless, there are families for whom center-based programs might not be desirable, such as families who prefer to keep their children at home or prefer family child care. As a result, further explorations of how to increase the effectiveness of home visits for long-term impact on children's later school success must become a high priority for researchers and professionals who serve these families.

The research to date does provide some directions for increasing the effectiveness of home-visiting programs. Studies of fidelity to intervention models are rarely conducted (Berlin, O'Neal, & Brooks-Gunn, 1998; Love et al., 2005), but such studies can lead to significant changes in how services are staffed and implemented. Adherence to program procedures can increase positive outcomes for parents and children (Love et al, 2005). Recent efforts directed toward developing instruments to assess the home visits have the potential to advance quality, fidelity, and training. Consideration should be given to including highly specific strategies for parents to use in facilitating their children's language and literacy development, building upon research that has demonstrated the value of helping parents learn specific strategies for helping children with early literacy, such as dialogic reading or for explicitly teaching early literacy skills. Quality controls related to hiring, training, and supervising home visitors can also lead to higher-quality programs

(Wasik & Bryant, 2009). Additional strategies for improving program quality and outcomes are addressed later in this chapter.

Family Literacy Interventions

Family literacy programs in the United States date from the 1980s, when two-generation programs were developed to provide services to parents with low literacy skills and their young children (Wasik & Herrmann, 2004). These programs are most commonly defined as including four components: parent education, early childhood education, parent–child literacy interaction time, and adult education. In 1989, the federal Even Start Family Literacy Program (Even Start), an initiative of the U.S. Department of Education, was established to provide services to low-income, low-literacy families with young children (from birth to 8 years). Beginning with the first funding effort, the government required an evaluation of these programs. Ultimately three major evaluations were conducted in which local sites collected data using nationally established reporting procedures (St.Pierre et al., 2003; St.Pierre et al., 1995). Although these evaluations obtained some positive child outcomes, the overall findings did not result in lasting positive treatment outcomes for parents or children. In a randomized test of Even Start with 18 projects and 463 families, no significant outcomes were obtained. The researchers attributed this result to two factors: a lack of full participation by families and instructional services that might be ineffective due to the curriculum content or the instructional approach (St.Pierre, Ricciuti, & Rimdzius, 2005). These authors concluded by questioning whether the four-component model was an effective intervention. Continuing concerns about whether family literacy programs were in fact having a positive influence on parent outcomes and children's literacy outcomes resulted in a large-scale national experimental study of Even Start— the *Classroom Literacy Interventions and Outcomes (CLIO)*, which involved 120 local programs (Judkins et al., 2008). Programs were randomly assigned to one of five treatment groups and data from 112 sites were collected in 2004–2005 and 2005–2006. The two basic questions the researchers examined were, first, whether evidenced-based early childhood interventions would result in positive outcomes compared with existing Even Start instructional services and, second, whether parent education combined with early childhood education would add value over the early childhood education curricula alone. Each of two developers was responsible for developing and implementing one early childhood program and one parent-education intervention combined with the early childhood program. This design resulted in four treatment groups: two that received the early childhood interventions only and two that received parent education plus the early childhood program (the *CLIO* combined curricula); there was also one control group. To create the early childhood intervention, data for the children in the two separate early childhood interventions were combined. To create the overall combined curriculum, the two early childhood interventions and the two parent interventions were combined. Additional information on the curricula used in the *CLIO* study is presented in the Judkins et al. (2008) report.

To address the first question, the groups that received the *CLIO* combined curricula (i.e., the four treatment groups combined) were compared with the control group. To address the second question, the groups that received the *CLIO* combined curricula were compared with those who received the *CLIO* preschool intervention only.

Child outcome measures targeted seven different aspects of early language and literacy, including receptive vocabulary, phonological awareness, print knowledge, syntax, and grammar. Parent outcomes examined in the study included measures of parents' interactive reading skill, responsiveness to their children, English-reading skill, and vocabulary. The researchers also included a measure of children's social competence. The study measured various instructional outcomes in preschool classrooms, in parent-education classrooms, and during parent–child interaction time (Judkins et al., 2008).

Analysis of the first research question (i.e., whether children in the *CLIO* early childhood intervention would outperform children in the control group) did not result in significant outcomes on the seven different aspects of early literacy. In examining the effects for participation in preschool education with child outcomes, the researchers initially found a statistically significant and positive relation between participation in preschool and child scores on five out of six English emergent–literacy outcomes (Judkins et al., 2008). In examining these results in more depth, the researchers found that this relation appears to be limited to children who participated for about 85 hours per month, a participation level experienced by 26% of the study children. Children who attended the equivalent of a full school day, or approximately 120 hours per month, obtained a differential of one third of a standard deviation. This finding is consistent with findings from other early intervention studies that have shown that participation levels have a strong positive effect on outcomes (Barnett, 1995; Ramey et al., 1992). Because only 3% of the study children reached this level of participation, further analyses were conducted using conservative statistical adjustments for the limited number of children; under these conditions, no significant outcomes were associated with participation (Judkins et al., 2008). In future research, participation needs to continue to be examined for its potential significant effect on positive child outcomes.

Analyses for the second research question indicated that the *CLIO* combined curricula had a statistically significant positive additive effect on parents' interactive reading and responsiveness to their children, compared with the groups that were assigned to the *CLIO* preschool curricula. In addition, parents in the groups assigned to the *CLIO* combined curricula spent a significantly greater percentage of time discussing child literacy during the parent education groups. However, the analyses showed that the *CLIO* combined curricula did not add value to measures of children's emergent literacy or social competence above and beyond the *CLIO* preschool curricula. The researchers also found that impacts on children did not vary as a function of children's ethnicity or home language; similar analyses on parents' ethnicity and on instructional outcomes were not conducted.

It is disappointing that the *CLIO* study did not produce significant child outcomes from the comparison of children in the experimental groups with children in the control group, given the study's scope and expense. These results, however, need to take into account several factors. Although the *CLIO* study has characteristics associated with quality research, especially randomization of sites and the identification of curricula that had evidence of effectiveness, several situations potentially limited the findings. Staff participation in training was not a requirement for participation in the research study and one in five staff members did not attend any training on the curricula; others attended only one of the two summer training sessions. Sites were spread across the 48 contiguous states, limiting the amount of on-site consultation possible. Program directors were often stretched thin with multiple responsibilities. Consequently, staff training was not as intensive as was most likely needed to bring about change in instructional strategies or in the classroom environment. These situations are reflected in the evaluations of program fidelity that resulted in average ratings of 3 on a scale of 1–5, in which 5 indicated strong fidelity. Whether different outcomes could have been obtained with a more intensive intervention in which staff members were provided more individualized and intensive training with more opportunities for the developers to ensure that procedures were implemented as intended remains unknown.

In light of the moderate program fidelity among project sites, the *CLIO* study investigated whether child and parenting outcomes were better in project sites that had higher program fidelity (Judkins et al., 2008). Though the study's report concluded that there was no evidence to suggest a relationship between program fidelity in the classrooms and child outcomes, the researchers acknowledged that this relationship is difficult to determine for several reasons. First, teachers in the *CLIO* study were expected to make changes to many aspects of their classrooms, making the expression of fidelity in a single measure possibly inappropriate. Also, the two interventions differed in their expectations for the classrooms, the control group implemented some of the same practices as the experimental groups, and fidelity was measured without controlling for preexisting teacher skills, leaving open the question of whether program fidelity influenced outcomes.

Before it can be concluded that these interventions cannot be successful in bringing about meaningful change in children's language and literacy development, several factors need to be considered. First, the early childhood intervention should provide a more intensive program, offering services for at least 30 hours per week. This time frame ensures that there is adequate time for explicit and informal instruction and is consistent with the intensity of most other effective studies of early childhood intervention. Second, before beginning the intervention, teaching staff should have obtained skills in early childhood education, ensuring that the essentials of setting up and managing an early childhood classroom are present. Third, key administrative staff should be knowledgeable of the program and able to support and supervise staff.

Two components of most family literacy programs are parent education and parent–child literacy interaction time. Though these two components are considered essential to the overall program's success, they have been the subjects of considerably less research attention than early childhood interventions. Most programs have used the parent education time to address a wide range of parenting topics, such as concerns with immigration. The parent–child literacy time activities have also varied widely across programs. Because of the strong relation between parent–child interactions and later school success, ways to positively influence parent behavior remains a high priority. Parents can be reached essentially through home-based programs or through groups in center-based settings. There remains a strong rationale to continue to examine what is needed during parent education to make these types of parent interventions an effective way of enhancing children's language and literacy.

In summary, although the *CLIO* evaluation of Even Start produced several significant findings that suggest the efficacy and additive value of the *CLIO* combined curricula for parents, the published results are not impressive in regard to outcomes for children. Though this latter finding is discouraging, these data should result in reflection on what is needed to bring about significant changes in child language and literacy development, with an intense focus on the quality of the intervention itself; the professional development, coaching, and feedback needed for quality implementation; and the development of realistic expectations for parents in terms of modifying their interactions with their children.

Other family literacy programs designed to help parents develop their children's early literacy skills also are available throughout the United States. Some of these programs use the four-component model (National Center for Family Literacy, 2012) and others focus primarily on children and parenting. At times, studies of these programs have shown positive outcomes for children and parents, but these studies have generally not used rigorous research design.

CONCLUSION

Interest in reaching children by providing parent education, both in parent groups and in the home, remains very high. The PPACA calls for $1.5 billion, the largest infusion of money into home-visiting services in the history of the United States. The federal government is requiring that states use evidenced-based programs when receiving these funds, a stipulation that is driving the intensive reviews of the effects on home-visiting programs on parent and child outcomes. Because home visits and parent groups need not be mutually exclusive services by an agency, programs might find advantages in considering combinations of these interventions.

The field continues to examine the questions of who can benefit from these services, what services are most effective, how long services need to be provided, and to what intensity services should be provided. These questions are not new, but answers to them have been difficult to attain. Nevertheless, the need to assist parents in promoting their children's early language and literacy development has even more urgency in the 21st century as a result of the increased need for a literate society and the accumulated evidence on the detrimental social effects of low educational attainment (Campbell et al., 2008; Levin, Belfield, Muennig, & Rouse, 2000; Muennig et al., 2009). Furthermore, because a large percentage of adults in the United States who have low literacy skills are raising children under the age of 5, the question of how best to support these parents must become a priority. Many of these adults are also English language learners, thus increasing the risk for their children to have reading difficulties and low academic achievement (Farver, Lonigan, & Eppe, 2009; Van Horn & Forlizzi, 2004).

Research shows that highly targeted interventions with parents can bring about significant positive outcomes in children's literacy and language development. But not all interventions work, and the next generation of research must attempt to understand the barriers to success. Programs that are more broad based and focus on a wide range of parent and child needs may be stretched too thin, lacking the resources for adequate staff training and follow-up coaching to ensure the interventions are implemented as intended. One of the continuing concerns about services for parents, especially those that are provided in the home, is whether or not the services are provided as intended, both in terms of content and intensity. Extremely few studies have examined the fidelity of parent education or home visits in regard to literacy instruction. Those studies that have done so reveal concerns about fidelity to the program model. The consequences of not providing a strong focus on fidelity to the intervention can result in erroneous conclusions about the potential for positive parent and child outcomes. The lack of assessment instruments has been a limitation in assessing program fidelity, but increased attention to this need since 2010 should provide the field with several options for assessing the quality and fidelity of home visiting.

Another compelling concern is that very few parents participate in these programs (Goldenberg, 2001). Engaging parents in either parent-education groups or home-visiting programs is often difficult and is not always successful. Data show that the number of parents who participate in parent-education groups is a very small percentage of eligible parents. Parents who might be most in need of learning ways to help their children might be least inclined to participate; they also may have fewer means, such as transportation and child care, to participate in out-of-home education programs. In addition, considerations of data that suggest the value of mixed intervention models that combine home-visiting and center-based programs will need to take into account the low participation of immigrant families in center-based interventions for preschool children.

Social conditions at the beginning of the 21st century suggest that home-visiting services will continue to carry the responsibility of reaching many parents. Although research findings have led to questions about the effectiveness of home visits as a means to increase children's school readiness, the professional response should be to focus on those strategies and interventions that can make a significant difference. At the same time, future research must also extend the examination of other interventions to expand the available options for reaching families. For example, some research suggests that intervention programs should not focus narrowly on language and literacy development but should also include social and emotional development in order to maximize positive outcomes (Sylva, Totsika, Ereky-Stevens, & Crook, 2008). The documentation of interactions among children's language development, social behaviors, and cognitive development emphasizes the need to consider multiple child domains in early intervention.

Because the strategies for reaching out to parents of preschool children are usually provided either in the home or in other settings such as preschools, there is a need for more intensive research on variables for both parent education and home-visiting programs. The implementation science literature provides direction for this research, noting the importance of operationalizing the intervention, developing implementation teams that can provide support for the intervention, creating methods for developing competent staff, and establishing organizational supports for practitioners and organizations (Fixsen, Naoom, Blasé, Friedman, & Wallace, 2005; Naoom, Van Dyke, Fixsen, Blasé, & Villagomez, 2012). Participant recruitment and participation, program quality and fidelity, and outcomes must all be examined as part of any future funding efforts. Parent education through home-visiting services has a history of being rediscovered by new generations of professionals and researchers. Researchers, educators, and policy makers should not wait for another generation to obtain the knowledge needed to make this strategy a more effective way of assisting parents and their young children. Using the recommendations of the implementation science literature (Fixsen et al., 2005; Naoom et al., 2012) has the potential to support major advances in parent education and home-based services.

REFERENCES

Achenbach, T. (1992). *Manual for the Child Behavior Checklist/2–3 and 1992 Profile*. Burlington: University of Vermont Department of Psychiatry.

Achenbach, T. (1991). *Manual for the Child Behavior Checklist/4–18 and 1991 Profile*. Burlington: University of Vermont Department of Psychiatry.

Aram, D., & Levin, I. (2001). Mother-child joint writing in low SES: Sociocultural factors, maternal mediation and emergent literacy. *Cognitive Development, 16*(3), 831–852.

Aram, D., & Levin, I. (2004). The role of maternal mediation of writing to kindergartners in promoting literacy in school: A longitudinal perspective. *Reading and Writing: An Interdisciplinary Journal, 17*(4), 387–409.

Baker, A.J.L., & Piotrkowski, C.S. (1996). *The Home Instruction Program for Preschool Youngsters: An innovative program to prevent academic underachievement: Implementation study*. (Final report grant no. R215A00090 to the U.S. Department of Education). New York, NY: The National Council of Jewish Women Center for the Child.

Baker, A.J.L., Piotrkowski, C.S., & Brooks-Gunn, J. (1998). The effects of the Home Instruction Program for Preschool Youngsters (HIPPY) on children's performance at the end of the program and one year later. *Early Childhood Research Quarterly, 13*(4), 571–588.

Barnett, W.S. (1995). Long-term effects of early childhood programs on cognitive and school outcomes. *The Future of Children, 5*(3): 25–30.

Bayley, N. (1969). *Manual for the Bayley Scales of Infant Development*. San Antonio, TX: Harcourt Assessment.

Bennett, K.K., Weigel, D.J., & Martin, S.S. (2002). Children's acquisition of early literacy skills: Examining family contributions. *Early Childhood Research Quarterly, 17*(3), 295–317.

Berlin, L.J., O'Neal, C.R., & Brooks-Gunn, J. (1998). What makes early intervention programs work? The program, its participants, and their interaction. *Zero to Three, 18*, 4–15.

Blom-Hoffman, J., O'Neil-Pirozzi, T.M., & Cutting, J. (2006). Reading Together, Talk Together: The acceptability of teaching parents to use dialogic reading strategies via videotaped instruction. *Psychology in the Schools, 43*(1), 71–78.

Bradley, R.H., & Gilkey, B. (2002). The impact of the Home Instructional Program for Preschool Youngsters (HIPPY) on school performance in 3rd and 6th grades. *Early Education and Development, 13*(3), 301–311.

Briesch, A.M., Chafouleas, S.M., Lebel, T.J., & Blom-Hoffman, J.A. (2008). Impact of videotaped instruction in dialogic reading strategies: An investigation of caregiver implementation integrity. *Psychology in the Schools, 45*(10), 978–993.

Brooks-Gunn, J., & Markham, L. (2005). The contribution of parenting to ethnic and racial gaps in school readiness. *The Future of Children, 15*(2), 139–168.

Burgess, S. (1997). The role of shared reading in the development of phonological awareness: A longitudinal study of middle to upper class children. *Early Child Development and Care, 127–128*, 191–199.

Bus, A.G., van IJzendoorn, M.H., & Pellegrini, A.D. (1995). Joint book reading makes for success in learning to read: A meta-analysis on intergenerational transmission of literacy. *Review of Educational Research, 65*(1), 1–21.

Caldera, D., Burrell, L., Rodriguez, K., Crowne, S.S., Rohde, C., & Duggan, A. (2007). Impact of a statewide home visiting program on parenting and on child health and development. *Child Abuse & Neglect, 31*(8), 829–852.

Campbell, F.A., & Ramey, C.T. (1994). Effects of early intervention on intellectual and academic achievement: A follow-up study of children from low-income families. *Child Development, 65*(2), 684–698.

Campbell, F.A., Wasik, B.H., Pungello, E., Burchinal, M., Barbarin, O., Kainz, K., & Sparling, J. (2008). The effects of early educational intervention on young adult outcomes: A replication study. *Early Childhood Research Quarterly, 23*(4), 452–466.

Drotar, D., Robinson, J., Jeavons, L., & Lester Kirchner, H. (2009). A randomized, controlled evaluation of early intervention: The *Born to Learn* curriculum. *Child: Care, Health & Development, 35*(5), 643–649

Dunn, L.M., & Dunn, L.M. (1997). *Peabody Picture Vocabulary Test–Third Edition (PPVT-III)*. Circle Pines, MN: American Guidance Service.

Farver, J.A.M., Lonigan, C.J., & Eppe, S. (2009). Effective early literacy skill development for young Spanish-speaking English language learners: An experimental study of two methods. *Child Development, 80*(3), 703–719.

Fitton, L., & Gredler, G. (1996). Parental involvement in reading remediation with young children. *Psychology in the Schools, 33*(4), 325–332.

Fixsen, D.L., Naoom, S.F., Blasé, K.A., Friedman, R.M., & Wallace, F. (2005). *Implementation research: A synthesis of the literature.* Tampa: University of South Florida, Louis de la Parte Florida Mental Health Institute, National Implementation Research Network.

Goldenberg, C. (2001). Making schools work for low-income families in the 21st century. In S.B. Neuman & D.K. Dickenson (Eds.), *Handbook of early literacy research* (pp. 211–231). New York, NY: Guilford Press.

Gomby, D.S. (2012). Family literacy and home visiting programs. In B.H. Wasik (Ed.), *Handbook of family literacy* (2nd ed., pp. 103–117). New York, NY: Routledge.

Haney, M., & Hill, J. (2004). Relationships between parent-teaching activities and emergent literacy in preschool children. *Early Child Development and Care, 174*(3), 215–228.

Harding, K., Galano, J., Martin, J., Huntington, L., & Schellenbach, C.J. (2007). Healthy Families America effectiveness: A comprehensive review of outcomes. *Journal of Prevention & Intervention in the Community, 34*(1–2), 149–179.

Hart, B., & Risley, T.T. (1995). *Meaningful differences in the everyday lives of young American children.* Baltimore, MD: Paul H. Brookes Publishing Co.

Healthy Families America. (2012). Retrieved from http://healthyfamilies america.org

Henderson, G., & Garcia, A. (1973). The effects of parent training program on the question-asking behavior of Mexican-American children. *American Educational Research Journal, 10*(3), 193–201.

Hockenberger, E.H., Goldstein, H., & Haas, L.S. (1999). Effects of commenting during joint book reading by mothers with low SES. *Topics in Early Childhood Special Education, 19*(1), 15–27.

Home Instruction for Parents of Preschool Youngsters (HIPPY) International. (2012). *About us.* Retrieved from http://www.hippyusa.org

Hood, M., Conlon, E., & Andrews, G. (2008). Preschool home literacy practices and children's literacy development: A longitudinal analysis. *Journal of Educational Psychology, 100*(2), 252–271.

Johnson, J. (2009). *State-based home visiting: Strengthening programs through state leadership.* New York, NY: National Center for Children in Poverty.

Judkins, D., St.Pierre, R., Gutmann, B., Goodson, B., von Glatz, A., Hamilton, J.,...Rimdzius, T. (2008). *A study of Classroom Literacy Interventions and Outcomes in Even Start* (NCEE 20084028). Washington, DC: U.S. Department of Education, Institute of Education Sciences, National Center for Education Evaluation and Regional Assistance.

Kaufman, A.S. (1983). *Kaufman Assessment Battery for Children (K-ABC).* Circle Pines, MN: American Guidance Service.

Landsverk, J., Carrilio, T., Connelly, C.D., Ganger, W., Slymen, D., Newton, R., Leslie, L., & Jones, C. (2002). *Healthy Families San Diego clinical trial: Technical report.* San Diego: The Stuart Foundation, California Wellness Foundation, State of California Department of Social Services, Office of Child Abuse Prevention.

Lazar, I., Darlington, R., Murray, H., Royce, J., & Snipper, A. (1982). Lasting effects of early education: A report from the Consortium for Longitudinal Studies. *Monographs of the Society for Research in Child Development, 47*(2–3).

Leach, D., & Siddall, W. (1990). Parental involvement in the teaching of reading: A comparison of hearing reading, paired reading, pause, prompt, praise, and direct instruction methods. *British Journal of Educational Psychology, 60*(3), 349–355.

Levenstein, P. (1989). Which homes? A response to Scarr and McCartney (1988). *Child Development, 60*(2), 514–516.

Levin, H., Belfield, C., Muennig, P., & Rouse, C. (2000). *The price we pay: Eco-*

nomic and social consequences of inadequate education. Washington, DC: Brookings Institution Press.

Lonigan, C.J., & Whitehurst, G.J. (1998). Relative efficacy of parent and teacher involvement in a shared-reading intervention for preschool children from low-income backgrounds. *Early Childhood Research Quarterly, 13*(2), 263–290.

Love, J.M., Kisker, E.E., Ross, C., Raikes, H., Constantine, J., Boller, K.,...Vogel, C. (2005). The effectiveness of Early Head Start for 3-year-old children and their parents: Lessons for policy and programs. *Developmental Psychology, 41*(6), 885–901.

Missouri Department of Elementary and Secondary Education. (1999). *Missouri Assessment Program (MAP)*. Monterey, CA: McGraw-Hill. Available from http://dese.mo.gov/divimprove/assess/tech

Morgan, L., & Goldstein, H. (2004). Teaching mothers of low socioeconomic status to use decontextualized language during storybook reading. *Journal of Early Intervention, 26*(4), 235–252.

Muennig, P., Schweinhart, L., Montie, J., & Neidell, M. (2009). Effects of a prekindergarten educational intervention on adult health: 37-year follow-up results of a randomized controlled trial. *American Journal of Public Health, 99*(8), 1431–1437.

Naoom, S.F., Van Dyke, M., Fixsen, D.L., Blasé, K.A., & Villagomez, A.N. (2012). Developing implementation capacity of organizations and systems to support effective uses of family literacy programs. In B.H. Wasik (Ed.), *Handbook of family literacy* (2nd ed., pp. 447–464). New York, NY: Routledge.

National Center for Family Literacy. (2012). *Program profiles*. Retrieved from http://www.famlit.org

National Early Literacy Panel. (2008). *Developing early literacy: Report of the National Early Literacy Panel*. Washington, DC: National Institute for Literacy.

Necoechea, D.M. (2007). Children at-risk for poor school readiness: The effect of an early intervention home visiting program on children and parents. *Dissertation Abstracts International: Section A. Humanities and Social Sciences, 68*(6-A), 2311.

Neuman, S.B. (1996). Children engaging in storybook reading: The influence of access to print resources, opportunity, and parental interaction. *Early Childhood Research Quarterly, 11*(4), 495–513.

Nurse-Family Partnership. (2011). *Program history*. Retrieved from http://www.nursefamilypartnership.org

Olds, D.L., Henderson, C.R., & Kitzman, H. (1994). Does prenatal and infancy nurse home visitation have enduring effects on qualities of parental caregiving and child health at 25 to 50 months of life? *Pediatrics, 93*(1), 89–98.

Olds, D.L., Kitzman, H., Cole, R., Robinson, J., Sidora, K., Luckey, D.W.,...Holmberg, J. (2004). Effects of nurse home-visiting on maternal life course and child development: Age 6 follow-up results of a randomized trial. *Pediatrics, 114*(6), 1550–1559.

Olds, D.L, Kitzman, H., Hanks, C., Cole, R., Anson, E., Sidora-Arcoleo, K.,... Bondy, J. (2007). Effects of nurse home visiting on maternal and child functioning: Age 9 follow-up of a randomized trial. *Pediatrics, 120*(4), 832–845.

Olds, D.L., Robinson, J., Pettitt, L., Luckey, D.W., Holmberg, J., Ng, N.S.,... Henderson, C.R., Jr. (2004). Effects of home visits by paraprofessionals and by nurses: Age 4 follow-up results of a randomized trial. *Pediatrics, 114*(6), 1560–1568.

Parents as Teachers. (2010). *Vision/mission history.* Retrieved from http:// www.parentsasteachers.org

Parents as Teachers. (2011). *2010–2011 Affiliate Performance Report Data for Charts: Summary.* Retrieved from http://www.parentsasteachers.org /images/stories/documents/US_APR_1pgr_2010-2011_v.1.pdf

Patient Protection and Affordable Care Act of 2010, PL 111-148, 42 U.S.C. §§ 18001 *et seq.*

Pfannenstiel, J.C. (1999). *School Entry Assessment Project: Report of findings.* Retrieved from Missouri Department of Elementary and Secondary Education web site: http://dese.mo.gov/eel/el/seap.pdf

Pfannenstiel, J.C., Seitz, V., & Zigler, E. (2002). Promoting school readiness: The role of the Parents as Teachers Program. *NHSA Dialog: A Research-to-Practice Journal for the Early Intervention Field, 6,* 71–86.

Ramey, C.T., Bryant, D.M., Wasik, B.H., Sparling, J.J., Fendt, K.H., & LaVange, L.M. (1992). Infant Health and Development Program for low birth weight, premature infants: Program elements, family participation, and child intelligence. *Pediatrics, 89*(3), 454–465.

Rasinski, T.V., & Stevenson, B. (2005). The effects of Fast Start reading, a fluency-based home involvement reading program, on the reading achievement of beginning readers. *Reading Psychology, 26*(2), 109–125.

Resetar, J.L., Noell, G.H., & Pellegrin, A.L. (2006). Teaching parents to use research-supported systematic strategies to tutor their children in reading. *School Psychology Quarterly, 21*(3), 241–261.

Sénéchal, M., & LeFevre, J.A. (2002). Parental involvement in the development of children's reading skill: A five-year longitudinal study. *Child Development, 73*(2), 445–460.

Sénéchal, M., LeFevre, J.A., Thomas, E.M., & Daley, K.E. (1998). Differential effects of home literacy experiences on the development of oral and written language. *Reading Research Quarterly, 33*(1), 96–116.

St.Pierre, R.G., Ricciuti, A.E., & Rimdzius, T. (2005). Effects of a family literacy program on low-literate children and their parents: Findings from an evaluation of the Even Start Family Literacy Program. *Developmental Psychology, 41*(6), 953–970.

St.Pierre, R.G., Ricciuti, A.E., Tao, F., Creps, C., Swartz, J., Lee, W.,...Rimdzius, T. (2003). *Third national Even Start evaluation: Program impacts and implications for improvement.* Washington, DC: U.S. Department of Education, Planning and Evaluation Service, Elementary and Secondary Education Division.

St.Pierre, R.G., Swartz, J.P., Gamse, B., Murray, S., Deck, D., & Nickel, P. (1995). *National evaluation of the Even Start Family Literacy Program: Final report.* Washington, DC: U.S. Department of Education, Planning and Evaluation Service, Elementary and Secondary Education Division.

Sweet, M.A., & Appelbaum, M.L. (2004). Is home visiting an effective strategy? A meta-analytic review of home visiting programs for families with young children. *Child Development, 75*(5), 1435–1456.

Sylva, K., Totsika, V., Ereky-Stevens, K., & Crook, C. (2008). Training parents to help their children read: A randomized control trial. *British Journal of Educational Psychology, 78*(3), 435–455.

Taverne, A., & Sheridan, S.M. (1995). Parent training in interactive book reading: An investigation of its effects with families at risk. *School Psychology Quarterly, 10*(1), 41–64.

Toomey, D. (1993). Parents hearing their children read: A review. Rethinking the lessons of the Haringey Project. *Educational Research, 35*(3), 223–236.

U.S. Department of Health and Human Services, Administration for Children and Families. (2012). *Maternal, Infant, and Early Childhood Home Visiting (MIECHV) Program.* Retrieved from http://www.acf.hhs.gov/earlychildhood/index.html

Van Horn, B., & Forlizzi, L. (2004). Assessment of adult literacy skills. In B.H Wasik (Ed.), *Handbook of family literacy* (pp. 567–586). Mahwah, NJ: Lawrence Erlbaum Associates.

Wagner, M., Cameto, R., & Gerlach-Downie, S. (1996). *Intervention in support of adolescent parents and their children: A final report on the Teen Parents as Teachers Demonstration.* Menlo Park, CA: SRI International.

Wagner, M.M. & Clayton, S.L. (1999). The Parents as Teachers program: Results from two demonstrations. *The Future of Children, 9*(1), 91–115.

Wasik, B.H., & Bryant, D.M. (2001). *Home visiting: Procedures for helping families* (2nd ed.). Newbury Park, CA: Sage Publications.

Wasik, B.H., & Bryant, D. (2009). Essentials of funding home visiting programs: Hiring, training, and supervising home visitors. Commentary. *Social Policy Report, 23*(4), 15.

Wasik, B.H., & Herrmann, S. (2004). Family literacy programs: Development, theory, and practice. In B.H. Wasik (Ed.), *Handbook of family literacy* (pp. 1–22). Mahwah, NJ: Lawrence Erlbaum Associates.

Wasik, B.H., Ramey, C.T., Bryant, D.M., & Sparling, J.J. (1990). A longitudinal study of two early intervention strategies: Project CARE. *Child Development, 61*(6), 1682–1696.

Wasik, B.H., Villagomez, A., Berry, S., & Mulholkar, P. (2012). Home visiting programs. In J.L. Roopnarine & J.E. Johnson (Eds.), *Approaches to early childhood education* (6th ed., pp. 79–96). Boston, MA: Pearson Education.

Whitehurst, G.J., Arnold, D.S., Epstein, J.N., Angell, A.L., Smith, M., & Fischel, J.E. (1994). A picture book reading intervention in day care and home for children from low-income families. *Developmental Psychology, 30*(5), 679–689.

Whitehurst, G.J., Zevenbergen, A.A., Crone, D.A., Schultz, M.D., Velting, O.N., & Fischel, J.E. (1999). Outcomes of an emergent literacy intervention from Head Start through second grade. *Journal of Educational Psychology, 91,* 261–272.

Zigler, E., Pfannenstiel, J.C., & Seitz, V. (2008). The Parents as Teachers program and school success: A replication and extension. *The Journal of Primary Prevention, 29*(2), 103–120.

8

Significant Differences

Identifying the Evidence Base for Promoting Children's Early Literacy Skills in Early Childhood Education

Christopher J. Lonigan and Anne E. Cunningham

C hildren's developing early literacy skills are important precursors to the development of skilled reading (Whitehurst & Lonigan, 1998). Preschool children with more skills in the domains of print knowledge, phonological processing, and oral language develop conventional reading and writing skills earlier and better than children with fewer of these skills (Lonigan, Schatschneider, & Westberg, 2008a). From the early educational experiences of children through later development, there is substantial continuity of reading-related skills (Duncan et al., 2007), suggesting that early childhood is a critically important period for acquisition of these skills and for attempts to alter the course of children's development to increase the probability of later academic success.

Acknowledgment: Preparation of this work was supported, in part, by grants to Christopher J. Lonigan from the *Eunice Kennedy Shriver* National Institute of Child Health and Human Development (HD052120, HD060292) and the Institute of Education Sciences (R305F100027, R305A090169) and by grants to Anne E. Cunningham from the Institute of Education Sciences (R305A090183, R305J030037). The views expressed herein are those of the authors and have not been reviewed or approved by the granting agencies.

A primary goal of the National Early Literacy Panel (NELP) was to synthesize the research on early literacy skills to identify those intervention strategies with evidence of effectiveness, and a secondary goal was to identify any gaps in the current research base concerning children's early literacy skills. In this chapter, we begin by summarizing what NELP (2008) reported concerning early childhood programs. We then move beyond the evidence that NELP uncovered and provide a broader review of evidence for the effectiveness of different components of early childhood education practices, with a focus on the acquisition of language and literacy skills.

NELP reported effect sizes for the various analyses that it conducted. An effect size is a measure of the amount of impact that a treatment has on an outcome. Effect sizes are expressed in standard deviation units. For example, an effect size of 0.33 means that the experimental group gained one third of a standard deviation more than the control group on the outcome measure (e.g., a treatment group–control group difference of 5 standard-score points on a typical standardized measure, such as a vocabulary test, that has a standard deviation of 15). Effect sizes (ES) are usually thought to be small if they are less than 0.30, moderate if they are in the 0.30–0.79 range, and large if they are more than 0.80 (Cohen, 1988). Because effect sizes are standardized, they can be compared across studies. In a meta-analysis, effect sizes are computed for each study, and these are then averaged across studies to determine how much impact some treatment had upon particular outcomes. Generally, the more studies that are combined in a particular analysis, the more reliable the effect size is.

NELP's review of interventions to promote the development of early literacy skills included an initial meta-analysis of 33 published research reports concerning the effects of early childhood programs (Molfese & Westberg, 2008). Of these 33 reports, 10 involved different presentations of results of the Abecedarian Project, which were combined to yield a single independent estimate of the effects of the project; consequently, NELP's meta-analysis ultimately included 24 unique studies of early childhood programs. Statistically significant and positive effects for these programs overall were obtained on the outcomes of readiness (ES = 1.22, p = .04, 3 studies) and spelling (ES = 0.34, p = .01, 3 studies). There were not statistically significant overall effects of these programs on the outcomes of alphabet knowledge (ES = 0.23, p = .27, 4 studies), cognitive ability (ES = 0.35, p = .13, 4 studies), oral language (ES = 0.13, p = .17, 12 studies), or reading (ES = 0.75, p = .19, 9 studies).

The programs included in the review by Molfese and Westberg (2008) were diverse in terms of their foci and populations studied. Of the 16 early childhood education studies that included reading or oral language outcomes, 9 involved preschool children (3 of those studies were randomized controlled trials). The preschool studies examined 1) the outcomes of the Abecedarian Project (1 unique study; see the General Effectiveness of Early Childhood Education section later in this chapter), 2) the results of a multisensory language intervention (1 study), 3) the effects of a literacy-focused curriculum (1 study), 4) the effects of adding parent involvement to preschool participation (1 study), 5) the effects of participating in a language-enriched child care environment (1 study), 6) the effects of including children with and without disabilities in preschool classes (versus attending noninclusive classes; 2 studies), and 7) the effects of attending a bilingual preschool program (versus not attending any preschool; 2 studies).

When the reports of studies conducted with children in preschool were compared with reports of studies conducted with children in kindergarten, statistically significant and positive effects were obtained in the kindergarten studies for both oral language (ES = 0.28, p = .01, 3 studies) and reading (ES = 0.88, p = .03, 7 studies) but not in the preschool studies for either oral language (ES = -0.03, p = .67, 9 studies) or reading (ES = 0.33, p = .60, 2 studies). Additional analyses indicated that programs with a literacy focus were more likely to obtain positive effects on reading outcomes than were programs without a literacy focus and that programs with professional development support yielded larger effects than programs without such support, although this effect was not independent of the literacy-focus effect because all of the programs with a literacy focus also included professional development.

NELP's review was restricted to a summary of studies published in peer-reviewed journals. Although such a restriction provides a level of quality control for the studies included, it can create a problem if much of the literature on a particular topic is not published in peer-reviewed journals. This, to some extent, was the case for the review of studies of early childhood education programs. Many such studies are not published in peer-reviewed journals, fail to meet research-design standards that allow strong conclusions, or both. Consequently, whereas the summary provided by Molfese and Westberg (2008) indicated a positive effect of early childhood programs, it could not address many questions of primary interest to early childhood educators at the preschool level, such as questions of the more general effectiveness of early childhood education programs, the effectiveness of different preschool curricula, and the value of professional development for early childhood educators. In the remainder of this chapter, we focus on the state of the evidence concerning these three questions and discuss issues related to center-based early childhood education in terms of standards of practice and empirical support for specific instructional activities and developmentally appropriate practice.

GENERAL EFFECTIVENESS OF
EARLY CHILDHOOD EDUCATION

Although a relatively large number of studies have outcomes for children who participated in various early childhood interventions and education services (e.g., see review by Camilli, Vargas, Ryan, & Barnett, 2010), the majority of these studies were of the type in which the effects of participation in the educational activities could not be disentangled from the effects of the conditions or circumstances that led to some children receiving educational services whereas others did not. Most of these studies have involved some form of a quasi-experimental design in which obtained differences between children exposed or not exposed to some early childhood education program were used as estimates of the effects of the intervention program. However, the reasons that some children attend some early childhood programs whereas other children do not were determined by factors beyond the control of the study. In studies of this type, it is likely that there are differences between participants and non-participants on both measured and unmeasured variables before program participation (e.g., parents of participants differ on the services they seek or select for their children). This high probability of differences before program participation makes it impossible to determine whether outcome differences after program participation were the result of the program or the initial differences between participants and nonparticipants.

Studies that do allow attribution of measured differences to program variation offer evidence of the general effectiveness of early childhood programs on children's early academic skills. For instance, the evaluation of Early Reading First, a program of the U.S. Department of Education that granted funding to provide increased resources and professional development for early childhood education programs, found small positive effects on children's print knowledge, using a regression-discontinuity design (Jackson et al., 2007). Wong, Cook, Barnett, and Jung (2008) demonstrated that the five state-funded preschool programs they examined using this research approach had positive effects on 4-year-old children's skills, with the largest effects on measures of print knowledge and the smallest effects on measures of oral language. In addition, the Head Start Impact Study (U.S. Department of Health and Human Services [DHHS], 2010), a randomized evaluation of the effects of attending Head Start for 3- and 4-year-olds, found small positive effects on 3-year-old children's alphabet knowledge, phonological awareness, and vocabulary skills and on 4-year-old children's alphabet knowledge, spelling, and vocabulary skills at the end of one year of program participation. Overall, the evidence base indicates that some academic-related skills develop faster for children who attend various federal- or state-funded early childhood education programs than they do for children who do not attend these programs, at least in the short term.

Evaluation of Early Childhood Education in Historical Context

Two programs of research concerning early childhood programs have particular significance regarding demonstrations of effectiveness of early childhood education because of their placement in historical context and their impact on the field. One of these, the Abecedarian Project, was included in NELP's meta-analysis of early childhood programs. The other, the Perry Preschool Project, was not included in NELP's meta-analysis because the majority of the reports of this project were not published in peer-reviewed journals. The primary details of these projects are summarized in the sections that follow.

Abecedarian Project   In this project, 120 high-risk infants and their families were identified through screening social services agencies and public health clinics. Four cohorts of children from 1972 to 1977 were recruited for the study. Upon recruitment, children were randomly assigned to a child care/preschool condition or to a minimal-contact control condition (only 111 of the 120 children were retained in the study after assignment). Children assigned to the preschool condition began attending the program's child care center at an average age of 4.4 months. The child care center was available 8 hours a day, 5 days a week, for 50 weeks a year. In the child care program, children were exposed to a curriculum designed to promote cognitive, language, perceptual-motor, and social skills development when they were infants and toddlers. A greater curricular emphasis was placed on language and early literacy skills during their preschool years than during the infant and toddler period. Families of children assigned to the control condition were provided with iron-fortified formula, disposable diapers, and access to on-demand social work services. When all of the children reached school age, a second randomization was conducted, with one half of the children and families assigned to a school treatment group that received 3 additional years of educational support and the other half of children and families assigned to a school control group that received no additional support. Children enrolled in the project as infants were followed until early adulthood.

Reports of the effects of the Abecedarian Project represent a broad range of academic and socioemotional outcomes. Initial results indicated that children who participated in the child care/preschool program experienced higher levels of growth in overall cognitive functioning than did children in the control condition. In general, the effects of the early childhood component of the project were substantially greater than the effects of the school component of the project across all outcomes. At age 12 (Campbell & Ramey, 1994) and age 14 (Campbell & Ramey, 1995), children who participated in the early childhood component of the project had maintained their advantages in cognitive functioning over children in the early childhood control condition, and they scored significantly higher on measures of reading and math achievement than did the children in the early childhood control condition. In addition, by age 14 years, children who had participated in the early childhood component of the project had been retained in grade significantly less than had children in the early childhood control condition (31% versus 55% had been retained in grade), and they were significantly less likely than children in the early childhood control condition to have received special education services (25% versus 48% had received special education services). When the participants were 21 years of age, 94% of them took part in a follow-up assessment (Campbell, Ramey, Pungello, Sparling, & Miller-Johnson, 2002). Results indicated higher verbal and full-scale IQ scores, higher scores on measures of reading and math achievement, more years of school completed, high rates of college enrollment, higher levels of occupational attainment, lower levels of teen parenthood, and lower levels of substance use for the participants who had received the early childhood education component of the project compared with participants who were in the early childhood control condition.

Perry Preschool Project   In this project, 128 children who were 3 and 4 years old, living in Ypsilanti, Michigan, and judged to be at significant risk because of family socioeconomic demographics were randomly assigned to intervention or control conditions. Beyond the initial cohort of children, only 3-year-old children were recruited for the project. Recruitment took place in five waves, from Fall 1962 through Fall 1965. Of the 128 children originally selected for the project, 123 completed the preschool program. Children assigned to the intervention group participated in preschool classes for 2½ hours each day for 30 weeks a year. In each year, four teachers served the 20–25 children participating that year. Over the course of the project, the project staff developed what ultimately became known as the *High/Scope Curriculum* (Hohmann & Weikart, 2002; Schweinhart, Barnes, & Weikart, 1993). All teachers in the program were certified in elementary, early childhood, or special education. With the exception of the 4-year-old children who entered the program in 1962, children attended the preschool program for 2 consecutive years, beginning at 3 years old. In addition, these children and their families received weekly 1½-hour home visits that were designed to involve parents in the educational process and to have teachers and parents conduct aspects of the curriculum at home.

The children were followed into adulthood, such that data collection occurred from the point of entry into the program until participants were 27 years of age (Schweinhart et al., 1993). Indeed, a remarkable feature of the Perry Preschool Project was its ability to limit attrition across the 24 years of data collection. Like the reports on the effects of the Abecedarian Project, reports of the Perry Preschool Project provide information across a wide range of outcomes. In terms of academic outcomes, children who were in the intervention group outscored children in the control group on measures of IQ at the end preschool and 1–2 years following participation in the preschool program, depending on the specific IQ measure used, and these children's language skills were higher than those of children in the control group at the end of preschool. Results on reading-, math-, and language-achievement tests that were administered to children from age 7 to age 14 (measures were completed when children were 7, 8, 9, 10, and 14 years old) tended to favor children who had participated in the preschool program; however, these differences reached conventional levels of statistical significance only for the assessments conducted when children were 14. Surveys administered when the participants were 19 years old indicated that those who had attended the preschool program outscored those from the control group on various kinds of knowledge (e.g., occupational knowledge, health information) and on general literacy ability. However, this superiority was not evident when the participants were 27 years old. Participants who had attended the preschool program also completed more years of school, were more likely to graduate from high school, and had spent fewer years in special education classes than participants in the control condition.

Despite its significance in demonstrating the potential of early childhood education, the Perry Preschool Project is not without some complications that reduce its relevance for specific questions concerning early childhood education. To begin, although the study included randomization to condition, intentional postassignment transfers of children between groups weakened the design element most needed to draw valid causal influences. For example, although children were initially assigned randomly to two undesignated groups, group membership was adjusted to create balance on socioeconomic variables, intellectual performance, and sex ratios. These groups were then randomized to condition. Children from the same family were switched into the same condition, and two children were switched from the intervention group to the control group because their mothers could not participate in program activities.

The Perry Preschool Project is often cited as providing support for the effectiveness of the *High/Scope Curriculum;* however, the nature of the study does not allow any effects to be attributed to the *High/Scope Curriculum*. First, the curriculum was not finalized until the last year of the project; therefore, only the last cohort of children was exposed to a curriculum that could be labeled the *High/Scope Curriculum*. Second, in addition to preschool participation, all children in the intervention condition received weekly home visits; therefore, any obtained effects could be due to preschool participation, home visits (which by themselves have been shown to be effective for promoting children's academic and socioemotional skills—e.g., Olds et al., 2002), or the combination of the two. Finally, the counterfactual in the study was no participation in preschool or home visits (i.e., a no-treatment control group). The use of this type of counterfactual does not allow specific attribution of any obtained effects to the specific program used. The specific curriculum used is completely confounded with participation in preschool and home visits. Therefore, the obtained results could be because of preschool participation, the curriculum used, or both. A later study conducted by Schweinhart, Weikart, & Larner (1986) that compared the *High/Scope Curriculum* with the *Direct Instruction Strategies for Teaching Arithmetic and Reading (DISTAR) Curriculum* (Bereiter & Englemann, 1966) and traditional nursery school found few differences between the groups on children's cognitive or academic outcomes.[1] Overall, although this body of research further suggests that high-quality early childhood education in general can provide significant benefits for children, the methodological weaknesses limit any valid conclusion that can be made about the effectiveness of the *High/Scope Curriculum*.

EFFECTIVENESS OF SPECIFIC EARLY CHILDHOOD CURRICULA

The knowledge that early childhood education in general can promote early skill development and that different funding streams for early childhood education yield positive results is important for policy makers. However, such information does not provide the answers to questions about which *specific* programs yield positive effects for children—the types of questions that most interest practitioners. In addition, many of the early childhood programs included in NELP's review are too idiosyncratic to the populations served to be broadly applicable or are too expensive for implementation on a wide scale (e.g., the Abecedarian program). Although NELP provided evidence of effectiveness for specific instructional practices such as teaching phonological awareness and print-related skills (Lonigan, Schatschneider, & Westberg, 2008b) and

---

[1]As in the Perry Preschool Project, postassignment shifting of children in the groups and unclear procedures for assignment of the first of three waves of children substantially weakened the validity of any causal conclusions from the study.

shared reading (Lonigan, Shanahan, & Cunningham, 2008), answers to questions about the effectiveness of specific early childhood curricula can provide a means of identifying existing packages that can be used to enhance children's academic outcomes. As previously indicated by the summary of NELP's review, only a small number of published studies have examined the effects of specific early childhood curricula using the types of research designs that allow valid conclusions about the effects of the curricula studied. In fact, only one of the studies included in NELP's meta-analysis of early childhood programs concerned a specific curriculum, and it was conducted with kindergarten children. Therefore, other research must be examined to guide the field's current understanding of the effectiveness of preschool curricula.

Review of Preschool Curricula by the What Works Clearinghouse

In contrast to the methods used by NELP, the What Works Clearinghouse (WWC) of the Institute of Education Sciences, U.S. Department of Education, reviewed all available evidence—both published and unpublished—concerning the efficacy of specific early childhood curricula. The review criteria of WWC require that studies use either a randomized controlled trial or one of a few quasi-experimental designs that allow unbiased estimates of the causal impacts of a curriculum. Evidence for a curriculum was included in the review if the studies of that curriculum could be classified as "meets standards" or "meets standards with reservations." In the former category were studies that used randomized trials or regression-discontinuity designs that had attrition levels that were within the acceptable limit. In the latter category were studies that used 1) quasi-experimental designs in which the treatment and control groups were matched on the variables used to measure outcomes before the target- and control-curriculum conditions were implemented and that had attrition within an acceptable limit or 2) randomized trials or regression-discontinuity designs with attrition beyond the acceptable limit. These standards increase the likelihood that estimates of the effects of a curriculum—relative to the comparison curriculum—can be unambiguously attributed to the curriculum. Randomization ensures that groups are equal on measured and unmeasured variables before implementation because individuals end up in groups by chance. In regression-discontinuity studies, group assignment is based on scoring above or below a single known score that can be modeled accurately in the analyses. Matched quasi-experimental studies demonstrate that groups were equal on at least measured characteristics before implementation.

The WWC's Early Childhood Education Review (n.d.) involved a comprehensive search for reports on studies of preschool curricula that were produced between 1986 and August 2010 (the last update for early childhood education reports). For the preschool literacy or comprehensive curricula for which WWC conducted searches for evidence, 35 curricula had no studies concerning evidence of effectiveness, 15 had only studies that failed to meet evidence standards, and 13 had one or more studies that met evidence standards with or without reservations. WWC uses a tiered system for rating effects that takes into account the effect demonstrated by a study, replications of the effect, and the evidence standard met by the included studies. Within an outcome domain, curricula can be rated as having "no/mixed effects" (i.e., either no effects or some positive effects and some negative effects), "potentially positive/ potentially negative effects" (i.e., at least one study showing an overall positive/negative effect but studies that do not meet the highest evidence standards), or "positive/negative effects" (i.e., two or more studies showing an overall positive/negative effect and at least one study that meets the highest evidence standards).

A summary of the WWC's classification of effectiveness for the 13 preschool literacy or comprehensive curricula with studies that met evidence standards is shown in Table 8.1.[2] As can be seen in the table, seven of the curricula had studies that indicated that the children exposed to the target curriculum did not have better outcomes in the oral language, print knowledge, phonological processing, or early reading/early writing domain than did children exposed to the comparison curricula used in the studies. One target curriculum had evidence of a potentially negative effect on children's oral language skills relative to the comparison curriculum. Of the remaining five curricula, when compared with the respective control curricula used in the studies, one had evidence of a potentially positive effect on children's print knowledge, two had evidence of a potentially positive effect on children's oral language and print knowledge, one had evidence of a potentially positive effect on children's phonological awareness and early reading and writing, and one had evidence of positive effects on children's oral language, print knowledge, and phonological awareness.[3]

---

[2] Two early math curricula also had interpretable studies and showed positive effects on children's math skills.

[3] The first author of this chapter is the senior author of the *Literacy Express Comprehensive Preschool Curriculum* (Lonigan, Clancy-Menchetti, Phillips, McDowell, & Farver, 2008) rated by the WWC. He had no involvement with the WWC's review of the studies conducted on the curriculum; however, he was involved in conducting the studies of the curriculum that were reviewed by the WWC.

Table 8.1. Summary of ratings of early childhood curricula reviewed by What Works Clearinghouse

Curriculum	Emergent literacy outcome domain			
	Oral language	Print knowledge	Phonological awareness	Early reading/ writing
Bright Beginnings (Pellin & Edmonds, 2001)	0	+	0	N/A
Creative Curriculum (Trister Dodge, Colker, & Heroman, 2002)	0	0	0	0
Curiosity Corner (Success for All Foundation, 2003)	0	0	0	N/A
Direct Instruction Strategies for Teaching Arithmetic and Reading (DISTAR) Curriculum (Bereiter & Englemann, 1966)	0	0	N/A	N/A
Doors to Discovery (Wright Group/ McGraw-Hill, 2001)	+	+	0	N/A
Headsprout Early Reading (Layng, Twyman, & Stikeleather, 2003)	+	+	N/A	N/A
Ladders to Literacy (Notari-Syverson, O'Connor, & Vadasy, 1998)	-	0	0	N/A
Let's Begin with the Letter People (Abrams & Company, 2000)	0	0	0	N/A
Literacy Express Comprehensive Preschool Curriculum (Lonigan, Clancy-Menchetti, Phillips, McDowell, & Farver, 2008)	++	++	++	N/A
Ready, Set, Leap! (Leap-Frog School House, 2003)	0	0	0	0
Sound Foundations (Byrne & Fielding-Barnsley, 1991	0	0	+	+
Tools of the Mind (Bodrova & Leong, 2007)	0	N/A	0	N/A
Waterford Early Reading Program (Waterford Institute, 2001)	0	0	N/A	N/A

Note: All information is based on intervention reports from the What Works Clearinghouse (n.d.).

Key: ++ = positive effect; + = potentially positive effect; 0 = no discernible effect or mixed effect; - = potentially negative effect; N/A = no study meeting evidence standards included an outcome measure in this domain.

Studies by the Preschool Curriculum Evaluation Research Consortium

The Preschool Curriculum Evaluation Research Consortium (PCER-C; 2008) obtained results similar to those of the WWC review. PCER-C was a group of 12 independent investigators who were funded by the Institute of Education Services to evaluate the effects of early childhood curricula. In this group's studies, 15 preschool curricula or combinations of curricula were evaluated using randomized controlled designs. Some studies of individual curricula in PCER-C were among those included in the studies reviewed by WWC. Of these 15 evaluations, only 2 curricula or curriculum combinations showed clear evidence of positive effects at the end of pre-school relative to the comparison curricula used in the studies.[4] Moreover, only the combination of curricula generated effects on young children's literacy and language development. More specifically, the combination of the *DLM Early Childhood Express* curriculum (SRA/McGraw-Hill, 2003a) with the *Open Court Reading Pre-K* curriculum (SRA/McGraw-Hill, 2003b) resulted in statistically significant positive effects on measures of oral language, print knowledge, phonological awareness, and math, with effect sizes ranging from 0.32 to 0.68 for significant effects. Given that the positive effects provide evidence for the effectiveness of the combined curriculum, it should be noted that the results are not indicative of the effectiveness of either curriculum in isolation.

Additional Published Evaluations of Specific Early Childhood Curricula

Subsequent to the searches conducted for the WWC reviews and the PCER-C studies, some additional evaluations of preschool curricula, focused on children's language and literacy, were published. Bierman et al. (2008) reported the results on an evaluation of their *Head Start Research-Based, Developmentally Informed (REDI)* curriculum. In their study, 356 children attending one of 44 Head Start classrooms received either the standard curriculum in use in the centers (either the *High/Scope Curriculum* or *The Creative Curriculum* [Trister Dodge, Colker, & Heroman, 2002]) or that standard curriculum enhanced with the *REDI* curriculum's components—which included activities designed to promote oral language, phonological awareness, and print knowledge skills—and the *Promoting Alternative Thinking Strategies* curriculum (Domitrovitch, Cortes, & Greenberg, 2007). Reported analyses indicated

---

[4]The other study demonstrating positive effects in the PCER-C evaluated a math curriculum (*Pre-K Math*), with effect sizes of 0.44 and 0.96 on the two statistically significant math outcomes.

that children in classrooms using the *REDI* curriculum scored significantly higher than children in the standard curriculum classrooms on measures of vocabulary, phonological awareness, emotion recognition, and three scores from the Challenging Situations Task, with effect sizes ranging from 0.15 to 0.39 for significant effects. A potential concern with the Bierman et al. study, however, is a mismatch between the unit of assignment and the unit of analysis reported in statistical results. That is, centers were assigned to condition[5]; however, the analyses were conducted at the classroom level, which may have inflated statistical significance.

Wilcox, Gray, Guimond, and Lafferty (2011) conducted a randomized-assignment study to examine the effectiveness of their *Teaching Early Literacy and Language (TELL)* curriculum. In the study, 118 children who were 4 years old and had developmental speech and/or language impairments were randomly assigned to attend one of 32 classrooms, in which either the *TELL* curriculum was used or business was conducted as usual. Because three teachers withdrew before the conclusion of the study, analyses were based on 29 classrooms. Although the classrooms included children with and without speech and language impairments, the results focused solely on effects for students with developmental speech or language problems. Reported analyses indicated that children in classrooms using the *TELL* curriculum outscored children in the business-as-usual, control-condition classrooms on measures of phonological awareness, letter sounds, mean length of utterance, and a vocabulary measure aligned with the vocabulary targeted by the *TELL* curriculum, with effect sizes ranging from 0.47 to 1.32 for significant effects.

Raver and colleagues (Raver et al., 2011; Raver at al., 2009) reported the results of their Chicago School Readiness Project (CSRP), which did not involve an academic-skills-focused curriculum but did include measures of children's academic and socioemotional outcomes. The study employed a cluster-randomized design in which outcomes for children in classrooms using a traditional early childhood curriculum were compared with outcomes for children in classrooms in which teachers implemented an adaptation of Webster-Stratton's *Incredible Years* behavior-management curriculum (e.g., Webster-Stratton, Reid, & Hammond, 2004) for which teachers received 30 hours of training. In addition to the curriculum and training, each CSRP classroom was provided with a mental health consultant who provided teachers with weekly in-class coaching on use of the strategies outlined in the cur-

---

[5]Although the number of centers is not reported by Bierman et al. (2008), it appears that there were between 18 and 26 centers included in the project, based on their description of the distribution of classrooms in each condition from small (1–2 classrooms per center) and large (3–5 classrooms per center).

riculum, consultation regarding specific children, and a stress-reduction workshop; the consultant also provided direct intervention services for children identified as having the most significant behavior problems. A total of 18 Head Start sites (35 classrooms) were randomized to either the CSRP intervention or a business-as-usual control condition; classes in the control condition received a classroom aide to control for the addition of the mental health consultant in the CSRP classrooms. Outcomes for 467 children in these 18 Head Start sites demonstrated statistically significant differences favoring children in CSRP classrooms, compared with children in control classrooms, on receptive language, letter naming, and early math skills, with effect sizes ranging from 0.34 to 0.54 for significant effects. Children in CSRP classrooms also had lower levels of teacher-reported internalizing and externalizing problems and higher levels of executive functioning skills than did children in control classrooms.

Finally, Fantuzzo, Gadsden, and McDermott (2011) reported a cluster-randomized evaluation of their *Evidence-Based Program for Integrated Curricula* (*EPIC*) in 80 Head Start classrooms assigned to either the *EPIC* or business-as-usual control condition (classrooms were using the *DLM* curriculum prior to the study). *EPIC* was developed by adapting evidence-based instructional strategies for language, literacy, and math, including interactive shared reading, small-group instruction for phonological awareness and print knowledge, and mathematics. *EPIC* also included instruction in four preschool learning behaviors (i.e., attention control, frustration tolerance, group learning, task approach) and integrated assessments, a learning community model of professional development for teachers, and a home component that linked the instructional focus of classroom and home. End-of-year outcomes for 1,107 3- and 4-year-old children from 70 Head Start classrooms (10 classrooms dropped out of the study) revealed statistically significant and positive impacts of *EPIC* on a researcher-designed measure of listening comprehension and mathematics, with effect sizes of 0.17 and 0.22, respectively.

Long-Term Effects of Early Childhood Curricula

As previously described, early studies such as the Abecedarian Project (e.g., Campbell & Ramey, 1994, 1995; Campbell et al., 2002) and the Perry Preschool Project (Schweinhart et al., 1993) provided evidence of long-term positive effects of early childhood education programs in general. Longitudinal evaluations of preschool curricula further substantiate the potential for long-term benefits for children. First, the PCER-C curricular combination (i.e., *DLM Early Childhood Express* and *Open Court Pre-K*) that generated evidence of positive effects on oral language, print knowledge, and phonological awareness at the end of preschool extended positive effects on reading, phonological awareness, and oral language to the end of kindergarten as well, with effect sizes ranging from 0.41 to 0.76 for significant effects (PCER-C, 2008). Furthermore, two additional curricula evaluated in the PCER-C, *Curiosity Corner* (Success for All Foundation, 2003) and the *Early Literacy and Learning Model* (Wood, 2002), had significant positive effects at the end of kindergarten (effect sizes ranging from 0.34 to 0.44 for significant effects), despite the fact that no positive effects were found at the end of preschool (PCER-C, 2008). In addition, in follow-up evaluations of children exposed to the *Sound Foundations* phonological awareness curriculum (Byrne & Fielding-Barnsley, 1991), which was found to have potentially positive effects according to the WWC classification, Byrne and colleagues (Byrne & Fielding-Barnsley, 1993, 1995; Byrne, Fielding-Barnsley, & Ashley, 2000) reported sustained positive effects on children's reading skills 6 years after preschool. In contrast, the Head Start Impact Study (U.S. DHHS, 2010) reported that the positive impacts of Head Start participation on children's academic and cognitive skills were no longer present 1 or 2 years after children's participation.

Common Features of Effective Early Childhood Education Curricula

In the various sources reviewed in this chapter, a common feature of the curricula with demonstrated positive or potentially positive effects on preschool children's early language and literacy skills is that they involve specific, explicit, and sequenced instructional activities that target certain components of language and literacy. *Doors to Discovery* (Wright Group/McGraw-Hill, 2001) focuses on teaching specific vocabulary and other early literacy skills—including phonological awareness, concepts about print, alphabet knowledge, writing, and comprehension—through the use of a set of instructional routines surrounding eight thematic units that include big books and activities. Instructional strategies for this curriculum include teacher-directed activities, such as cloze techniques, think-aloud activities, and scaffolding, as well as opportunities for children to apply skills independently. *Headsprout Early Reading* (Layng, Twyman, & Stikeleather, 2003) is a computer-based curriculum that uses explicit instruction in letter–sound correspondence, phonological awareness, beginning phonics, vocabulary, and early reading skills in a set of interactive modules that adjust to a child's learning profile and needs. *Sound Foundations* focuses exclusively on teaching children phoneme-identity skills in the context of small-group games in which children need to identify a specific phoneme in a word (e.g., matching words starting with the same phoneme, coloring pictures of words that start with a specific phoneme).

The *Literacy Express, REDI, TELL,* and *EPIC* curricula all include some combination of the types of activities empirically demonstrated to improve children's language (Lonigan, Shanahan, & Cunningham, 2008) or code-related (Lonigan et al., 2008b) skills. For instance, all four curricula make use of a variant of dialogic reading (e.g., see Arnold, Lonigan, Whitehurst, & Epstein, 1994; Lonigan & Whitehurst, 1998; Whitehurst et al., 1988) to promote the development of children's oral language skills. In dialogic reading, the teacher uses picture books as an organizing prop to assess, teach, and model vocabulary and grammar. For example, instead of just reading a book, the teacher asks children to label objects, actions, and attributes of items pictured in the book by responding to *wh-* questions (e.g., What is this called? What is she doing? What color is the duck?). Once children have learned the vocabulary of the book, the teacher encourages children to help with the reading of the book by using open-ended prompts (e.g., What's happening on this page? Why do you think she is doing this?). During this process, the teacher uses repetition, correction, and expansions of children's answers to model increasingly complex verbal exchanges.

The *Literacy Express, REDI, TELL,* and *EPIC* curricula also include developmentally sequenced and explicit activities and games, as well as center-based tasks that teach children phonological awareness skills and print-related knowledge, such as letter names, letter sounds, and writing. It should be noted that for these curricula, the code-based instruction, and in particular the phonological awareness instruction, is conducted with small groups of children. Given that NELP's report found evidence supporting small-group instruction for code-based interventions (Lonigan et al., 2008b), the more powerful effects generated by these curricula are likely due in part to the alignment with the research base.

Overall, with the use of randomized designs, it has become more evident that certain curricula, and moreover, certain common curricular features, are in fact causally related to substantial language and literacy growth in young children. Given this emerging body of research, it is unfortunate that the early childhood curricula most commonly utilized in Head Start and other early childhood education programs that serve children who are at risk for academic difficulties have no causally interpretable evidence regarding effective early childhood curricula. That is, the *High/Scope Curriculum* and *The Creative Curriculum* are used in between 59% and 70% of these classrooms (Jackson et al., 2007; U.S. DHHS, 2005). To promote more optimal rates of early language and literacy development on a large scale, early childhood education programs should look to the more rigorous research base as they determine which curriculum packages to adopt.

EFFECTIVENESS OF EARLY CHILDHOOD EDUCATION PROFESSIONAL DEVELOPMENT

In part because of the increased emphasis placed on educational objectives for early childhood programs, there has been an increase in calls for more and higher quality professional development for the early childhood educator work force (e.g., Pianta, 2006; Ramey & Ramey, 2006). As with preschool curricula, however, the depth of the research base for identifying and selecting effective professional development programs or models is shallow. A number of studies have attempted to affect preschool teachers' instructional behaviors related to language and early literacy within the classroom via professional development, in-class coaching, or both; yet many of these studies have employed the types of study designs that make interpretation difficult. Nonetheless, they provide some direction to early childhood educators regarding effectiveness of professional development.

Quasi-Experimental Studies of Early Childhood Education Professional Development

A number of quasi-experimental studies on professional development have provided mixed results. Dickinson and Caswell (2007) examined the effects of providing Head Start teachers with a professional development program in the form of a course on language and literacy for which the teachers were given college credit. The course consisted of two 3-day sessions. The first session occurred in late October or early November, and the second session occurred in late February. Support for teachers applying the newly learned material was provided between sessions. Classroom observations of the 30 teachers who took the course indicated significant growth from fall to spring in classroom characteristics and instructional activities related to language and literacy compared with observations of the 40 teachers who did not take the course. Child outcomes were not reported, however, and that lack of information prevents attaching the model of professional development to the outcome of primary interest—improved outcomes for children. Although an earlier report of the project suggested positive effects on children (Dickinson & McCabe, 2001), insufficient information was provided in that report to determine if the effects could be attributed in part to the professional development.

Incorporating an analysis of effects on both teachers and children, Schwanenflugel et al. (2010) conducted a quasi-experimental study involving 22 teachers and 350 children that compared a business-as-usual control condition with a program that offered preschool teachers a range of literacy- and language-focused professional development components, including a summer institute, after-school workshops, and classroom support from preliteracy specialists. Although analyses suggested that children's early literacy and decoding skills were enhanced to a greater degree if their teacher had participated in some aspect of the professional development program, the greatest overall effects were observed for the full package of professional development. More specifically, children in classrooms in which teachers received the full program of professional development scored higher than children in the control group on language, phonological awareness, and letter–sound knowledge at the end of preschool. For the vocabulary outcome, children in classrooms in which teachers received one of the reduced versions of the professional development package had higher scores than did children in control classrooms. Overall, however, potential differences in schools, teachers, and children at the outset of the study make it difficult to attribute any of the observed differences to the specific components of professional development included.

Cusumano, Armstrong, Cohen, and Todd (2006) examined the effects of the *HeadsUp! Reading* professional development program, which is intended to support teachers' use of an explicit literacy-focused curriculum via a college-level course, with and without the addition of in-class literacy coaching. Jackson et al. (2006) also examined the effects of *HeadsUp! Reading* with and without coaching in a quasi-experimental study involving teachers self-selecting to participate in the program and coaching condition. Effects of the *HeadsUp! Reading* professional development program on child outcomes have been negligible. Cusumano et al. (2006) reported a significant impact of professional development on only one of three child early literacy outcome measures. The findings regarding the additional benefit of in-class coaching have been mixed, with limited effects observed on child outcomes but some indication of an impact on teachers. Results from both Cusumano et al. (2006) and Jackson et al. (2006) suggested that in-class coaching did not yield a significant impact on teacher or child outcomes; however, a more recent study (Armstrong, Cusumano, Todd, & Cohen, 2008) indicated that teachers who received in-class coaching demonstrated greater growth in their knowledge base, teaching skills, and reported confidence in use of the new instructional strategies relative to control teachers. It is unclear why effects of in-class coaching have not translated to child outcomes or consistently to teacher outcomes. Moreover, given the design of the studies, the few significant findings are again more parsimoniously interpreted as a result of preexisting differences at the outset of the studies than as a result of the type of professional development.

Promising results were reported by Landry, Swank, Smith, Assel, and Gunnewig (2006) from their quasi-experimental study of a large-scale, statewide initiative to improve children's language and literacy outcomes through professional development and in-class coaching. In this project, teachers from 20 Head Start programs were provided with 4 days of training before the start of the school year, 1 hour each week of in-class coaching, access to professional development staff throughout the year for problem solving, at least two site visits each year by training staff, and ongoing small-group professional development led by the site coordinator of coaches throughout the year. In the first year of the program, 500 teachers from the 20 Head Start programs received the training, and 250 teachers did not receive the training. In the second year of the program, all teachers received the training. Estimates of the impacts of the program on classroom observations and child outcomes were made by comparing classrooms of teachers who received the training in either the first or second year with the classrooms of teachers who did not receive the training in the first year. Landry et al. reported positive changes in teachers' instructional behaviors related to language and literacy, and greater growth in children's language, phonological awareness, and print knowledge skills. Unfortunately, selection criteria for teachers to receive or not receive the professional development were not reported, and insufficient information was reported to determine the degree of match between treated and untreated classrooms in terms of teachers or children, hence limiting the possibility of making strong causal conclusions from this study.

Randomized Studies of Early Childhood Education Professional Development

Given the shortcomings of the quasi-experimental research base on professional development, it is necessary to examine the results of several recent randomized studies that have evaluated the effectiveness of specific professional development programs for early childhood educators. Neuman and Cunningham (2009) investigated the effects of coursework-based language and literacy professional development with and without the addition of year-long, in-class literacy coaching on teachers' knowledge and practices in center- and home-based early childhood education settings. Participants from 304 sites were stratified by setting (168 were center-based) and randomly assigned to receive the course only or the course with coaching, or to be part of the control group. For teachers who received the course alone, no significant effects were found on any teacher outcomes. For teachers providing center-based early childhood education, those who received the course with coaching had significantly better language and literacy instructional practices than did those in the control group. Without the inclusion of child outcomes, however, the implications of this study for enhancing children's language and literacy development are limited.

Landry, Anthony, Swank, and Monseque-Bailey (2009) reported the results of a large multistate study in which they experimentally evaluated professional training and type of progress-monitoring assessments used by teachers. In their study, 262 early childhood educators from 158 schools in four states were randomly assigned to a business-as-usual control group or one of four experimental groups that varied both on 1) whether they used a pencil-and-paper progress-monitoring tool or a computerized version of the same progress-monitoring tool that provided immediate feedback and instructional suggestions based on each child's score and 2) whether teachers received in-class coaching or not. The types of progress-monitoring conditions and the coaching conditions were fully crossed in the four experimental groups, and all teachers in the four experimental groups were provided with an online early literacy professional development course and supplemental materials. Observations in the classrooms of a randomly selected subset of teachers revealed substantial differences in teachers' classrooms and behaviors that were due to the professional development support. There was evidence that both coaching and access to computerized progress monitoring had larger impacts on classroom quality and instructional behavior than did no coaching and pencil-and-paper progress monitoring. Results suggest, however, that the type of progress monitoring had a larger impact than did coaching across teacher outcomes. With respect to children's language and literacy outcomes, the results were complex, with many of the outcomes moderated by the state in which teachers taught and children's initial skills levels; there was little evidence that either coaching or computerized progress monitoring was consistently superior to no coaching or pencil-and-paper progress monitoring, respectively.

Although the experimental studies previously discussed examined professional development programs that included literacy coaching, a few other randomized evaluations have investigated whether coaching can enhance curriculum-focused professional development. Across the studies, the effects of coaching again appear to be somewhat limited. Assel, Landry, Swank, and Gunnewig (2006) randomly assigned preschool centers from Head Start, Title I, and universal pre-K programs to a control group or one of two literacy-focused curricula groups (i.e., *Let's Begin with the Letter People* [Abrams & Company, 2000]; *Doors to Dis-*

covery). Teachers received a 4-day summer workshop on the respective curriculum and were randomly assigned to receive in-class coaching or no literacy coaching. Although Assel et al. reported positive impacts of curriculum condition, they found no clear advantage of in-class coaching on growth in children's skills over the preschool year. That is, both positive and negative effects were observed and moderated by the child outcome measured, the type of preschool program, and the assigned curriculum. Similarly, Lonigan, Farver, Phillips, and Clancy-Menchetti (2011) randomly assigned Head Start and Title I preschool teachers to a business-as-usual control condition or to professional training for the *Literacy Express Comprehensive Preschool Curriculum* either as workshop training only or as workshop training with in-class coaching. Whereas all of the child outcome measures were positively impacted by the curriculum itself, the in-class coaching comparison had a significant effect on only one child outcome. Overall, both Assel et al. (2006) and Lonigan et al. (2011) demonstrated that implementation of an explicit and systematic literacy-focused curriculum generated the largest impacts on child outcomes, whereas the type of professional development used had limited impact.

Pianta and colleagues (e.g., Mashburn, Downer, Hamre, Justice, & Pianta, 2010; Pianta, Mashburn, Downer, Hamre, & Justice, 2008) have conducted studies of their web-mediated professional development program MyTeachingPartner (MTP),[6] which includes web-based materials describing classroom and teaching principles and activities theoretically and empirically linked to growth in language, literacy, and socioemotional outcomes for children, and a web-based library of annotated video clips of teachers enacting these activities in the classroom. In Pianta et al. (2008), 173 preschool teachers from 24 school districts were all given access to MTP but were randomly assigned at the district level to conditions with or without consultation about their own teaching practices via web-based feedback on submitted video exemplars of their classroom teaching. Classroom teaching practices and teacher–child interactions of teachers in districts that received consultation improved more across the preschool year than did the practices and interactions of teachers in school districts that had access to MTP but without consultation.

Mashburn et al. (2010) randomly assigned 41 school districts that included a total of 182 participating preschool teachers to one of three professional training conditions. One group of teachers received access

---

[6] To our knowledge, no study examining the overall impacts of this professional development program (e.g., a comparison to standard or alternative professional development) has been published to date. Consequently, it is currently unknown whether or not use of the program benefits children in terms of academic or socioemotional outcomes compared with standard, alternative, or no professional development practices.

to the web-based MTP activities with no access to the video exemplars; a second group of teachers received access to the MTP activities and the video library of high-quality teaching exemplars; and a third group of teachers received access to the MTP activities, access to the video library, and consultation. Mashburn et al. reported a comparison of child language and literacy outcomes for children in classrooms in which teachers received access to the MTP materials with and without consultation (outcomes for children in classrooms in which teachers received only the language and literacy activities were not included in the analyses). Across four child outcome measures and a composite measure, significant positive effects of the addition of consultation were reported only for children's receptive vocabulary scores.[7]

Finally, Powell, Diamond, Burchinal, and Koehler (2010)[8] randomly assigned 88 classrooms in 24 preschool centers from five Head Start programs to an experimental professional development condition or a control condition. The training focused on instructional practices to promote children's language, phonological awareness, and print knowledge skills. Teachers received a 2-day workshop, materials to use for phonological awareness and print knowledge activities, access to a hypermedia professional development course that included text and video exemplars of specific teaching practices, and either in-class coaching or remote coaching (i.e., teachers received feedback on submitted videos of their classroom practices). Teachers received an average of seven in-class coaching visits or feedback on seven submitted videotapes, depending on their coaching condition. Professional development activities, classroom observations, and child assessments were conducted within a semester (i.e., beginning of fall to midyear and midyear to end of spring). The overall quality and amount of language and literacy activities for teachers who received the training increased substantially more than did that of teachers in the control group. In addition, children in the classrooms of teachers who received the training experienced significantly higher gains in their print knowledge, phonological awareness, and writing skills than did children in classrooms of teachers who did not receive the professional development support; effect sizes ranged from 0.17 to 0.29 for statistically sig-

---

[7]Like Bierman et al. (2008), Mashburn et al. (2010) conducted their analyses at the classroom level. Because assignment took place at the school-district level, there was a mismatch between unit of assignment and unit of analysis that might have inflated levels of statistical significance.

[8]Wasik and Hindman (2011) have also reported a randomized evaluation of a professional development program. In their study, three Head Start centers were randomized to condition. Because center and assigned condition were confounded (i.e., one condition had a single center assigned), it is not possible to disentangle the effects of the professional development program from the center. Therefore, the study cannot provide meaningful evidence concerning the potential benefit of the professional development program.

nificant effects. There was no effect of professional development on children's oral language. However, remote coaching resulted in more gains on children's oral-language (ES = 0.13) and sound-matching skills than did on-site coaching, suggesting that coaching provided via technology can be a promising alternative to the more traditionally used model of in-class coaching.

The Current State of Professional Development and a More Promising Future

Although it is clear that professional development has positive effects on teachers' classroom practices, the research has not yet yielded compelling evidence that just providing early childhood educators with professional development will always result in better language and literacy outcomes for children. In particular, studies that have examined the effects of adding various levels of coaching to professional development have not found consistent differences on child outcome measures in favor of the enhanced professional development model (e.g., Assel et al., 2006; Landry et al., 2009; Lonigan et al., 2011; Mashburn et al., 2010). Moreover, only one study to date has shown unequivocal evidence that high-quality professional development results in increased language and literacy skills for children. This study (Powell et al., 2010) included professional training with a much higher level of intensity and support than teachers typically receive, including workshop training, the use of text- and video-based instructional materials concerning teaching practices, materials to support literacy-teaching activities, and in-class or remote coaching sessions that occurred frequently and for a sustained duration of time.

Consequently, at present there is limited support for a conclusion that substantial improvements in children's developmental trajectories can be obtained solely using professional development, especially models of development without a high degree of intensity, which are likely to be difficult for most early childhood education programs to implement successfully. It is unclear why research produces mixed and limited evidence regarding the effectiveness of professional development on child outcomes, especially given the more consistent link to some teacher outcomes. In part, it is difficult to disentangle the mechanisms that could potentially contribute to, or hinder, effective professional training models, for a variety of reasons. For instance, vast differences in duration (e.g., 2 months or weeks versus 2 years) or intensity (e.g., number and frequency of sessions), due to either the design of programs or self-selection by teachers, and differences in workshop or coaching models themselves (e.g., type of feedback provided, fidelity required, opportunities for collaborative reflection) could affect how professional development functions. Ongoing research efforts may clarify features of professional training that have positive effects on children's literacy and language development, beyond what can be generated by high-quality curricula. Recent reports (e.g., Cunningham, Platas, Boyle, Wheeler, & Raher, 2010; Diamond & Powell, 2011) have provided examples of the iterative development of refined professional development approaches that are intended to uncover and incorporate the active ingredients needed to support preschool teachers in implementing language and literacy instructional practices that can foster significant gains in children's skills. Ultimately, research that employs designs allowing for valid causal conclusions will need to be conducted on these theoretically driven professional development models.

EARLY CHILDHOOD EDUCATION AND DEVELOPMENTALLY APPROPRIATE PRACTICE

A significant influence on early childhood education has been the variation in the National Association for the Education of Young Children's (NAEYC) guide to developmentally appropriate practice. Therefore, it is important to consider this variation in light of the current evidence base for promoting children's language and literacy development in early childhood education. The most recent version of the guide (Copple & Bredekamp, 2009) and the organization's accompanying position statement (NAEYC, 2009), "Developmentally Appropriate Practice in Early Childhood Programs Serving Children from Birth through Age 8," provides guidance on 1) various teaching practices that take into account children's specific educational needs, developmental levels, and backgrounds; 2) a framework for matching instructional practices to those needs, strengths, and limitations; and 3) educational expectations based on developmental research and state accountability standards. Earlier versions of the NAEYC's position statement (1986) and guide to developmentally appropriate practice (Bredekamp & Copple, 1986, 1997), however, were far more prescriptive about appropriate types of instructional practices, including the limitation of a focus on skills in early childhood education. In general, an intentional instructional focus on specific skills was deemed "developmentally inappropriate."

Accumulating research evidence has highlighted that the developmental sequence of skills important for educational success originates before children begin formal schooling (e.g., Lonigan et al., 2008a; Whitehurst & Lonigan, 1998). Moreover, increasing research evidence indicates that significant gaps exist in the development of early language and literacy skills and subsequent educational achievement among children from different socioeconomic backgrounds (e.g., Hart

& Risley, 1995; Lonigan, Burgess, Anthony, & Barker, 1998). The body of research evidence also has demonstrated the value of early intervention for promoting development of these skills. In this regard, the NAEYC's position statement (2009) has evolved with the evolving research base concerning development, developmental outcomes, and effective early intervention. An unfortunate legacy of the early versions of the NAEYC's position statement (e.g., 1986), however, seems to be that a philosophy of early childhood education has been fixed in a vague constructivist, child-directed notion of learning that eschews a focus on specific skill outcomes and teacher-directed learning opportunities (as opposed to teacher-created environments in which a child selects the learning to be done). Teacher-directed instruction and a focus on specific skills quickly earn the pejorative label "developmentally inappropriate" and are deemed harmful to children's development.

Addressing Concerns About Possible Negative Impacts of Early Intervention

Objections to providing young children more or more directed early educational experiences are often rooted in concerns that early instruction in academic skills will result in negative consequences, particularly in the domains of children's socioemotional development and motivation. Time spent in early childhood education is, in fact, associated with lower scores on socioemotional indicators, such as higher levels of behavior problems (e.g., Belsky, 2001; Belsky et al., 2007; Magnuson, Ruhm, & Waldfogel, 2007). However, this effect is independent of the type of instructional practices, and the levels of behavior problems observed are not within a level of clinical significance (Belsky et al., 2007). Significant attention has been given to results from two nonexperimental studies that suggested a link between an academic focus in preschool and worse socioemotional outcomes for children. Stipek and colleagues (Stipek et al., 1998; Stipek, Feiler, Daniels, & Milburn, 1995) reported a variety of less positive motivational and behavioral outcomes for children who attended preschools with a more academic and didactic focus than did children who attended more child-centered preschools. As previously noted, however, nonexperimental studies that cannot establish the equivalence of groups before exposure to the variable of interest (in this case, more child-centered versus more didactic instructional activities) are open to alternative and equally plausible explanations. For instance, in the studies of Stipek and colleagues, factors associated with worse behavior outcomes (e.g., poverty, less skilled parenting) may be the same factors that determine if, when, for how long, and in what type of child care a child is enrolled.

There are a few experimental studies that have compared behavioral or socioemotional outcomes for early childhood programs with more versus less of a focus on systematic and explicit instruction. The study of the *REDI* curriculum (Bierman et al., 2008) demonstrated that children in classrooms using that curriculum had more positive outcomes on socioemotional indicators than did children in classrooms using only traditional early childhood curricula, indicating that having a focus on academic skills does not diminish efforts to support socioemotional development. Within the PCER-C (2008), measures of children's socioemotional development, including behavior problems, were collected at the end of preschool and at the end of kindergarten. Across the 14 different preschool curricula studied, there were no significant effects (negative or positive) on children's prosocial or problem behaviors at the end of preschool, and only one curriculum yielded significant negative effects on children's prosocial and problem behaviors at the end of kindergarten; however, the comparison curriculum for this effect was a skills-based curriculum, whereas the target curriculum involved a more child-centered approach, a fact that further warrants the claim that skills-based curricula are not more likely to affect socioemotional development negatively. Moreover, an absence of results for socioemotional outcomes was observed for each of the curricula that produced positive impacts on children's academic skills, all of which had an academic skills focus. Consequently, available causally interpretable evidence does not support a link between early childhood curricula with a systematic and explicit instructional focus (i.e., teacher directed) and negative socioemotional outcomes for children. Therefore, such curricula are in fact consistent with the most recent NAEYC position statement (2009) and guidelines on developmentally appropriate practice (Copple & Bredekamp, 2009), and early childhood programs can be assured that their use of evidence-based curricula can generate positive language and literacy outcomes without hindering socioemotional development.

CONCLUSION

The evidence base pointing to the continuity of development of skills important to academic success from early in the life of a child throughout his or her educational tenure is large and consistent in its findings (e.g., Duncan et al., 2007; Lonigan et al., 2008a). A significant number of children, however, arrive at school with skills that are on a developmental trajectory that places them at risk for educational difficulties both early on and throughout their school experiences. Evidence also points to the promise of early childhood education as a means to alter the developmental trajectories of many of these children, putting them on a footing to take full advantage of the educational opportunities available to them in school and throughout life. At present, however, there are only a few high-quality studies that identify specific instructional programs (i.e., preschool curricula) that are effective for promoting these developmental precursors to academic achievement.

It is unfortunate that there remains a mismatch between this promising evidence base, albeit still growing, and the prevalent use of the *High/Scope Curriculum* and *The Creative Curriculum*, neither of which have evidence of effectiveness, in Head Start and other early childhood education programs around the nation (Jackson et al., 2007; U.S. DHHS, 2005). Reasons for this mismatch between evidence and current practice are not entirely clear. One reason might be historical precedent. These two curricula were among the first full-fledged curricula to be available to early childhood educators. A second reason is likely the "philosophical rut" of early childhood education described previously. That is, both of these curricula have a clear focus on child-directed practices. However, as summarized in the previous section, there is no credible evidence that could be used to argue for a child-directed instructional approach over an instructional approach that makes use of appropriate teacher-directed, explicit, and systematic practices—either in terms of negative effects of the latter or clear positive outcomes of the former. In fact, studies of specific preschool curricula with evidence of effectiveness provide some support that the teacher-directed, explicit, and systematic approach is clearly superior to the child-directed approach. In many cases, the business-as-usual comparison condition for the target curriculum tested in a study was either *High/Scope* or *The Creative Curriculum* (e.g., Bierman et al., 2008; Lonigan et al., 2011; Wilcox et al., 2011). To be fair, however, the level of support and professional development for teachers using the target curricula was typically higher than that for teachers in the business-as-usual conditions, and it is not clear whether fidelity of implementation for the *High/Scope Curriculum* or *The Creative Curriculum* was at the same level as the target curricula or at a level that the developers of these curricula would consider sufficient. Regardless, it seems that there is a clear need for developers of curricula to demonstrate the effectiveness of their curricula and a need for the field to move toward use of preschool curricula with credible evidence of effectiveness as more of it becomes available.

As of 2012, whereas the research on curricula has demonstrated a few causally effective programs, there is too little evidence to suggest that adding professional development to existing early childhood programs will result in dramatically more positive outcomes. As summarized earlier, there is only a single study of professional development showing clear positive effects on children's outcomes, and the scope of that training was more substantial than the forms of professional development typically available to early childhood educators. In fact, the scope of the professional development provided in that study makes it difficult to distinguish from the materials and practices included in a typical curriculum evaluation study. Clearly, if there are to be continuing calls to improve the quality of early childhood education through the use of increased and improved professional development, substantially more research is needed to define the necessary content and scope of professional development to achieve that end and to develop and identify professional development programs with credible evidence of effectiveness.

As this research base grows, we believe that it is time to move beyond dichotomized views of developmentally appropriate versus developmentally inappropriate practice. Most teacher-directed instructional activities that have proved to be effective are consistent with current NAEYC guidelines on developmentally appropriate practice. That is, they are most often individualized to the needs and abilities of individual children, take into account children's backgrounds, involve significant scaffolding of children's skill development, and take into account children's attentional, motivational, and motoric strengths and limitations. The majority of these approaches involve relatively brief hands-on activities and games conducted individually or in small groups that fit well with models of teaching to individual children's needs and within their zone of proximal development. They use warm, sensitive, and responsive interactions, and appropriate varying of group sizes and instructional modalities. None of these instructional approaches fits a model of instruction that involves lengthy whole-group drill, choral responding, and worksheets, or that includes an expectation that all children will produce the same products. Most of these approaches are focused on balancing adult-guided and child-guided learning experiences and are designed to provide children with the tools necessary to take advantage of child-guided learning experiences. Such approaches therefore represent an appropriate way to foster the language and literacy development needed for young children to achieve future reading and academic success.

REFERENCES

Abrams & Company. (2000). *Let's Read with the Letter People*. Waterbury, CT: Author.

Armstrong, K., Cusumano, D.L., Todd, M., & Cohen, R. (2008). Literacy training for early childhood providers: Changes in knowledge, beliefs, and instructional practices. *Journal of Early Childhood Teacher Education, 29,* 297–308.

Arnold, D.S., Lonigan, C.J., Whitehurst, G.J., & Epstein, J.N. (1994). Accelerating language development through picture-book reading: Replication and extension to a videotape training format. *Journal of Educational Psychology, 86,* 235–243.

Assel, M.A., Landry, S.H., Swank, P.R., & Gunnewig, S. (2006). An evaluation of curriculum, setting, and mentoring on the performance of children enrolled in pre-kindergarten. *Reading and Writing: An Interdisciplinary Journal, 20*, 463–494.

Belsky, J. (2001). Emanuel Miller lecture: Developmental risks (still) associated with early child care. *Journal of Child Psychology & Psychiatry & Allied Disciplines, 42*, 845–859.

Belsky, J., Vandell, D.L., Burchinal, M., Clarke-Stewart, K.A., McCartney, K., Owen, M.T., & the NICHD Early Child Care Research Network. (2007). Are there long-term effects of early child care? *Child Development, 78*, 681–701.

Bereiter, C., & Englemann, S. (1966). *Teaching the disadvantaged child in the preschool.* Englewood Cliffs, NJ: Prentice-Hall.

Bierman, K.L., Domitrovich, C.E., Nix, R.L., Gest, S.D., Welsh, J.A., Greenberg, M.T.,...Gill, S. (2008). Promoting academic and social-emotional readiness: The Head Start *REDI* Program. *Child Development, 79*, 1802–1817.

Bodrova, E. & Leong, D.J. (2007). *Tools of the Mind: The Vygotskian approach to early childhood education* (2nd ed.). Upper Saddle River, NJ: Prentice-Hall.

Bredekamp, S., & Copple, C. (Eds.). (1986). *Developmentally appropriate practice for early childhood programs.* Washington, DC: National Association for the Education of Young Children.

Bredekamp, S., & Copple, C. (Eds.). (1997). *Developmentally appropriate practice for early childhood programs* (Rev. ed.). Washington, DC: National Association for the Education of Young Children.

Byrne, B., & Fielding-Barnsley, R.F. (1991). *Sound Foundations.* Artarmon, New South Wales, Australia: Leyden Educational Publishers.

Byrne, B., & Fielding-Barnsley, R.F. (1993). Evaluation of a program to teach phonemic awareness to young children: A 1-year follow-up. *Journal of Educational Psychology, 85*, 104–111.

Byrne, B., & Fielding-Barnsley, R. (1995). Evaluation of a program to teach phonemic awareness to young children: A 2- and 3-year follow-up and a new preschool trial. *Journal of Educational Psychology, 87*, 488–503.

Byrne, B., Fielding-Barnsley, R., & Ashley, L. (2000). Effects of preschool phoneme identity training after six years: Outcome level distinguished from rate of response. *Journal of Educational Psychology, 92*, 659–667.

Camilli, G., Vargas, S., Ryan, S., & Barnett, W.S. (2010). Meta-analysis of the effects of early education interventions on cognitive and social development. *Teachers College Record, 112*, 151–179.

Campbell, F.A., & Ramey, C.T. (1994). Effects of early intervention on intellectual and academic achievement: A follow-up study of children from low-income families. *Child Development, 65*, 684–698.

Campbell, F.A., & Ramey, C.T. (1995). Cognitive and school outcomes for high-risk African-American students at middle adolescence: Positive effects of early intervention. *American Educational Research Journal, 32*, 743–772.

Campbell, F.A., Ramey, C.T., Pungello, E., Sparling, J., & Miller-Johnson, S. (2002). Early childhood education: Young adult outcomes from the Abecedarian Project. *Applied Developmental Science, 6*, 42–57.

Cohen, J. (1988). *Statistical power analysis for the behavioral sciences* (2nd ed.). Hillsdale, NJ: Lawrence Erlbaum Associates.

Copple, C., & Bredekamp, S. (Eds.). (2009). *Developmentally appropriate practice in early childhood programs serving children from birth through age 8*. Washington, DC: National Association for the Education of Young Children Books.

Cunningham, A.E., Platas, L., Boyle, K., Wheeler, S., & Raher, K. (2010, June). *Providing opportunities to acquire the knowledge and practices necessary in supporting early literacy: The role of teacher study groups.* Paper presented at the Fifth Annual Institute of Education Sciences Conference, Washington, DC.

Cusumano, D.L., Armstrong, K., Cohen, R., & Todd, M. (2006). Indirect impact: How early childhood educator training and coaching impacted the acquisition of literacy skills in preschool students. *Journal of Early Childhood Teacher Education, 27*, 363–377.

Diamond, K.E., & Powell, D.R. (2011). An iterative approach to the development of a professional development intervention for Head Start teachers. *Journal of Early Intervention, 33*, 75–93.

Dickinson, D.K., & Caswell, L. (2007). Building support for language and early literacy in preschool classrooms through in-service professional development: Effects of the Literacy Environment Enrichment Program. *Early Childhood Research Quarterly, 22*, 243–260.

Dickinson, D.K., & McCabe, A. (2001). Bringing it all together: The multiple origins, skills, and environmental supports of early literacy. *Learning Disabilities Research and Practice, 16*, 186–202.

Domitrovitch, C.E., Cortes, R., & Greenberg, M.T. (2007). Improving young children's social and emotional competence: A randomized trial of the *PATHS* curriculum. *Journal of Primary Prevention, 28*, 67–91.

Duncan, G.J., Dowsett, C.J., Claessens, A., Magnuson, K., Huston, A.C., Klebanov, P.,...Japel, C. (2007). School readiness and later achievement. *Developmental Psychology, 43*, 1428–1446.

Fantuzzo, J.W., Gadsden, V.L., & McDermott, P.A. (2011). An integrated curriculum to improve mathematics, language, and literacy for Head Start children. *American Educational Research Journal, 48*, 763–793.

Hart, B., & Risley, T.R. (1995). *Meaningful differences in the everyday experience of young American children.* Baltimore, MD: Paul H. Brookes Publishing Co.

Hohmann, M., & Weikart, D.P. (2002). *Educating young children: Active learning practices for preschool and child care programs.* Ypsilanti, MI: High/Scope Press.

Jackson, B., Larzelere, R., St. Clair, L., Corr, M., Fichter, C., & Egertson, H. (2006). The impact of *HeadsUp! Reading* on early childhood educators' literacy practices and preschool children's literacy skills. *Early Childhood Research Quarterly, 21*, 213–226.

Jackson, R., McCoy, A., Pistorino, C., Wilkinson, A., Burghardt, J., Clark, M.,... Swank, P. (2007). *National evaluation of Early Reading First: Final report to Congress.* Washington, DC: Institute of Education Sciences.

Landry, S.H., Anthony, J.L., Swank, P.R., & Monseque-Bailey, P. (2009). Effectiveness of comprehensive professional development for teachers of at-risk preschoolers. *Journal of Educational Psychology, 101*, 448–465.

Landry, S.H., Swank, P.R., Smith, K.E., Assel, M.A., & Gunnewig, S.B. (2006). Enhancing early literacy skills for preschool children: Bringing a professional development model to scale. *Journal of Learning Disabilities, 39*, 306–324.

Layng, J., Twyman, J., & Stikeleather, G. (2003). *Headsprout Early Reading:* Reliably teaching children to read. *Behavioral Technology Today, 3*, 7–20.

LeapFrog School House. (2003). *Ready, Set, Leap!* Emeryville, CA: Author.

Lonigan, C.J., Burgess, S.R., Anthony, J.L., & Barker, T.A. (1998). Development of phonological sensitivity in two- to five-year-old children. *Journal of Educational Psychology, 90,* 294–311.

Lonigan, C.J., Clancy-Menchetti, J., Phillips, B.M., McDowell, K., & Farver, J.M. (2008). *Literacy Express Comprehensive Preschool Curriculum.* Tallahassee, FL: Literacy Express.

Lonigan, C.J., Farver, J.M., Phillips, B.M., & Clancy-Menchetti, J. (2011). Promoting the development of preschool children's emergent literacy skills: A randomized evaluation of a literacy-focused curriculum and two professional development models. *Reading and Writing, 24,* 305–337.

Lonigan, C.J., Schatschneider, C., & Westberg, L. (with the National Early Literacy Panel). (2008a). Identification of children's skills and abilities linked to later outcomes in reading, writing, and spelling. In *Developing early literacy: Report of the National Early Literacy Panel* (pp. 55–106). Washington, DC: National Institute for Literacy.

Lonigan, C.J., Schatschneider, C., & Westberg, L. (with the National Early Literacy Panel). (2008b). Impact of code-focused interventions on young children's early literacy skills. In *Developing early literacy: Report of the National Early Literacy Panel* (pp. 107–151). Washington, DC: National Institute for Literacy.

Lonigan, C.J., Shanahan, T., & Cunningham, A. (with the National Early Literacy Panel). (2008). Impact of shared-reading interventions on young children's early literacy skills. In *Developing early literacy: Report of the National Early Literacy Panel* (pp. 153–171). Washington, DC: National Institute for Literacy.

Lonigan, C.J., & Whitehurst, G.J. (1998). Relative efficacy of parent and teacher involvement in a shared-reading intervention for preschool children from low-income backgrounds. *Early Childhood Research Quarterly, 17,* 265–292.

Magnuson, K.A., Ruhm, C., & Waldfogel, J. (2007). Does prekindergarten improve school preparation and performance? *Economics of Education Review, 26,* 33–51.

Mashburn, A.J., Downer, J.T., Hamre, B.K., Justice, L.M., & Pianta, R.C. (2010). Consultation for teacher and children's language and literacy development during pre-kindergarten. *Applied Developmental Psychology, 14,* 179–196.

Molfese, V., & Westberg, L. (with the National Early Literacy Panel). (2008). Impact of preschool and kindergarten programs on young children's early literacy skills. In *Developing early literacy: Report of the National Early Literacy Panel* (pp. 189–209). Washington, DC: National Institute for Literacy.

National Association for the Education of Young Children. (1986). Position statement on developmentally appropriate practice in programs for 4- and 5-year-olds. *Young Children, 41,* 20–29.

National Association for the Education of Young Children. (2009). *Developmentally appropriate practice in early childhood programs serving children from birth through age 8: A position statement of the National Association for the Education of Young Children.* Retrieved from http://www.naeyc.org/files/naeyc/file/positions/PSDAP.pdf

National Early Literacy Panel. (2008). *Developing early literacy: Report of the National Early Literacy Panel.* Washington, DC: National Institute for Literacy.

Neuman, S.B., & Cunningham, L. (2009). The impact of professional development and coaching on early language and literacy instructional practices. *American Educational Research Journal, 46,* 532–566.

Notari-Syverson, A., O'Connor, R.E., & Vadasy, P.F. (1998). *Ladders to Literacy: A preschool activity book.* Baltimore, MD: Paul H. Brookes Publishing Co.

Olds, D.L., Robinson, J., O'Brien, R., Luckey, D.W., Pettitt, L.M., Henderson, C.R.,...Talmi, A. (2002). Home visiting by paraprofessionals and by nurses: A randomized, controlled trial. *Pediatrics, 110,* 486–497.

Pellin, B., & Edmonds, E. (2001). *Bright Beginnings, 1997–2001.* Charlotte, NC: Charlotte–Mecklenburg Schools.

Pianta, R.C. (2006). Standardized observation and professional development: A focus on individualized implementation and practices. In M. Zaslow & I. Martinez-Beck (Eds.), *Critical issues in early childhood professional development* (pp. 231–254). Baltimore, MD: Paul H. Brookes Publishing Co.

Pianta, R.C., Mashburn, A.J., Downer, J.T., Hamre, B.K., & Justice, L. (2008). Effects of web-mediated professional development on teacher-child interactions in pre-kindergarten programs. *Early Childhood Research Quarterly, 23,* 431–451.

Powell, D.R., Diamond, K.E., Burchinal, M.R., & Koehler, M.J. (2010). Effects of an early literacy professional development intervention on Head Start teachers and children. *Journal of Educational Psychology, 102,* 299–312.

Preschool Curriculum Evaluation Research Consortium. (2008). *Effects of preschool curriculum programs on school readiness* (NCER 2008-2009). Washington, DC: National Center for Education Research, Institute of Education Sciences, U.S. Department of Education.

Ramey, S.L., & Ramey, C.T. (2006). Creating and sustaining a high-quality workforce in child care, early intervention, and school readiness programs. In M. Zaslow & I. Martinez-Beck (Eds.), *Critical issues in early childhood professional development* (pp. 355–368). Baltimore, MD: Paul H. Brookes Publishing Co.

Raver, C.C., Jones, S.M., Li-Grining, C., Zhai, F., Bub, K., & Pressler, E. (2011). CSRP's impact on low-income preschoolers' preacademic skills: Self-regulation as a mediating mechanism. *Child Development, 82,* 362–378.

Raver, C.C., Jones, S.M., Li-Grining, C., Zhai, F., Metzger, M.W., & Solomon, B. (2009). Targeting children's behavior problems in preschool classrooms: A cluster-randomized controlled trial. *Journal of Consulting and Clinical Psychology, 77,* 302–316.

Schwanenflugel, P.J., Hamilton, C.E., Neuharth-Pritchet, S., Restrepo, M.A., Bradley, B.A., & Webb, M. (2010). *PAVEd for Success:* An evaluation of a comprehensive preliteracy program for four-year-old children. *Journal of Literacy Research, 42,* 227–275.

Schweinhart, L.J., Barnes, H.V., & Weikart, D.P. (1993). *Significant benefits: The High/Scope Perry Preschool Study through age 27.* Ypsilanti, MI: High/Scope Press.

Schweinhart, L.J., Weikart, D.P., & Larner, M.B. (1986). Consequences of three preschool curriculum models through age 15. *Early Childhood Research Quarterly, 1,* 15–45.

SRA/McGraw-Hill. (2003a). *DLM Early Childhood Express.* Desoto, TX: Author.

SRA/McGraw-Hill. (2003b). *Open Court Reading Pre-K.* Desoto, TX: Author.

Stipek, D.J., Feiler, R., Byler, P., Ryan, R., Milbuiw, S., & Salmon, J.M. (1998). Good beginnings: What difference does the program make in preparing young children for school? *Journal of Applied Developmental Psychology, 19*, 41–66.

Stipek, D., Feiler, R., Daniels, D., & Milburn, S. (1995). Effects of different instructional approaches on young children's achievement and motivation. *Child Development, 66*, 209–223.

Success for All Foundation. (2003). *Curiosity Corner.* Baltimore, MD: Author.

Trister Dodge, D., Colker, L.J., & Heroman, C. (2002). *The Creative Curriculum for Preschool* (4th ed.). Bethesda, MD: Teaching Strategies.

U.S. Department of Health and Human Services, Administration for Children and Families. (2005). *Head Start Impact Study: First year findings.* Washington, DC: Author.

U.S. Department of Health and Human Services, Administration for Children and Families. (2010). *Head Start Impact Study: Final report.* Washington, DC: Author.

Wasik, B.A., & Hindman, A.H. (2011). Improving vocabulary and pre-literacy skills of at-risk preschoolers through teacher professional development. *Journal of Educational Psychology, 103*, 455–469.

Waterford Institute (2001). *Waterford Early Reading Program, level I.* New York, NY: Pearson School.

Webster-Stratton, C., Reid, M.J., & Hammond, M. (2004). Treating children with early-onset conduct problems: Intervention outcomes for parent, child, and teacher training. *Journal of Consulting and Clinical Psychology, 33*, 105–124.

What Works Clearinghouse. (n.d.). *Early childhood education intervention reports.* Retrieved on March 1, 2011, from http://ies.ed.gov/ncee/wwc/reports/topicarea.aspx?tid=13

Whitehurst, G.J., Falco, F.L., Lonigan, C.J., Fischel, J.E., DeBaryshe, B.D., Valdez-Menchaca, M.C., & Caulfield, M. (1988). Accelerating language development through picture book reading. *Developmental Psychology, 24*, 552–559.

Whitehurst, G.J., & Lonigan, C.J. (1998). Child development and emergent literacy. *Child Development, 69*, 848–872.

Wilcox, M.J., Gray, S.L., Guimond, A.B., & Lafferty, A.E. (2011). Efficacy of the *TELL* language and literacy curriculum for preschoolers with developmental speech and/or language impairment. *Early Childhood Research Quarterly, 26*, 278–294.

Wong, V.C., Cook, T.D., Barnett, W.S., & Jung, K. (2008). An effectiveness-based evaluation of five state pre-kindergarten programs. *Journal of Policy Analysis and Management, 27*, 122–154.

Wood, J. (2002). *Early Literacy and Learning Model.* Jacksonville: Florida Institute of Education and the University of North Florida.

Wright Group/McGraw-Hill. (2001). *Doors to Discovery: A new prekindergarten program.* Bothhell, WA: Author.

9

Methodological and Practical Challenges of Curriculum-Based Language Interventions

David K. Dickinson and Catherine L. Darrow

The report issued by the National Early Literacy Panel (NELP; 2008) makes clear that there is a set of abilities present in the preschool years that provides the basis for later reading success. As the NELP report establishes, early language ability is associated with later reading, and measures of complex and discourse-level skills are particularly strong predictors. This finding is consistent with the fact that language is a complex, multidimensional system that is recruited to support decoding and comprehension as children learn to read (Dick-

Acknowledgment: Funding for the research reported in this study came from a grant from the Institute for Educational Sciences, U.S. Department of Education (R324E060088A). We thank our Head Start partners for their support during this project and especially acknowledge the efforts of Ann Kaiser, Jill Freiberg, Tanya Flushman, Erica Barnes, Ragan McCleod, and Megan Roberts.

inson, Golinkoff, & Hirsh-Pasek, 2010; Dickinson, Golinkoff, & Hirsh-Pasek, 2010; Dickinson, McCabe, Anastasopoulos, Peisner-Feinberg, & Poe, 2003; Vellutino, Tunmer, Jaccard, & Chen, 2007). Vocabulary is the component of language competence that is most commonly studied, partly because of the availability of easily used, reliable, and predictive measures of it. In this chapter, we focus on vocabulary because it is important to long-term literacy and because there have been many reported efforts to bolster it through interventions.

Studies that have been successful in supporting vocabulary growth most often have been done as part of relatively narrowly focused interventions, whereas curriculum-based interventions, often delivered on a large scale, have met with significantly less success in substantially increasing vocabulary gains. We argue that our understanding of these problems is limited by weaknesses in how fidelity of implementation is measured. Drawing on analyses of results from our own randomized controlled study in which we failed to find evidence of consistent main effects on language (Kaiser et al., 2010), we argue that the limited success of such efforts may be partly due to the low level of implementation of strategies known to support language or to lack of consistency across settings.

LANGUAGE AND READING

Language is a complex system that encompasses processing skills and knowledge that are central to reading. By the later elementary school years, reading comprehension is highly dependent on language abilities as described by the simple view of reading model (Hoover & Gough, 1990) and the more recent convergent skills model of reading (Vellutino et al., 2007). The convergent skills model hypothesizes that there is a shift in the importance of different abilities as children learn to read, with language becoming increasingly important among older children. This theory was tested by administering to students a battery of tests that included two subtests from the Wechsler Intelligence Scale for Children–Revised (Wechsler, 1974), Vocabulary and Similarities. The Vocabulary subtest evaluates the child's ability to provide oral definitions of words that increase in difficulty and degree of abstractness. The Similarities subtest evaluates the child's ability to detect and describe commonalities between two words representing objects or concepts. Data collected from 468 children revealed that semantic knowledge was an equally important predictor of reading among both the younger and the older readers, supporting the contention that knowledge associated with complete understanding of words makes an important contribution to reading even when children are refining basic decoding skills.

Vocabulary also plays an important role in fostering reading development in the years before formal reading instruction, providing further urgency to the need to find successful ways of intervening to foster its growth. Several decades of research summarized by the NELP report establish that phonological awareness is a key contributor to children's ability to learn to read. Of course, phonological representations are part of the linguistic system, and the ability to gain access to these representations may in part be a by-product of early vocabulary development. One indication of this is the fact that during the preschool years, the size of a child's vocabulary is associated with improvements in the ability to attend to the sounds of language (Adams, 1990; Munson, Kurtz, & Windsor, 2005; Storkel, 2001; Storkel & Adlof, 2009). One line of investigation has examined the hypothesis that phonological awareness is facilitated by a reorganization in how lexical knowledge is stored (Metsala, 1999, 2011; Metsala & Walley, 1998), and recent studies suggest that as increasing numbers of words with similar phonological representations are acquired, a reorganization of the neural representation of that cluster of words occurs, with the result being that words are decomposed into smaller sound units that in turn are more readily accessed as discrete units.

Further reason to attend to the challenge of finding effective ways to foster vocabulary learning comes from evidence indicating that children's abilities to learn new words is partially conditioned by how many words they already know; children learn new words faster when words are similar to those already in their lexicon (Storkel, 2001, 2003). Thus, when intervention studies use book reading to build vocabulary knowledge, children with stronger vocabularies tend to be more able to learn the words that are being taught (Penno, Wilkinson, & Moore, 2002). This self-perpetuating cycle of early language begetting later language acquisition begins long before children enter preschool, because toddlers' speed of lexical access—their ability to quickly interpret language—is related to early vocabulary and language acquisition (Fernald, Perfors, & Marchman, 2006), an ability that is related to the amount of linguistic input young children experience (Hurtado, Marchman, & Fernald, 2007, 2008). Language-processing speed and receptive vocabulary size at age 25 months are predictive of vocabulary when children are 8 years old (Marchman & Fernald, 2008). Research has not explored possible contributions of effective preschool interventions to children's lexical processing and capacity to learn new vocabulary, but these findings make apparent the fact that children enter preschool with a long history of language learning that conditions their ability to benefit from classroom experiences.

CHALLENGES FACED BY LANGUAGE-FOCUSED INTERVENTIONS

Interventions that seek to foster language face a substantial challenge because the interconnected and complex nature of language means that the language system that is one target of these interventions has a long developmental history and draws on a broad range of linguistic and cognitive capacities. Furthermore, interventions occur in a social context in which motivational, behavioral, and social factors heavily condition the nature of the learning climate. Children's attention to language input and their willingness to respond to it are affected by a host of factors, including their interest in the topic of the conversation, their relationship to the speaker, the number and identities of other conversational participants, and the setting. Potentially more vexing is the fact that teachers, the most important source of language input in preschool classrooms, have a lifetime history of using language in ways of which they are largely unaware. Their habitual ways of interacting with children may or may not be consistent with the types of interactions found by research to be optimally conducive to language learning: conversations that stay on a single topic, that provide children opportunities to talk, that encourage analytical thinking, and that give information about the meanings of words (Dickinson & Porche, 2011). Many of these elements are rare in spontaneous teacher–child conversations in preschools (Dickinson, Darrow, & Tinubu, 2008); the fact that they are not naturally part of patterns of teacher–child interactions means that the introduction of them likely will require significant changes in patterns of talk in classrooms.

In sum, we hypothesize that preschool classrooms can foster vocabulary learning but that interventions often fail to provide the intensity of support that is required to make a substantial impact on a system with such a long history of development prior to the intervention. The problem is further exacerbated by the fact that the teachers who provide the input may need to use language in ways that are discrepant from their standard ways of conversing at the same time that they are striving to learn to use new materials and implement new instructional routines. Unfortunately, studies of curriculum-based interventions have not included the types of measures of fidelity of implementation that we believe are necessary to determine in detail why efforts were or were not effective.

INTERVENTIONS THAT TARGET VOCABULARY

Examination of broadly targeted preschool programs has revealed that improving levels of vocabulary in children is difficult. NELP (2008) reports an analysis of the results of 15 shared-reading interventions that had outcomes for language whose results were reliable. These interventions were delivered in a variety of settings and studied in the context of rigorously conducted studies. The overall effect size of these studies was 0.57, a relatively large impact. Follow-up analyses failed to find any characteristic of interventions or populations that had a reliable impact on the benefits of shared reading, but there was a trend suggesting that children at risk of later learning challenges in school, often due to the effects of poverty, showed fewer benefits than others (for a similar result see Mol, Bus, de Jong, & Smeets, 2008). Although these are encouraging results, it is important to realize that the effects come from interventions that often were delivered by parents, one to one, or in small-group settings. The authors of the NELP report include the following caveat:

> Notably, the estimated [effect sizes] for shared reading do not reflect the impact of the typical program of shared reading conducted in early childhood settings (e.g., whole-group shared reading during circle time), which was typically the comparison condition in studies of shared reading in schools. Consequently, the results of this analysis do not provide evidence that typical classroom practices in early childhood education promote the development of oral language and print knowledge skills (NELP, 2008, p. 163).

Evidence from the type of preschool settings that serve large numbers of children is less encouraging. A study of the efficacy of Head Start in bolstering preacademic growth found that vocabulary levels are generally stable from early ages to later grades. The recent Head Start Impact Study (U.S. Department of Health and Human Services, 2010) found that children who attended Head Start had slightly higher vocabulary by the end of preschool than did children who attended other child care programs or had no child care experience. The effect size of Head Start was 0.09, an effect that dropped to 0.04 the following year. Another federal program that funded programs seeking to support early literacy growth, the Early Reading First project, was evaluated early in its existence and evaluators found only a hint of evidence of effects on language outcomes (Jackson et al., 2007).

To better understand effects of preschool curriculum interventions on vocabulary development, Darrow (2011) conducted a meta-analysis designed to measure the effect of preschool curriculum interventions on the vocabulary development of children at the end of preschool and the end of kindergarten. Random-effects analysis produced a grand mean effect size for vocabulary at the end of preschool of 0.038 ($p > .05$), an effect that is not statistically significant. The majority of interventions analyzed had little to no effect on vocabulary, as their individual effect sizes hovered around 0. Similar results were obtained when calculating the grand mean effect size for vocabulary at the end of kindergarten. The grand mean effect size across 13 studies was 0.048. Similar to the impact of the curriculum interventions at the end of preschool, the impact of the interventions at the end of kindergarten was positive, but the effect size was neither significant nor much above 0. In a similar vein, NELP (2008) reported on 10 studies that sought to teach vocabulary, most of which were studies involving small groups and interventions that lasted several weeks. These studies collectively had an insignificant result for children's expressive and receptive vocabulary as compared with comparison/control groups.

Conversely, when language interventions are targeted to provide language support at selected times and involve relatively well-specified methods, significantly stronger results have been observed. For example, Mol, Bus, and de Jong (2009) found that interactive book-reading instruction produced an overall effect size of 0.62 on children's expressive vocabulary across 20 studies and an overall effect size of 0.45 on receptive vocabulary across 23 studies. It is important to note the differential patterns of effects between these meta-analyses because they provide some clues regarding the disappointing pattern of results found in the NELP and Darrow meta-analyses. The Mol et al. (2009) study examined only book-reading interventions, and all of the studies were implemented by teachers and/or graduate students. Of the 31 studies Mol et al. reviewed, only 9 included the entire class, with 5 studies involving interventions that included one-to-one interventions. In contrast, the interventions in the studies that Darrow (2011) reviewed included the entire class and were delivered by classroom teachers. The interventions reviewed by Mol et al. (2009) almost certainly were delivered with much greater fidelity to the intended model than those reviewed by Darrow (2011) or the NELP report, because they targeted specific language skills in a particular activity (i.e., book reading) and were more often delivered by experimenters or their graduate students.

However, a meta-analysis that examined vocabulary enhancement interventions delivered through intensive small-group or one-to-one efforts found more encouraging results. Marulis and Neuman (2010) reviewed results of 67 studies and found an overall effect size of 0.88. Likewise, McLeod and Kaiser (2009) found differential effects on children's language outcomes when researchers rather than teachers delivered the instruction. The overall effect size for researcher-delivered interventions was 0.44 ($p < .05$) on receptive language and 0.31 ($p < .01$) on expressive language. Interventions delivered by teachers brought smaller effects, producing a grand mean effect of 0.07 ($p = .10$) on receptive language and 0.14 ($p = .17$) on expressive language.

Thus, the differential success of efforts to foster language learning in preschool settings suggests that, although vocabulary is difficult to support, some interventions have demonstrated that it is possible to speed growth through interventions. The variability in the effectiveness of different approaches suggests that there are factors specific to interventions delivered primarily by classroom teachers and spanning the entire classroom day that may account for the small magnitude of effects of these approaches.

Unfortunately, the research methods employed to examine interventions have yielded relatively little information regarding the reasons that effects were not observed. For example, we know little about the degree to which the interventions were delivered as intended or whether fidelity of implementation varied across the day, we know little about the nature of children's experiences in control classrooms, and we have scant knowledge regarding the "active ingredients" in interventions, the features of interventions that are most important in bringing about improved learning. In short, little has been learned about the processes of intervention delivery or mechanisms by which classrooms might affect development. One reason for the lack of progress in understanding how to deliver effective, full-class interventions is that until recently, the concept of fidelity of implementation was weakly conceptualized by educational researchers (Darrow, 2010; Mowbray, Holter, Teague, & Bybee, 2003). To address that concern, we briefly review literature on fidelity of implementation and then describe the approach that we are using that addresses many of the typical shortcomings.

FIDELITY OF IMPLEMENTATION

Dane and Schneider (1998) provided a framework that has helped researchers in educational settings more clearly understand the different, yet related, dimensions of fidelity. They reviewed published reports of prevention-based interventions that were delivered to schoolchildren in primary and early secondary grades. The focus of the interventions reviewed was on behavioral and academic problems demonstrated by children in school settings. Dane and Schneider analyzed the reports, published between 1980 and 1994, and synthesized the ways in which fidelity had been understood and measured. Their analysis allowed them to identify five major components of fidelity: exposure (i.e., the length of the program and the frequency with which it was delivered), adherence (i.e., the extent to which specific elements of the program were delivered), quality of delivery (i.e., the attitudes of program deliverers), program differentiation (i.e., confirmation that the program was delivered to the intended group), and participant responsiveness (i.e., levels of enthusiasm and participation in the program). This categorization is often cited in literature on fidelity of implementation, although individual interpretation of these categories varies. Dane and Schneider found no real consensus among researchers related to the types of measures needed to accurately assess fidelity of implementation and, as a result, no solid understanding of how to define and then measure program integrity. Their review clarified the ways in which fidelity had been defined but also illustrated the gaps in understanding among researchers working with school-age children. They found that few researchers included all five components of fidelity that they had identified and that researchers had varied, and sometimes, contradictory definitions of these components.

Dusenbury, Brannigan, Falco, and Hansen (2003) arrived at similar conclusions from their review of studies of mental health, drug abuse prevention, personal and social competence promotion, and education that were delivered in school settings. They categorized 25 years of studies using Dane and Schneider's (1998) framework and found inconsistencies across studies with regard to how treatment was defined and measured. Only 24% of 162 studies assessed fidelity of implementation. Of those, only one third looked at the effect of fidelity on outcomes. Dusenbury et al. were unable to identify a single published study that included all five components of fidelity defined by Dane and Schneider. Moreover, they found that researchers more typically described the methods they used to ensure higher levels of fidelity than details about the measures used to assess it.

Inconsistencies in the way fidelity is defined and ambiguity around how to measure it also exist in K–12 curriculum intervention studies. In a review of 23 studies of K–12 curriculum interventions, O'Donnell (2008) found that few reports of curriculum interventions included details on measures of fidelity of implementation, but she did note that more attention had been paid to issues around fidelity beginning in the early 2000s with the passing of No Child Left Behind Act of 2001 (PL 107-110). In addition to the paucity of available studies, O'Donnell found that very few studies (5 of 23) linked levels of fidelity to outcomes. Thus, O'Donnell's review provided evidence that K–12 research has yet to suitably account for implementation fidelity and its inherent relationship with treatment outcomes.

More recently, Hulleman and Cordray (2009) developed a new way of thinking about fidelity in which they call for researchers to determine the relative strength of any intervention. They argue that researchers must use measures of fidelity in both the treatment and the control classroom in determining the quality of delivery of the intervention in the control and experimental conditions. The approach developed by Darrow and adopted by our team uses measures of fidelity of key elements of curricula implemented in both the treatment and the control classrooms. These measures help to differentiate the nature of instruction delivered in each case.

ASSESSING FIDELITY OF IMPLEMENTATION

Although funded to carry out a randomized controlled study, we were interested in capturing the details of teacher–child interaction; therefore, we videotaped classrooms, and these tapes supplied us with video records that we could use to analyze fidelity of implementation and to describe patterns of language use in a fine-grained manner. Our ultimate intention was to seek to identify specific classroom behaviors that predict enhanced language learning.

Data were collected in a large Head Start program in a medium-sized Southern city. Classrooms were randomly assigned to teachers who implemented the *Opening the World of Learning (OWL)* curriculum (Schickedanz & Dickinson, 2005) in conjunction with *The Creative Curriculum for Preschool* (Dodge, Colker, & Heroman, 2001; $n = 36$) and those who used *The Creative Curriculum for Preschool* alone (i.e., business as usual, $n = 16$). Multilevel models that examined the effects of the intervention by controlling for relevant variables revealed no consistent pattern of effects of the intervention on fall-to-spring growth or on end-of-kindergarten outcomes (Kaiser et al., 2010). Thus, we are in a situation similar to that of other curriculum-based interventions, except that we have more detailed information about the fidelity of implementation that we can use to help us understand possible reasons for our failure to bring about the desired results.

OWL is a comprehensive curriculum that emphasizes language and literacy skills across six thematically integrated units. The day is organized into six activity periods: morning meeting, centers, small-group instruction, book reading, group literacy instruction, and group content-oriented instruction. Here, we report data only from 1) small-group instruction, 2) book reading, and 3) group literacy instruction because they are core settings for instruction related to language and literacy. During small-group instruction, teachers work with children in three small groups, two of which are supervised by a teacher. The focus of activities varies considerably, as some lessons relate to language and literacy and others are associated with mathematical and scientific concepts. Book reading is a key element in the *OWL* program, with five storybooks being provided for each of the six thematic units. Teachers are expected to read each book four separate times, with each reading having a different purpose. The purpose of the first reading is to introduce the story and present the story's main events and new vocabulary. In the second reading, teachers are to encourage children to recall events and characters while continuing to use and define suggested vocabulary. In the third and fourth readings, teachers are asked to encourage children to chime in during the reading and to act out scenes from the story.

Finally, group literacy instruction involves several different elements, such as songs, poems, and games, to teach phonological and alphabet awareness as well as letter recognition.

The business-as-usual condition was *The Creative Curriculum,* the approach the Head Start program had used for many years. Although it is called a curriculum, it was referred to by the director of the program as being more of a framework that governed how the teachers approach working with children. It stresses the socioemotional, cognitive, creative, and physical development of children. Teachers assigned to the treatment condition were asked to employ *OWL* while maintaining core elements of *The Creative Curriculum;* therefore, we expected that the instruction in treatment classrooms would represent components of both *OWL* and *The Creative Curriculum,* whereas the teaching in control classrooms would reflect only elements of *The Creative Curriculum.* In the year before data collection began, program leadership had all teachers in *Creative Curriculum* classrooms adopt the structure of the classroom day used by *OWL.* Although this shift represented a serious and systemic form of contamination, it facilitated collection of parallel fidelity-of-implementation data, because in all classrooms we were able to videotape and code for the same general kinds of activities.

INSTRUMENTS TO DETERMINE FIDELITY OF IMPLEMENTATION

Darrow devised an approach to determining fidelity of implementation that addressed several of the problems present in many educational studies. She created checklists for each daily activity setting that included four categories of items: 1) *OWL*-specific fidelity, 2) *Creative Curriculum* fidelity, 3) general instruction, and 4) general management. Tools were created to code fidelity by activity settings from videotapes that were made at two times during the school year (fall, spring) and were averaged to create a classroom score.

Instructional items uniquely related to the objectives of *OWL* were identified, with input from the coauthor of *OWL* (Dickinson). The number of items varied across activities. The book-reading checklist had 12 items, while the small-group and group literacy instruction checklists contained 11 items each. Activity-specific checklists also were created to assess *Creative Curriculum* items by drawing on items included in *The Creative Curriculum for Preschool Implementation Checklist* (Dodge, Colker, & Heroman, 2003). Darrow asked the director of education and two education specialists employed by the Head Start program and involved in the intervention to identify items representing instructional and environmental elements included in *The Creative Curricu-*

lum checklist that they would expect to see occurring in classrooms during the selected activities. When all three agreed about a proposed item, it was included in the *Creative Curriculum* section of our checklist. The number of *Creative Curriculum* items varied across activities: book reading had seven, small-group instruction had seven, and group literacy instruction included four.

We also coded for general instructional quality. These items were developed by identifying items that were common across the original *OWL* fidelity items (created by Dickinson) and *The Creative Curriculum for Preschool Implementation Checklist*. For example, both curricula noted that when teachers read aloud, they should hold the book so the children can see it. Such behavior was deemed to be an example of generally accepted good instructional practice. The checklists for book reading, small-group instruction, and group literacy instruction contained seven, six, and four items representing instructional quality, respectively. Finally, we coded for general management skill, believing that the ability to maintain order and momentum might be a dimension distinct from instructional quality. Teachers were rated on the same nine items for all activities. For each activity, we trained coders to criterion (85% or greater exact percentage agreement), and they independently coded four video sessions. Then they again coded a tape that was checked by a verifier. If they were at least 85% reliable, the coders worked independently for another four sessions before being checked again.

This approach to evaluating the fidelity of implementation was devised to enable us to address three questions:

1. Was the intervention curriculum delivered as intended in each activity setting? (adherence)

2. Were there differences between control and intervention classrooms in the use of intervention strategies in each setting? (differentiation)

3. Was there a difference between implementing the curriculum and simply being a good teacher? (specificity)

Our approach allowed us to see whether the intervention was delivered and to assess the consistency of implementation across instructional settings (adherence), to determine the extent to which *OWL* was delivered in intervention and not in control classrooms (differentiation), and to distinguish between good teaching and good implementation (specificity).

When we examined patterns of fidelity of implementation across three settings that were evaluated in both intervention and control classrooms, we observed three important findings. First, we found evidence of differentiation in delivery of the curriculum between intervention and control classrooms. As shown in Figure 9.1, in each setting, the use of strategies associated with the intervention was more common in intervention classrooms than in comparison classrooms, with implementation of *OWL* strategies being roughly 20% more common in intervention classrooms. This difference was statistically significant, $t(50) = -8.08$, $p = .000$. Although this provides evidence of differentiation, it is sobering to note that on average, strategies of particular importance to delivery of the intervention were seen in control classrooms more than 30% of the time. Second, intervention classrooms fell far short of ideal levels, with average scores in small-group instruction, the setting with the strongest average implementation, not reaching 70%. In book reading, the setting most critical for language instruction, average rates of implementation in intervention classrooms were only slightly above 29% ($M = 29.55$, $SD = 10.0$), a rate that was about double what was seen in control classrooms ($M = 14.41$, $SD = 7.12$). Third, fidelity varies by setting, with implementation scores being markedly stronger in small-group instruction and group literacy instruction than in book reading.

Thus, for this curriculum with multiple instructional settings, each of which has sets of instructional strategies that are specific to it, the consistency of implementation could vary for the same teacher across the day.

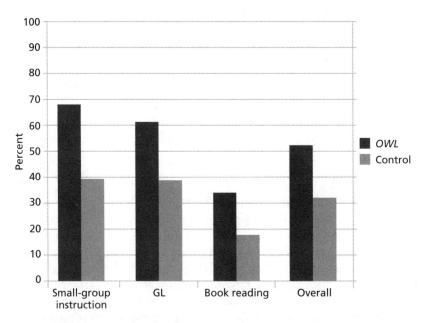

Figure 9.1 Fidelity of implementation of *Opening the World of Learning (OWL;* Schickedanz & Dickinson, 2005) in small-group instruction, group literacy instruction, and book reading. (*Key:* GL, Group literacy instruction focusing on letters and phonological awareness.)

Within-teacher variability in fidelity is an issue that has not previously been discussed in the literature, possibly because many interventions are more likely to target behaviors required in one activity setting. When fidelity is reported, and when, on the rare occasions, it is used as a moderator in analyses of intervention effectiveness, researchers tend to enter a single score for a classroom. The potential for this to obscure between-teacher differences when teachers are asked to adopt novel methods across multiple instructional settings is illustrated when one considers the patterns of implementation of three teachers, each of whom achieved average fidelity-of-implementation scores of 56% (see Figure 9.2). Note the shifting rank orderings in the strength of instruction across the three settings. For example, Teacher 1 was the strongest in delivering instruction in reading, in the middle in small-group instruction, and the lowest in group literacy instruction. Similar reversals of ranking were seen for the other two teachers. The complexity of the situation is compounded when one realizes that for this curriculum, there are three other activity settings, with each having its own cluster of recommended strategies. The generality of this challenge is made evident when average fidelity ratings are charted across these three settings. When tracking three classrooms' relative fidelity ratings across the three settings, we find the following reversals in relative orderings: small group A > B > C; group content C > A > B; and in book reading C > B > A. Thus, with more careful and detailed

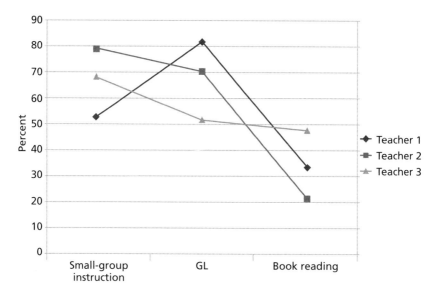

Figure 9.2. Fidelity scores, by instructional setting, of three teachers with the same overall level of implementation (56%). (*Key:* GL, Group literacy instruction focusing on letters and phonological awareness.)

descriptions of the fidelity with which an intervention is delivered come complex, analytical challenges as we strive to distill observations into a relatively small set of measures of instructional fidelity.

A vexing problem that classroom intervention studies face is determining whether observed instructional practices simply reflect good teaching as opposed to adoption of methods associated with a new curriculum. By looking at all four scores—group management, general instruction, use of *OWL* methods, and use of *The Creative Curriculum*—we are able to determine whether the ratings for implementing the intervention are simply alternative ways of identifying effective teachers. That is, we can distinguish between good teaching and adoption of the curriculum—a feature we call the specificity of the impact of the intervention on teacher practice. Results shown in Table 9.1 give reason to believe we are able to at least partially disentangle these dimensions of instructional quality. As noted before, intervention teachers were higher in the use of relevant strategies but were essentially the same as control teachers in effective management, a hallmark of good teaching, and were only slightly better than control teachers in general instructional quality. The slightly higher general instruction scores in intervention classrooms may partially reflect the impact of the intervention on instruction more generally, because it is an approach that places a higher premium on teaching than does the business-as-usual approach. Support for this hypothesis comes from looking at specific items included in the general instruction scale, in which there were noteworthy differences between intervention- and control-group teachers. For example, nearly 64% of intervention teachers explicitly defined educationally useful words three to five times during book reading. In contrast, 81% of all control teachers defined such words two or fewer times during book reading. Thus, we conclude that our approach was

Table 9.1. Overall fidelity and quality scores (by percentage) for teachers by experimental condition

	OWL		Control	
	M	SD	M	SD
OWL fidelity	53.90	9.20	32.11	7.34
Creative Curriculum fidelity	63.07	6.42	63.70	10.59
General instruction	72.73	7.52	64.82	5.70
General management	81.37	10.67	82.74	6.81

Key: OWL, *Opening the World of Learning*. (Dodge, Colker, & Heroman, 2001; Schickedanz & Dickinson, 2005).

at least partially successful in distinguishing between overall good instruction and high-level implementation of the intervention.

A final interesting question that we can ask is the extent to which the existing curriculum was implemented in all the classrooms. Note that because the program viewed *OWL* as a curricular overlay on *The Creative Curriculum*, we hypothesized that *OWL* would be more common in *OWL* classrooms but that *The Creative Curriculum* would be roughly equally present across sites. Indeed, this is what we found, as average use of the existing curriculum was the same across conditions (see Table 9.1), whereas use of *OWL* was more common in intervention classrooms. We calculated scores for multiple components of instruction and management across the day and found that higher levels of intervention fidelity across program settings correlate with higher general instruction scores in intervention classrooms ($r = .491$, $p = .002$). However, fidelity to *The Creative Curriculum* calculated in the same manner does not have a significant association with general instruction ($r = .38$, $p = .147$). Because we lacked observational data before the intervention was implemented, we cannot know for certain whether the intervention helped bring about stronger scores on our general instruction measure or the classrooms started with stronger instruction. But the fact that we used random assignment and that management scores were the same suggests that the intervention was partially responsible for better general instruction. The methodological takeaway point is that this approach to evaluating interventions equips researchers with tools to answer important questions that typically cannot be addressed.

USE OF FIDELITY-OF-IMPLEMENTATION DATA FOR DIAGNOSTIC PURPOSES

The approach to evaluating implementation quality that we employed has the added benefit of enabling a relatively nuanced examination of patterns of implementation that can shed light on aspects of the intervention that were relatively difficult to adopt by determining relative rates of effective use of recommended methods. Such information can be valuable as a means to guide professional development as well as curriculum development. Indeed, in our work, we have given teachers and coaches implementation checklists that are quite similar to those we used for research purposes because they describe valued strategies in a concrete manner that is readily understood by practitioners. Because the checklists describe specific instructional strategies, they provide concrete guidance regarding what teachers are doing and with what areas they need help. Such detailed, item-level information provides important, precise insight into areas of instruction where teachers need help and can shed light on the weak points of entire interventions.

In Table 9.2, we report the frequency with which teachers used behaviors that prior research indicates are likely to result in improved vocabulary learning. These items are taken from the fidelity-of-implementation checklists; therefore, they reflect averages from two observation points in three instructional settings—book reading, small-group instruction, and group literacy instruction. To simplify interpretation, we have translated the results into a 3-point scale: yes = 60% or more of the teachers were observed to use a behavior; sometimes (S) = 41%–59% of the time teachers used the behavior; and no = less than 40% of the teachers were observed using the strategy described.

Examination of the results reveals the disappointingly low frequency of use of instructional behaviors related to vocabulary teaching in book reading, with this being apparent across both conditions. On average, intervention-specific items related to vocabulary teaching were never observed with high frequency, and only two strategies were observed "sometimes" in intervention classrooms (gives or elicits definitions of vocabulary targeted by the intervention; gives information about analytical issues). The coding for general instruction, which included attention to words that were not specifically highlighted by the intervention curriculum but that were deemed to be words with instructional value, revealed a stronger pattern in intervention classrooms, with teachers often being observed giving definitions explicitly and sometimes providing implicit definitions (e.g., pointing to pictures, gesturing) and engaging in analytical discussions. Vocabulary-related instruction in other settings was relatively common in intervention classrooms but rare in control classrooms.

The observations from control classrooms provide strong evidence that in this Head Start program, teachers tend not to draw children's attention to the meanings of words and that the intervention resulted in some increase in the frequency with which this occurred. This item-level data also makes evident the difficulty of getting this type of instruction to occur with the consistency that may be needed to substantially improve children's vocabulary learning. It is striking that in book reading, the setting for which there is the strongest evidence of potential of classroom instruction to build vocabulary (Wasik & Bond, 2001; Wasik, Bond, & Hindman, 2006; Dickinson & Porche, 2011), there was uneven adoption of recommended methods even though scripted guidance was provided. The fact that more teachers defined words that were not highlighted by the curriculum than words that were identified and that attention to word meanings was seen in other settings, suggests that teachers began to grasp the importance of teaching vocabu-

Table 9.2. Frequency of use of behaviors hypothesized as being associated with stronger vocabulary instruction, by condition and instructional setting

Selected items from fidelity-of-implementation checklists

Book reading: *OWL* fidelity items	Control	*OWL*
Teacher gives or elicits accurate definitions of *OWL* targeted vocabulary words (No = 0–2)*	No	S
Teacher defines words using implicit strategies (No = 0–2)	No	No
Teacher prompts children to say words (No = 0–2)	No	No
Teacher gives information about analytical issues (No = 0–2)	No	S

Book reading: general instruction		
Teacher defines educationally useful words explicitly (No = 0–2)	No	Yes
Teacher defines words implicitly (No = 0–2)	No	S
During the reading, teacher elicits information from children about analytical issues (No = 0–2)	No	S

Group literacy instruction: *OWL* fidelity items		
Teaches word meanings: points to objects/pictures, says words, defines words, gives clear hints/meanings (No = 0–3)	No	Yes
Teacher encourages children to say key words (No = 0–3)	No	S

Small-group instruction: *OWL* fidelity items		
Uses precise vocabulary (No = 0–3)	No	Yes
Prompts children to use vocabulary (No = 0)	No	Yes
Goals are conceptually based	No	Yes
Makes brief presentation to introduce concepts	No	S

Key: OWL, Opening the World of Learning. (Schickedanz & Dickinson, 2005).

Note: Yes = Across two observed sessions, 60% or more of the teachers were coded as having used the stated behavior. No = Across two observed sessions, 60% or more of the teachers were coded as not having used the stated behavior. S = sometimes; the described behavior was observed in 41%–59% of the coded lessons. * indicates teachers were scored "no" on certain items based on the number of times the particular behavior was observed. Using the first item as an example, teachers received a "no" score if they gave or elicited accurate definitions of *OWL* targeted vocabulary words 0–2 times in the course of the observation.

lary and made efforts to do it. However, they lacked precision in attending to specified words that the curriculum targeted in book reading and in other contexts during the day.

This shift toward recognizing the need for explicit instruction about vocabulary throughout the day is potentially quite important. To determine the possible impact of such an orientation on vocabulary learning, we looked at our teachers' efforts to teach vocabulary throughout the day, using a simple index of vocabulary instruction. At midyear, we visited classrooms and coded teachers' instructional engagement with children in three settings—book reading, centers, and lunchtime. Teachers were coded for several behaviors, one of which was whether they made an explicit effort to teach children meanings of words. The criterion number of attempts varied by setting (book reading: 5 or more; lunchtime and centers: 3 or more). We also used our videotaped book-reading sessions of reading events that occurred on other days to determine the frequency of vocabulary teaching. We constructed a 5-point scale and used general linear model analyses to examine the predictive power of these efforts to teach vocabulary during small-group instruction, lunchtime, centers, and book reading. Children were nested within classrooms and controlled for gender, age, fall score on the same measure, and summer language (Preschool Language Scale–3 [PLS-3]; Zimmerman, Steiner, & Pond, 1992). Explicit efforts to teach vocabulary predicted growth in Peabody Picture Vocabulary Test–Third Edition ($F = 5.30$, $p < .05$; Dickinson, Freiberg, Darrow, Hofer, & Kaiser, 2009). Of particular interest is the fact that the increase in word learning was associated only with highest scoring teachers, and only 6 of the 52 teachers received scores of 4 or 5. Thus, improvement in vocabulary may occur only when levels of exposure across the day reach levels that are not commonly observed.

Therefore, our approach to coding fidelity of implementation provides insights to why so few comprehensive interventions have much impact on language learning. Initial levels of language teaching likely are low in many classrooms, adoption of strategies may be relatively low and may lack precision when it occurs, and attention to vocabulary may vary across the day. Finally, vocabulary, and rates of language acquisition in general, may be difficult to change without substantial and consistently adopted changes in classroom practice.

CONCLUSION: IS THERE HOPE?

Results from prior meta-analyses and our description of the difficulties we have in achieving high fidelity in implementation make evident the challenges we face when attempting to use full-day, curriculum-based interventions as a means to spur growth of language ability. That is the general picture, but there are indications that comprehensive interventions can achieve success, given the right conditions. Early Reading First is a government program that has sought to create high-quality preschool programs by supplying substantial funding to projects for 3 years, requiring a focus on a relatively small number of classrooms (e.g., 10–20), providing coaching and professional development, ensuring use of a curriculum deemed to have an educational focus and research backing, and working with external evaluators who collect and supply the project with ongoing data about program delivery and child growth.

We conducted a secondary data analysis of results collected by eight independent research teams working with Early Reading First programs that had been in operation 2 or more years and had been using the *OWL* curriculum. The total sample of children assessed was roughly 3,000 (Ashe, Reed, Dickinson, Morse, & Wilson, 2009). The only measure that was used in common across these sites that had national norms was the Peabody Picture Vocabulary Test–Fourth Edition (Dunn & Dunn, 2007), so we used it as our yardstick of program effectiveness because there were no control groups. During the first year of funding in four of the eight sites, classrooms were in operation only about half of the year. Evaluators found only modest changes (gains of 2.6 standard score points) that year. However, over the next 2 years, vocabulary growth in these same programs was roughly twice as great as was observed the first year, with mean gains of 5.5 and 6.6 standard score points in Years 2 and 3, respectively. These results fall far short of the gold standard because there were no control groups, but they give hope to those who seek to intervene using comprehensive approaches. However, these results occurred in the context of a federally funded initiative that supplied substantially more money to programs than is available to local school districts and states. These funds made it possible for programs to have research partners who could supply information about their effectiveness, professional development that helped teachers understand early literacy, and coaches who sought to ensure that teachers implemented recommended strategies consistently and with precision. Even more encouraging are results of an analysis of one Early Reading First program that used *OWL* in which a method called regression discontinuity was used to test for causal evidence that the intervention had beneficial effects. Significant and sizable effects on language and print knowledge were found for both English language learners and native speakers of English (Wilson, Dickinson, & Rowe, under review).

Knowing that it is possible to bring about growth in language using a comprehensive approach is encouraging, but it raises a host of questions: Can we achieve such results with less funding? Can such results be achieved with any curriculum? What elements of the approach are of critical importance? Can such successes be sustained? We surmise that answers to such questions will only come as researchers adopt more consistent and precise means of tracking the implementation of interventions and as curriculum developers and researchers find ways to make more evident to teachers the instructional strategies that are of critical importance for supporting children's language learning.

REFERENCES

Adams, M. (1990). *Beginning to read: Thinking and learning about print.* Cambridge, MA: MIT Press.

Ashe, M.K., Reed, S., Dickinson, D.K., Morse, A.B., & Wilson, S.J. (2009). Cross-site effectiveness of *Opening the World of Learning* and site-specific strategies for supporting implementation. *Early Childhood Research Services, 3*(3): 179–191.

Dane, A.V., & Schneider, B.H. (1998). Program integrity in primary and early secondary prevention: Are implementation effects out of control? *Clinical Psychology Review, 18*(1), 23–45.

Darrow, C.L. (2010). *Measuring fidelity in preschool interventions: A micro-analysis of fidelity instruments used in curriculum interventions.* Manuscript submitted for publication.

Darrow, C.L. (2011). *Language and literacy effects of curriculum interventions for preschools serving economically disadvantaged children: A meta-analysis.* Manuscript submitted for publication.

Dickinson, D.K., Darrow, C.L., & Tinubu, T. (2008). Patterns of teacher–child conversations in Head Start classrooms: Implications for an empirically grounded approach to professional development. *Early Education and Development, 19*(3), 396–429.

Dickinson, D.K., Freiberg, J.B., Darrow, C.L., Hofer, K.G., & Kaiser, A.P. (2009, June). *Toward identifying an "active ingredient" responsible for improving receptive vocabulary in preschool children.* Paper presented at the Annual Conference of the Institute for Educational Sciences, Washington, DC.

Dickinson, D.K., Golinkoff, R., & Hirsh-Pasek, K. (2010). Speaking out for language: Why language is central to reading development. *Educational Researcher, 39*(4), 305–310.

Dickinson, D.K., McCabe, A., Anastasopoulos, L., Peisner-Feinberg, E., & Poe, M.D. (2003). The comprehensive language approach to early literacy: The interrelationships among vocabulary, phonological sensitivity, and print knowledge among preschool-aged children. *Journal of Educational Psychology, 95*(3), 465–481.

Dickinson, D.K., & Porche, M.V. (2011). The relationship between teacher–child conversations with low-income four-year-olds and grade four language and literacy development. *Child Development, 82*(3) 870–886.

Dodge, D.T., Colker, L., & Heroman, C. (2001). *The Creative Curriculum for Preschool.* Washington, DC: Teaching Strategies.

Dodge, D.T., Colker, L., & Heroman, C. (2003). *The Creative Curriculum for Preschool Implementation Checklist.* Washington, DC: Teaching Strategies.

Dunn, L.M., & Dunn, D.M. (2007). *Peabody Picture Vocabulary Test, Fourth Edition (PPVT-4).* Minneapolis, MN: NCS Pearson.

Dusenbury, L., Brannigan, R., Falco, M., & Hansen, W.B. (2003). A review of research on fidelity of implementation: Implications for drug abuse prevention in school settings. *Health Education Research, 28,* 237–256.

Fernald, A., Perfors, A., & Marchman, V.A. (2006). Picking up speed in understanding: Speech processing efficiency and vocabulary growth across the 2nd year. *Developmental Psychology, 42*(1), 98–116.

Hoover, W.A., & Gough, P.B. (1990). The simple view of reading. *Reading and Writing, 2*(2), 127–160.

Hulleman, C.S., & Cordray, D.S. (2009). Moving from the lab to the field: The role of fidelity and achieved relative intervention strength. *Journal of Research on Educational Effectiveness, 2,* 88–110.

Hurtado, N., Marchman, V.A., & Fernald, A. (2007). Spoken word recognition by Latino children learning Spanish as their first language. *Journal of Child Language, 34*(2), 227–249.

Hurtado, N., Marchman, V.A., & Fernald, A. (2008). Does input influence uptake? Links between maternal talk, processing speed, and vocabulary size in Spanish-learning children. *Developmental Science, 11*(6), F31–F39.

Jackson, R., McCoy, A., Pistorino, C., Wilkinson, A., Burghardt, J., Clark, M.,... Swank, P. (2007). *National evaluation of Early Reading First: Final report.* Washington, DC: Institute of Educational Sciences.

Kaiser, A.P., Dickinson, D.K., Hofer, K.G., Roberts, M., Darrow, C.L., McCleod, R., & Freiberg, J.B. (2010, March). *The effects of two language-focused preschool curricula on children's achievement in preschool and kindergarten.* Paper presented at the meeting of grantees of the Institute for Educational Sciences, Washington, DC.

Marchman, V.A., & Fernald, A. (2008). Speed of word recognition and vocabulary knowledge in infancy predict cognitive and language outcomes in later childhood. *Developmental Science, 11*(3), F9–F16.

Marulis, L.M., & Neuman, S.B. (2010). The effects of vocabulary intervention on young children's word learning: A meta-analysis. *Review of Educational Research, 80*(3), 300–335.

McLeod, R.H., & Kaiser, A.P. (2009, November). *Curriculum effects on vocabulary outcomes.* Symposium presented at American Speech-Language-Hearing Association conference, New Orleans, LA.

Metsala, J.L. (1999). Young children's phonological awareness and nonword repetition as a function of vocabulary development. *Journal of Educational Psychology, 91*(1), 3–19.

Metsala, J. (2011). Lexical reorganization and the emergence of phonological awareness. In S.B. Neuman & D.K. Dickinson (Eds.), *Handbook of early literacy research* (pp. 66–84). New York, NY: Guilford Press.

Metsala, J.L., & Walley, A.C. (1998). Spoken vocabulary growth and the segmental restructuring of lexical representations: Precursors to phonological awareness and early reading ability. In J.L. Morrison, F.J. Smithe, & M. Dow-Ehrensberger (Eds.), *Education and cognitive development: A natural experiment* (pp. 789–799). Mahwah, NJ: Lawrence Erlbaum Associates.

Mol, S.E., Bus, A.G., & de Jong, M.T. (2009). Interactive book reading in early education: A tool to stimulate print knowledge as well as oral language. *Review of Educational Research, 79*(2), 979–1007.

Mol, S.E., Bus, A.G., de Jong, M.T., & Smeets, D.J.H. (2008). Added value of dialogic parent–child book reading: A meta-analysis. *Early Education and Development, 19,* 7–26.

Mowbray, C.T., Holter, M.C., Teague, G.B., & Bybee, D. (2003). Fidelity criteria: Development, measurement, and validation. *American Journal of Evaluation, 24*(3), 315–340.

Munson, B., Kurtz, B.A., & Windsor, J. (2005). The influence of vocabulary size, phonotactic probability, and wordlikeness on nonword repetitions of children with and without specific language impairment. *Journal of Speech, Language, and Hearing Research, 48*(5), 1033–1047.

National Early Literacy Panel. (2008). *Developing early literacy: Report of the National Early Literacy Panel.* Washington, DC: National Institute for Literacy.

No Child Left Behind Act of 2001, PL 107-110, 115 Stat. 1425, 20 U.S.C. §§ 6301 *et seq.*

O'Donnell, C.L. (2008). Defining, conceptualizing, and measuring fidelity of implementation and its relationship to outcomes in K–12 curriculum intervention research. *Review of Educational Research, 78*(1), 33–84.

Penno, J.F., Wilkinson, I.A.G., & Moore, D.W. (2002). Vocabulary acquisition from teacher explanation and repeated listening to stories: Do they overcome the Matthew effect? *Journal of Educational Psychology, 94*(1), 23–33.

Schickedanz, J., & Dickinson, D.K. (2005). *Opening the World of Learning: A comprehensive literacy program.* Parsippany, NJ: Pearson Early Learning.

Storkel, H.L. (2001). Learning new words: Phonotactic probability in language development. *Journal of Speech, Language, and Hearing Research, 44*(6), 1321–1337.

Storkel, H.L. (2003). Learning new words II: Phonotactic probability in verb learning. *Journal of Speech, Language, and Hearing Research, 46*(6), 1312–1323.

Storkel, H.L., & Adlof, S.M. (2009). The effect of semantic set size on word learning by preschool children. *Journal of Speech, Language, and Hearing Research, 52*(2), 306–320.

U.S. Department of Health and Human Services. (2010). *Head Start Impact Study: Final report.* Washington, DC: Author.

Vellutino, F.R., Tunmer, W.E., Jaccard, J.J., & Chen, R.S. (2007). Components of reading ability: Multivariate evidence for a convergent skills model of reading development. *Scientific Studies of Reading, 11*(1), 3–32.

Wasik, B.A., & Bond, M.A. (2001). Beyond the pages of a book: Interactive book reading and language development in preschool classrooms. *Journal of Educational Psychology, 93*(2), 243–250.

Wasik, B.A., Bond, M.A., & Hindman, A. (2006). The effects of a language and literacy intervention on Head Start children and teachers. *Journal of Educational Psychology, 98*(1), 63–74.

Wechsler, D. (1974). *Wechsler Intelligence Scale for Children–Revised.* New York, NY: Psychological Corporation.

Wilson, S.J., Dickinson, D.K., & Rowe, D.R. (under review). *Impact of an Early Reading First program on the language and literacy achievement of children from diverse language backgrounds.*

Zimmerman, I., Steiner, V., & Pond, R. (1992). *Preschool Language Scale–3 (PLS-3).* San Antonio, TX: Harcourt Assessment.

10

Young Children's Oral Language Abilities and Later Reading Comprehension

Tiffany P. Hogan, Kate Cain, and Mindy Sittner Bridges

There is possibly no current educational issue raising more interest than the role of oral language in literacy development. The National Early Literacy Panel (NELP; 2008), in its study of precursors to reading comprehension, found that more complex aspects of oral language were clearly related to later reading comprehension—but that simpler measures of oral language (e.g., the widely used Peabody Picture Vocabulary Test–Third Edition [PPVT-III; Dunn & Dunn, 1997], a measure of receptive vocabulary) had very limited and undifferentiated

Acknowledgment: The creation of this chapter was supported in part by the Institute of Education Sciences, U.S. Department of Education, through Grant R305F100002 to The Ohio State University as part of the Reading for Understanding Research Initiative. The opinions expressed are those of the authors and do not represent views of the institute or the U.S. Department of Education.

associations with reading comprehension. NELP also examined the effectiveness of specific approaches used to teach early oral language development to establish a solid foundation for later reading comprehension. This chapter reviews and extends NELP's findings on oral language and reading comprehension.

EARLY ORAL LANGUAGE AND LATER READING COMPREHENSION: A DEVELOPMENTAL FRAMEWORK

In this chapter, we present an overview of the NELP meta-analysis of oral language and reading comprehension within the framework of the simple view of reading. The simple view is a model that describes reading comprehension as the product of decoding printed text (i.e., word reading) and understanding language accessed through the process of decoding (i.e., language comprehension; Gough & Tunmer, 1986). Put simply, a child comprehends written text when he or she is able to translate print into spoken language accurately and fluently to enable comprehension. Numerous studies support the simple view by showing that word reading and language comprehension are relatively independent skills but that both contribute significantly to reading comprehension (e.g., Aaron, Joshi, & Williams, 1999; Catts, Hogan, & Fey, 2003; de Jong & van der Leij, 2002; Hoover & Gough, 1990; Singer & Crouse, 1981). Moreover, word reading and language comprehension have independent genetic influences on reading comprehension (Keenan, Betjemann, Wadsworth, DeFries, & Olson, 2006).

Germane to the topic of oral language and literacy, good comprehension is dependent on language abilities that have been developing since birth. For example, basic vocabulary and grammar are clearly essential to comprehension because each enables understanding of the words and individual sentences in a text that supports the construction of a representation of the literal meaning of that text (Kintsch & Kintsch, 2005). However, children with good reading comprehension go beyond word and sentence comprehension to construct a representation of the text's meaning that represents the situation or state of affairs described by the text, referred to as a *mental model* (Kintsch & Kintsch, 2005). The construction of a mental model involves organizing a text's multiple propositions into an integrated whole while incorporating prior world knowledge. To do this, successful comprehenders draw upon a set of higher-level language skills, including inferencing, monitoring comprehension, and using text structure knowledge. These higher-level language skills are particularly crucial to accurate comprehension because of the integrative role they play in creating a mental model (Cain, Oakhill, & Bryant, 2004; Perfetti, 2007). Consider the following short story:

Johnny carried a jug of water. He tripped on a step. Mom grabbed the mop.

The literal representation of the individual words and sentences does not enable the reader to integrate their meanings and construct a mental model. Successful comprehenders have knowledge of narrative structure and will use this knowledge coupled with their world knowledge to infer that Johnny spilled the water. They then understand why Mom grabbed a mop. Successful comprehenders monitor their comprehension of stories, written or spoken, and in doing so, realize the need to make an inference—that Johnny spilled the water—to make sense of Mom's response.

The higher-level language skills used to create a mental model of a text are not exclusive to reading; children begin developing these language skills well before formal reading instruction in a range of language comprehension situations. For example, young children make inferences and monitor their comprehension as well as rely on knowledge of narrative structure to follow a set of instructions; understand spoken stories, cartoons, and movies; and relate autobiographical accounts of everyday activities around the dinner table.

Adding to the complexity of developing reading comprehension is that the skills underpinning reading comprehension change over time, as illustrated in Figure 10.1. In the early grades, reading comprehension is heavily dependent on emerging word-reading skills. As children automatically and fluently read printed words, language comprehension begins to contribute more to individual differences in reading comprehension (Adlof, Catts, & Little, 2006; Catts, Hogan, & Adlof, 2005). Most children who score poorly on reading comprehension tests have

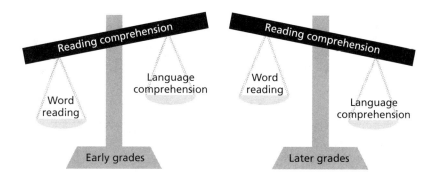

Figure 10.1.   The changing nature of reading comprehension. The scales illustrate that reading comprehension is mostly associated with individual differences in word reading in the early grades, whereas it is mostly associated with individual differences in language comprehension in the later grades. (*Sources:* Adlof, Catts, & Little, 2006; Catts, Hogan, & Adlof, 2005.)

difficulty decoding words and understanding language. However, those
with poor word-reading abilities in spite of good language comprehension (i.e., poor decoders) lag behind their typically developing peers on
reading comprehension measures in the early grades. Those with poor
language comprehension in spite of relatively proficient word-reading
ability do not lag behind their typically developing peers on reading
comprehension tests until they have had one or two years of reading
instruction (Catts et al., 2005).

This complex relation between reading comprehension, word reading, and language comprehension in poor comprehenders and poor
decoders is illustrated in Figure 10.2. Of particular importance is the fact
that what appears to be a decline in reading comprehension for these
poor comprehenders is not the result of declining language skills; on the
contrary, these students' language skills were already poor compared
with their typically developing peers at the onset of schooling (Catts,
Adlof, & Weismer, 2006). In fact, a recent report found that poor comprehenders in fifth grade (i.e., those with poor reading comprehension despite good word-reading abilities) evidenced weak language
skills as early as 15 months of age (Justice, Mashburn, & Petscher, in
press) compared with their age-matched peers who went on to become

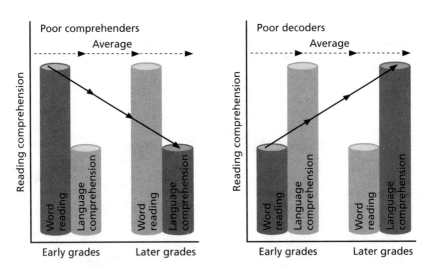

Figure 10.2. Reading comprehension declines over time for poor comprehenders, whereas it
increases over time for poor decoders. Note that poor comprehenders have consistent deficiencies in language comprehension across the grades and that poor decoders have consistent deficiencies in word reading across the grades. Their change in reading comprehension abilities
is likely due to the changing nature of reading comprehension assessments. In early grades,
successful reading comprehension is most reliant on word reading, putting the poor decoders at
a disadvantage. In later grades, successful reading comprehension is most reliant on language
comprehension, putting the poor comprehenders at a disadvantage.

good comprehenders and poor decoders. Moreover, many poor comprehenders were labeled as clinically language impaired prior to or when just beginning formal education, in preschool or kindergarten (Catts, Fey, Tomblin, & Zhang, 2002). It is hypothesized that their decline in reading comprehension over time is related to the changing nature of reading comprehension assessments: The texts used to assess reading comprehension in the early grades require less complex mental models, allowing those with weak language skills to answer basic comprehension questions as accurately as their typically developing peers (Catts et al., 2005). Indeed, poor comprehenders are often good at answering questions that tap memory for facts in a text (Cain & Oakhill, 1999). In the later grades, reading comprehension assessments contain more difficult passages that require more complex mental models than were required of texts in the early grades. Poor comprehenders lack the language skills needed to construct these complex mental models and thus begin to score more poorly on reading comprehension assessments than their typically developing peers in the later grades. The increase in poor decoders' reading comprehension scores support this view as well; their good language comprehension abilities may serve as compensation for weak word-reading abilities in the later grades, such that as long as they can read most of the words in a text to bootstrap their way to the text's meaning, they are able to use their good language skills to construct complete mental models to correctly answer both basic and more complex comprehension questions (Stanovich, 1980). With these ideas in mind, we now describe NELP's findings on oral language and reading comprehension within the framework of the simple view of reading.

SUMMARY OF FINDINGS OF THE NATIONAL EARLY LITERACY PANEL: ORAL LANGUAGE LINKS TO LATER READING COMPREHENSION

The purpose of NELP was to identify both interventions and practices for preschoolers that would result in positive literacy outcomes. In line with the framework of the simple view of reading, the panel focused on two reading outcomes: word recognition/decoding and reading comprehension. Clearly, because few preschool-age children are able to read words, it follows that comprehension cannot be evaluated by testing how well the students understand what they read. Thus, the focus of any comprehension study of this age group would need to be on the precursors that predict later reading comprehension rather than on direct tests of reading comprehension itself.

There has been a wealth of research on the early predictors of word reading. The results of the NELP meta-analysis for word reading found strong support for the picture that has emerged over the past decade (e.g., see de Jong & van der Leij, 2002; Kendeou, van den Broek, White, & Lynch, 2009; Muter, Hulme, Snowling, & Stevenson, 2004; Storch & Whitehurst, 2002). Knowledge of the alphabet assessed in kindergarten or earlier was the strongest predictor of later word-reading success. Phonological awareness, rapid naming, knowledge about print conventions and concepts, the ability to write letters or names, and oral language skills were moderate predictors. Of note, visual motor skills and visual memory were not strongly related to word reading or reading comprehension.

Although several studies have demonstrated a dissociation between the skills that predict word reading and those that predict later reading comprehension (e.g., Catts et al., 2003; Kendeou et al., 2009; Muter, et al., 2004; Oakhill & Cain, in press; Oakhill, Cain, & Bryant, 2003; Storch & Whitehurst, 2002), the NELP analysis revealed a surprising consistency in the skills that predicted each component. The predictors NELP found for word reading also predicted reading comprehension. There were two additional predictors of reading comprehension—short-term memory and print awareness. Although word reading and reading comprehension shared predictors, the *strongest* predictors of success were different for each. Whereas a code-related skill—knowledge of the alphabet—was the most important predictor of later word reading, the strongest predictor of reading comprehension was concepts about print, knowledge that is indicative of a rich home literacy environment (Van Steensel, 2006).

One reason for the overlap in the predictors of word reading and reading comprehension is that word reading itself is a significant predictor of reading comprehension, particularly in the early stages of reading development, as illustrated in Figure 10.1 (Adlof et al., 2006; Catts et al., 2005; Gough, Hoover, & Peterson, 1996). One of the key challenges facing the beginning reader is learning to "crack the code," that is, learning how written language maps onto spoken language. Better decoders will be able to devote greater cognitive resources to the processes involved in comprehending text (Perfetti, 1985), whereas poor decoders will have limited access to these processes as they laboriously and inefficiently read words. Another basis for this relation is that a child's oral language skills serve as the foundation for both aspects of reading ability—word reading and language comprehension (Dickinson, Golinkoff, & Hirsh-Pasek, 2010). There is perhaps an intuitive association between oral language and language comprehension, but the relation between oral language and word reading is less straightforward. For example, oral language, specifically oral vocabulary growth, is causally linked to the development of phonological awareness (but not vice versa; Lonigan, 2010), a skill associated with successful early word reading. In sum, NELP's results show that oral language was predictive of both word reading and language comprehension.

With that said, another surprising NELP finding was that oral language skills were only moderately predictive of later word reading and reading comprehension. Oral language is a broad and complex construct; measures of it can assess vocabulary, grammar, and discourse, and these measures can be assessments of a child's comprehension, production, or both. If the aim is to identify the critical language skills to foster in a preschool intervention, a more fine-grained analysis is required. NELP provided one. A breakdown of the studies that included oral language revealed that composite measures of oral language (i.e., those that included measures of vocabulary, syntax, and/or listening comprehension) were the strongest predictors of both word reading and reading comprehension, followed by single predictors such as vocabulary and grammar, with simple receptive and expressive vocabulary measures among the weakest predictors. The overall language composite measures accounted for nearly 50% of the variance in reading comprehension and 34% of the variance in decoding.

NELP notes that a composite or multicomponent measure would have increased reliability to measure a complex skill, such as language. In addition, inspection of commonly used composite measures of oral language also suggests that it is the nature of the constructs assessed by these batteries that drives the relation, particularly when considering the processes involved in reading comprehension. For example, composite measures tend to include assessment of conceptual knowledge and vocabulary definitions, morphological knowledge and sentence grammar, and understanding language in context. Clearly, basic knowledge of word meanings is essential to comprehend sentences and create a mental model. However, the NELP findings suggest that measures that go beyond comprehension of single words in isolation are key predictors of reading comprehension. Thus, we agree with NELP's conclusion that vocabulary knowledge alone may be "insufficient" for successful reading comprehension.

Finally, developmental changes in reading comprehension may also explain the modest relation between oral language and reading comprehension. As noted, reading comprehension changes over time such that individual differences in word reading are most predictive of early reading comprehension, whereas individual differences in language comprehension are most predictive of later reading comprehension, as illustrated in Figure 10.1 (Catts et al., 2005). NELP's findings were based mainly on studies of the relation between oral language and reading comprehension outcomes in the early grades, when reading comprehension is driven mostly by individual differences in word reading. Studies examining the relation between oral language and reading comprehension outcomes in the later grades find the predicted, stronger association between oral language and reading comprehension. Adlof et al. (2006) showcase this relation in an analysis of the skills underpinning reading comprehension in a large, longitudinal data set of children matriculating from second grade to eighth grade. They found that a composite of language, comprising vocabulary, grammar, and discourse measures, was indistinguishable from reading comprehension in eighth grade, but the correlation of these same abilities with reading comprehension was only .53 for fourth graders and was even lower (.31) for second graders.

POOR COMPREHENDERS: EVIDENCE THAT ORAL LANGUAGE IS RELATED TO READING COMPREHENSION

A review of the oral language weaknesses associated with specific reading comprehension difficulties supports NELP's analysis that successful reading comprehension depends on skills beyond single-word reading and comprehension. Children with specific reading comprehension difficulties (i.e., poor comprehenders) develop good word-reading skills, but their language comprehension and reading comprehension lag behind those of their typically developing peers (Cain, Oakhill, & Bryant, 2000; Catts et al., 2006; Stothard & Hulme, 1992). Although some poor comprehenders have weak vocabulary skills (e.g., Catts et al., 2006; Nation & Snowling, 1999), others have vocabulary knowledge comparable to their age-matched peers (Cain et al., 2000; Stothard & Hulme, 1992). These findings are in line with NELP's analysis (and with longitudinal studies of reading development), which shows that whereas single-word vocabulary knowledge is related to reading comprehension, it alone is not sufficient to ensure adequate comprehension.

As noted, NELP's analysis found that composite measures of oral language were the best predictors of reading comprehension. A comparison of good and poor comprehenders' performance on discourse tasks reveals the nature and extent of the difficulties of poor comprehenders and why oral language beyond vocabulary contributes to reading comprehension outcomes. In essence, these studies converge on two findings: first, good comprehenders construct good mental models of text (presented in either written or oral form) and poor comprehenders do not (e.g., Cain & Oakhill, 1999; Cain, Oakhill, Barnes, & Bryant, 2001; Catts et al., 2006; Megherbi & Ehrlich, 2005); second, good comprehenders are better able to produce coherent and integrated narratives compared with poor comprehenders (e.g., Cain, 2003).

Two studies demonstrate the importance and critical features of a good mental model of text. Catts and colleagues (2006) assessed good and poor comprehenders' inference-making abilities in a listening comprehension task with two conditions: in one, the critical information was presented in either the same or adjacent sentences (near inference condition); in the other, the critical information was separated by four intervening sentences (far inference condition). Poor comprehenders did particularly poorly in the far inference condition. Similarly, a listening comprehension study by Cain and colleagues (2001) found weaknesses in poor comprehenders' inference-making ability. Of note, both studies revealed that the differences in performance between good and poor comprehenders remained even when differences in memory for explicit details in the text were statistically equated. Thus, these studies and others (e.g., Cain & Oakhill, 1999; Megherbi & Ehrlich, 2005) suggest that poor comprehenders fail to go beyond the word or sentence level to make connections between different events in a text. Such connections are critical for constructing an integrated and coherent mental model of a text's meaning.

A study of poor comprehenders' narrative skills by Cain (2003) complements these findings, showing that poor comprehenders fail to make causal links between episodes in narratives that they produce. Good and poor comprehenders produced oral narratives in three prompt conditions: a picture sequence, a goal-directed title (e.g., how the pirates lost their treasure), and a topic title (e.g., pirates; Cain, 2003). The poor comprehenders' narratives were rated as being less structurally coherent than those produced by the age-matched good comprehenders. In particular, their narratives typically lacked a causal sequence of events and were instead temporally bound. The poor comprehenders did produce more structurally coherent narratives in the two supported conditions, which provided an outcome for their stories—picture sequence and goal-directed title—compared with the less supported condition—topic title; however, even in the supportive condition, their narratives were not as causally coherent as those produced by good comprehenders. Similarly, a study by Cragg and Nation (2006) of written narrative production using a picture book prompt found that poor comprehenders obtained lower global structure scores for their stories and included fewer main points than good comprehenders.

In both the Cain (2003) and Cragg and Nation (2006) studies, the good and poor comprehenders produced narratives of similar lengths; what differed was the structural quality of their narrative productions. Together with the evidence of poor comprehenders' poor inference skills, this work suggests that poor comprehenders have a fundamental difficulty establishing links between events and episodes in texts that they read, hear, or produce. Thus, their inability to use and understand complex discourse is a fundamental feature of their poor language and reading comprehension—limitations not likely to be evident during the early years of their schooling because the text demands they confront do not exceed these limits. Nevertheless, early language limitations do appear to presage those later comprehension problems.

IMPLICATIONS FOR LITERACY INSTRUCTION: INCREASING ORAL LANGUAGE TO IMPROVE LATER READING COMPREHENSION

Most researchers and educators support the notion that appropriate environmental inputs can reduce individual differences in reading ability. Thus, numerous studies have examined the effectiveness of various approaches for young-child reading instruction, often focusing solely on explicit skills that are likely to affect word-reading ability, such as letter identification and phonological awareness. However, considerably less research attention has been paid to oral language abilities that impact later reading comprehension. This is surprising, given our knowledge that language structures such as grammar and vocabulary are significant contributors to reading comprehension (Catts, Fey, Zhang, & Tomblin, 1999; Kendeou et al., 2009; Verhoeven & van Leeuwe, 2008). This disparity is reflected in the NELP report, which identified 78 studies with an emphasis on code-focused instruction and only 28 studies with an emphasis on language enhancement. Additionally, there were 16 studies on shared book reading that primarily focused on oral language improvement, and several of the other interventions, including some of the code-focused ones, at least attempted to measure the effects of their approaches on language attainment. Of the 28 studies focused specifically on language enhancement, outcome measures were typically limited to increased ability in proximal skills (i.e., the language ability targeted by a specific intervention) instead of improvements in distal skills (i.e., reading comprehension; the ability to comprehend written text).

A thorough review of the intervention studies included in the NELP report shows that overall, interventions that focused on enhancing oral language through explicit and direct instruction were effective, although the reported effect sizes were modest; such approaches tended to be more effective with younger children. The report also suggested that a variety of interventions led to positive increases in language ability, primarily through the improvement of vocabulary skills. One of the most prevalent early literacy interventions is shared book reading. Shared book reading involves an adult reading a book to one child or a small group of children with a focus on actively engaging children in the reading process. In the past decade, many studies have used shared book reading as the basis for interventions to promote language and literacy skills (e.g., Bus, van IJzendoorn, & Pellegrini, 1995; Justice & Ezell, 2000; Wasik & Bond, 2001; Whitehurst et al., 1994). NELP analyses revealed that shared book reading had the largest impact on children's oral language abilities (again, usually receptive vocabulary), with a moderate mean effect size of 0.68. Because book reading is a common early childhood activity utilized by both parents and center-based teachers, intervention focused on this type of exchange should be relatively easy to implement in a variety of settings.

One evidence-based reading practice designed around books that has been shown to support language and literacy skills of young children is dialogic reading (Whitehurst & Lonigan, 1998). Dialogic reading is a specific type of intervention aimed at stimulating oral language skills. During shared book reading, an adult provides children with multiple opportunities to verbally communicate by using a range of techniques, such as asking open-ended questions, repeating and expanding a child's response to questions, and modeling good word reading and comprehension. In essence, the child becomes actively engaged in reading by becoming the storyteller, and the adult serves as an active listener and questioner. Studies that have utilized dialogic reading techniques during shared book reading have been found to positively affect oral language development (e.g., Arnold, Lonigan, Whitehurst, & Epstein, 1994; U.S. Department of Education, 2006; Wasik & Bond, 2001; Whitehurst et al., 1988; Whitehurst & Lonigan, 1998), including improvements for those who are at high-risk for reading disabilities (Valdez-Menchaca & Whitehurst, 1992) due to impoverished language environments.

One particularly positive finding from the NELP report showed that parents could effectively provide language-focused intervention around book reading. The studies that showed the most consistent positive impacts of dialogic reading were those in which a home reading component was included, with and without a concomitant center-based intervention (Lonigan & Whitehurst, 1998; Whitehurst et al., 1994). Reading books to children is a fairly common activity undertaken by families in the United States. In 2001, a home literacy survey revealed that approximately 50% of young children whose mother had a high school degree and 73% of young children whose mother had a college degree had been read to by a family member every day of the previous week (U.S. Department of Education, 2003). Thus, an intervention focused on improving book reading should be one that is easily integrated into families' daily lives.

The intervention studies reviewed by NELP were most often focused on a single domain of language (e.g., vocabulary). However, as noted previously, text comprehension involves the creation of a mental model constructed by not only comprehension of single words but also comprehension of connected words within sentences and within a narrative structure. That is, to comprehend a story, a child must be able to interconnect multiple events in a text (Trabasso, Secco, & van den Broek, 1984) to create the mental model needed to comprehend that text. The causal connections in a story are a crucial component for building an adequate, accurate mental model (e.g., Mandler & Johnson, 1977; Trabasso et al., 1984). Attending to the text structure of a story, and in particular the causal relationships in a narrative, has positive effects on a child's ability to comprehend narratives, building a foundation for later reading comprehension (Kendeou et al., 2009; Oakhill & Cain, in press). Knowledge and use of narrative structure is found to be weak in poor comprehenders unless adequate external support is provided (Cain, 2003), further suggesting that intervention focused on improving knowledge and use of narrative skills will lead to improved comprehension as these children become readers.

Dialogic reading, with its focus on active discussions around a shared book reading activity, may be ideal for helping children create complex mental models, but more research is needed to confirm this prediction. Moreover, caregivers could facilitate the creation of mental models of text by asking questions during shared book reading that focus on connections made in the story, such as "Why did he build a house of brick?" or "How did the boy feel when he lost his money?" A related field of research on autobiographical memory and personal narratives supports this possibility. Reese and Newcombe (2007) found that children of parents who were trained to use a more interactive style when reminiscing about past events produced narratives of better quality. More research is needed to determine if caregivers' use of dialogic reading around shared book reading supports the creation of the mental models that lead to successful early and later reading comprehension.

CONCLUSION

The simple view of reading model emphasizes the importance of both decoding and oral language ability; decoding is used to go from text to language, and then a reader's ability to make sense of oral language becomes central. Accordingly, the NELP report, along with other studies of children's early language development, suggests that early oral language makes a relatively large and growing contribution to later reading comprehension and that this contribution is separate from the important role played by the alphabetic code. This means that improving young children's oral language development should be a central goal during the preschool and kindergarten years. Although various approaches have been found to improve young children's language, the approach with the greatest research support so far is shared book reading, particularly when such reading is carried out dialogically, that is, with a lot of language interaction between the reader and the child.

REFERENCES

Aaron, P.G., Joshi, M., & Williams, K.A. (1999). Not all reading disabilities are alike. *Journal of Learning Disabilities, 32*, 120–137.

Adlof, S.M., Catts, H.W., & Little, T.D. (2006). Should the simple view of reading include a fluency component? *Reading and Writing: An Interdisciplinary Journal, 19*, 933–958.

Arnold, D.H., Lonigan, C.J., Whitehurst, G.J., & Epstein, J.N. (1994). Accelerating language development through picture book reading: Replication and extension to videotape training format. *Journal of Educational Psychology, 86*, 235–243.

Bus, A.G., van IJzendoorn, M.H., & Pelligrini, A.D. (1995). Joint book reading makes for success in learning to read: A meta-analysis on intergenerational transmission of literacy. *Review of Educational Research, 65*, 1–21.

Cain, K. (2003). Text comprehension and its relation to coherence and cohesion in children's fictional narratives. *British Journal of Developmental Psychology, 21*, 335–351.

Cain, K., & Oakhill, J.V. (1999). Inference-making ability and its relation to comprehension failure. *Reading and Writing: An Interdisciplinary Journal, 11*, 489–503.

Cain, K., Oakhill, J.V., Barnes, M.A., & Bryant, P.E. (2001). Comprehension skill, inference-making ability, and the relation to knowledge. *Memory and Cognition, 29*, 850–859.

Cain, K., Oakhill, J.V., & Bryant, P.E. (2000). Investigating the causes of reading comprehension failure: The comprehension–age match design. *Reading and Writing, 12*, 31–40.

Cain, K., Oakhill, J., & Bryant, P. (2004). Children's reading comprehension ability: Concurrent prediction by working memory, verbal ability, and component skills. *Journal of Educational Psychology, 96*, 31–42.

Catts, H.W., Adlof, S.M., & Weismer, S.E. (2006). Language deficits in poor comprehenders: A case for the simple view of reading. *Journal of Speech, Language, and Hearing Research, 49*, 278–293.

Catts, H.W., Fey, M.E., Tomblin, B.J., & Zhang, X. (2002). A longitudinal investigation of reading outcomes in children with language impairments. *Journal of Speech, Language, and Hearing Research, 45*, 1142–1157.

Catts, H.W., Fey, M.E., Zhang, X., & Tomblin, B.J. (1999). Language basis of reading and reading disabilities: Evidence from a longitudinal investigation. *Scientific Studies of Reading, 3*, 331–361.

Catts, H.W., Hogan, T.P., & Adlof, S.M. (2005). Developmental changes in reading and reading disabilities. In H.W. Catts & A.G. Kamhi (Eds.), *The connections between language and reading disabilities* (pp. 25–40). Mahwah, NJ: Lawrence Erlbaum Associates.

Catts, H.W., Hogan, T.P., & Fey, M.E. (2003). Subgrouping poor readers on the basis of individual differences in reading-related abilities. *Journal of Learning Disabilities, 36*, 151–164.

Cragg, L., & Nation, K. (2006). Exploring written narrative in children with poor reading comprehension. *Educational Psychology, 26*, 55–72.

de Jong, P.F., & van der Leij, A. (2002). Effects of phonological abilities and linguistic comprehension on the development of reading. *Scientific Studies of Reading, 6,* 51–77.

Dickinson, D., Golinkoff, R., & Hirsh-Pasek, K. (2010). Speaking out for language: Why language is central to reading development. *Educational Researcher, 39,* 305–310.

Dunn, L.M., & Dunn, L.M. (1997). *Peabody Picture Vocabulary Test–III (PPVT-III).* Circle Pines, MN: American Guidance Service.

Gough, P.B., Hoover, W.A., & Peterson, C.L. (1996). Some observations on a simple view of reading. In C. Cornoldi & J. Oakhill (Eds.), *Reading comprehension difficulties: Processes and interventions* (pp. 1–13). Mahwah, NJ: Lawrence Erlbaum Associates.

Gough, P.B., & Tunmer, W.E. (1986). Decoding, reading, and reading disability. *Remedial and Special Education, 7,* 6–10.

Hoover, W.A., & Gough, P.B. (1990). The simple view of reading. *Reading and Writing, 2,* 127–160.

Justice, L.M., & Ezell, H.K. (2000). Enhancing children's print and word awareness through home-based parent intervention. *American Journal of Speech-Language Pathology, 7,* 33–47.

Justice, L.M., Mashburn, A., & Petscher, Y. (in press). Very early language skills of fifth-grade poor comprehenders. *Journal of Research in Reading.*

Keenan, J.M., Betjemann, R.S., Wadsworth, S.J., DeFries, J.C., & Olson, R.K. (2006). Genetic and environmental influences on reading and listening comprehension. *Journal of Research in Reading, 29,* 75–91.

Kendeou, P., van den Broek, P., White, M.J., & Lynch, J.S. (2009). Predicting reading comprehension in early elementary school: The independent contributions of oral language and decoding skills. *Journal of Educational Psychology, 101,* 765–778.

Kintsch, W., & Kintsch, E. (2005). Comprehension. In S.G. Paris & S.A. Stahl (Eds.), *Current issues in reading comprehension and assessment* (pp. 71–92). Mahwah, NJ: Lawrence Erlbaum Associates.

Lonigan, C.J. (2010). Vocabulary development and the development of phonological awareness skills in preschool children. In R.K. Wagner, A.E. Muse, & K.R. Tannenbaum (Eds.), *Vocabulary acquisition: Implications for reading comprehension* (pp. 15–31). New York, NY: Guilford Press.

Lonigan, C.J., & Whitehurst, G.J. (1998). Examination of the relative efficacy of parent and teacher involvement in a shared-reading intervention for preschool children from low-income backgrounds. *Early Childhood Research Quarterly, 13,* 263–290.

Mandler, J.M., & Johnson, N.S. (1977). Remembrance of things parsed: Story structure and recall. *Cognitive Psychology, 9,* 111–151.

Megherbi, H., & Ehrlich, M.F. (2005). Language impairment in less skilled comprehenders: The on-line processing of anaphoric pronouns in a listening situation. *Reading and Writing, 18,* 715–753.

Muter, V., Hulme, C., Snowling, M.J., & Stevenson, J. (2004). Phonemes, rimes, vocabulary, and grammatical skills as foundations of early reading development: Evidence from a longitudinal study. *Developmental Psychology, 40,* 665–681.

Nation, K., & Snowling, M.J. (1999). Developmental differences in sensitivity to semantic relations among good and poor comprehenders: Evidence from semantic priming. *Cognition, 70,* 81–83.

National Early Literacy Panel. (2008). *Developing early literacy: Report of the National Early Literacy Panel*. Washington, DC: National Institute for Literacy.

Oakhill, J.V., & Cain, K. (in press). The precursors of reading ability in young readers: Evidence from a four-year longitudinal study. *Scientific Studies of Reading*.

Oakhill, J.V., Cain, K., & Bryant, P.E. (2003). The dissociation of word reading and text comprehension: Evidence from component skills. *Language and Cognitive Processes, 18*, 443–468.

Perfetti, C.A. (1985). *Reading ability*. New York, NY: Oxford University Press.

Perfetti, C.A. (2007). Reading ability: Lexical quality to comprehension. *Scientific Studies of Reading, 11*, 357–383.

Reese, E., & Newcombe, R. (2007). Training mothers in elaborative reminiscing enhances children's autobiographical memory and narrative. *Child Development, 78*, 1153–1170.

Singer, M.H., & Crouse, J. (1981). The relationship of context-use skills to reading: A case for an alternative experimental logic. *Child Development, 52*, 1326–1329.

Stanovich, K.E. (1980). Toward an interactive-compensatory model of individual differences in the development of reading fluency. *Reading Research Quarterly, 16*, 32–71.

Storch, S.A., & Whitehurst, G.J. (2002). Oral language and code-related precursors to reading: Evidence from a longitudinal structural model. *Developmental Psychology, 38*, 934–947.

Stothard, S.E., & Hulme, C. (1992). Reading comprehension difficulties in children: The role of language comprehension and working memory skills. *Reading and Writing, 4*, 245–256.

Trabasso, T., Secco, T., & van den Broek, P.W. (1984). Causal cohesion and story coherence. In H. Mandl, N.L. Stein, & T. Trabasso (Eds.), *Learning and comprehension of text* (pp. 83–111). Mahwah, NJ: Lawrence Erlbaum Associates.

U.S. Department of Education, Early Childhood Education, Institute of Education Sciences. (2006). *Dialogic reading* (What Works Clearinghouse intervention report). Washington, DC: Author.

U.S. Department of Education, National Center for Education Statistics. (2003). *Early childhood education program participation surveys of the National Household Education Surveys Program: 2001*. Retrieved from http://nces.ed.gov/pubsearch/getpubcats.asp?sid=004

Valdez-Menchaca, M.C., & Whitehurst, G.J. (1992). Accelerating language development through picture book reading: A systematic extension to Mexican day-care. *Developmental Psychology, 28*, 1106–1114

Van Steensel, R. (2006). Relations between socio-cultural factors, the home literacy environment, and children's literacy development in the first years of primary education. *Journal of Research in Reading, 29*, 367–382.

Verhoeven, L., & van Leeuwe, J. (2008). Predictors of text comprehension development. *Applied Cognitive Psychology, 22*, 407–423.

Wasik, B., & Bond, M.A. (2001). Beyond the pages of a book: Interactive book reading and language development in preschool classrooms. *Journal of Educational Psychology, 93*, 243–250.

Whitehurst, G.J., Arnold, D.S., Epstein, J.N., Angell, A.L., Smith, M., & Fischel, J.E. (1994). A picture book reading intervention in day-care and home for children from low-income families. *Developmental Psychology, 30*, 679–689.

Whitehurst, G.J., Falco, F.L., Lonigan, C.J., Fischel, J.E., DeBaryshe, B.D., Valdez-Menchaca, M.C., & Caulfield, M. (1988). Accelerating language development through picture book reading. *Developmental Psychology, 24,* 552–559.

Whitehurst, G., & Lonigan, C.J. (1998). Child development and emergent literacy. *Child Development, 69,* 848–872.

11

Early Literacy Intervention for Young Children with Special Needs

Judith J. Carta and Coralie Driscoll

D o young children with special needs require special instruction in early literacy? The meta-analyses of early literacy interventions carried out and reported on by the National Early Literacy Panel (NELP; 2008) revealed few differences in instructional effectiveness for special populations of any kind. The NELP methodology did not include studies with single-case designs, which are often used in the field of special education. Until direct tests of special instructional strategies for children with special needs are addressed with large randomized trials or there is a careful review of the existing studies with single-case designs, it is impossible to say with certainty whether practices identified as effective for enhancing the early literacy of the general population will work for young children with special needs. In this chapter we review empirical studies that focus on the instructional effectiveness of a variety of interventions for promoting the early literacy development of young children with special needs, highlight areas in which evidence is strongest, and point to areas in which more research is needed.

EARLY LITERACY INTERVENTIONS
FOR YOUNG CHILDREN WITH SPECIAL NEEDS

Professionals as well as the general public are becoming increasingly aware of the importance of early literacy development. A number of reports and large studies have fueled this interest (National Institute of Child Health and Development Early Child Care Research Network, 2005; Storch & Whitehurst, 2002), but a significant factor spurring the attention is the growing understanding of the vast differences in children's early literacy skills when they enter kindergarten, and how children's experiences before school set the stage for these differences. Unfortunately, most children who begin kindergarten with a deficiency in vocabulary and reading skills rarely catch up (Biemiller, 2006). As a result, researchers and policy makers have advocated for programs that focus on the prevention of reading problems by providing young children with the type of early experiences that can be implemented before children enter kindergarten. Over the past decade, much research has been carried out and many model programs have been developed to address this gap by using specific intervention strategies. The NELP report (2008) and other studies (Bus & van IJzendoorn, 1999; Mol, Bus, & de Jong, 2009; U.S. Department of Education, 2007, 2008) have begun to shed light on the most effective strategies for shoring up children's early literacy skills before they begin to experience reading failure.

Although empirical information about the instructional effectiveness of strategies for promoting children's early literacy is growing at a rapid rate, little is known about how strategies identified as "evidence-based" work for young children with special needs. Neither the NELP report nor a report published by the National Academy of Sciences (Snow, Burns, & Griffin, 1998) identified strategies that work to improve the early literacy performance or the reading readiness of young children with developmental problems. Although we have long known that a variety of disabilities and developmental problems place children at significant risk for difficulties in learning to read, very little research exists on early literacy intervention that specifically targets young children with special needs. Likewise, few larger studies of early literacy interventions have examined effects on young children with disabilities by disaggregating outcomes on specific subgroups.

The purpose of this chapter is to report on the instructional effectiveness of intervention strategies that have specifically targeted young children with special needs. For this chapter, children with special needs include children with disabilities, with general delays in development, or with sensory impairments. A broader question relevant to early literacy intervention science is whether interventions that are found to be effective for typically developing children will work for all groups of children. Although NELP's meta-analyses found few differences in instructional effectiveness for special populations of any kind, the authors pointed out that group differences identified in studies were often confounded with other study features. Seldom were studies conducted with enough power to allow an analysis of subgroup impacts. Moreover, the NELP analysis specifically excluded studies employing single-case designs to examine the effectiveness of early literacy and language interventions. Ruling out studies using single-case designs essentially eliminated the research methodology that has been used most often to validate intervention practices for students with disabilities (Horner et al., 2005; Tankersley, Harjusola-Webb, & Landrum, 2008). In this chapter, we include studies using both group and single-case designs to summarize what is known about early literacy and language interventions that have targeted young children with a range of special needs. We identify areas in which the preponderance of empirically based knowledge has been generated about what works and for whom, and we also point out where the largest gaps in the literature exist. We conclude with a discussion of the implications of this analysis for classroom practice.

STUDIES OF EARLY LITERACY INTERVENTIONS FOR CHILDREN WITH SPECIAL NEEDS

Although a few researchers began studying early literacy for preschool-age children with special needs more than a decade ago (e.g., Katims, 1994; O'Connor, Jenkins, Leicester, & Slocum, 1993), it has only been in the last 5 years that researchers have published findings on the efficacy of explicit interventions for special populations of young children. This more recent research has focused primarily on examinations of the code-based instruction or early language teaching described in the NELP report. The work consists largely of studies on interventions for children with specific speech or language impairments (e.g., Lovelace & Stewart, 2007; Munro, Lee, & Baker, 2008). Other studies have focused on the effectiveness of early literacy instruction for children with a variety of developmental delays (O'Connor et al., 1993) or intellectual disabilities (Mechling, Gast, & Langone, 2002) or specifically for children with Down syndrome (van Bysterveldt, Gillon, & Moran, 2006). Finally, a small set of studies of early literacy has been carried out with older children with specific disabilities, such as autism (Eikeseth & Jahr, 2001), or with sensory impairments, such as impairments in hearing or vision (e.g., Bergeron, Lederberg, East-erbrooks, Miller, & Connor, 2009; Monson & Bowen, 2008). Most studies describing early literacy outcomes for special populations, however, have been descriptive in nature. Only a few intervention studies have been con-ducted with children who have sensory impairments, and almost all of these have been with children who are in the elementary grades or older (e.g., Trezek, Wang, Woods, Gampp, & Paul, 2007). We therefore focus primarily on those intervention studies involving preschool-age children that have targeted any of the areas of early literacy (i.e., phonological awareness, print awareness, or alphabet knowledge) or any language skills related to early literacy. We begin with a summary of studies that focus on teaching phonological awareness.

Phonological Awareness Interventions

More than any other component of early literacy, phonological aware-ness has been identified as an important predictor of later success in reading decoding (NELP, 2008; Storch & Whitehurst, 2002), and inter-ventions in this area have been shown to improve most children's read-ing (Troia, 1999). Phonological awareness has been defined as "the conscious awareness that words are made up of segments of our own speech that are represented with letters in an alphabetic orthography" (Moats, 2000, p. 234). Phonemic awareness is a subset of phonological awareness and includes both the understanding that words are made up of individual phonemes and the ability to manipulate phonemes. Researchers have identified several subgroups of children who have dif-ficulty developing phonemic awareness, and among them are children with language impairment (Boudreau & Hedberg, 1999), children with speech impairment (Rvachew, Ohberg, Grawburg, & Heyding, 2003), and children with intellectual disabilities (Sun & Kemp, 2006). There-fore, it is not surprising that phonemic awareness skills have constituted an area of intervention research.

The instructional approaches for phonological awareness and the specific populations targeted have varied considerably across the inter-vention studies. Early work by O'Connor and colleagues (1993) targeted young children with a variety of disabilities and employed a 7-week classroom-based program of phonological awareness focusing on sound identification and manipulation. Children ages 4–6 years were randomly assigned to one of three treatments—rhyming, blending, or segmenting. Results from mastery tests suggested that the children's performance was highest in the skill area for which they received phonological aware-ness intervention. Children did not demonstrate generalization to other phonological awareness skills. An important finding in this study was the considerable variation in children's gains in response to treatment. Almost all children learned to rhyme (92%), but only 54% learned to segment, and just 64% demonstrated acquisition of blending. O'Connor and her colleagues reported that although children's cognitive skills predicted several phonological awareness outcomes, most children demonstrated some growth resulting from phonological awareness training, regardless of their developmental level. Many children with low cognitive scores demonstrated gains in phonological awareness in response to treatment. The child's cognitive ability did not appear to limit learning.

In a similar intervention study focusing on kindergarten-age children with language impairments, Warrick, Rubin, and Rowe-Walsh (1993) implemented an 8-week intervention focusing on a developmental hierarchy of phonological awareness skills. These skills included syllable awareness, initial sound segmentation, onset–rime and rhyme recognition, and phoneme segmentation. Children with language impairments were randomly assigned to the intervention or control conditions. Children receiving the treatment outperformed children in the control group at posttest on several phonological awareness measures and were performing similarly to typically developing children 1 year postintervention on most of the measures.

Another intervention study that is noteworthy for the duration and intensity of the phonological awareness treatment focused specifically on preschool-age children with moderate and severe language impairment. In a single-subject, alternating-treatment design, Major and Bernhardt (1998) tested a treatment that targeted syllable structure, phonemes, rhyming, alliteration, and segmentation and that was conducted in individual sessions led by speech-language pathologists three times per week for 16 weeks. Children made important gains in the targeted phonological awareness skills. Worth noting is a descriptive follow-up of the original 12 children 3 years after the initial treatment. Bernhardt and Major (2005) found that 10 of the original 12 children demonstrated sustained improvement on the skills that had been the focus of the intervention, as well as average or above-average reading decoding, sight word reading, and reading comprehension, indicating a degree of transfer of originally learned skills.

Roth, Troia, Worthington, and Dow (2002) carried out one of the first examples of an intervention study testing the efficacy of a comprehensive and explicit phonological awareness curriculum. Aimed at preschoolers with speech and language impairments, this curriculum focused specifically on rhyming. The curriculum offered a number of design features that may be especially important for children with disabilities, including 1) explicit instruction that incorporated clear explanation of the tasks and target behaviors, modeling by the instructors, and positive reinforcement and corrective feedback for each response on a series of progressively more difficult tasks; 2) a balance of teacher-directed activities and child-centered activities, such as songs, games, and movement, that provided children with more opportunities to be engaged in the target behavior; 3) a criterion-based approach for a child's individual progress through the curriculum; 4) scripted lessons or "metascripts," detailed lesson plans that the instructor could tailor to meet the individual needs of students; and 5) alternate lessons for accommodating children with diverse learning rates, and lessons for teaching prerequisite skills to children who could not demonstrate the minimum threshold of rhyming ability. The intervention was implemented in individual 30-minute sessions 3 days per week for 6–8 weeks. Using a single-subject design for eight students, the researchers found that all children demonstrated significant gains on rhyming—the skill targeted for the intervention.

Until recently, most phonological awareness interventions for young children with speech and language impairments have been treatments of high intensity and relatively long duration and have been offered in individual sessions, often by speech and language pathologists. In the past few years, some researchers have attempted to determine whether low-intensity interventions offered in classrooms might also be effective in improving phonological awareness skills in children with language impairments. Laing and Espeland (2005) tested the effectiveness of a classroom-based treatment of relatively low intensity that was delivered twice weekly in 15-minute sessions to small groups of children with sensory or language impairments. The program, which ran for only 8 weeks, focused on rhyme identification, rhyme production, sound categorization, letter identification, and letter–sound correspondence. Children receiving treatment in this quasi-experimental study demonstrated greater postintervention gains than children in the comparison group in rhyme identification, rhyme production, and sound categorization. Gains were achieved in spite of the fact that the treatment group had significantly lower cognitive skills than the comparison group. The researchers noted that this provides some evidence that children with limited cognitive skills can benefit from phonological awareness training.

Ziolkowski and Goldstein (2008) evaluated a novel approach to phonological awareness intervention involving repeated shared book reading. These researchers targeted 13 preschool-age children with language delays who came from high-poverty communities. Explicit instruction in rhymes and letter sounds was embedded multiple times within shared book–reading sessions. The intervention—consisting of two intervention conditions, Rhyme Time and Initial Sound Off—was implemented three times a week for 13 weeks in small reading groups of three children. The single-subject design provided evidence that the children improved their rhyme production and sound identification skills when they received the rhyme intervention and that they improved their alliteration and initial-sound fluency skills as a consequence of the initial-sound intervention. Effects were replicated for all 13 children. The authors believe that an important result of this study is the demonstration that children with language delays who come from low-income settings can improve their phonological awareness skills if interventionists provide them with multiple opportunities for learning those skills when they are embedded in the context of frequently used shared book reading in the classroom.

Justice, Kaderavek, Bowles, and Grimm (2005) tested for feasibility a similar intervention based on repeated shared storybook readings that were implemented with parents of children with specific language impairments. In this study, children with specific language impairments were randomly assigned to the home-based, parent-implemented intervention targeting phonological awareness skills. Comparison-group children also received a parent-implemented intervention, one that that focused on vocabulary building. Intervention took place in 40 sessions over a 10-week period. Analysis of the results revealed that children receiving the experimental treatment improved on rhyming but not on alliteration measures. The researchers speculated that because alliteration is more difficult than rhyming, children may need to achieve a threshold of syllable-level awareness (as demonstrated by their performance on rhyming measures) before they will begin to show growth on onset–rime skills (as measured by their performance on alliteration tasks).

In summary, researchers have demonstrated that preschool children with speech and language impairments or disabilities can learn phonological awareness skills. Interventions that targeted specific skills and those that embedded teaching into repeated shared book reading in the home or at school were effective in improving most phonological awareness skills. Teaching children in groups or individually was also successful. The most critical components of the interventions appeared to be the use of explicit teaching strategies and giving children multiple opportunities to learn the skills. Researchers are examining the intensity of instruction and experimenting with the minimum amount of instructional time needed for children with special needs to learn particular phonological awareness skills. The hierarchy of phonological awareness tasks for special populations is yet to be determined.

It is vital that once phonological awareness skills are acquired, they should be maintained and generalized. Few researchers have reported longitudinal effects of phonological awareness interventions for young children with special needs. In one study (Bernhardt & Major, 2005), most of the participants with speech and language impairments who received follow up 3 years after the initial intervention performed reading and phonological awareness tasks at a level similar to that of children with typical development. However, in an earlier study, O'Connor and colleagues (1993) found that generalization to untaught skills was not observed for children with various disabilities. Research is needed to determine whether these different outcomes are due to the nature of children's disabilities or to the specific intervention techniques for teaching or promoting generalization. More short-term and long-term research that looks at the acquisition, maintenance, and generalization of skills using both single-case and group designs for children with a range of special needs is needed.

Interventions Focusing on Print Awareness and Alphabet Knowledge

Although phonological awareness is the target for the preponderance of intervention studies focusing on young children with disabilities, a substantial set of studies have been conducted on interventions that focus on other areas of early literacy, such as print knowledge. Print knowledge is a multidimensional construct that refers to children's understanding of the forms and functions of written language (Whitehurst & Lonigan, 1998). It includes print concept knowledge, or how print is organized and the function it serves in texts; alphabet knowledge, or the names and features of letters of the alphabet; and emergent writing, the expression of meaning through writing (Justice, Kaderavek, Fan, Sofka, & Hunt, 2009). In multiple studies, researchers have found that these sets of skills are important predictors of children's later reading achievement (Scarborough, 1998; Tunmer, Herriman, & Nesdale, 1988). Print knowledge is strongly shaped by young children's home environments and the interactions they share with their parents around books and other print material (Senechal, LeFevre, Thomas, & Daley, 1998). Children with disabilities, and in particular those with language impairments, have been found to have fewer high-quality interactions with their parents during shared book reading (Marvin & Wright, 1997).

Recent studies have focused on improving the print knowledge of children with language impairments. Lovelace and Stewart (2007) examined the efficacy of a nonevocative, explicit strategy during shared storybook reading. This strategy, based on work by Justice and Kaderavek (2005), employs explicit teaching to "the literacy targets through the use of direct, sequenced instructional opportunities with aspects of an embedded approach where adults serve as facilitators of children's literacy learning" (p. 18). More specifically, the procedure employs dialogic reading and explicit print referencing to direct "children's attention to print concepts that are embedded into book reading interactions" (p. 18). Using a single-subject design, Lovelace and Stewart examined the effects of this nonevocative print-referencing strategy during 10-minute storybook readings that were incorporated into individualized language intervention sessions and took place twice weekly in children's classrooms. Participants, who were children with language impairments, demonstrated gains in their knowledge of print concepts. All three participants demonstrated gains on print concepts after only four 10-minute sessions, and they continued, on periodic probes, to demonstrate growth with repeated training. This finding, along with its demonstration of generalization of print knowledge, showed that children with language impairments can acquire print knowledge through a nonevocative, explicit referencing technique implemented within the nonintrusive and frequently used context of shared book reading.

Storybook reading with print referencing has also been used with parents of children with Down syndrome as implementers. In a study by van Bysterveldt, Gillon, and Moran (2006), parents were taught how to use print referencing to bring their children's attention to targeted letters and sounds within words and to initial phonemes in words. After a 6-week intervention, the children receiving treatment showed significant improvement on phonological awareness and letter knowledge. One finding that may have practical implications is that knowledge of letter names and letter sounds appeared to be a prerequisite to children's phonological awareness skills (specifically, to identifying initial phonemes). Other researchers have suggested this sequence of skills in their literature as well (e.g., Bowey, 1994; Johnston, Anderson, & Holligan, 1996).

Another aspect of early literacy that is a strong predictor of later reading achievement is alphabet knowledge (Catts, Fey, Zhang, & Tomblin, 2001; Stevenson & Newman, 1986). Alphabet knowledge refers to children's understanding of the names, features, and details of letters (Lomax & McGee, 1987), an area of learning that some researchers have indicated is an area of weakness for young children with special needs (Boudreau & Hedberg, 1999). Lafferty, Gray, and Wilcox (2005) studied the effectiveness of a 7-week intervention for teaching alphabet knowledge to two children with developmental language delay and two typically developing children. The intervention employed an explicit teaching approach incorporating modeling, imitation, and feedback within play activities. The one-to-one teaching session emphasized repeated learning opportunities to produce letter names and sounds. Using a single-subject design, the researchers found that three of the four children successfully learned to produce and recognize some of the targeted letter names and sounds. All children demonstrated gains between baseline and posttest on their ability to name and produce letters. Although each child learned at a different rate, an overall higher accuracy was found in children's acquisition of letter name and production compared with sound recognition and production. This study provided a preliminary demonstration that a short-term intervention could be successful in improving alphabet knowledge for preschoolers with language delays.

Integrated Early Literacy Interventions

Several researchers have acknowledged that early literacy is composed of skills in different areas and have combined two or more skill areas within treatment sessions. Gillon (2000, 2002, 2005) and her colleagues focused on children with speech impairments in a series of studies that targeted phonological awareness and knowledge of letter names and sounds as well as improvement in speech intelligibility. The intervention they devised, delivered in individual treatment sessions, systematically targeted rhyming, manipulation and identification of phonemes, segmenting, blending, and phoneme–grapheme correspondence in 6-year-old children with speech impairments. In a quasi-experimental study, Gillon (2000) found the integrated intervention to be more effective in improving children's growth in phonological awareness and reading skill compared with an intervention in which children received a more traditional treatment targeting speech alone. In a follow-up study 1 year later (Gillon, 2002), children who had received the integrated intervention were still maintaining their edge in phonological awareness and were performing comparably to typically developing peers in reading. In a later study, Gillon (2005) tested the same integrated intervention combining phonological awareness, letter naming, and speech intelligibility, but this time the intervention was delivered to 3- to 5-year-old children in small groups twice per week over 18 weeks. Activities involved interventionist-directed activities that promoted children's active participation. The integrated approach focused on therapy sessions in which activities for simulating phonological awareness and letter knowledge were interspersed with activities targeting speech production. Once again, in a quasi-experimental study, children with speech impairments who received the integrated intervention demonstrated higher levels of growth in phonological awareness as they reached kindergarten entry and were comparable to typically developing children in these skills.

This integrated approach to early literacy was subsequently employed successfully with preschool children with Down syndrome (van Bysterveldt, Gillon, & Foster-Cohen, 2010). In this particular study, the intervention included three components: the integrated therapy sessions that interspersed phonological awareness and letter knowledge goals with speech production goals, a parent-implemented home program using a print-referencing technique four times per week, and a learning-through-computer component. In a single-subject design involving 10 participants, 6 participants improved on letter knowledge and 9 participants improved on identifying initial phonemes in words. All participants demonstrated gains on speech measures.

In summary, combining speech articulation training with phonological awareness and letter knowledge has been shown to be effective on short-term measures for the majority of children with speech impairments and children with Down syndrome. Moreover, for children with speech impairments, literacy outcomes have persisted for up to 3 years. Although randomized trials with larger samples have yet to be conducted, these studies demonstrate that the skills can be taught and that their effects persist at least up to school entry.

Vocabulary and Other Oral Language Interventions

There has been a growing recognition of the contribution of oral language skills, such as vocabulary knowledge, as important precursors to the development of children's reading comprehension (e.g., Catts & Kamhi, 2005; McGregor, 2004). The manner in which vocabulary might be related to word recognition and reading comprehension is still unfolding. Vocabulary abilities, for example, have been shown to be highly related to phonological awareness skills in both preschool- and school-age children (Bowey, 1994; Lonigan, Burgess, Anthony, & Barker, 1998). Other studies have shown vocabulary growth to be related to word recognition (Walley, Metsala, & Garlock, 2003). In spite of substantial literature linking language to reading, relatively fewer studies of early literacy interventions focusing on vocabulary development have been carried out compared with the vast number of studies focusing on phonological awareness and print knowledge. Dickinson, Golinkoff, and Hirsh-Pasek (2010) lamented this lack of attention to vocabulary interventions and speculated that language may be overlooked in preschool interventions because it is generally more difficult to teach than the more specific code-related early literacy skills.

Children with developmental delays often experience difficulties in vocabulary and other areas of oral language (Boudreau & Hedberg, 1999; Kaderavek & Sulzby, 2000). Vocabulary has been a challenging area for getting intervention effects for children who are struggling learners. NELP (2008) found no significant language differences for preschool children participating in programs that implemented class-wide early literacy curricula. Targeted interventions, on the other hand, such as shared book reading or dialogic reading, have demonstrated some success in improving children's language (e.g., Mol et al., 2009; Whitehurst et al., 1994). These positive effects have not been as robust with children with special needs as they have been with less vulnerable learners. For example, Dale, Crain-Thoreson, Notari-Syverson, and Cole (1996) studied the effectiveness of dialogic reading when implemented by parents of children with mild to moderate language delays. The researchers randomly assigned 33 children and their parents to either a dialogic reading intervention or a control group in which the parents were trained to implement the *Conversational Language Training Program,* which taught parents how to interact responsively with their children but did not include a book-sharing component. Children who received the dialogic reading intervention showed significant increases in lexical diversity during a play activity and in their total number of utterances while sharing books with their parents. When Crain-Thoreson and Dale (1999) carried out another study of dialogic reading, they failed to replicate the effects of the earlier study.

Another area of early literacy intervention that has been relatively ignored for young children with special needs is comprehension. A handful of studies have been conducted to investigate the effectiveness of interventions targeting literal and inferential language skills. For example, studies conducted by Bradshaw, Hoffman, and Norris (1998) and by van Kleeck, Vander Woude, and Hammett (2006) have found that book sharing can be used as the context for embedding questions that target literal and inferential language skills. In a small-group randomized study, van Kleeck and colleagues randomly assigned 30 children with language impairments to either a comprehension intervention or a control group. The treatment consisted of a twice-weekly, 15-minute, one-to-one book-sharing session during which adults embedded scripted questions into storybook text and then modeled appropriate responses as necessary. After 8 weeks of intervention, children receiving the treatment showed gains in both literal and inferential language skills.

In another related area of research on comprehension strategies, studies have been conducted to examine the effectiveness of narrative intervention for young children with language impairments. Children's narrative abilities, or their skills in retelling a story or in describing causally related events, have been documented as strong predictors of later school success (e.g., Catts, Fey, Tomblin, & Zhang, 2002; Griffin, Hemphill, Camp, & Wolf, 2004). Although some studies have been conducted to evaluate the effectiveness of narrative interventions for older children to improve reading (e.g., Carnine & Kinder, 1985), this type of intervention has been relatively untested for preschool-age children. In an exploratory study, Hayward and Schneider (2000) produced some promising findings, suggesting that prekindergarten- and kindergarten-age children with moderate to severe language impairments who received a narrative intervention improved in their abilities to provide more relevant and more complex information about stories. Similarly, Spencer and Slocum (2010) found that children with narrative language delays demonstrated improved abilities to retell stories after receiving a narrative intervention consisting of increasingly independent practice delivered in a small group. These are encouraging results, because all children showed storytelling improvements despite the fact that they were at risk for learning problems and were also culturally and linguistically diverse. We expect that this study will lead to more research on the much-ignored area of comprehension as a target for intervention.

Hybrid Language/Literacy Interventions

Whereas some studies have targeted the specific component of vocabulary or comprehension in interventions for children with speech and language impairments (McGregor & Leonard, 1989), others have included oral language as one of multiple components in interventions that include both phonological awareness and vocabulary knowledge. For example, Munro et al. (2008) carried out a feasibility study of a hybrid intervention targeting both phonological awareness and vocabulary that involved drill-based games and oral narrative storybook reading for children with speech and language impairments. This 6-week intervention demonstrated significant postintervention gains in children's skills in expressive vocabulary, rhyme, and alliteration awareness.

This type of hybrid intervention is an example of what Justice and Kaderavek (2005) have termed an embedded-explicit model of emergent literacy intervention. This model emphasizes the use of a combination of approaches, including 1) embedded, or child-directed, contextualized and meaningful interactions around literacy concepts that are incorporated into classroom activities throughout the day (e.g., Clay, 1998) and 2) explicit, or structured, adult-directed, instructions focused on discrete skills taught through modeling, elicitation, and repeated guided practice (Chard & Dickson, 1999). The embedded-explicit model combines both child- and teacher-directed approaches within a multitiered model so that a foundational tier of high-quality, embedded and explicit sets of activities are provided to all children (i.e., Tier 1). Children who are slow to progress in this universal tier of instruction receive a second tier of instruction implemented in small groups or one to one. A more intensive tier of instruction may be delivered to children who still need additional literacy support.

This multitiered approach, called response to treatment or response to intervention (RTI; Greenwood et al., 2008; Koutsoftas, Harmon, &

Gray, 2009; Vaughn, Linan-Thompson, & Hickman, 2003) assumes that in a given classroom, children will have different needs for additional support or instructional intensity. Children are identified for that additional support not through an eligibility process that identifies them as having a disability but through their performance in response to the instruction they have received. Although this approach has been employed for a number of years with older students and is written into the Individuals with Disabilities Education Improvement Act (IDEA) of 2004 (PL 108-446), its application to preschool children is just beginning. Early research on RTI for young children has been conducted by Bailet, Repper, Piasta, and Murphy (2009); Kousoftas et al. (2009); and VanDerHeyden, Snyder, Broussard, and Ramsdell (2007). Researchers are attempting to determine efficient approaches for identifying children who may need higher tiers of instructional support, effective interventions that can be used to supplement the instruction struggling learners are receiving in Tier 1, and strategies for monitoring the progress of children who are receiving those interventions (Center for Response to Intervention in Early Childhood, 2010). Overarching questions that remain to be answered are what proportion of children in classrooms will need higher tiers of intervention, who will implement the assessment and intervention at those higher levels, and whether comprehensive RTI models will be feasible across the wide array of early education programs. In spite of the challenges, RTI has the advantage of offering a systematic way of addressing the individual differences in children's emergent literacy development.

CONCLUSION

In this chapter, we have reviewed the instructional effectiveness of early literacy and language interventions that have specifically targeted young children with special needs. We have questioned whether various approaches for teaching phonological awareness, print knowledge, alphabet knowledge, and vocabulary that have been documented as effective with typically developing or children at risk for reading difficulties are also effective for teaching young children with identified disabilities and developmental delays. Because the prevailing zeitgeist in early literacy instruction in preschools is early intervention aimed at preventing later reading problems, it is worth examining whether the same philosophy of preventing reading failure can be applied to children who already have identified developmental problems. Furthermore, practitioners who serve young children in general early education settings need to know whether evidence-based strategies that they employ for children in their classrooms might also be effective for children with a variety of disabilities.

What can we learn from this review about the state of the evidence regarding early literacy instruction for young children with special needs?

1. Our review of empirical studies highlights that young children with special needs can learn early literacy skills. Although this field of research is still very new, preliminary evidence shows that young children with identified disabilities have demonstrated gains in response to early literacy interventions. It should be noted that the great preponderance of studies to this point have been conducted with children with speech and language impairments. Relatively fewer studies of preschoolers with general developmental delays or specific cognitive or sensory impairments have been carried out.

2. The largest proportion of studies have focused on phonological awareness interventions or integrated interventions that include phonological awareness instruction. A trend seems to be the integration of child- and teacher-initiated activities. Many of the most successful interventions for children with disabilities have featured explicit and systematic instruction that includes modeling by the instructors, positive reinforcement, and corrective feedback on a sequence of progressively more difficult tasks.

3. The context for many of the interventions across these studies has been speech and language clinics or small groups within classrooms, sites at which the interventions have been conducted by research staff. A limited number of studies have engaged parents or classroom teachers as implementers. An important next step in this research will be to translate promising practices and test their feasibility and effectiveness when implemented by classroom teachers.

4. Very few longitudinal studies have been carried out to document the lasting effects of early literacy interventions and whether or not they improve the probability that children will be successful readers who can comprehend text. These types of studies as well as those that illustrate the types of continuing instructional support that children with special needs may need to maintain early literacy gains will be an important future step in research in the next few years.

5. The research designs employed in the studies we have reviewed had some significant methodological constraints. Although some single-case designs are providing evidence of promising intervention strategies for some children with specific disabilities, the generalizability of these findings is limited in the absence of randomized trials with larger sample sizes. An important fact worth noting in the group experimental studies reviewed was the wide variation in children's responses to the interventions. This finding points to the critical need for individualizing

instruction on the basis of a child's response to the intervention that he or she has received and not on the child's disability. Children's performance on specific early literacy skills should be monitored regularly in order to ascertain their level of growth and to adjust the level of instructional support in response to their demonstrated performance.

Implications for Practice

One important implication for practitioners is that we have no evidence at this point that children with special needs will *not* benefit from evidence-based practices in early literacy. Although children with general developmental delays or disabilities or with sensory problems may struggle to learn literacy skills, they should not be ruled out of classwide instruction by virtue of their special needs status. Instead, teachers should monitor their progress in response to instruction and provide them with a higher level of literacy support if that is indicated.

A second important take-home message from this summary is that instructional strategies were demonstrated as effective for children with special needs when implemented in a variety of contexts. Although many interventions were carried out in one-to-one situations in clinic settings by speech and language pathologists, some strategies worked when implemented in small groups in classrooms by teachers. Others strategies implemented by parents in home settings, such as shared storybook reading with print referencing (e.g., Justice et al., 2005; van Bysterveldt et al., 2006), showed some preliminary evidence of effectiveness. Practitioners should be encouraged to carry out these interventions in settings in which learning and play typically occur for young children.

A third important implication relevant to practice is the importance of increasing opportunities for learning through a balance of child- and teacher-initiated activities. Research thus far appears to indicate that when children with special needs are first acquiring literacy skills, they benefit from explicit teaching (i.e., giving children clear instructions supplemented with modeling or demonstration, and reinforcing correct responses or giving corrective feedback). Complementing this type of intentional teaching with the provision of multiple opportunities for children to practice newly acquired skills in games and songs and developmentally appropriate activities throughout the day promotes the maintenance and generalization of the acquired skills.

Some of the studies we have reviewed demonstrate the potential promise of early literacy interventions for young children with special needs, but it is clear that this field of research is still emerging. Much more research is needed on children with a variety of characteristics and in a variety of settings before we can offer many recommendations to practitioners. We expect that as more evidence-based intervention to promote early literacy is implemented with young children in general, researchers as well as teachers will be able to see how children with a variety of disabilities respond to instruction and how best to offer greater intensity of support. Such demonstrations will allow us to improve the science and practice relevant to special groups of young learners.

REFERENCES

Bailet, L.L., Repper, K.K., Piasta, S.B., & Murphy, S.P. (2009). Emergent literacy intervention for prekindergarteners at risk for reading failure. *Journal of Learning Disabilities, 42,* 336–355.

Bergeron, J.P., Lederberg, A.R., Easterbrooks, S.R., Miller, E.M., & Connor, C.M. (2009). Building the alphabetic principle in young children who are deaf or hard of hearing. *The Volta Review, 109*(2–3), 87–119.

Bernhardt, B., & Major, E. (2005). Speech, language and literacy skills 3 years later: A follow-up study of early phonological and metaphonological intervention. *International Journal of Language and Communication Disorders, 40,* 1–27.

Biemiller, A. (2006). Vocabulary development and instruction: A prerequisite for school learning. In D.K. Dickinson & S.B. Neuman (Eds.), *Handbook of early literacy* (Vol. 2, pp. 41–51). New York, NY: Guilford Press.

Boudreau, D.M., & Hedberg, N.L. (1999). A comparison of early literacy skills in children with specific language impairment and their typically developing peers. *American Journal of Speech-Language Pathology, 8,* 249–259.

Bowey, J.A. (1994). Phonological sensitivity in novice readers and non-readers. *Journal of Experimental Child Psychology, 58,* 134–159.

Bradshaw, M.L., Hoffman, P.R., & Norris, J.A. (1998). Efficacy of expansions and close procedures in the development of interpretations by preschool children exhibiting delayed language development. *Language, Speech, and Hearing Services in Schools, 29,* 85–95.

Bus, A.G., & van IJzendoorn, M.H. (1999). Phonological awareness and early reading: A meta-analysis of experimental training studies. *Journal of Education Psychology, 91,* 403–414.

Carnine, D., & Kinder, D. (1985). Teaching low-performing students to apply generative and schema strategies to narrative and expository material. *Remedial and Special Education, 6*(1), 20–30.

Catts, H.W., Fey, M.E., Tomblin, J.B., & Zhang, X. (2002). A longitudinal investigation of reading outcomes in children with language impairments. *Journal of Speech and Hearing Research, 45,* 1142–1157.

Catts, H.W., Fey, M.E., Zhang, X., & Tomblin, J.B. (2001). Estimating the risk of future reading difficulties in kindergarten children: A research-based model and its clinical implications. *Language, Speech, and Hearing Services in Schools, 32,* 38–50.

Catts, H.W., & Kamhi, A.G. (2005). *Language and reading disabilities* (2nd ed.). Boston, MA: Allyn & Bacon.

Center for Response to Intervention in Early Childhood. (2010). *Research agenda.* Retrieved from http://www.crtiec.org/Research/crtiecsfocused programofresearch.shtml

Chard, D.J., & Dickson, S.V. (1999). Phonological awareness instructional assessment guidelines. *Intervention in School and Clinic, 19*, 261–270.

Clay, M. (1998). *By different paths to common outcomes*. York, ME: Stenhouse Publications.

Crain-Thoreson, C., & Dale, P.S. (1999). Enhancing linguistic performance: Parents and teachers as book-reading partners for children with language delays. *Topics in Early Childhood Special Education, 19*, 28–40.

Dale, P.S., Crain-Thoreson, C., Notari-Syverson, A., & Cole, K. (1996). Parent–child book reading as an intervention technique for young children with language delays. *Topics in Early Childhood Special Education, 16*, 213–235.

Dickinson, D.K., Golinkoff, R.M., & Hirsh-Pasek, K.K. (2010). Speaking out for language: Why language is central to reading development. *Educational Researcher, 39*, 305–310.

Eikeseth, S., & Jahr, E. (2001). The UCLA reading and writing program: An evaluation of the beginning stages. *Research in Developmental Disabilities, 22*, 289–307.

Gillon, G.T. (2000). The efficacy of phonological awareness intervention for children with spoken language impairment. *Language, Speech, and Hearing Services in Schools, 31*, 126–141.

Gillon, G. (2002). Follow-up study investigating benefits of phonological awareness intervention for children with spoken language impairment. *International Journal of Language and Communication Disorders, 37*, 381–400.

Gillon, G.T. (2005). Facilitating phoneme awareness development in 3- and 4-year-old children with speech impairment. *Language, Speech, and Hearing Services in Schools, 36*, 308–324.

Greenwood, C.R., Carta, J.J., Baggett, K., Buzhardt, J., Walker, D., & Terry, B. (2008). Best practices integrating progress monitoring and response-to-intervention concepts into early childhood. In A. Thomas, J. Grimes, & J. Gruba (Eds.), *Best practices in school psychology* (Vol. 5, pp. 535–548). Washington, DC: National Association of School Psychology.

Griffin, T.M., Hemphill, L., Camp, L., & Wolf, D.P. (2004). Oral discourse in the preschool years and later literacy skills. *First Language, 24*, 123–147.

Hayward, D., & Schneider, P. (2000). Effectiveness of teaching story grammar knowledge to pre-school children with language impairment: An exploratory story. *Child Language Teaching and Therapy, 16*, 255-284.

Horner, R., Carr, E.G., Halle, J., McGee, G., Odom, S., & Wolery, M. (2005). The use of single-subject research to identify evidence-based practice in special education. *Exceptional Children, 71*, 165–179.

Individuals with Disabilities Education Improvement Act (IDEA) of 2004, PL 108-446, 20 U.S.C. §§ 1400 *et seq.*

Johnston, R.S., Anderson, M., & Holligan, C. (1996). Knowledge of the alphabet and explicit awareness of phonemes in pre-readers: The nature of the relationship. *Reading and Writing: An Interdisciplinary Journal, 8*, 217–234.

Justice, L.M., & Kaderavek, J.N. (2005, August). *Embedded-explicit model of emergent literacy intervention*. Paper presented at the Inclusive and Supportive Special Education Congress, Glasgow, Scotland.

Justice, L.M., Kaderavek, J., Bowles, R., & Grimm, K. (2005). Language impairment, parent–child shared reading, and phonological awareness: A feasibility study. *Topics in Early Childhood Special Education, 25*, 143–156.

Justice, L.M., Kaderavek, J.N., Fan, X., Sofka, A., & Hunt, A. (2009). Accelerating preschoolers' early literacy development through classroom-based teacher–

child storybook reading and explicit print referencing. *Language, Speech, and Hearing Services in Schools, 40,* 67–85.

Kaderavek, J.N., & Sulzby, E. (2000). Narrative productions by children with and without specific language impairment: Oral narratives and emergent readings. *Journal of Speech, Language, and Hearing Research, 43,* 34–49.

Katims, D.S. (1994). Emergence of literacy in preschool children with disabilities. *Learning Disabilities Quarterly, 17*(1), 58–69.

Koutsoftas, A.D., Harmon, M.T., & Gray, S. (2009). The effect of Tier 2 intervention for phonemic awareness in a response-to-intervention model in low-income preschool classrooms. *Language, Speech, and Hearing Services in Schools, 40,* 116–130.

Lafferty, A.E., Gray, S., & Wilcox, M.J. (2005). Teaching alphabetic knowledge to pre-school children with developmental language delay and with typical language development. *Child Language Teaching and Therapy, 21,* 263–277.

Laing, S.P., & Espeland, W. (2005). Low intensity phonological awareness training in a preschool classroom for children with communication impairments. *Journal of Communication Disorders, 38,* 65–82.

Lomax, R.G., & McGee, L.M. (1987). Young children's concepts about print and reading: Toward a model of word reading acquisition. *Reading Research Quarterly, 22,* 237–256.

Lonigan, C., Burgess, S.R., Anthony, J.L., & Barker, T.A. (1998). Development of phonological sensitivity in 2- to 5-year-old children. *Journal of Educational Psychology, 90,* 294–311.

Lovelace, S., & Stewart, S.R. (2007). Increasing print awareness in preschoolers with language impairment using non-evocative print referencing. *Language, Speech, and Hearing Services in Schools, 38,* 16–30.

Major, E., & Bernhardt, B. (1998). Metaphonological skills of children with phonological disorders before and after phonological and metaphonological intervention. *International Journal of Language and Communication Disorders, 33,* 413–444.

Marvin, C.A., & Wright, D. (1997). Literacy socialization in the homes of preschool children. *Language, Speech, and Hearing in Schools, 28,* 154–163.

McGregor, K.K. (2004). Developmental dependencies between lexical semantics and reading. In C.A. Stone, E.R. Silliman, B.J. Ehren, & K. Apel (Eds.), *Handbook of language and literacy: Development and disorders* (pp. 302–317). New York, NY: Guilford Press.

McGregor, K.K., & Leonard, L.B. (1989). Facilitating word-finding skills of language-impaired children. *Journal of Speech and Hearing Disorders, 54,* 141–147.

Mechling, L.C., Gast, D.L., & Langone, J. (2002). Computer-based video instruction to teach persons with moderate intellectual disabilities to read grocery aisle signs and locate items. *The Journal of Special Education, 35,* 224–240.

Moats, L. (2000). *Speech to print: Language essentials for teachers.* Baltimore, MD: Paul H. Brookes Publishing Co.

Mol, S.E., Bus, A.G., & de Jong, M.T. (2009). Interactive book reading in early education: A tool to stimulate print knowledge as well as oral language. *Review of Educational Research, 79,* 979–1007.

Monson, M.R., & Bowen, S. (2008). The development of phonological awareness by braille users: A review of the research. *Journal of Visual Impairment and Blindness, 102,* 210–220.

Munro, N., Lee, K., & Baker, E. (2008). Building vocabulary knowledge and phonological awareness skills in children with specific language impairment through hybrid language intervention: A feasibility study. *International Journal of Language and Communication Disorders, 43,* 662–682.

National Early Literacy Panel. (2008). *Developing early literacy: Report of the National Early Literacy Panel.* Washington, DC: National Institute for Literacy.

National Institute of Child Health and Development Early Child Care Research Network. (2005). Pathways to reading: The role of oral language in the transition to reading. *Developmental Psychology, 41,* 428–442.

O'Connor, R.E., Jenkins, J., Leicester, N., & Slocum, T. (1993). Teaching phonological awareness to young children with learning disabilities. *Exceptional Children, 59,* 532–546.

Roth, F.P., Troia, G.A., Worthington, C.K., & Dow, K.A. (2002). Promoting awareness of sounds in speech: An initial report of an early intervention program for children with speech and language impairments. *Applied Psycholinguistics, 23,* 535–565.

Rvachew, S., Ohberg, A., Grawburg, M., & Heyding, J. (2003). Phonological awareness and phonemic perception in 4-year-old children with delayed expressive phonology skills. *American Journal of Speech-Language Pathology, 12,* 463–471.

Scarborough, H.S. (1998). Early identification of children at risk for reading difficulties: Phonological awareness and some other promising predictors. In B.K. Shapiro, P.J. Accardo, & A.J. Capute (Eds.), *Specific reading disability: A view of the spectrum* (pp. 75–199). Timonium, MD: York Press.

Senechal, M., LeFevre, J.A., Thomas, E., & Daley, K. (1998). Differential effects of home literacy experiences on the development of oral and written language. *Reading Research Quarterly, 32,* 96–116.

Snow, C.E., Burns, S., & Griffin, P. (Eds.). (1998). *Preventing reading difficulties in young children.* Washington, DC: National Academy Press.

Spencer, T.D., & Slocum, T.A. (2010). The effect of a narrative intervention on story retelling and personal story generation skills of preschoolers with risk factors and narrative language delays. *Journal of Early Intervention, 32*(3), 178–199.

Stevenson, H.W., & Newman, R.S. (1986). Long-term predictions of achievement and attitudes in mathematics and reading. *Child Development, 57,* 646–659.

Storch, S.A., & Whitehurst, G.J. (2002). Oral language and code-related precursors to reading: Evidence from a longitudinal structural model. *Developmental Psychology, 38,* 934–947.

Sun, K.K., & Kemp, C. (2006). The acquisition of phonological awareness and its relationship to reading in individuals with intellectual disabilities. *The Australasian Journal of Special Education, 30,* 86–99.

Tankersley, M., Harjusola-Webb, S., & Landrum, T. (2008). Using single-subject research to establish the evidence base of special education. *Intervention in School and Clinic, 44,* 83–90.

Trezek, B.J., Wang, Y., Woods, D.G., Gampp, T.L., & Paul, P.V. (2007). Using visual phonics to supplement beginning reading instruction for students who are deaf or hard of hearing. *Journal of Deaf Studies and Deaf Education, 12,* 373–384.

Troia, G.A. (1999). Phonological awareness intervention research: A critical review of the experimental methodology. *Reading Research Quarterly, 34,* 28–52.

Tunmer, W., Herriman, M., & Nesdale, A. (1988). Metalinguistic abilities and beginning reading. *Reading Research Quarterly, 23,* 134–158.

U.S. Department of Education, Early Reading First. (2007). *National evaluation of Early Reading First.* Washington, DC: Author.

U.S. Department of Education, Institute of Education Sciences, Preschool Curriculum Evaluation Research Consortium. (2008). *Effects of preschool curriculum programs on school readiness.* Washington, DC: Author.

van Bysterveldt, A.K., Gillon, G., & Foster-Cohen, S. (2010). Integrated speech and phonological awareness intervention for pre-school children with Down syndrome. *International Journal of Language and Communication Disorders, 45,* 320–335.

van Bysterveldt, A.K., Gillon, G.T., & Moran, C. (2006). Enhancing phonological awareness and letter knowledge in preschool children with Down syndrome. *International Journal of Disability, Development and Education, 53,* 301–329.

VanDerHeyden, A., Snyder, P., Broussard, C., & Ramsdell, K. (2007). Measuring response to early literacy intervention with preschoolers at risk. *Topics in Early Childhood Special Education, 27,* 232–249.

van Kleeck, A., Vander Woude, J., & Hammett, L. (2006). Fostering inferential language skills in Head Start preschoolers with language impairment using scripted book-sharing discussions. *American Journal of Speech-Language Pathology, 15,* 85–95.

Vaughn, S., Linan-Thompson, S., & Hickman, P. (2003). Response to instruction as a means of identifying students with reading/learning disabilities. *Exceptional Children, 69,* 391–409.

Walley, A.C., Metsala, J., & Garlock, V.M. (2003). Spoken vocabulary growth: Its role in the development of phoneme awareness and early reading ability. *Reading and Writing, 16,* 5–20.

Warrick, N., Rubin, H., & Rowe-Walsh, S. (1993). Phoneme awareness in language-delayed children: Comparative studies and intervention. *Annals of Dyslexia, 43,* 153–173.

Whitehurst, G.J., Epstein, J.N., Angell, A.L., Payne, A.C., Crone, D.A., & Fischel, J.E. (1994). Outcomes of an emergent literacy intervention in Head Start. *Journal of Educational Psychology, 86,* 542–555.

Whitehurst, G.J., & Lonigan, C.J. (1998). Child development and emergent literacy. *Child Development, 69,* 848–872.

Ziolkowski, R.A., & Goldstein, H. (2008). Effects of an embedded phonological awareness intervention during repeated book reading on preschool children with language delays. *Journal of Early Intervention, 31,* 67–90.

12

Content, Concepts, and Reading Comprehension

What's Missing in the National Early Literacy Panel Report

Tanya Kaefer, Susan B. Neuman, and Ashley M. Pinkham

F ew issues in reading are more contentious than views on how children come to be successful readers and writers. Theories abound, yet we know surprisingly little about the factors that lead to success (or failure) in learning to read. This was the charge of the National Early Literacy Panel (NELP): to examine interventions, programs, and instructional practices that promote children's early literacy development as a means of identifying specific factors that may predict their long-term literacy achievement.

Admittedly, this was an ambitious task. Panel members had to carefully review published scientific studies that could provide evidence of a relationship between early skill attainment and later achievement. Their goal was to examine how these early skills might best predict conventional literacy skill—decoding, oral reading fluency, reading comprehension, writing, and spelling. The demanding and rigorous review process yielded important information about the early skills implicated in later learning. However, meta-analytic studies may be limited in their ability to provide specific guidance for instructional practice in the early childhood years. Therefore, although *Developing Early Literacy* (NELP, 2008) is not without its strengths, it is perhaps better interpreted as a report of what current practice *is* rather than what current practice *should be.*

In this chapter, we first consider the key findings of the meta-analysis. Although we firmly acknowledge the soundness of the report, we suggest that researchers and educators must use more than meta-analysis to determine what instruction should look like in the early years. To illustrate our argument, we provide an extended example involving reading comprehension. We then focus on the importance of in-depth examinations of related foundational skills and suggest how research into these foundational skills may influence our understanding of children's early literacy development. Finally, we suggest that although meta-analysis represents an important methodological tool for synthesizing research, it is not without its limitations.

KEY FINDINGS OF THE NATIONAL EARLY LITERACY PANEL

Charged with synthesizing the extant research on early literacy development, the primary goal of NELP was the identification of interventions, parenting practices, and instructional strategies that promote children's skill attainment. This certainly required considerable diligence and effort. In fact, the panel's search procedures yielded more than 8,000 potential articles, which were then screened for relevance and rigor. Their final inclusion process identified approximately 500 studies that were subsequently categorized and analyzed to examine the strength of the effects the approaches had on children's outcomes.

The resulting meta-analysis revealed that a wide range of interventions may potentially impact children's literacy development. Code-focused instructional interventions designed to teach alphabetic skills were most prevalent ($n = 78$) and consistently demonstrated positive effects, with moderate to large effects reported for a broad spectrum of early literacy outcomes. Shared book reading displayed less dramatic findings: Analysis of 19 studies of book-reading interventions revealed only moderate effects. In fact, these results are consistent with other meta-analyses of storybook reading that reported only modest effects (Mol, Bus, de Jong, & Smeets, 2008; Scarborough & Dobrich, 1994). NELP also found moderate effects for interventions using parents ($n = 32$). Studies examining prekindergarten programs ($n = 33$), such as the Abecedarian Project, were statistically significant, with long-term, follow-up evidence of effects. Finally, language-enhancement programs ($n = 28$) yielded large effects, particularly on oral language development.

Overall, the news was good. The NELP report provided a rich set of findings for the domains of early literacy skills. More specifically, the report identified 11 distinct factors that consistently predicted children's literacy achievement as preschoolers and later as kindergartners. These skills included alphabet knowledge, phonological awareness, rapid automatic naming, rapid automatized naming of objects, writing, phonological memory, concepts about print, print knowledge, reading readiness, oral language, and visual processing. The panel also identified specific practices that supported child outcomes. Taken together, the NELP report provides compelling evidence for policy makers that given effective, high-quality instruction, we can significantly enhance literacy development.

LIMITATIONS OF THE NATIONAL EARLY LITERACY PANEL REPORT

Like the earlier National Reading Panel (National Institute of Child Health and Human Development, 2000), NELP adopted the methodology of meta-analysis. This approach enabled the panel to synthesize 1) correlational data on relationships between children's early abilities and skills and later literacy development and 2) experimental data on the impact of instructional interventions on children's learning. The panel used these experimental and quasi-experimental studies to determine the efficacy of instructional strategies, programs, and practices on either conventional literacy skills or any of the precursors to these skills.

Meta-analysis is undoubtedly a highly regarded and useful tool for synthesizing research evidence. The method provides a rigorous and systematic approach for the exclusion and inclusion of quantitative studies, as well as a useful metric (i.e., effect size) for measuring the strength of the effect on children's outcomes. Researchers are increasingly turning to meta-analysis as a means of analyzing comprehensive sets of obtainable data in an unbiased way and determining the moderators and mediators that might affect the outcome measures.

But like any methodology, meta-analysis has its limitations. Meta-analyses are reports of the status quo; they can speak only to what has already been conducted in the field. Because reviews and meta-analyses can examine only the extant research literature, they are necessarily limited to the studies conducted in a particular area that provide quantitative evidence and have sufficient control procedures to allow their inclusion in the synthesis. If a particular area is sparsely researched (e.g., a new or highly resource-intensive field of study) or underreported (e.g., the so-called file-drawer problem), the area may be overlooked by meta-analytic procedures, regardless of its potential impact on outcomes. In the case of the NELP report, code-focused interventions were more prevalent than any other intervention type, enabling the panel to closely examine the relationship between code-based factors and children's outcomes. By contrast, given that only a handful of interventions focusing on writing development were available for study, it was difficult to determine whether writing development may also be a powerful intervention tool.

Meta-analyses may also be influenced by the methods of exclusion and inclusion. For example, Mol, Bus, and de Jong (2009) conducted a meta-analysis on the impact of storybook reading on children's receptive language, expressive language, and print concepts. In contrast to NELP's meta-analysis, theirs included both published and unpublished studies in English and in other languages. Moreover, it focused on children's outcomes prior to conventional literacy. Their search strategy led to 37 studies with an average effect size of 0.28, whereas NELP examined 19 studies with an average effect size of 0.57 (after the removal of an outlier). As this comparison demonstrates, the conclusions drawn based upon a meta-analysis may be influenced by researchers' goals, philosophies, and approaches to the selection criteria when initially constructing the meta-analysis. Consider, for instance, classic articles by Scarborough and Dobrich (1994) and Bus, van IJzendoorn, and Pellegrini (1995), who were among the first to provide narrative summaries and meta-analyses of the impact of book reading on early literacy skills. Their results provided contrasting views of the effects for shared book reading, with Scarborough and Dobrich calling into question the positive effects often claimed for reading and Bus and colleagues arguing for more substantial effects.

Furthermore, meta-analysis may exclude certain types of studies a priori. For example, single-subject design, an experimental design that uses a single case in a series of experiments, is frequently excluded from meta-analyses (Neuman, 2011). Although such a design may represent an awkward fit for meta-analytic techniques, it is nonetheless a potentially strong and internally valid approach to examining the impact of interventions, especially for children in special education.

These concerns are legitimate and represent some of the pitfalls of meta-analysis. Like any other methodology (Lipsey & Wilson, 2001), meta-analysis must overcome difficulties: Among other issues, publication bias, missing data, quality of the individual research studies, and what researchers chose to report and not report will continue to raise concerns. Those conducting recent meta-analyses—Mol et al. (2009) and NELP (2008)—have used increasingly sophisticated methods to address these issues and have also been careful to delineate the limitations of the analyses.

But meta-analysis has often been the subject of unfair criticism as well. Some critics, for instance, have argued that the method does not reflect a "balanced" perspective of reading (e.g., Garan, 2002). However, such an argument essentially ignores that the purpose of a meta-analysis is to examine the average effects of a collection of quantitative studies designed to measure the impact of environments, child characteristics, and interventions. The methodology is specifically designed to examine quantitative evidence; qualitative studies are excluded by definition. Critics are quite right, therefore, when they argue that a meta-analysis does not reflect all of the extant literature in the field. They are also correct in suggesting that important work that has advanced our understanding of early literacy, such as Elizabeth Sulzby's classic work on emergent storybook reading (1985), cannot be adequately represented in a meta-analysis. Therefore, as promising a methodology as it is, meta-analysis is not designed to address or theoretically challenge different perspectives in instruction. Some would wish for the exclusion of studies because they are based on a "medical model" or a narrow view of what constitutes (pre)literacy outcomes (e.g., Dail & Payne, 2010). However, by being inclusive, meta-analysis can help prevent subjectivity in examining the research evidence.

Nevertheless, there are legitimate concerns over how the results of a meta-analysis translate to classrooms or programs. For example, Joanne Yatvin (2002), a member of the National Reading Panel and a vocal critic of the findings in its report (National Institute of Child Health and Human Development, 2000), argued that the findings failed her taste test for usefulness because there were no teachers on the panel who might be able to translate these findings into instructional activities. Similarly, Dail and Payne (2010) questioned whether the family literacy programs reviewed in the NELP report could adequately translate to culturally relevant interventions for minority families.

Whether the results of a meta-analysis can be translated to the real world may be one of the most important concerns of both advocates and critics of the methodology. We agree with this point and believe that it is crucial that the findings of the NELP report are carefully and thoughtfully implemented.

READING COMPREHENSION: AN EXTENDED EXAMPLE OF THE LIMITATIONS OF META-ANALYSIS

To illustrate the potential limitations of meta-analysis, we examine one literacy outcome in detail. Because comprehension is the ultimate outcome of reading development, it provides a particularly valuable example. After all, reading to understand is the fundamental goal of every reader (National Institute of Child Health and Human Development, 2000). It is therefore especially important that we have a full understanding of the early predictors of success in reading comprehension. In this section, we ask three questions: 1) What did *Developing Early Literacy* (NELP, 2008) find out about comprehension? 2) Does the nature of comprehension make current research incomplete? 3) Can a different approach supplement the knowledge gleaned from the report?

Of course, the NELP report was necessarily much broader in scope than our example. The report considered many interventions for reading comprehension, oral language comprehension, and other oral language skills. However, for the purposes of illustration, we focus primarily on the early indicators of reading comprehension.

Developing Early Literacy and Comprehension

To answer the question, What early skills predict later reading comprehension? NELP (2008) synthesized 151 correlations that included reading comprehension as a factor (see p. 62, Table 2.2, of the report). The analysis revealed 18 variables that significantly predicted children's comprehension outcomes. Readiness and concepts about print were the strongest predictors of comprehension, followed by alphabet knowledge, print awareness, phonological awareness, and rapid naming. Although the panel concluded that the readiness variable was the strongest predictor of comprehension, they also admitted that the variable contained a mix of skills that were not well defined in the original studies. In particular, the panel noted that it was unclear what skill or combination of skills was driving the effect sizes noted.

The panel also found that the oral language skills variable was a relatively weak predictor of comprehension. They noted that studies including oral language skills as a predictor of comprehension showed a great deal of heterogeneity in the magnitude of reported correlations. When oral language skills were decomposed into distinct measures, the panel found that overall language comprehension, receptive language comprehension, expressive language comprehension, grammar, definitional vocabulary, listening comprehension, and verbal knowledge were all strong predictors of reading comprehension; by contrast, measures of expressive vocabulary, receptive vocabulary, and "language not otherwise specified" were relatively weak predictors of reading comprehension. The panel suggested that variables measuring complex oral language skills may be better predictors of reading comprehension than measures of simple oral language skills, indicating a need for more careful study of the role of oral language in literacy development. As the panel noted, although oral language skills may not be *sufficient* for reading comprehension, they are certainly *necessary*.

Consider these results in comparison with decoding. NELP (2008) synthesized 426 correlations predicting decoding skill—nearly three times the number synthesized for comprehension—and identified 25 predictors of decoding (see p. 59, Table 2.1, of the report). Decoding nonwords, spelling, and invented spelling were the best predictors of children's literacy outcomes. According to the panel, this finding attests to the strength and stability of conventional literacy skills over time. As a result, the panel was able to make clear recommendations for future research and practice related to decoding: Specifically, improving children's skills in producing and decoding print will facilitate their ability to decode.

Why were the findings regarding comprehension not similarly rich? The report explicitly highlights one reason: The majority of studies were conducted within a brief window of development. By correlating skills at the beginning of kindergarten with reading comprehension at the end of kindergarten, the panel argued that studies measured reading comprehension at a point in development when decoding is also strongly implicated. Reading comprehension is typically assessed by asking children to read and answer questions about a text. But prior to the fifth birthday or so, only the most precocious children can meaningfully engage in text reading, particularly when it is assessed through inquiry, synthesis, and thinking-aloud measures. As a consequence, we cannot easily measure children's reading comprehension before they can adequately decode the text. In fact, studies suggest that comprehension as an independent process can be examined only when children have become skilled decoders, usually after age 8 (Kendeou, van den Broek, White, & Lynch, 2007; Nation, Cocksey, Taylor, & Bishop, 2010). With this in mind, the panel endeavored to find long-term studies that examined the effect of preschool or kindergarten predictors on reading comprehension in later elementary school, but very few studies of this type were found.

The Problem with Comprehension

Comprehension presents a unique problem for a meta-analytic technique. It is not a straightforward skill that can be easily assessed at younger ages or compared across age groups; rather, comprehension is a complex process, and its measurement may be inextricably bound to other skills, such as decoding. In many studies, young children's reading comprehension is measured at a point in development when it is presumably confounded by other reading skills. This creates a unique source of difficulty for meta-analyses, including the NELP report, that are interested in possible predictive relationships between early literacy (or preliteracy) skills and later literacy development. Moreover, this may explain why the NELP report included relatively few studies of comprehension and why those that were included had difficult-to-interpret or ambiguous results.

In addition to developmental issues, the interconnectedness of skills necessary for comprehension may make it more complex than other conventional literacy skills. At its most general level, comprehension requires the reader to construct a mental representation of the information contained in a text (Kendeou, van den Broek, White, & Lynch, 2009). The reader must connect sentences to form events, connect events to build a plot, and so forth, ultimately resulting in an integrated representation of the overall text (Mandler & Goodman, 1982). The text is thereby mentally represented as an integrated network of individual units of information.

Consider the following text:

> Four children lived in a house. One day, they were getting ready to play in the snow. They needed to find their hats.

To read this passage, the reader must successfully decode the text. But to comprehend the story, the reader must also understand the meaning of individual words, build connections between words to form sentences, understand the individual sentences, and build connections between the sentences to construct an integrated representation of the whole passage. Without understanding that the four children wanted to play in the snow, the reader might be puzzled as to why the children needed to find their hats.

To read the passage, you likely relied upon your decoding skills, your vocabulary knowledge, and your grammatical understanding. All of these skills were necessary, but none of them was solely sufficient for comprehension. You needed to make connections between the sentences (e.g., Who wanted to play in the snow? The four children living in the house wanted to play in the snow.) and draw inferences (e.g., Why did they need their hats? Snow is cold.). A reader's ability to draw causal inferences is crucial because it links individual units to a larger representation, facilitating overall comprehension (Cain & Oakhill, 2007; Kendeou et al., 2007).

For skilled readers, this process of decoding, making inferences, integrating, and comprehending occurs so rapidly that it seems automatic. But for young children and individuals with comprehension difficulties, this process can be extremely difficult. Poor comprehenders, for instance, are frequently able to integrate pieces of information at the sentence level but exhibit difficulty making inferences. This, in turn, leads to difficulty integrating the text as a whole (Cain & Oakhill, 1999). Although poor comprehenders may understand that 1) some children want to play in the snow and 2) some children are looking for their hats, these readers cannot pull these pieces of information together to understand that 3) the children need their hats so that they can play in the snow.

If a problem in making inferences is a distinguishing feature of comprehension difficulties, the issue becomes identifying the source of this impairment. Making inferences requires integrating new information (i.e., the text) with relevant background knowledge (Cain & Oakhill, 2007). In other words, children must possess sufficient background knowledge to draw the inferences necessary for successful comprehension. For example, Recht and Leslie (1988) asked seventh graders to read a grade-level passage describing a half inning of a baseball game. Half of the children were classified as good readers, and the other half as poor readers, based on a standardized reading test. The passage was divided into five parts, and the children were asked, in a task analogous to a think-aloud protocol, to use a replica of a baseball field with players to describe and interpret what they had read after each part. An important finding was that children's understanding of the passage hinged on having appropriate background knowledge: Poor readers with high knowledge of baseball displayed better comprehension than good readers with low knowledge of baseball.

This effect of background knowledge on children's reading comprehension may be specifically linked to their ability to make inferences. Kendeou and van den Broek (2007) examined the inferences made by individuals with accurate background knowledge about science as compared with individuals who held misconceptions about science. Readers who held misconceptions made a greater number of incorrect inferences about a text than those with accurate background knowledge. All of the readers were able to integrate the newly encountered information with their existing background knowledge. However, because the readers who held misconceptions possessed erroneous background knowledge, they integrated the new information with incorrect information, resulting in incorrect inferences. Although these readers formed an integrated representation of the text, because the inferences were misguided by incorrect background knowledge, the entire text was misunderstood. Whereas the Recht and Leslie (1988) study demonstrated that background knowledge influences reading comprehension, the Kendeou and van den Broek (2007) study suggests that this relationship may be mediated by the reader's ability to draw correct inferences about a text.

The breadth and depth of a reader's background knowledge are certainly crucial to his or her ability to make inferences, but the knowledge also must be accessible and must be used appropriately in order to benefit comprehension. For example, Cain, Oakhill, Barnes, and Bryant (2001) provided children with relevant background knowledge prior to giving them a text passage to read. Even when background knowledge was equalized, some children were still consistently poor at drawing inferences based upon the text. Why was this the case? Cain and colleagues proposed three possible explanations: 1) the children may have been unable to recall the relevant background information, 2) they may have failed to integrate the background information with the text, or 3) they may have failed to realize that inferences needed to be made. The source of children's difficulties in making inferences remains an open question. Regardless of the source, however, this study confirms that a combination of higher-order cognitive processes is necessary for successful reading comprehension.

We believe that this relationship between children's background knowledge and skill in making inferences may help explain some of the mixed results for oral language skills reported by NELP (2008). The panel argued that measures of complex skills may be better predictors of reading comprehension than measures of simple oral language skill. Considering the processes necessary for making inferences, it is perhaps unsurprising that complex skills are better predictors than discrete skills. That is, measures of complex skills may capture the higher-order skills necessary for reading comprehension, whereas measures of simpler skills do not. We agree with the panel's recommendation that future research must address the potential effects of oral language skills on children's reading development. In particular, we propose that possible interactions between the various components of oral language skills should be examined and evaluated for their contribution to reading comprehension in particular and literacy development in general.

In fact, research has already taken a step in that direction. Kendeou et al. (2007), for example, propose that children's ability to comprehend other modalities (e.g., oral language) and media (e.g., televised narratives) may be key factors in their reading comprehension. They argue that children's listening and multimedia comprehension utilize many of the complex skills involved in reading comprehension and are therefore a better indicator of children's early literacy (or preliteracy) abilities than simple oral language measures. Listening and multimedia comprehension are not dependent upon children's decoding skills, thus allowing comprehension to be examined as an independent process at an earlier age than it has usually been done (see Nation et al., 2010). Kendeou and colleagues further suggest that children's vocabulary knowledge may indirectly affect their reading comprehension by influencing the concurrent development of decoding skills and comprehension skills in other media. Rather than waiting until the elementary school years to detect possible reading comprehension failures, this theory suggests that researchers and educators may be able to facilitate reading comprehension through alternative types of media in the preschool and early elementary school years.

Longitudinal behavioral research supports this argument. As NELP (2008) acknowledges in the report, comprehension problems are usually not apparent until relatively late in elementary school, making the early experiences of children with comprehension problems difficult to ascertain. However, in an ambitious study, Nation et al. (2010) were able to examine the early listening comprehension skills of children who later exhibited poor reading comprehension skills. Researchers measured the phonological, decoding, listening comprehension, reading comprehension, and overall language skills of a large sample of children multiple times starting at age 5. When the children were 8 years old, the researchers identified 15 "poor comprehenders": children with average decoding ability but limited comprehension skills. When the poor comprehenders' early skills were examined, Nation and colleagues discovered that although their decoding skills developed normally throughout the elementary school years, their listening comprehension skills were well below matched controls as early as kindergarten. In other words, children who had reading comprehension difficulties at age 8 displayed listening comprehension difficulties at age 5.

Neuroimaging research further supports the idea that children's comprehension in other modalities may be a strong indicator of their reading comprehension skills. Researchers have reported some overlap in brain activation during listening and reading comprehension tasks (Jobard, Vigneau, Mazoyer, & Tzourio-Mazoyer, 2007), particularly for higher-order cognitive processes such as making inferences (Booth et al., 2002). By contrast, there are marked differences in neural activation during lower-level processes (Jobard et al., 2007). Taken together, these results suggest that listening and reading comprehension are distinct but highly related processes and that each is rooted in similar cognitively complex processes (Kendeou et al., 2007).

In summary, reading comprehension is clearly a complex cognitive process, an intricate interaction among decoding, vocabulary, background knowledge, inference making, and listening comprehension skills. Until recently, most of what we knew about the processes involved in reading comprehension resulted from studies with older children and adults, wherein decoding and comprehension could be decomposed into relatively independent processes. Recent research, however, indicates that the processes underlying listening and reading comprehension may be quite similar, suggesting that listening comprehension may be a promising means of examining children's early comprehension skills independent of their decoding abilities.

Supplemental Understanding of Comprehension

From this perspective, we can begin to understand why NELP had difficulty isolating relevant findings related to reading comprehension. Much of the research we have discussed was able to draw conclusions about the processes involved in comprehension by studying older children and adults. Looking at these findings, we can speculate that the factors associated with these processes in older children and adults can be fostered earlier in development. If background knowledge significantly contributes to middle-schoolers' inference-making ability and text comprehension (Kendeou & van den Broek, 2007; Recht & Leslie, 1988), for example, then perhaps children's background knowledge can be cultivated in early education as a means of facilitating reading development down the line. Unfortunately, such promising findings could never have been included in the NELP report as they are drawn from studies peremptorily excluded from the meta-analysis because of the age of the sample population.

If we assume that background knowledge is necessary for successful reading comprehension, the next question becomes, What are the sources of children's knowledge? Firsthand experience is one valuable source of information. Children can learn that cats have four legs by observing various cats or that chairs are for sitting by observing how adults interact with chairs. However, not all information is available through direct experience. Children cannot directly observe germs, witness the Battle of Waterloo, or remember their own birth—yet they need to know about science, history, and their birthday. Luckily, young children are also able to rely upon a variety of indirect sources, such as what other people tell them (Harris, 2007; Harris & Koenig, 2006) or books and television (Ganea, Pickard, & DeLoache, 2008; Hayne, Herbert, & Simcock, 2003), to build their background knowledge (see Gelman, 2009, for further discussion).

Moreover, children are natural knowledge seekers (Neuman, Roskos, Wright, & Lenhart, 2007); their desire to acquire knowledge and become experts in a given domain often guides their behavior. As Kelemen (1999) points out, it is natural for children to ask questions such as "What is it for?" when encountering unfamiliar objects. When given the opportunity to freely explore a series of photographs and ask a knowledgeable adult any questions they might have, children asked a variety of questions about the functions of artifacts and about the category membership, diets, and habitats of animals (Greif, Kemler Nelson, Keil, & Gutierrez, 2006). Furthermore, when they asked about an object and were provided with only the object's name, children frequently repeated their inquiry until the function or purpose of the object was also provided (Kemler Nelson, Egan, & Holt, 2004). Through this active, persistent pursuit of knowledge (Neuman, 2006), children begin to acquire the background knowledge necessary for making inferences and, by extension, reading comprehension.

In addition to examining children's background knowledge, we may gain a deeper understanding of the processes involved in reading comprehension through examining the factors underlying children's complex oral language skills. Vocabulary and working memory may be two important components of the listening comprehension task. In fact, children's vocabulary and verbal IQ scores account for approximately 22% of the variance in their listening comprehension scores (Florit, Roch, Altoè, & Levorato, 2009), and their vocabulary knowledge in kindergarten accounts for approximately 8% of the variance in listening comprehension in first grade (Sénéchal, Ouellette, & Rodney, 2006). Phonological awareness, by comparison, accounts for less than 1% of the variance in children's listening comprehension abilities (Sénéchal et al., 2006). By examining young children's listening comprehension and avoiding decoding skills as a possible confound, the picture of children's early comprehension skills becomes increasingly clearer.

CONCLUSION

Meta-analysis has many advantages as a method for synthesizing research. It provides a fair and systematic approach for determining the average results of a collection of independent studies. It also examines the variation in results and can report on the mediators and moderators that might influence these results. But like any other methodology, meta-analysis has its limitations. It cannot account for interrelationships between predictor variables. It can report on variability but is not particularly able to explain it. Finally, meta-analysis can examine only the current literature base. These limitations are particularly problematic for reading comprehension, given its complex nature and the current body of research to date.

It is for some of these reasons that researchers have increasingly turned to using multiple methods to synthesize data. A synthesis from the field of public health (Thomas et al., 2004), for example, suggests an approach for integrating a qualitative analysis with a meta-analysis review. This approach began with a traditional meta-analysis: Studies were subjected to exclusion and inclusion strategies and pooled to determine their effect sizes. Heterogeneity was examined by carrying out subgroup analyses on a limited range of categories specified in advance. But in this case, the researchers reexamined their studies to look for qualitative patterns—patterns that might be missed in an a priori determination of categories. Their final analysis provided a finer-grained analysis of studies that gave more specific guidance to policy makers, practitioners, and researchers.

This is the procedure we carried out in a recent meta-analysis on the effects of vocabulary interventions on word learning (Marulis & Neuman, 2010). Combining the results of the trials using a random-effects model, we found that on average, the interventions described were able to increase children's vocabulary by more than three quarters of a standard deviation. However, there was great variability among studies. For example, one intervention was able to increase vocabulary by more than two standard deviations, whereas most others were able to do so by less than one. Because all but a few of the studies evaluated different interventions, the summary statistic and moderator analyses seemed to conceal more than they revealed. We were unable to explain the statistical heterogeneity using prespecified categories covering study quality, study design, setting, and type of intervention.

We then conducted a more qualitative analysis of the studies. We began to read and reread articles to look for patterns that might reveal aspects of the studies to account for these differences. We assigned codes to describe relevant words, such "rich instruction," that might inform our analyses. As an example, one theme that emerged in the analysis was that interventions that provided multidimensional instruction rather than a single format appeared to be more effective. Using this information, we then returned to our codebook to create a category that allowed systematic examination of this characteristic in a revised meta-analysis. In this way, qualitative analysis can allow researchers to discover categories underlying more effective interventions.

There are additional strategies that may contribute important information to meta-analytic studies. For example, Greenhalgh et al. (2005) have recommended a meta-narrative approach for examining large data sets drawn from heterogeneous sources. Drawing on Kuhn's (2005) notion of scientific paradigms, they developed the meta-narrative review to sort and interpret different traditions of research. These research narratives were mapped in order to bring together seminal theoretical and empirical studies, both qualitative and quantitative, to build a rich picture of a particular field of study: its history, contributions, and outcome data. The authors thus produced a synthesis that embraced the many complexities and ambiguities of a particular research tradition. We suggest that this type of analysis might be particularly useful for reading research by allowing us to move forward in our research enterprises rather than our having to reinvent the wheel or fall victim to the infamous pendulum shift.

Others have also conducted complementary meta-analyses and narrative reviews. Borman and Dowling (2008), for example, conducted a meta-analysis and narrative review of teacher retention and attrition, looking at features that could not be explained entirely by a meta-analysis. Similarly, Cooper, Charlton, Valentine, and Muhlenbruck (2000) conducted an important analysis of summer learning using both meta-analysis and narrative review—an analysis that proved to be highly relevant for policy makers and practitioners. By combining traditions, such strategies can thereby enhance both the rigor and the practicality of a review.

Consequently, the strengths of the meta-analysis (Borenstein, Hedges, Higgins, & Rothstein, 2009)—specifically, its narrow focus, comprehensive search for evidence, criterion-based selection of relevant evidence, and rigorous appraisal of validity and the evidence-based inferences it derives—are clearly important and critical to the field of reading. But, as we have discussed, for some review topics, such as reading comprehension, the strengths of the systematic review may actually be weaknesses. Perhaps the narrow focus at times is just too narrow. When skills and processes are potentially confounded, as is the case for reading comprehension, it is crucial to explore the more complex antecedents and relationships. Under such circumstances, approaching the data from a theoretical and analytic perspective may complement rather than hinder the meta-analytic approach.

REFERENCES

Booth, J.R., Burman, D.D., Meyer, J.R., Gitelman, D.R., Parrish, T.B., & Mesulam, M.M. (2002). Modality independence of word comprehension. *Human Brain Mapping, 16*(4), 251–261.

Borenstein, M., Hedges, L., Higgins, J., & Rothstein, H. (2009). *Introduction to meta-analysis.* West Sussex, United Kingdom: Wiley & Son.

Borman, G., & Dowling, N. (2008). Teacher attrition and retention: A meta-analysis and narrative review. *Review of Educational Research, 78*(3), 367–409.

Bus, A.G., van IJzendoorn, M.H., & Pellegrini, A.D. (1995). Joint book reading makes for success in learning to read: A meta-analysis on intergenerational transmission of literacy. *Review of Educational Research, 65*(1), 1–21.

Cain, K., & Oakhill, J.V. (1999). Inference making and its relation to comprehension failure. *Reading and Writing, 11*, 489–503.

Cain, K., & Oakhill, J.V. (2007). Reading comprehension difficulties: Correlates, causes, and consequences. In K. Cain & J. Oakhill (Eds.), *Children's comprehension problems in oral and written language: A cognitive perspective* (pp. 41–70). New York, NY: Guilford Press.

Cain, K., Oakhill, J.V., Barnes, M.A., & Bryant, P.E. (2001). Comprehension skill, inference-making ability, and their relation to knowledge. *Memory and Cognition, 29*(6), 850–859.

Cooper, H., Charlton, K., Valentine, J., & Muhlenbruck, L. (2000). Making the most of summer school: A meta-analytic and narrative review. *Monographs of the Society for Research in Child Development, 65*(1, Serial No. 260), 1–118.

Dail, A., & Payne, R. (2010). Recasting the role of family involvement in early literacy development: A response to the NELP report. *Educational Researcher, 39,* 300–303.

Florit, E., Roch, M., Altoè, G., & Levorato, M.C. (2009). Listening comprehension in preschoolers: The role of memory. *British Journal of Developmental Psychology, 27*(4), 935–951.

Ganea, P.A., Pickard, M.B., & DeLoache, J.S. (2008). Transfer between picture books and the real world by very young children. *Journal of Cognition and Development, 9*(1), 46–66.

Garan, E. (2002). *Resisting reading mandates.* Portsmouth, NH: Heinemann.

Gelman, S.A. (2009). Learning from others: Children's construction of concepts. *Annual Review of Psychology, 60*(1), 115–140.

Greenhalgh, T., Robert, G. Macfarlane, F., Bate, P., Kyriakidou, O., & Peacock, R. (2005). Storylines of research in diffusion of innovation: A meta-narrative approach to systematic review. *Social Science & Medicine, 61*(2), 417–430.

Greif, M., Kemler Nelson, D., Keil, F.C., & Gutierrez, F. (2006). What do children want to know about animals and artifacts? Domain-specific requests for information. *Psychological Science, 17*(6), 455–459.

Harris, P.L. (2007). Trust. *Developmental Science, 10,* 135–138.

Harris, P.L., & Koenig, M.A. (2006). Trust in testimony: How children learn about science and religion. *Child Development, 77*(3), 505–524.

Hayne, H., Herbert, J., & Simcock, G. (2003). Imitation from television by 24- and 30-month-olds. *Developmental Science, 6*(3), 254–261.

Jobard, G., Vigneau, M., Mazoyer, B., & Tzourio-Mazoyer, N. (2007). Impact of modality and linguistic complexity during reading and listening tasks. *NeuroImage, 34*(2), 784–800.

Kelemen, D. (1999). The scope of teleological thinking in preschool children. *Cognition, 70*(3), 241–272.

Kemler Nelson, D.G., Egan, L.C., & Holt, M.B. (2004). When children ask, "What is it?" what do they want to know about artifacts? *Psychological Science, 15*(6), 384–389.

Kendeou, P., & van den Broek, P. (2007). The effects of prior knowledge and text structure on comprehension processes during reading of scientific texts. *Memory and Cognition, 35*(7), 1567–1577.

Kendeou, P., van den Broek, P., White, M.J., & Lynch, J.S. (2007). Comprehension in preschool and early elementary children: Skill development and strategy interventions. In D.S. McNamara (Ed.), *Reading comprehension strategies: Theories, interventions, and techniques* (pp. 27–45). Mahwah, NJ: Lawrence Erlbaum Associates.

Kendeou, P., van den Broek, P., White, M.J., & Lynch, J.S. (2009). Predicting reading comprehension in early elementary school: The independent contributions of oral language and decoding skills. *Journal of Educational Psychology, 101*(4), 765–778.

Kuhn, D. (2005). *Education for thinking.* Cambridge, MA: Harvard University Press.

Lipsey, M.W., & Wilson, D.B. (2001). *Practical meta-analysis.* Thousand Oaks, CA: Sage Publications.

Mandler, J.M., & Goodman, M.S. (1982). On the psychological validity of story structure. *Journal of Verbal Learning and Verbal Behavior, 21*(5), 507–523.

Marulis, L.M., & Neuman, S.B. (2010). The effects of children's vocabulary intervention on young children's word learning: A meta-analysis. *Review of Educational Research, 80*(3), 300–335.

Mol, S., Bus, A., & de Jong, M. (2009). Interactive book reading in early education: A tool to stimulate print knowledge as well as oral language. *Review of Educational Research, 79*(2), 979–1007.

Mol, S.E., Bus, A.G., de Jong, M.T., & Smeets, D.J.H. (2008). Added value of dialogic parent–child book readings: A meta-analysis. *Early Education and Development, 19*(1), 7–26.

Nation, K., Cocksey, J., Taylor, J.S.H., & Bishop, D.V.M. (2010). A longitudinal investigation of early reading and language skills in children with poor reading comprehension. *Journal of Child Psychology and Psychiatry, 51*(9), 1031–1039.

National Early Literacy Panel. (2008). *Developing early literacy: Report of the National Early Literacy Panel.* Washington, DC: National Institute for Literacy.

National Institute of Child Health and Human Development. (2000). *Report of the National Reading Panel: Teaching children to read: An evidence-based assessment of the scientific research literature on reading and its implications for reading instruction* (NIH Publication No. 00-4769). Washington, DC: Government Printing Office.

Neuman, S.B. (2006). The knowledge gap: Implications for early literacy development. In D. Dickinson & S.B. Neuman (Eds.), *Handbook of early literacy research* (Vol. 2, pp. 29–40). New York, NY: Guilford Press.

Neuman, S.B. (2011). Single-subject experimental design. In N. Duke & M. Mallette (Eds.), *Literacy research methodologies* (pp. 383–404). New York, NY: Guilford Press.

Neuman, S.B., Roskos, K., Wright, T., & Lenhart, L. (2007). *Nurturing knowledge: Linking literacy to science, math, social studies, and much more.* New York, NY: Scholastic.

Recht, D.R., & Leslie, L. (1988). Effect of prior knowledge on good and poor readers' memory of text. *Journal of Educational Psychology, 80*(1), 16.

Scarborough, H.S., & Dobrich, W. (1994). On the efficacy of reading to preschoolers. *Developmental Review, 14*(3), 245–302.

Sénéchal, M., Ouellette, G., & Rodney, D. (2006). The misunderstood giant: On the predictive role of early vocabulary to future reading. In D. Dickinson & S.B. Neuman (Eds.), *Handbook of early literacy research* (Vol. 2, pp. 173–183). New York, NY: Guilford Press.

Sulzby, E. (1985). Children's emergent reading of favorite storybooks: A developmental study. *Reading Research Quarterly, 20*(4), 458–481.

Thomas, J., Harden, A., Oakley, A., Oliver, S., Sutcliffe, K., Rees, R.,… Kavanagh, J. (2004). Integrating qualitative research with trials in systematic reviews. *British Medical Journal, 328*(7446), 1010–1012.

Yatvin, J. (2002). Babes in the woods: The wanderings of the National Reading Panel. *Phi Delta Kappan, 83*(5), 364–369.

13

Reflections on the National Early Literacy Panel

Looking Back and Moving Forward

Christopher J. Lonigan and Timothy Shanahan

As the last chapter in this book, this chapter is both the final summary of the work of the National Early Literacy Panel (NELP) and the symbolic bringing to a close of almost a decade of work involving the panel. It has been a long and winding path, from the first meeting of the panel, during which two of the three members quit (both ultimately continued), to now, as the final words of this book are edited. Along the way, the panel spent countless hours in windowless hotel meeting rooms in both interesting and uninteresting places, reading, rating, and sorting research abstracts and articles; working through

Acknowledgment: Preparation of this work was supported, in part, by grants to Christopher J. Lonigan from the *Eunice Kennedy Shriver* National Institute of Child Health and Human Development (HD052120, HD060292) and the Institute of Education Sciences (R305F100027, R305A090169, R324E060086). The views expressed herein are those of the authors and have not been reviewed or approved by the granting agencies.

many different configurations of analyses and reporting of results; and considering comments, feedback, and reactions of colleagues and those in attendance at presentations of the findings. Some aspects of the NELP report have started to have an effect on the field of early childhood education. None of this would have been possible without the members of the panel:

- Timothy Shanahan (Distinguished Professor of Urban Education and Chair, Department of Curriculum & Instruction, at the University of Illinois at Chicago [UIC] and Director of the UIC Center for Literacy)

- Anne Cunningham (Professor, Cognition and Development, in the Graduate School of Education at the University of California, Berkeley)

- Kathy C. Escamilla (Professor of Education at the University of Colorado at Boulder)

- Janet Fischel (Professor of Pediatrics and Psychology at the State University of New York at Stony Brook)

- Susan Landry (Michael Matthew Knight Professor in the Department of Pediatrics at the University of Texas Health Science Center at Houston)

- Christopher J. Lonigan (Distinguished Research Professor in the Department of Psychology and Associate Director of the Florida Center for Reading Research at Florida State University)

- Victoria J. Molfese (Chancellor's Professor in Child, Youth, and Family Studies at the University of Nebraska–Lincoln)

- Chris Schatschneider (Professor of Psychology and Associate Director of the Florida Center for Reading Research at Florida State University)

- Dorothy Strickland (Professor Emeritus in the Graduate School of Education at Rutgers University).

Although everyone who participated in this effort contributed to the report in important ways, two individuals stand out as central to reaching this point, because without their efforts, there would never have been a NELP report. Laura Westberg at the National Center for Family Literacy (NCFL), though not a member of the panel, had the unenviable task of managing the panel from start to finish. She directed, coordinated, motivated, and, when absolutely necessary, begged to keep the process moving forward. Dr. Chris Schatschneider at Florida State University was responsible for conducting almost every analysis in the report. He was dubbed the "NELP Sherpa" by the panel because of his work with NCFL research assistants on the coding of studies, his work with members of each subgroup to help define and refine analyses, and his efforts to produce and explain the results of the analyses. *(Note to the reader from Tim Shanahan:* My coeditor, Chris Lonigan, wrote this thoughtful paragraph. Unfortunately, it contains the only misleading statement in this volume. What he wrote about Laura and Chris S. is correct, but actually *three* NELP participants, not two, performed remarkably throughout this panel review process. Chris Lonigan—with his intellectual integrity, hard-edged irascible skepticism, seemingly boundless energy and selflessness, and deep and abiding commitment to the idea that all children deserve literate lives—was the driving force and moving spirit behind NELP. Ultimately, his ideas formed the most basic conception of the study, and he wrote more of the report than anyone else, some of which was even credited to him. It is fair to say that without Chris Lonigan the NELP report would not exist. This modestly misleading statement has now been corrected.)

You learn a lot of things from being a member of a panel such as NELP, including the depth of knowledge, the diversity of experiences, and the multiple perspectives that colleagues from different disciplines and backgrounds bring to the interpretive context necessary to synthesize such a large body of research. You learn who talks and who writes. You learn who answers your e-mails at all hours versus those who typically do so only during business hours. Synthesizing extant research in an area forces you to see everything about a literature. Some of this is exciting. Some of this is disheartening. It is exciting when someone has executed and written about a complex study with competence, precision, and accessibility to provide novel and compelling information. It is disheartening when the critical flaws that prevent meaningful conclusions to be drawn from a study apparently did not prevent the study from being published, even in well-regarded, peer-reviewed journals. In fact, you learn just how many published research studies have major flaws in design, execution, analysis, and reporting. At various points, we seriously considered a possible outcome of NELP to be the creation of a "research tribunal" able to summon authors and journal editors to answer for their actions. Often we worked too late into the night.

The resultant product of NELP sheds light on many aspects of early literacy. For a number of areas, there is a deep and consistent research base. This category includes predictors of conventional reading and writing skills, instructional activities that help children develop skills associated with word decoding—as well as word decoding itself—and perhaps the effect of shared book reading on children's vocabulary skills. For other areas, what stands out in sharpest relief are the research questions that need to be addressed by future research. In the remainder of this chapter, we briefly summarize the evidence used to produce the NELP report, note some of the major findings and potential uses of the report, discuss some of the areas the report identified as needing additional research, and highlight some of the central issues raised by the authors of the chapters in this book, including a number of issues that cut across the specific areas covered by individual chapters.

SCOPE OF EVIDENCE FOR EARLY LITERACY SKILLS AND INTERVENTIONS

The original charge to NELP was similar to the charge to the National Reading Panel (NRP; National Institute of Child Health and Human Development, 2000): to identify the instructional practices with evidence of effectiveness. In contrast to the NRP, however, the outcomes of interest were not clearly defined for NELP. Whereas the NRP's focus was on reading outcomes for which there was significant consensus in the field (e.g., word decoding, reading comprehension), NELP's focus was on early literacy skills for which there was less general agreement. That is, although there had been a number of previous attempts to define the universe of developing skills that were central to becoming a skilled reader (e.g., Adams, 1990; Clay, 1966; Sénéchal, LeFevre, Smith-Chant, & Colton, 2001; Sulzby & Teale, 1991; Teale & Sulzby, 1986; Whitehurst & Lonigan, 1998), these accounts differed in how they defined emergent or early literacy, in the importance given to different literacy-like behaviors, and in the degree to which research evidence was used to help define the domain. Instead of adopting one of the existing definitions of early literacy or defining the domain based on panel members' expertise and ideas, NELP decided to use available research to identify the set of skills that could be called early literacy skills. Adopting Whitehurst and Lonigan's (1998) perspective that emergent literacy skills were the developmental precursors of conventional forms of reading and writing (i.e., word decoding, reading comprehension, spelling, and composition), NELP sought empirical evidence for any skills or behaviors that 1) were present prior to the emergence of conventional reading and writing and 2) were related to these later conventional literacy skills. That is, NELP attempted to identify the universe of early childhood skills that predicted how well children learned to read and write after the onset of formal schooling.

Unlike earlier attempts to define early literacy, NELP used a comprehensive empirical approach. Using a large set of search terms ($N = 351$) to cast a wide net over the research literature, NELP conducted multiple electronic searches of published research articles and identified 7,313 articles with possible relevance to the question. Setting aside articles that were not published in English or in peer-reviewed journals, that were not about learning to read in English or another alphabetic language, and that did not analyze and present quantitative data drawn from children in the appropriate age range resulted in the identification of 1,824 articles, which then had to be reviewed by at least two members of NELP. This step winnowed the results down to 275 articles judged relevant to the question, and this number was reduced further, to 234, because 41 articles did not provide sufficient information about the data. A second search with an expanded definition of the population studied resulted in an additional 622 articles, which, after review, added 65 relevant articles to the total. Consequently, 299 published studies were used to identify skills that could be considered developmental precursors to conventional literacy skills. From these 299 studies, the correlations between a potential early literacy skill and some conventional literacy skill were summarized by using meta-analytic techniques.

This initial meta-analysis identified 13 skills or behaviors (i.e., alphabet knowledge, concepts about print, environmental print, invented spelling, language, listening comprehension, name writing, phonological awareness, phonological short-term memory, rapid automatized naming, verbal IQ, visual memory, and visual perception) that had been reported in at least three studies, were present prior to the emergence of conventional forms of reading and writing (i.e., studies included children who were kindergarten age or younger), and that had nontrivial average correlations with a conventional literacy outcome (i.e., word decoding, reading comprehension, and spelling) measured in kindergarten or later. These 13 outcomes defined the scope of learning outcomes for which an attempt would be made to identify interventions. Consequently, along with conventional literacy outcomes, these 13 skills identified the focus of studies of aimed at identifying instructional practices with evidence of effectiveness. A search for studies of potentially effective instructional practices yielded 931 articles from which 136 were judged relevant to the question. Another, modified search resulted in an additional 55 articles. Therefore, 191 published articles were used to determine the effectiveness of various instructional practices to improve young children's early literacy skills. Ultimately, these 191 articles were categorized into five domains of interventions based on the focus of the intervention or the type of instructional program (i.e., code-focused interventions, shared-reading interventions, parent and home programs, preschool and kindergarten programs, and language-enhancement interventions). Unlike the NRP, which preselected intervention topics to summarize, NELP included all possible interventions with outcome targets within the domain of early literacy skills that were identified by the initial meta-analysis.

THE NATIONAL EARLY LITERACY PANEL REPORT

As articulated throughout this book, the NELP report provided a comprehensive summary of the evidence for the relations between early literacy skills and later conventional literacy skills, and it provided a summary of the evidence for the size, scope, and limits of the effects of interventions intended to affect these early literacy skills and, by extension, later conventional literacy skills. The evidence indicated that 1) print-related skills (i.e., alphabet knowledge, concepts about print, and print awareness) and phonological-processing abilities (i.e., phonological awareness, phonological access to lexical store [rapid naming tasks], phonological and short-term memory) were strong to moderate predictors of all aspects of conventional literacy (i.e., word decoding, reading comprehension, and spelling), 2) oral language skills were moderate predictors of all aspects of conventional literacy skills, and 3) visual-perceptual skills were weak predictors. Additional analyses did not yield strong support that these predictive relations were limited by child characteristics such as demographics, age, or skill level. Further analysis of the phonological awareness and oral language variables revealed that some aspects of these skills or ways of assessing them yielded significantly stronger relations with conventional literacy outcomes than did other aspects or methods of assessment. Of particular note was the finding that some aspects of oral language were more closely related to conventional literacy skills and had different strengths of relations with word decoding versus reading comprehension. Several types of measures of oral language were significantly more associated with reading comprehension than with word decoding, whereas simple vocabulary skills (the measure of language most likely to appear in these studies) had relatively weak predictive relations with both word decoding and reading comprehension.

With respect to evidence for interventions to promote early literacy skills, the NELP report summarized a large body of evidence concerning code-focused interventions, a moderate amount of evidence concerning shared-reading interventions, and much smaller amounts of evidence for home and parent programs, preschool and kindergarten programs, and general language instruction. Most code-focused interventions included training on some phonological awareness skill, and the results were large, consistent, and extended, in many cases, to conventional literacy outcomes. Evidence for shared-reading interventions was consistently positive, primarily for oral language outcomes, and shared-reading interventions appeared to have larger effects for vocabulary than for other oral language outcomes. Dialogic reading had larger effects than did simple shared reading. Whereas the difference in effect sizes between dialogic reading and simple shared reading was not statistically significant, it is likely that dialogic reading does, in fact, have a larger effect than simple shared reading, given that the comparison group in many dialogic-reading studies uses simple shared reading; thus, in these studies, the effect of dialogic reading is the effect over that of simple shared reading. Parent and home programs had evidence of positive effects on children's cognitive abilities and oral language outcomes—again, with seemingly larger effects for vocabu-lary than for other oral language outcomes. Preschool and kindergar-ten programs yielded a variety of small but positive effects, with more consistent effects from kindergarten than from preschool programs. Language-enhancement interventions yielded positive effects on oral language outcomes, including vocabulary as well as other oral language outcomes.

As with the release of the NRP report, the release of the NELP report resulted in significant controversy. Much of the critique of the NELP report emphasized things that were not said. Pearson and Hiebert (2010) declared the report a failure because it "adds little new knowl-edge or insight about teaching reading to young children" (p. 287). They went on to say,

> Because the scope of the NELP review did not allow examination of its findings in relation to key contemporary research and evaluation efforts (e.g., the implementation and evaluation of Reading First and Early Read-ing First and the Early Childhood Longitudinal Study [ECLS]), it does not provide insights or recommendations that can move the field of early literacy instruction ahead. (p. 287)

A host of other commentators claimed that NELP had overempha-sized findings related to code-focused outcomes and interventions rela-tive to an emphasis on oral language outcomes and interventions (e.g., Dickinson, Golinkoff, & Hirsh-Pasek, 2010; Neuman, 2010; Paris & Luo, 2010; Teale, Hoffman, & Paciga, 2010). Still others faulted NELP for not focusing enough on children whose home language was not English or for suggesting that the findings were likely applicable to this population of children (e.g., Gutiérrez, Zepeda, & Castro, 2010). Some even sug-gested that the NELP report included "serious confounding factors in the analyses that lead to exaggerated and perhaps incorrect conclusions in the report" (Paris & Luo, 2010, p. 316) or simply failed to include the appropriate research (Dail & Payne, 2010; Orellana & D'warte, 2010). The specifics of many of these critiques have been answered previously (see Lonigan & Shanahan, 2010; Schatschneider & Lonigan, 2010); how-ever, the recurrent themes highlight many of the issues that we believe the NELP report brings to the fore, including uses of the report and areas in which more research is needed.

Uses of the National Early Literacy Panel Report

Some of the critics of the NELP report suggested that we should have been more prescriptive based on the summary of empirical evidence, the expertise included on the panel, or conventional wisdom within the field (e.g., Neuman, 2010; Pearson & Hiebert, 2010; Teale et al., 2010). In fact, given the intensity of some of the reactions to the NRP report, we explicitly decided to separate the summary of the evidence from any extensive recommendations to the practice community based on that summary. The federal agency overseeing the NELP's work, the National Institute for Literacy, conducted a call for proposals to produce a practitioner-oriented guide based on the summary of evidence prepared by NELP. NCFL and several members of NELP put together a proposal to complete this work, but a different group was selected to produce that guide. NELP members did not work on the guide that was produced, and it would be fair to say that the guide failed to capture much of the nuance and cross-area implications of the evidence summarized by the NELP report.

The recommendations that were included in the NELP report were tightly tied to the evidence summarized. There is a difference between producing a research synthesis (as NELP did) and engaging in speculation based on little to no evidence (as these critics often did). NELP set out to provide a comprehensive summary of available evidence concerning the skills related to developing literacy and of instructional practices that had positive effects on those skills. Such a summary, we thought, would represent a starting point for adapting educational practice to better align with empirical evidence and a means of determining where the gaps in the empirical evidence were. We also recognized that the NELP report represented a snapshot in time—an examination of what things look like now. In some cases, it seemed unlikely that the picture would change much, given the extensiveness, depth, and varied texture included in the empirical evidence summarized. In other cases, it seemed likely that the picture would change as additional details were added by further research. Although the literature summarized in the report represented empirical studies completed across a substantial period of time, it is perhaps correct to conclude that what we found were more gaps in the knowledge base than highly refined answers to questions. However, there were some findings from the synthesis that can and should influence educational practice.

Assessment of Early Literacy Skills   Results from the synthesis of skills that predict conventional literacy skills (Lonigan, Schatschneider, & Westberg, 2008a) provide strong and consistent evidence of what can be assessed to gauge children's early literacy development for purposes of identification and instruction. The synthesis produced compelling evidence for the importance of print knowledge and phonological-processing abilities for word decoding, reading comprehension, and spelling, and strong evidence for the importance of oral language skills for later conventional literacy skills, particularly reading comprehension. Assessments of these early skills can provide educators with information about whether a child is on track to develop conventional literacy skills without difficulty and can identify children who are likely to need additional or more intensive instruction to achieve the goal of reading well as they progress through school (see Chapter 3).

Targets of Early Intervention and Preschool Instruction In addition to identifying areas for assessment, the synthesis of skills that predict conventional literacy skills provides direction concerning the skills that should be targeted by early intervention and instruction in early childhood education settings. However, regarding the use of the synthesis for identifying instructional targets, educators need to consider both the strength of the predictors and the likely value and success of instruction aimed at those skills. For instance, there is evidence that print knowledge, phonological awareness, and oral language skills can be taught (e.g., see Chapter 5 as well as Lonigan, 2006; Marulis & Neuman, 2010; Piasta, Purpura, & Wagner, 2010), but there is little evidence that instruction on skills such as rapid naming or phonological short-term memory is likely to be effective (i.e., increase the skills) or result in enhanced conventional literacy skills. Hence, the use of the results of NELP's synthesis should not be to identify the strongest predictors and try to intervene to affect them but to combine knowledge of what skills are predictive, what skills are likely malleable, and what skills are accompanied by a set of instructional practices that are effective.

Identification of Effective Instructional Practices NELP's syntheses of empirical evidence of instructional practices in five broad domains provided the basis for determining what types of instructional activities are likely to be successful in increasing children's early literacy skills. Without doubt, the largest body of evidence for instructional practices that was synthesized by NELP concerned code-focused instruction (Lonigan, Schatschneider, & Westberg, 2008b). This evidence indicated that instruction directed at teaching children to be able to perform phonological awareness tasks (e.g., blend or delete parts of words, isolate individual sounds in words) resulted in both increased phonological awareness skills and increased conventional literacy skills and that the effects were largest when instruction in phonological awareness was combined with instruction in some aspect of print, such as letter knowledge or rudimentary phonics. Most of these interventions were created by researchers; other than the general instructional focus and the fact that they usually were conducted with individual children or small groups of children and were of brief duration, they did not share many common features. Secondary analyses failed to find instructional features that resulted in stronger or weaker outcomes; thus, for example, whether phonemes or subphoneme units were the target, or whether the task taught included analysis or synthesis, did not seem to matter.

The second largest domain of instructional activities reviewed consisted of studies involving shared-reading interventions (Lonigan, Shanahan, & Cunningham, 2008). This evidence indicated that shared-reading interventions resulted in increased oral language skills for children, particularly vocabulary skills, and that interactive shared reading in which an adult used books as a prop with which to engage children in conversations resulted in larger effects than did simply reading to children. Similarly, oral language interventions yielded positive results for oral language outcomes, and the positive effects were present for both vocabulary and other language skills (Fischel & Landry, 2008). As was the case for code-focused interventions, the shared-reading activities or oral language interventions in many of these studies were conducted with small groups of children or with individual children. Notably, the outcomes included in the shared-reading studies typically included only oral language outcomes and never included conventional literacy outcomes. Consequently, in contrast to code-focused interventions, there was no direct evidence that shared-reading or oral language interventions promote conventional literacy skills.

The syntheses of parent and home programs (Lonigan, 2008) and preschool and kindergarten programs (Molfese & Westberg, 2008) found positive effects of programs in both domains; however, the number of studies available was small, and the commonalities among the different programs evaluated within each domain were few. Consequently, it was not possible to identify characteristics of programs in either domain that were associated with stronger or weaker effects.

Overall, NELP's synthesis of instructional programs yielded evidence of positive effects; however, many of the instructional practices were not those aligned with the dominant philosophy of instruction in most early childhood education programs (see Chapter 8). That is, the majority of instructional practices shown to yield positive effects on children's early literacy or conventional literacy skills involved focused, explicit, teacher-directed instruction that was conducted in small groups or individually. This contrasts with a model of instruction that promotes implicit, child-directed, and whole-class instructional activities—the type of instructional practice most commonly observed in early childhood education settings (e.g., Bracken & Fischel, 2006) or embodied in traditional early childhood curricula (Phillips, Clancy-Menchetti, & Lonigan, 2008). At present, there is no evidence that implicit, whole-class strategies such as reading rhyming stories, clapping-out syllables in words, or singing word-play songs yield positive outcomes for children's early literacy skills.

Such findings do not imply that early childhood education should involve whole-group, lengthy, drill, or worksheet-based practices—a concern often voiced by early childhood education "experts." In fact, the instructional practices with evidence of positive impacts on children's skills involve small-group, brief, hands-on activities that fit well with models of differentiated and scaffolded instruction. Nor do such findings imply that these are the only instructional activities that should be a part of early childhood education. That is, evidence of significant positive effects for certain instructional activities that promote code-related early literacy skills and some aspects of oral language development should not prevent early childhood educators from doing things that are traditionally found in early childhood settings (i.e., center time, singing songs, word games, or pretend play) or novel approaches (e.g., increasing background knowledge, high-quality language interactions). However, these findings indicate that the early childhood education environment should also include those things that are essential to learning to read (e.g., alphabet knowledge, phonological awareness) and that the instructional activities should look like those that have been shown to work. In contrast to emphasizing code-focused instruction to the exclusion of instruction to promote language development or other skills and knowledge central to becoming a skilled reader, the identification of a clear set of instructional practices that effectively and efficiently provide children with the elements of code-related skills needed to become skilled readers opens up the early childhood education environment to develop, investigate, and evaluate replicable instructional activities that enhance skills other than code-related skills.

Areas Needing More Research

The NELP report provided a rich set of findings about the relationship between early developing child skills and later literacy attainment and the effectiveness of interventions for helping young children to progress toward successful literacy learning. The analyses carried out by the panel also reveal important gaps in the empirical research record that future research should address. The areas in which NELP's synthesis suggests a need for additional research include specific populations of children, early writing skills, reading comprehension, the effect of shared reading on conventional literacy skills, interventions that positively impact oral language skills beyond vocabulary, and translational research.

Specific Populations of Children   One of the consistent difficulties encountered in the NELP analyses was the inability to disaggregate the analyses of predictors and intervention effects by subgroups of children. Early childhood educators have specific questions about predictive relationships between early literacy skills and later conventional literacy skills across different groups, and they would like to know which interventions will work best for children living in poverty, children from traditionally underrepresented ethnic groups, children who are English language learners, or children with identified disabilities. However, there are few extant studies that focus on these specific subpopulations or that report results in a way that allows an examination of these subpopulations to answer these questions. Although many of the prediction and intervention studies included in the NELP syntheses had mixed samples of children from different socioeconomic backgrounds, ethnic groups, and living environments, the data in these studies were usually not reported separately for different subgroups. Consequently, we were usually unable to address our questions about whether child characteristics moderated predictive relations between early literacy skills and later conventional literacy skills or whether interventions were more or less effective depending on characteristics of children. Because results from studies of diverse groups of children suggest that predictive relations and impacts of interventions generalize across many of these child characteristics, future research should directly address these questions, either by focusing on specific subgroups or by specifically testing questions of the degree to which findings generalize across subgroups.

Early Writing Skills   NELP's analyses revealed that children's early writing skills were one of the moderately strong predictors of later conventional literacy skills. Relative to studies on the predictive relations for variables such as alphabet knowledge or phonological awareness, there were relatively few studies of early writing (i.e., 10 studies relating early writing to word decoding, 4 studies relating early writing to reading comprehension, and 3 studies relating early writing to spelling), and many of these studies were about children's name writing only. Although the early education field has often seen name writing as an important skill, recent studies indicate that preschool children have a broad array of early writing skills (e.g., Puranik & Lonigan, 2011). Moreover, some evidence indicates that it is not name writing itself that is responsible for the predictive relation with conventional literacy skills.

Other dimensions of early writing are important both for name writing and for conventional literacy skills (e.g., Puranik, Lonigan, & Kim, 2011). Consequently, it appears that name writing is a useful summary variable but is not the skill important for developing literacy competencies. Such findings have instructional implications (e.g., it is likely more beneficial to teach the component writing skills than name writing); however, more research is needed to better understand the degree to which early writing skills are distinct competencies from other early literacy skills (e.g., alphabet knowledge, phonological awareness), how much they contribute to specific conventional literacy skills, and whether they are beneficial targets of instruction.

Reading Comprehension   Most studies in the NELP synthesis to identify early literacy skills took place over a brief period of time. Assessments of reading comprehension appear to leverage different component skills at different ages (see Chapter 10). Specifically, measures of reading comprehension in the early grades appear to rely heavily on children's word-decoding skills, whereas measures of reading comprehension in later grades depend more on language processes. NELP's analyses demonstrated that some oral language skills were more strongly related to reading comprehension than to decoding skills. Although subsequent analyses of just the longer-term longitudinal studies that were included in NELP did not find evidence that the influence of oral language on reading increased over a longer period of time or that the influence of code-related skills diminished (Lonigan & Shanahan, 2010), additional research on the development of reading comprehension and the links between early literacy skills and later reading comprehension is needed. In fact, the Institute of Education Sciences of the U.S. Department of Education recently funded a large-scale research initiative (2010–2015) to better understand reading comprehension, skills that contribute to reading comprehension, and interventions that effectively improve reading comprehension (see Institute of Education Sciences, 2010).

Shared-Reading Interventions   Given the ubiquity with which shared reading is recommended as an important practice for helping children develop good reading skills, it is surprising that none of the studies of shared-reading interventions synthesized by NELP had conventional literacy outcomes, a weakness evident in most studies conducted with school-age children too (Sénéchal & Young, 2008). Although it is clear that shared reading can promote the development of oral language skills, particularly vocabulary, it would be useful to know the extent to which shared-reading practices influence word decoding and reading comprehension. Understanding the scope of the effects of shared-reading practices will help better refine the types of instructional practices that are necessary in early childhood education environments. Consequently, research examining potential longer-term effects of shared-reading interventions on children's conventional reading skills is needed.

Oral Language Interventions   Given the potential importance of oral language skills to later reading, particularly reading comprehension, it was surprising that substantially fewer studies had investigated oral language interventions than the number of studies investigating code-focused interventions. In a more recent meta-analysis, Marulis and Neuman (2010) summarized results from 67 published and unpublished studies of vocabulary teaching involving about 6,000 children (ages birth to 9) that included preschool and kindergarten children who were classified both as "at risk" and "not at risk" (the students in a study were classified as being at risk if more than half the children were in one or more risk categories, including low socioeconomic status, low parent education, English as a second language status, or low academic achievement). They reported an average effect size of 0.88 (a large effect) for the preschool and kindergarten portion of the studies. Moderator analyses indicated that larger effects were obtained when researchers, teachers, or parents delivered the intervention than when child care workers did; when explicit (versus implicit) instruction was used; when researcher-created measures were used rather than standardized language measures; and when children were from families of higher socioeconomic status. Children's risk status, the intensity and duration of intervention, the focus of the vocabulary measure (receptive versus expressive vocabulary), and group size used in the intervention were not associated with differences in effect sizes. For almost two thirds of the studies, the intervention involved some variation of shared reading. This meta-analysis demonstrates how few nonshared-reading oral language interventions have been evaluated. Children from populations known to be at risk for later reading difficulties (e.g., children from low-income backgrounds, children whose home language is not English) often have substantially lower levels of oral language skills at school entry than their peers. Therefore, it seems like a valuable area of research would be the development and evaluation of oral language interventions that are not shared-reading interventions and that improve outcomes beyond vocabulary. This seems particularly warranted given the fact that the NELP synthesis found that vocabulary skills were relatively weak predictors of conventional literacy skills and that the effects of shared-reading interventions were larger for vocabulary outcomes than for other oral language outcomes.

Translational Research   A significant proportion of the studies concerning code-focused interventions that were synthesized by NELP involved instruction carried out by researchers. In addition, most of these interventions were conducted as either individual or small-group intervention, and there was no evidence that whole-class or large-group, code-focused interventions produced the same positive effects on children's reading-related skill. These types of instructional practices are not those typically seen in early childhood education settings. There is a significant need for research that investigates how to move research findings to practice. That is, studies are needed that address how well instructional practices that produce large positive impacts on children's literacy-related skills transfer to typical early childhood education environments, as well as studies that investigate the conditions necessary for these instructional practices to be successful in typical early childhood education environments. As noted in several of the chapters, there is far less evidence concerning the effectiveness of programs in typical education settings than in research settings. The lack of translational research may be one reason that results from curriculum studies are not more positive (Chapter 8) or that specific types of early literacy programs have not yielded evidence of success (Chapter 7).

BEYOND THE NATIONAL EARLY LITERACY PANEL

The chapters of this book build on the findings of NELP. They highlight emerging research in topics summarized by NELP, offer additional perspective on the findings reported by NELP, and suggest additional areas in which the knowledge base of early literacy and professional practice must be increased. In this section, we summarize some of these key points and identify some crosscutting issues raised by the authors of the chapters.

NELP restricted its review and synthesis to empirical studies published in peer-reviewed journals. In part, this was done to limit the scope of searches conducted (i.e., alternative search strategies could have included conference reports, dissertations, and other unpublished work), to ensure that searches within a literature were comprehensive (i.e., many alternative literatures are not abstracted and cannot be systematically searched), and to provide some level of quality control over the studies that were included (i.e., peer review ensures that work included meets some quality standard, however slight). In Chapter 2, Griffin and McCardle point out several large-scale projects supported

by the U.S. government that have relevant data concerning the development and promotion of early literacy skills. Many of these data sets can
be used to answer questions based on the analyses of large and often
nationally representative samples of children and families. Regarding
some of these data sets, one can question the degree to which depth was
sacrificed for breadth in the design of assessment batteries or can be
concerned that the measurement operations below the construct labels
are, by design, black boxes (e.g., specific item content is not available for
most measures used in the data sets for the Early Childhood Longitudinal Study). However, there is no question that these data sets and the
reports derived from them to date provide useful information concerning young children's development. Many of the studies noted by Griffin
and McCardle are embedded in the findings reported in other chapters
of this book (e.g., Chapter 8).

In Chapter 3, Spencer, Spencer, Goldstein, and Schneider provide
a review of assessments that can be used for different purposes. They
note that the NELP report identifies skill domains in which assessment
would provide useful information for purposes of screening, identification, and progress monitoring children's literacy levels and proficiency.
These skill domains also are relevant to child and classroom assessment
systems that could be used to identify teachers who might need support
and professional development to achieve the goal of supporting children's
development. Although the chapter authors identify a host of measures
for these different purposes, data on the appropriateness and validity of
many of these measures for these purposes are, in most cases, weak or
nonexistent (Lonigan, Allan, & Lerner, 2011; Wilson & Lonigan, 2009,
2010). A number of standardized diagnostic measures are validated for
use with preschool-age children. However, the cost, training, and administration time required for most of these measures make them impractical
for widespread use in most early childhood environments. The best use of
these measures is to provide in-depth assessments of children's relative
strengths and weaknesses in specific skill domains.

Additional work is needed on the development and validation of
measures that can be used for screening and progress monitoring of a
subset of skills identified by NELP. As an example of such work, the State
of Florida, in 2009–2010, developed a set of assessments that teachers
in its state-funded preschool program can use to screen and monitor
children's progress related to oral language, phonological awareness,
print knowledge, and mathematics (see Florida Department of Education, 2008), in line with Florida's Early Learning Standards. These
assessments are part of an effort by the state to create assessment systems that can be used by teachers to inform instruction. For example,
the state previously developed the Florida Assessment for Instruction

in Reading, which is a system of screening, progress monitoring, and diagnostic measuring of children in kindergarten through Grade 12. A large-scale field trial of the preschool measures indicated that they can be administered reliably by children's preschool teachers and are valid for identifying children at risk of not meeting Florida's school-readiness classification in the fall of kindergarten.

In Chapter 4, Spinrad, Valiente, and Eisenberg highlight the growing number of research findings of a connection between children's self-regulation and their academic skills. As noted by Spinrad and colleagues, studies have shown that a variety of socioemotional constructs are related to children's language, reading, and math skills, including effortful control, executive function, social competence, peer relationships, teacher relationships, motivation, emotionality, emotion understanding, and emotion regulation. These constructs were not a part of the NELP report's set of predictor variables because 1) many of the studies of these variables involve children in elementary school or 2) the studies were not published until after the cutoff date for NELP's literature review (e.g., Blair & Razza, 2007; McClelland et al., 2007). This area of research raises a number of interesting questions concerning the dynamic interaction of academic skills and behavioral and cognitive development. At present, there are many questions concerning definitions of constructs (e.g., Allan & Lonigan, 2011; Willoughby, Blair, Wirth, & Greenberg, 2010) and the degree to which these self-regulation constructs independently influence academic skills, including growth in academic skills (see Duncan et al., 2007; Ponitz, McClelland, Matthews, & Morrison, 2009).

As previously noted, a frequent criticism of the NELP report is that it emphasized evidence concerning code-related skills and instruction; however, this was a function of the amount of higher-quality published evidence concerning these skills and instructional activities and not a decision on the part of the panel to focus on one area and not another. In Chapter 5, Phillips and Piasta expand the evidence summarized by NELP on code-focused outcomes and interventions to include more recent studies. They confirm the NELP findings regarding the predictive nature of phonological awareness and alphabet knowledge. In addition, they summarize some more recent work on teaching phonological awareness and print knowledge. By the cutoff date of NELP's literature review, there were few studies identified that examined the effect of teaching children about the alphabet only—in contrast to studies that taught the alphabet in conjunction with phonological awareness instruction. Having looked at the results of more recent studies on the effects of teaching alphabet knowledge, Phillips and Piasta conclude that teaching both letter names and letter sounds is important. They also discuss issues surrounding whole-class versus small-group instructional methods and note that current data suggest a need to increase attention to phonological awareness instruction in preschool classrooms.

The NELP synthesis of studies concerning interventions involving shared reading is just one of a number of such syntheses that have been reported. In Chapter 6, Pentimonti, Justice, and Piasta review some of these other summaries of the effects of shared reading, and they summarize the effects of interventions involving shared reading that also involve word elaborations and print referencing. They make a point of noting that the effects of these shared-reading strategies may be substantially reduced when used by teachers instead of parents or researchers and that the effects seem to vary as a function of child age and risk status. They note that despite longstanding calls for shared book reading in early childhood education settings, there is considerable variability in how often book reading takes place in preschools and child care centers, with a not small number of preschool and child care classrooms with low levels of book-reading activity. Pentimonti and colleagues also discuss a relatively underresearched area, that is, the types of books that are used in shared reading with young children (e.g., narrative versus expository), and they make suggestions for types of books to be used. They also highlight the need for more research on the relative benefits of small-group versus whole-class shared reading, on types of books used in shared reading, and on optimal ways to promote language skills beyond vocabulary.

In Chapter 7, Wasik and Feldman summarize results from additional studies of parent and home programs. They provide a detailed summary of the history of evaluations of the now-defunct Even Start program, which was the U.S. government's two-generation ("family literacy") program. Several randomized evaluations of Even Start failed to demonstrate positive benefits of the program on most child or parent outcomes. The last randomized evaluation of Even Start, the *Classroom Literacy Interventions and Outcomes [CLIO]* study (Judkins et al., 2008), evaluated the impact of deploying evidence-based classroom and parent interventions in Even Start programs; however, the *CLIO* study yielded few positive findings. Wasik and Feldman discuss one possible reason for the lack of consistent positive effects from family literacy programs—fidelity. That is, for an intervention to be effective, those it is intended to affect must receive it in some minimally potent dose. Teachers in classrooms may not implement evidence-based practices as intended, and parents may not participate in the available program components with sufficient frequency for those components to make a difference. Wasik and Feldman also discuss findings from research with older children in which parents are provided with explicit instructional strategies to teach reading skills, and they suggest that it may be useful to develop and evaluate explicit instructional practices for parents of preschool children to use—beyond shared reading—that will help their children acquire early literacy skills.

Few preschool curriculum or professional development studies were included in the NELP synthesis because there are few empirical evaluations of preschool curricula that are published in peer-reviewed journals or that meet standards of quality that allow causal conclusions. In Chapter 8, Lonigan and Cunningham provide a summary of current evidence concerning preschool curricula and professional development programs. Beyond studies of programs that suggest the value of high-quality early childhood education, there is a relative dearth of well-designed studies that evaluate specific preschool early literacy curricula. Most commercially available curricula have no available studies, or they have studies from which valid conclusions about the effects of the curricula cannot be drawn, and there are relatively few positive results from the few well-designed studies available. Such findings indicate that substantially more work is needed to develop and evaluate preschool curricula. At present, most of the curricula adopted by preschools either have no evidence of effectiveness or no evidence that a particular curriculum is better than a generic alternative. As for professional development programs, the available evidence indicates that professional development for teachers seems unlikely to offer an easy solution, with most studies of professional development failing to show better outcomes for children whose teachers received the professional development than for children whose teachers did not receive the professional development; the one study demonstrating a significant advantage of professional development involved a scope and intensity of professional development well beyond that which programs typically adopt or can afford. Commonalities among curricula and professional development with evidence of effectiveness include explicit instruction that is at odds with the historical philosophy of early childhood education.

In Chapter 9, Dickinson and Darrow highlight the significance of language development for becoming a skilled reader and note the relative paucity of interventions shown to be effective in promoting language development skills. They note that most studies showing positive effects on language development involve relatively narrow and short-term interventions and have not involved language-focused curricula. They discuss a number of impediments to deploying effective, literacy-focused curricula and also discuss aspects of fidelity of implementation that may be associated with more versus less positive outcomes for children, including the fact that in many classrooms, initial levels of language teaching are low—requiring large changes to move into effective levels of instruction—adoption of effective strategies may be low and variable in application, and use of strategies may be highly variable throughout the day.

In Chapter 10, Hogan, Cain, and Bridges provide an expanded description on the ways in which oral language skills contribute to skilled reading, particularly reading comprehension. Based upon the simple view of reading model (Gough, Hoover, & Peterson, 1996; Hoover & Gough, 1990), they describe a changing situation for skilled reading that initially draws heavily on code-related skills and simple language processes in children's early years but that increasingly relies on a variety of more complex language processes to yield good reading comprehension skills. Given the changing nature of the reading task as children progress through school, difficulties may not be apparent until the more complex language processes are required. Hogan and colleagues discuss the need to promote these more complex language skills that allow children to integrate multiple elements within a text, develop a mental model of the text that can be interrogated and modified, and identify causal relations in text to provide children with the language skills that will ultimately be needed to have skilled reading once the reading tasks make increasing demands on more complex language processes.

One area that NELP noted it was unable to provide significant evidence for concerned special populations, including children with disabilities. This was because few group-design studies reported results in ways that allowed effects to be isolated within a part of the study sample and because studies with single-subject designs were excluded from the NELP synthesis because they do not yield effect sizes that can be combined with effect sizes of group-design studies. In Chapter 11, Carta and Driscoll summarize the evidence of the effectiveness of interventions with special needs populations. As with the NELP summary, the largest number of interventions evaluated with special needs populations concerned code-focused instruction. These interventions, which typically include a large component of explicit instruction, are effective at promoting the skills they target (i.e., phonological awareness or print knowledge). However, most of the studies of these interventions have involved children who have speech and language impairments rather than more general developmental delays or other cognitive/sensory impairments. Carta and Driscoll note the need for additional studies in this area—studies that involve a broader inclusion of children with special needs, instruction that targets more than code-focused skills, instruction that takes place in typical educational settings, and inclusion of longitudinal outcomes so that the longer term effects of these interventions on children's conventional literacy skills can be evaluated.

Finally, in Chapter 12, Kaefer, Neuman, and Pinkham highlight some of the strengths and weaknesses of using meta-analysis to identify important correlates of an outcome and effective instructional practices for promoting development of an outcome. They correctly note, as we have elsewhere (Lonigan & Shanahan, 2010), that any meta-analysis is limited by the research that has been completed and reported by the time the analysis is done. Clearly, a meta-analysis cannot provide a synthesis of research not yet conducted or a synthesis of good ideas. Moreover, different sets of inclusion and exclusion criteria can affect the conclusions of a synthesis; Kaefer and colleagues use the example of the effects of shared-reading interventions in which different meta-analyses have supported stronger or weaker effects, in part because of the studies included. They highlight a "mixed methods" approach to meta-analysis in which qualitative aspects of studies are evaluated in an attempt to understand patterns. Such an approach is likely what happens in most meta-analyses, however, and it certainly describes most of the meta-analyses reported by NELP. That is, once the primary meta-analysis is completed, features of individual studies (e.g., methods, population, components of intervention) are analyzed to try to explain reliable and replicable features associated with variations in effect sizes. Although some of these features typically are envisioned at the outset of a meta-analysis, it is also usually the case that other, unanticipated features are evaluated after the studies have been examined first. The essential elements here, however, are reliability and replicability. Any study may produce larger or smaller effects and have unique features; however, those unique features may not be responsible for the larger or smaller effects. To link any feature to an outcome, it is necessary that the feature be evident in multiple studies, and then its presence or absence has to correlate with the outcome variations. Kaefer and colleagues also posit aspects important to the development of reading comprehension, one of the crosscutting issues that we turn to next.

Crosscutting Issues

Each chapter in this book explores important specific ideas and issues on the major topic addressed by those chapters. However, the chapter authors also collectively managed to address a number of crosscutting issues; issues that arose repeatedly through the varied lenses of these different chapter topics.

Fidelity of Implementation   Even a powerful set of instructional techniques will be ineffective if they are not implemented with sufficient intensity and adherence to provide children with the necessary exposure. Quite a few of the chapters highlight issues related to fidelity of implementation (e.g., Chapters 6, 7, and 9). The issue of fidelity is an important one, not in the sense of pointing to low fidelity to explain why a particular intervention or curriculum did not produce the expected or desired results, but in the sense of asking questions about conditions required to achieve a level of fidelity of implementation that is sufficient to produce the expected or desired results.

Inadequate fidelity can result from a host of factors, including characteristics of the personnel who are implementing the intervention, aspects of the organization in which the intervention is delivered, components of the training required to implement the intervention, and the nature of the intervention itself. Much has been written about the qualifications of early childhood educators (e.g., Burchinal, Cryer, Clifford, & Howes, 2002; National Institute of Child Health and Human Development, 2002). It may be that teachers with lower educational attainment are less able to successfully implement some or all of the instructional practices that are a part of an intervention. In general, however, teacher education itself does not appear to account for higher or lower outcomes for children, once factors common to both are taken into account (e.g., Early et al., 2007). Background characteristics of teachers may inhibit adequate fidelity of implementation. Dickinson and Darrow (Chapter 9) suggest this issue in their discussion of the potential impact of teachers' own history of language use (e.g., if the language usage requirements of an intervention are in opposition to teachers' typical usage, low fidelity may result). It may also be the case that the organizations in which specific instructional activities, including curriculum, are imbedded are not structured in a way that supports high-quality implementation. Organizational impediments may include insufficient personnel such that classroom teachers have little support to manage their classes or are expected to coordinate other center activities, making it difficult to plan and execute an instructional routine consistently. Organizational obstacles also may include administrative issues, such as effective management that includes consistent routines, expectations, supervision, and effective support of classroom teachers.

Inadequate fidelity—particularly in evaluation studies—can also be construed as a failure of the intervention itself or of the implementation model in which it is embedded. That is, an intervention program may not be structured in a way that is sufficiently clear to allow teachers to implement it with the degree of intensity or adherence needed to yield desired outcomes. Instructional activities may be overly complex or rely too heavily on teachers to bridge the gap between expected outcome and specific mechanisms of delivery. Obviously, instructional programs or curricula that cover many areas of development or that involve complex instructional routines (i.e., activities scaffolded to children's existing and developing skills) require more substantial training than do narrower and simpler programs. Consequently, inadequate fidelity can result from insufficient professional development about the instruction. Of course, either of these reasons can be dependent on characteristics of the personnel expected to deliver the instruction to children or on characteristics of the organizations in which they work. In some of our own research, we have seen these factors—alone and in combination—reduce the degree to which instruction was implemented the way it was designed to be implemented.

Questions about fidelity and its impact on child outcomes, however, probably are best situated in the context of interventions that are known to produce the desired outcomes. That is, a study in which a particular set of instructional activities or a curriculum is evaluated in a field setting—typically referred to as "effectiveness research"—as an initial test of whether the intervention works is probably an inefficient use of complex and expensive field research. In cases in which outcomes fail to show an effect of the intervention, the cause may be inadequate fidelity; however, the failure to show positive effects may also be the result of an ineffective intervention, and it is impossible to disentangle the two.

A more efficient approach would be to establish the potential of the intervention in a more highly controlled evaluation study (e.g., those that deliver the intervention work for and are supervised by the researcher)—typically referred to as "efficacy research." Interventions that prove efficacious can be moved to the field, where many factors are out of the researcher's control (e.g., qualifications of teachers, supervision of teachers, teacher buy in), to determine the degree to which the intervention is robust to variations found in typical educational environments. In these types of studies, questions of fidelity make more sense because variations in fidelity can be studied in the context of an intervention with known positive outcomes, and questions concerning variations in personnel, settings, materials, and required training can be evaluated. This type of field research that addresses questions concerning elements necessary to produce a level of fidelity necessary for desired outcomes is typically referred to as "scale up." Ultimately, this sequence of evaluation is necessary to understand which interventions are likely to produce positive outcomes for children outside of a research context because they evaluate the match between the necessary elements of effective implementation with the practical realities of typical early childhood education environments.

The variation in instructional research findings is important to consider from a practical vantage as well. Just because research finds a particular instructional approach to be effective does not mean that it will be effective automatically if you adopt it at your school. Although it is evident from a meta-analysis that on average, some approach to teaching has conferred an advantage to children, such analyses rarely provide a clear idea of what sufficient implementation intensity would be needed to obtain a similar result. "Research-based instruction" is what has worked under some set of circumstances, not what will necessarily work under one's own circumstances (Shanahan, 2002). Meta-analyses can reveal which interventions have provided students with some comparative learning advantage (the significance and size of the average effect size), how reliably such interventions have done this (how often, out of all the times tried, did this intervention work), how big the effects might be (average effect and range of effects), and which features were usually associated with success. It is then up to future researchers and practitioners to try to match the original intensity of the effort and to ensure that the circumstances (e.g., nature of the population, instructional supports) are sufficiently equivalent to lead to a similar result.

Special Populations   As noted by Carta and Driscoll (Chapter 11), there is far less research on the assessment, development, and promotion of the early literacy skills of children from special populations, including children with disabilities and children whose home language is not English (i.e., English language learners). Research in this area is clearly needed. Although there is a growing body of research concerning the development of early literacy skills (e.g., Anthony et al., 2009; Anthony et al., 2011), the influence of home environments (Farver, Xu, Eppe, & Lonigan, 2006; Mancilla-Martinez & Lesaux, 2011) and effective interventions for children who are English language learners (e.g., Farver, Lonigan, & Eppe, 2009), many questions remain, including how children's home language influences their development of early literacy skills in English, the best ways to assess these children's skills, and what effective instruction would be. Moreover, most work to date on young English language learners has involved children whose home language is Spanish. Although this is the largest single group of English language learners in the United States (McCardle, Mele-McCarthy, Cutting, Leos, & D'Emilio, 2005), there are other significant groups of English language learners in U.S. schools.

Spencer and colleagues (Chapter 3) discuss response to intervention (RTI) in the context of available assessment measures. RTI approaches are increasingly common in grade school, both as a way of identifying children with disabilities and as a model of instruction (Fletcher & Vaughn, 2009). The use of RTI approaches in preschool holds promise for identifying and intervening with children with special needs. Findings from studies in which interventions are used in an RTI approach, however, suggest several key issues to be considered before a wide-scale adoption of the RTI approach in preschools (Lonigan & Phillips, 2009).

One issue is that the majority of preschool curricula have no evidence of effectiveness from rigorous studies (e.g., Chapter 8). The RTI approach calls for the use of effective Tier 1, that is, classroom instruction that meets the educational needs of the majority of children in a classroom; however, the majority of preschool programs—particularly those serving children at highest risk for education difficulties—use curricula that have no evidence of effectiveness. Given the resources required to implement high-quality and effective Tier 2 (or Tier 3) instruction, it may be more cost effective to first focus on improving the quality of the Tier 1 instruction to which most children are exposed.

Another issue concerns the effectiveness of instructional activities with children specifically identified as not making adequate progress within the context of effective Tier 1 classroom instruction. Although a number of the instructional activities identified by NELP as effective for promoting early literacy skills have been evaluated with children who could be classified as at risk for educational difficulties, results from studies in which a classroom curriculum known to be effective was used (see Lonigan & Phillips, 2009) suggest that effective Tier 2 instruction for children who fail to make adequate progress with effective Tier 1 instruction needs to be more individualized, more intensive, and conducted in smaller groups than the instructional activities identified by the NELP report.

Finally, it is often the case that preschools serve relatively homogeneous groups of students, often grouped by factors that aggregate higher or lower levels of risk for later educational difficulties (e.g., Head Start programs, Title I preschool programs). Some of our work suggests that more than 50% of children in centers serving disadvantaged populations qualify for enhanced instruction (i.e., Tier 2 or 3), despite receiving a high-quality, evidence-based classroom curriculum, delivered in most cases by degreed and certified teachers. Such numbers fail to achieve the oft-stated RTI expectation that Tier 1 instruction will serve the educational needs of 75%–80% of children in a classroom. Substantial additional research is needed to investigate how best to integrate an RTI approach into existing preschool contexts, particularly those that serve disproportionate numbers of children who are at risk for later reading difficulties.

Defining Reading Comprehension Several chapters in this book (e.g., Chapters 10 and 12) highlight significant issues concerning reading comprehension that confront researchers, practitioners, and policy makers interested in the development of skilled reading.

Measures designed to assess reading comprehension appear to leverage different skills at different points in children's development of reading skills, with measures used with older children requiring increasingly well-developed, language-related skills relative to measures used with younger children (e.g., Keenan, Betjemann, Wadsworth, DeFries, & Olson, 2006). Although on its face it seems easy to define reading comprehension, translating that definition into a psychometrically sound measure is substantially more complex. For instance, the RAND report *Reading for Understanding* (Snow, 2002) defined reading comprehension as

> The process of simultaneously extracting and constructing meaning through interaction and involvement with written language. We use the words *extracting* and *constructing* to emphasize both the importance and the insufficiency of the text as a determinant of reading comprehension. Comprehension entails three elements:
> - The *reader* who is doing the comprehending
> - The *text* that is to be comprehended
> - The *activity* in which comprehension is a part.
>
> In considering the reader, we include all the capacities, abilities, knowledge, and experiences that a person brings to the act of reading. Text is broadly construed to include any printed text or electronic text. In considering activity, we include the purposes, processes, and consequences associated with the act of reading. (p. 11, emphasis in the original)

When considering this definition of reading comprehension, it is hard to imagine how it could be measured in a reliable way. How does one measure "extracting meaning," and which meaning must be extracted? How does one measure "constructing meaning," and which meaning must be constructed? Do assessments need to take into account aspects of the reader? (And if so, what aspects should be taken into account?) Do we expect that comprehension will vary across different activities in which comprehension might be measured? (And if it does not, should questions about the validity of the measure be raised?) These questions highlight some of the complexities of knowing what the outcomes should look like in terms of assessments, and they provide some indication of how the processes involved in skilled reading might have more or less of an influence depending on how the reading comprehension outcome is operationalized.

There are also questions concerning the boundaries between reading comprehension and the underlying skills that make comprehension more or less likely when reading. For instance, Hogan and colleagues (Chapter 10) note that inference making is often seen as a component of comprehension. However, is the ability to make accurate inferences a part of reading comprehension, a skill necessary for high levels of reading comprehension, or an indicator that a high level of reading comprehension occurred? Kaefer and colleagues (Chapter 12) argue for the importance of background knowledge to high levels of reading comprehension. However, it may be that high levels of background knowledge are typically the result and not the cause of high levels of reading comprehension, and the distinction between background knowledge and other knowledge—particularly general language abilities, such as vocabulary—is not clear. In preliminary analyses of data from an ongoing study concerning component processes associated with reading comprehension in children in preschool through fifth grade, we found that background knowledge, as measured by standardized measures of background knowledge, could not be separated from a factor representing children's vocabulary knowledge at any age. Ultimately, the ability to identify the skills that contribute to reading comprehension, and the instructional activities that can increase those skills for children at risk of poor reading comprehension, will require a definition of reading comprehension that is refined and that can be operationalized.

CONCLUSION

The attainment of skilled literacy is a complex and multifaceted process that unfolds over a relatively long period of time—not unlike the NELP report. Also, like the attainment of skilled literacy, the NELP report is not an end point in a process but a means to attain more knowledge. This chapter has highlighted areas in which the NELP report summarized a deep body of research in which findings are unlikely to change much (e.g., predictors of conventional literacy skills, code-focused interventions). The chapter has also outlined several areas in which the NELP report indicated that much more research is needed in order to understand developing literacy and to identify effective interventions that can help maximize the educational success of all children. The other chapters in this book expand the information included in the NELP report by summarizing more recent research findings or research that fell outside of the scope of NELP's synthesis, highlighting points of departure between the findings of the NELP report and those of other syntheses and raising a number of important questions that need to be addressed to move the field forward. We have highlighted a number of these as crosscutting issues. Evidence summarized by NELP and the chapters in this book included the past 30-plus years of research on the development and promotion of early literacy. We hope that as the field digests this information and adopts practices based on strong evidence, that the foundation has been built for the next 10 years of research and that this progress enhances young children's ultimate success in school and beyond.

REFERENCES

Adams, M.J. (1990). *Learning to read: Thinking and learning about print.* Cambridge, MA: MIT Press.

Allan, N.P., & Lonigan, C.J. (2011). Examining the dimensionality of effortful control in preschool children and its relation to academic and socio-emotional indicators. *Developmental Psychology, 47,* 905–915.

Anthony, J.L., Solari, E.J., Williams, J.M., Schoger, K.D., Zhang, Z., Branum-Martin, L., & Francis, D.J. (2009). Development of bilingual phonological awareness in Spanish-speaking English language learners: The roles of vocabulary, letter knowledge, and prior phonological awareness. *Scientific Studies of Reading, 13,* 535–564.

Anthony, J.L., Williams, J.M., Durán, L.K., Gillam, S.L., Liang, L., Aghara, R.,... Landry, S.H. (2011). Spanish phonological awareness: Dimensionality and sequence of development during the preschool and kindergarten years. *Journal of Educational Psychology, 103,* 857–876.

Blair, C., & Razza, R.P. (2007). Relating effortful control, executive function, and false belief understanding to emerging math and literacy ability in kindergarten. *Child Development, 78,* 647–663.

Bracken, S.S., & Fischel, J.E. (2006). Assessment of preschool classroom practices: Application of Q-sort methodology. *Early Childhood Research Quarterly, 21,* 417–430.

Burchinal, M.R., Cryer, D., Clifford, R.M., & Howes, C. (2002). Caregiver training and classroom quality in child care centers. *Applied Developmental Science, 6,* 2–11.

Clay, M.M. (1966). *Emergent reading behavior* (Unpublished doctoral dissertation). University of Auckland, New Zealand.

Dail, A., & Payne, R.L. (2010). Recasting the role of family involvement in early literacy development: A response to the NELP Report. *Educational Researcher, 39*(4), 330–333.

Dickinson, D., Golinkoff, R.M., & Hirsh-Pasek, K. (2010). Speaking out for language: Why language is central to reading development. *Educational Researcher, 39,* 305–310.

Duncan, G.J., Dowsett, C.J., Claessens, A., Magnuson, K., Huston, A.C., Klebanov, P.,...Japel, C. (2007). School readiness and later achievement. *Developmental Psychology, 43,* 1428–1446.

Early, D.M., Maxwell, K.L., Burchinal, M., Bender, R.H., Ebanks, C., Henry, G.T.,...Zill, N. (2007). Teacher's education, classroom quality, and young children's academic skills: Results from seven studies of preschool programs. *Child Development, 78,* 558–580.

Farver, J.M., Lonigan, C.J., & Eppe, S. (2009). Effective early literacy skill development for young English language learners: An experimental study of two methods. *Child Development, 80,* 703–719.

Farver, J.M., Xu, Y., Eppe, S., & Lonigan, C.J. (2006). Home environments and young Latino children's school readiness. *Early Childhood Research Quarterly, 21,* 196–212.

Fischel, J., & Landry, S. (with the National Early Literacy Panel). (2008). Impact of language-enhancement interventions on young children's early literacy skills. In *Developing early literacy: Report of the National Early Literacy Panel* (pp. 211–231). Washington, DC: National Institute for Literacy.

Fletcher, J.M., & Vaughn, S. (2009). Response to intervention: Preventing and remediating academic difficulties. *Child Development Perspectives, 3,* 48–50.

Florida Department of Education. (2008). *VPK assessment.* Retrieved from http://www.fldoe.org/earlylearning/assessments.asp

Gough, P.B., Hoover, W.A., & Peterson, C.L. (1996). Some observations on a simple view of reading. In C. Cornoldi & J. Oakhill (Eds.), *Reading comprehension difficulties: Processes and interventions* (pp. 1–13). Mahwah, NJ: Lawrence Erlbaum Associate.

Gutiérrez, K.D., Zepeda, M., & Castro, D.C. (2010). Advancing early literacy learning for all children: Implication of the NELP report for dual-language learners. *Educational Researcher, 39*(4), 334–339.

Hoover, W.A., & Gough, P.B. (1990). The simple view of reading. *Reading and Writing, 2,* 127–160.

Institute of Education Sciences. (2010). *Reading for understanding research initiative.* Retrieved from http://ies.ed.gov/ncer/projects/program.asp?ProgID=62

Judkins, D., St.Pierre, R., Gutmann, B., Goodson, B., von Glatz, A., Hamilton, J.,...Rimdzius, T. (2008). *A study of classroom literacy interventions and outcomes in Even Start.* (NCEE 2008-4028). Washington, DC: Institute of Education Sciences, U.S. Department of Education.

Keenan, J.M., Betjemann, R.S., Wadsworth, S.J., DeFries, J.C., & Olson, R.K. (2006). Genetic and environmental influences on reading and listening comprehension. *Journal of Research in Reading, 29,* 75–91.

Lonigan, C.J. (2006). Conceptualizing phonological processing skills in prereaders. In D.K. Dickinson & S.B. Neuman (Eds.), *Handbook of early literacy research* (2nd ed., pp. 77–89). New York, NY: Guilford Press.

Lonigan, C.J. (with Escamilla, K., Strickland, D., & the National Early Literacy Panel). (2008). Impact of parent and home programs on young children's early literacy skills. In *Developing early literacy: Report of the National Early Literacy Panel* (pp. 173–188). Washington, DC: National Institute for Literacy.

Lonigan, C.J., Allan, N.P., & Lerner, M.D. (2011). Assessment of preschool early literacy skills: Linking children's educational needs with empirically supported instructional activities. *Psychology in the Schools, 48,* 488–501.

Lonigan, C.J., & Phillips, B.M. (2009). Reducing children's risk for later reading disabilities: The role of Tier I and Tier II instruction in preschool. *Perspectives on Language and Literacy, Special,* 21–26.

Lonigan, C.J., Schatschneider, C., & Westberg, L. (with the National Early Literacy Panel). (2008a). Identification of children's skills and abilities linked to later outcomes in reading, writing, and spelling. In *Developing early literacy: Report of the National Early Literacy Panel* (pp. 55–106). Washington, DC: National Institute for Literacy.

Lonigan, C.J., Schatschneider, C., & Westberg, L. (with the National Early Literacy Panel). (2008b). Impact of code-focused interventions on young children's early literacy skills. In *Developing early literacy: Report of the National Early Literacy Panel* (pp. 107–151). Washington, DC: National Institute for Literacy.

Lonigan, C.J., & Shanahan, T. (2010). Developing early literacy skills: Things we know we know and things we know we don't know. *Educational Researcher, 39*(4), 340–346.

Lonigan, C.J., Shanahan, T., & Cunningham, A. (with the National Early Literacy Panel). (2008). Impact of shared-reading interventions on young children's early literacy skills. In *Developing early literacy: Report of the National Early Literacy Panel* (pp. 153–171). Washington, DC: National Institute for Literacy.

Mancilla-Martinez, J., & Lesaux, N.K. (2011). Early home language and later vocabulary development. *Journal of Educational Psychology, 103*, 535–546.

Marulis, L.M., & Neuman, S.B. (2010). The effects of vocabulary intervention on young children's word learning: A meta-analysis. *Review of Educational Research, 80*, 300–335.

McCardle, P., Mele-McCarthy, J., Cutting, L., Leos, K., & D'Emilio, T. (2005). Learning disabilities in English language learners: Identifying the issues. *Learning Disabilities Research and Practice, 20*, 1–5.

McClelland, M.M., Cameron, C.E., Connor, C.M., Farris, C.L., Jewkes, A.M., & Morrison, F.J. (2007). Links between behavioral regulation and preschoolers' literacy, vocabulary, and math skills. *Developmental Psychology, 43*, 947–959.

Molfese, V., & Westberg, L. (with the National Early Literacy Panel). (2008). Impact of preschool and kindergarten programs on young children's early literacy skills. In *Developing early literacy: Report of the National Early Literacy Panel* (pp. 189–209). Washington, DC: National Institute for Literacy.

National Institute of Child Health and Human Development. (2000). *Report of the National Reading Panel: Teaching children to read: An evidence-based assessment of the scientific research literature on reading and its implications for reading instruction* (NIH Publication No. 00-4769). Washington, DC: Government Printing Office.

National Institute of Child Health and Human Development, Early Child Care Research Network. (2002). Childcare structure → process → outcome: Direct and indirect effects of child-care quality on young children's development. *Psychological Science, 13*, 199–206.

Neuman, S.B. (2010). Lessons from my mother: Reflections of the National Early Literacy Panel Report. *Educational Researcher, 39*(4), 301–304.

Orellana, M.F., & D'warte, J. (2010). Recognizing different kinds of "head starts." *Educational Researcher, 39*(4), 295–300.

Paris, S.G., & Luo, S.W. (2010). Confounded statistical analyses hinder interpretation of the NELP Report. *Educational Researcher, 39*(4), 316–322.

Pearson, P.D., & Hiebert, E.H. (2010). National reports in literacy: Building a scientific base for practice and policy. *Educational Researcher, 39*(4), 286–294.

Phillips, B.M., Clancy-Menchetti, J., & Lonigan, C.J. (2008). Successful phonological awareness instruction with preschool children: Lessons from the classroom. *Topics in Early Childhood Special Education, 28*, 3–17.

Piasta, S.B., Purpura, D.J., & Wagner, R. (2010). Developing emergent literacy skills: The impact of alphabet instruction. *Reading and Writing, 23*, 607–626.

Ponitz, C.C., McClelland, M.M., Matthews, J.S., & Morrison, F.J. (2009). A structured observation of behavioral self-regulation and its contribution to kindergarten outcomes. *Developmental Psychology, 45*, 605–619.

Puranik, C.S., & Lonigan, C.J. (2011). From scribbles to scrabble: Preschool children's developing knowledge of written language. *Reading and Writing, 24*, 567–589.

Puranik, C.S., Lonigan, C.J., & Kim, Y. (2011). Contributions of emergent literacy skills to name writing, letter writing, and spelling in preschool children. *Early Childhood Research Quarterly, 26*, 465–474.

Schatschneider, C., & Lonigan, C.J. (2010). Misunderstood statistical assumptions undermine criticism of the National Early Literacy Report. *Educational Researcher, 39*(4), 347–351.

Sénéchal, M., LeFevre, J., Smith-Chant, B.L., & Colton, K.V. (2001). On refining models of emergent literacy: The role of empirical evidence. *Journal of School Psychology, 39*, 439–460.

Sénéchal, M., & Young, L. (2008). The effect of family literacy interventions on children's acquisition of reading from kindergarten to Grade 3: A meta-analytic review. *Review of Educational Research, 78*, 880–907.

Shanahan, T. (2002). What reading research says: The promises and limitations of applying research to reading education. In A.E. Farstrup & S.J. Samuels (Eds.), *What research has to say about reading instruction* (pp. 8–24). Newark, DE: International Reading Association.

Snow, C.E. (2002). *Reading for understanding: Toward a research and development program in reading comprehension.* Santa Monica, CA: RAND Corporation.

Sulzby, E., & Teale, W. (1991). Emergent literacy. In R. Barr, M. Kamil, P. Mosenthal, & P.D. Pearson (Eds.), *Handbook of reading research: Volume 2* (pp. 727–758). New York, NY: Longman.

Teale, W.H., Hoffman, J.L., & Paciga, K.A. (2010). Where is NELP leading preschool literacy instruction? Potential positives and pitfalls. *Educational Researcher, 39*(4), 311–315.

Teale, W.H., & Sulzby, E. (Eds.). (1986). *Emergent literacy: Writing and reading.* Norwood, NJ: Ablex.

Whitehurst, G.J., & Lonigan, C.J. (1998). Child development and emergent literacy. *Child Development, 69*, 848–872.

Willoughby, M.T., Blair, C.B., Wirth, R.J., & Greenberg, M. (2010). The measurement of executive function at age 3 years: Psychometric properties and criterion validity of a new battery of tasks. *Psychological Assessment, 22*, 306–317.

Wilson, S.B., & Lonigan, C.J. (2009). Emergent literacy screeners for preschool children: An evaluation of Get Ready to Read! and individual growth and development indicators. *Annals of Dyslexia, 59*, 115–131.

Wilson, S.B., & Lonigan, C.J. (2010). Identifying preschool children at risk of later reading difficulties: Evaluation of two emergent literacy screening tools. *Journal of Learning Disabilities, 43*, 62–76.

Index

Tables, figures, and notes are indicated by *t, f,* and *n,* respectively.